New Forms of Human Trafficking

Anabela Miranda Rodrigues • Maria João Guia
Editors

New Forms of Human Trafficking

Global South Highlights and Local Contexts on Sexual and Labor Exploitation

Springer

Editors
Anabela Miranda Rodrigues
Faculty of Law
University of Coimbra
Coimbra, Portugal

Maria João Guia
Centre for Legal Research of
Faculty of Law
University of Coimbra
Coimbra, Portugal

ISBN 978-3-031-39731-8 ISBN 978-3-031-39732-5 (eBook)
https://doi.org/10.1007/978-3-031-39732-5

This Springer imprint is published by the registered company Springer Nature Switzerland AG
The registered company address is: Gewerbestrasse 11, 6330 Cham, Switzerland

Paper in this product is recyclable.

Acknowledgments

The publication of this volume has been prepared within the framework of the research project "Societal Challenges, Uncertainty and Law: Plurality | Vulnerability | Undecidability" [University of Coimbra Institute for Legal Research (UCILeR), Coimbra, Project I&D, UID/DIR/04643/2020].

Contents

List of Abbreviations

BC	Before Christ
BPC	Brazilian Penal Code
CPS	Criminal Police Service
ECHR	European Convention on Human Rights
ECtHR	European Court of Human Rights
EUMS	European Union Member States
EUROPOL	European Police Office
EUROSTAT	Statistical Office of the European Communities
EUTF	European Union Trust Fund
GAMM	Global Approach to Migration and Mobility
GDP	Gross Domestic Product
GNI	Gross National Income
GRETA	The Group of Experts on Action against Trafficking in Human Beings
HRSC	(South African) Human Sciences Research Council
ILO	International Labour Organization
IOM	International Organization for Migration
JHA	Justice and Home Affairs
MPF	Migration Partnership Framework
MS	Member States
NAPTIP	Nigerian National Agency for the Prohibition of Trafficking in Persons
NATIP	National Agency against Trafficking in Persons (Romania)
NGO	Non-Governmental Organisations
NPA	National Prosecuting Authority
OCG	Organized Crime Groups
PESTRAF	Survey on Trafficking in Women, Children and Adolescents for the Purposes of Commercial Sexual Exploitation
PPC	Polish Penal Code
PPO	Public Prosecutor Office
PTDS	Post-Traumatic Stress Disorder
SADC	Southern African Development Community

SANDF	South African National Defence Force
SAPS	South African Police Services
SELEC	South East European Law Enforcement Center
SOCTA	Serious and Organized Crime Threat Assessment
SSA	Sub-Saharan Africa
THB	Trafficking in Human Beings
TIP	(US) Trafficking in Persons
TVPA	(US) Trafficking Victims Protection Act 2000
UDHR	Universal Declaration of Human Rights
UNICEF	United Nations International Children's Emergency Fund
UNGIFT	United Nations Global Initiative to Fight Human Trafficking
UNODC	United Nations Office on Drugs and Crime
VoT	Victims of Trafficking

Brief Introductory Chapter: New Forms of Human Trafficking

Anabela Miranda Rodrigues and Maria João Guia

Trafficking in human beings (THB) is not a new phenomenon, it has roots in a number of different practices that threaten the fundamental rights of its victims, particularly slavery and more specifically the trafficking of women. There are also some intersections with other types of criminal actions, such as the exploitation of sexual practices, commonly known as 'pimping'. As this criminal phenomenon has not followed the same path internationally, there are still many countries and areas in the world where it is not even seen as a criminal act. Many violations of fundamental rights still happen in the twenty-first century and many victims are still manipulated and exploited by criminal agents acting by themselves or at a higher level, often following a specific *modus operandi* as part of an organised crime group (OCG).

THB has caught the attention of the international community, especially because ever since its impact in numbers and types of victims exploited have been known, there has been a greater focus from a legal, criminological and sociological point of view, and new legal, judicial and law enforcement tools have been set up, into leading to a global movement against its commission. THB has been a priority of the European Union (EU), Member States and the international community, as mentioned in United Nations 'Transforming Our World: 2030 Agenda for Sustainable Development' (2015).

In fact, the designation of the different forms of THB victims' exploitation has been so substantially widened, that the European Directive 2011/36/EU has tried to encompass some of the most recognised and common exploitation forms, requesting the EU Member States to enlarge their own national legislation to harmonise

A. M. Rodrigues
Faculty of Law, University of Coimbra, Coimbra, Portugal
e-mail: anarod@fd.uc.pt

M. J. Guia (✉)
Centre for Legal Research of Faculty of Law, University of Coimbra, Coimbra, Portugal
e-mail: maria.joao.guia@ij.uc.pt

A. M. Rodrigues, M. J. Guia (eds.), *New Forms of Human Trafficking*,
https://doi.org/10.1007/978-3-031-39732-5_1

procedures and, especially, to amend legal texts where this crime is provided for, to enable more effective prevention and combat against this crime and also aiming a better support for its' victims. Point 11 of the preamble points to the need for employing a more comprehensive concept of THB than outlined in the previous Framework Decision 2002/629/JAI, focusing on the inclusion of new forms of exploitation, such as a clear mention to forced begging, organ removal, illegal adoption, forced marriage or the exploitation of other criminal activities, such as exploiting THB victims to commission theft, robberies and drug trafficking. A number of different provisions have been added and legislation amended in several countries, while experts continue to describe tendencies and the *modus operandi* used to exploit victims.

Since 2011, a remarkable new stage has been signalled in the prevention and combat against THB, resulting in a better approach to victims, with a better framing of the unknown forms of exploitation. Point 25 of the preamble to the Directive expressly mentions the need for EU Member States to adopt or reinforce THB prevention policies, including measures that reduce the demand for victims or increase the investigation tools for a better application of justice.

Within this context, many different questions have been raised and the authors contributing to this book have touched extensively on different unexplored topics and forms of exploitation, while performing statistical and qualitative analysis of the effects of exploiting human beings, focusing on a wide variety of issues related to our chosen topic of 'New Forms of Exploitation', debating current problems, using a multi-disciplinary approach that takes a legal, sociological, and criminological point of view, while also intersecting with other sciences such as psychology and political sciences.

The book chapters reflect each author's individual background and unique point of view and are enriched by this transdisciplinary technique furthering the knowledge of those willing to delve deeper into this type of crime. This combination of the authors' scientific backgrounds and variety of topics on the same issue is the only way to achieve the required effective prevention and fight against THB. Nevertheless, it should be stressed that we sought to achieve a strong departure from the legal field as the initial goal of each article, and this is why we are back with this fresh and unique book combining the different approaches, touching on several national points of view and giving the reader the opportunity to reflect upon a set of issues from different geographical origins and national frameworks, on outcomes as international awareness and attention to this crime has increased. We believe that these reflections should lead to more questions being raised and that the penal system will benefit from the variety of approaches and analysis from across the world; from South Africa to Brazil, to Europe with particular emphasis on Portugal, The Netherlands, Norway, Romania, Poland, Spain, Slovenia and Italy.

The way in which the book has been organised provides the reader with a fresh induction to the theme, starting with the theoretical legal debate in the penal field, progressing through the chapters in order towards a more empirical reflection, taking into account public policy issues. Nevertheless, all of them are oriented by the main goal of analysing the new forms of human trafficking so most of them present specific cases where the reader can learn about the diverse forms of THB. As a brief introduction to this book with this chapter 1, a short summary of each chapter will be briefly presented.

In the second chapter, Anabela Miranda Rodrigues and Maria João Guia present a juridical reflection of the crime of THB and by studying its origins, they explore the legal debate surrounding amendments to the Portuguese penal code and the interesting discussion over the moral issue. This chapter presents research into the approach to prostitution from Before Christ up until recent times in Portuguese criminal history, analysing different periods in which regulations and procedures have been implemented to assess it and prohibit it, enabling the reader to understand why the divergent evolution of both crimes (TBH and pimping) followed its way, taking into account the most recent amendments to the penal code, after the transposition of the Directive 2011/36/EU.

Laura Zúñiga Rodriguez is the author of Chap. 3 entitled "Cross-Border Organized Crime and Human Rights: The Awfulness of Trafficking in Human Beings" which highlights the difficulties facing the treatment by the law of THB crime due to its invisibility and illegality. The author highlights THB as a phenomenon full of specificities, conflicting interests, and generalisations that is often concealed by other phenomena such as prostitution, sexual exploitation and illegal migration crimes, taking examples from the Spanish context. The author reports on the way in which contradictory criminal policies have been designed which violate victims' rights. The difficulty of differentiating between free and coercive prostitution increases the struggle to identify the victim's autonomy. However as human dignity, a core fundamental right, must be protected, the author mentions that in THB there is always an asymmetric reality between the dealer and the victim, adversely affecting the victim's human dignity. The author reflects on the juridical legal good and the validity of the victim's consent in cases in Spain, after which the author provides some conclusions and recommendations within the scope of criminal law and from a criminological perspective.

Nina Mollema presents chapter "Combating Human Trafficking in South Africa" exploring THB's root causes and specific types of trafficking and exploitation in South Africa. It bridges the gap between on the one hand amendments to the law on THB and its results in terms of better action, with an analysis of the characteristics of this particular region, its borders and coastlines, and social factors such as poverty, inequality and the overall inefficiency of its institutions and structures. The flow patterns of human trafficking in South African society, taking into account its legal innovations, is what distinguishes this region from other African ones, bearing in mind that it is currently one of the few nations in this continent actively engaged in the prevention and fight against this crime. Among these reflections, the specificity of the so-called '*marche du petit vagin*' (literally 'the market of the small vagina') is explained with its relations to the exploitation of human trafficking.

Moving to human trafficking policies in Scandinavia, May-Len Skilbrei authors the chapter "Human Trafficking Policies in Scandinavia: What Happens When International Obligations Meet National Problem Definitions?" discussing various shifts in how Denmark, Norway and Sweden have approached human trafficking since the inception of the UN Trafficking Protocol in 2000. This chapter examines how the definition of THB has changed over time in governmental white papers and statements, identifying common factors in the trajectories of the three countries' trafficking policies, where the author identifies a reproduced bias towards prostitution-related trafficking and female victims, intertwined with migration. This comparative chapter leads the author to conclude that scholars should not become locked into their understanding of how a country manages trafficking, since comparisons demonstrate that policies on paper are not the same as policies in practice, and that this relationship may be very different even in empirical contexts that appear similar in many respects, as is the case with the Scandinavian countries.

Chapter "Fight Against Human Trafficking in Poland: From Theory to Practice" is written by Joanna Banach-Gutierrez and it focus specifically on the case of Poland and human trafficking with an analysis of the statistics. This author shows us how much this crime needs 'a comprehensive and interdisciplinary approach', clarifying its links with organised crime. The vulnerability of its victims is highlighted along with some protection measures, but also the roots of human trafficking and the new forms of male exploitation are also analysed, among the most common forms, such as sexual exploitation and forced labour (agriculture, textile industry, food processing and other forms). The specific case of Poland and Polish law is mentioned in detail, with reference to other nationals who have been recently detected as victims in THB criminal networks, mainly of Eastern Europe origin. Some cases, mainly analysed in the ECtHR are used to the arguments presented. This chapter concludes that the Polish government has increased financing for assisting victims of THB, including medical and psychological care, among other provisions such as legal aid, food and clothing. Also trends in this THB analysis shows us that sexual and labour exploitation as still the most common forms of exploitation in Poland.

Chapter "The Silenced Coercion of voodoo over Nigerian Women sexually exploited in Europe", authored by Maria João Guia and Sandra Dumitrescu, focuses on EU's externalisation of border control to third countries and its impact on traditional forms of coercion into THB. Analysing a concrete case, that of Nigerian women coerced into sexual exploitation by means of voodoo practices, the authors explore the added value of European Union (EU)-funded projects, which are seldom fully adapted to the specific needs of local communities and persons entitled to international protection. Externalisation of EU border control measures through the EU Emergency Trust Fund for Africa remains a controversial policy decision. The authors plea for a more tailored design of EU-funded projects – in the specific case of voodoo-trafficked Nigerian women – by building contextual analysis into aid projects, but also by providing European justice officials with the adequate tools to correctly identify and support these victims.

Chapter "Transvestites and Transwomen in Human Trafficking for Sexual Exploitation: A Study in Brazil" is authored by Andreza Pantoja Smith who presents an analysis of a study conducted in Brazil: the victimisation of transvestites and transwomen trafficked for sexual exploitation, mainly using examples from Belém do Pará and São Paulo, Brazil. Among other points of analysis, the author argues around inequality, discrimination and prejudice to which they are subjected due to their sexual orientation, gender identity and the body they construct for their assumed gender. It focuses on the invisibility they experience due to being stigmatised as there are no data on this topic although it seems to be an increasing trend in the sexual exploitation of Brazilian victims. Andreza Pantoja Smith concludes that many studies focusing on women and children as victims of THB for sexual exploitation are available because of the influence of national legislation that is in line with international regulations. Nevertheless, the increasing THB victimisation of transvestites and transwomen of a Brazilian origin should also be considered, since the numbers are increasing, but still invisible because of the bias and intolerance of general society towards this group of victims who suffer double violence.

Rafaela Pascoal and Adina Schwartz present the chapter "Romania: Trendstetter in European Human Trafficking?", where they mostly lead the reader through the consequences of the specific new forms of human trafficking by which the organised crime groups have exploited Romanian victims and how over the past two decades the European legislative framework has evolved to maximise judicial efforts to prevent and repress THB, as well as increase the revictimisation and assistance mechanisms for victims. Furthermore, this chapter debates interesting issues related to the definition of exploitation, as well as reflections upon the elements of trust and the false consciousness of exploitation often felt by its victims, leading them to remain to silent and invisible while they are exploited. Finally, these authors explain how the 'lover boy' method, exploitation for begging and for petty crimes commission are often used in Romanian THB cases and they present and analyse some Romanian legal cases that were European landmarks in this specific form of recruitment and exploitation.

Chapter 10 is written by Cláudia Cruz Santos, entitled 'Individuals Treated as Nonpersons and the Challenge to Criminal Justice: The Specific Problems Facing Victims of Trafficking in Human Beings'. It analyses the specific problems experienced by victims of human trafficking and outlines a brand new approach to victims of human trafficking, especially taking into account the vulnerability approach. The author debates the issues of criminal, protective and assistance origins, combining these reflections with the violent organisation characteristics of THB crime. The author concludes challenging the penal system is the best way forward and at the same time become more effective at punishing the THB agents of crime.

Rita Penedo is the author of chapter "Trafficking in Human Beings as an Hourglass Paradigm" which addresses issues of continued victimisation. The author tries to understand whether THB victims detected and registered in some Member States are not the same that are continuously being exploited in another or other several countries (or Member States). The author affirms that this challenge is empirically very difficult, especially collecting data and supporting evidence, so she decided to explore the *modus operandi* of the path to victimisation to discover whether there was an uninterrupted cycle, using the image of an hourglass to illustrate the image of THB. The case of Portuguese victims is used to exemplify what would be important to collect at a European and international level, in order to allow the justice system to function better. After detailed analysis of the different phases, Rita Penedo concludes that a harmonised monitoring system would be the best way to assess this topic while the prevention policies and national and transnational referral mechanisms would enhance all the variables listed in the revictimisation topic.

Chapter "The Formal Institutions of Control and the Victims of Human Trafficking: From Frequency to Impunity" is written by Maria João Guia and is a reflection from a criminological and victimological approach to human trafficking victims, mainly connected to the formal institutions of control. This chapter seeks to analyse the failure of convictions in human trafficking cases, mainly due to the loss of trust in the judicial system. As it is known, in human trafficking cases, the criminal evidence is based primarily on the testimony of its victims. Nevertheless, if victims do not trust the judicial system, they will not cooperate and testify as needed to make the judicial system effective. Consequently, trials in human trafficking cases collapse and again the spiral of lack of trust in its victims increases. The chapter concludes with some recommendations on how to improve the formal institutions of control, respecting the victims of human trafficking and acting to repress this grievous crime.

Meško, Bojan Dobovšek, & Katja Eman are the authors of the following chapter, chapter "Human Trafficking in Slovenia: Contemporary Issues", which focuses mainly on Slovenia, a country located on the Balkan Route, and presented as the main human trafficking route in this part of Europe, and which has recorded an increased number of victims since the 1990s. Trafficking in women for sexual exploitation has been reported as the most common form of exploitation. Slovenia is shown by the authors primarily as a transit country for human trafficking, albeit it sometimes acts as a country of origin and destination. Not only does this chapter focus of women forced into prostitution as forms of exploitation for THB, but also contemporary types and purposes of human trafficking including forced begging and petty crimes, trafficking in human organs, tissues and cells, child trafficking, and human trafficking for labour exploitation or forced labour. Briefly, this chapter presents the various types of human trafficking in the twenty-first century encountered in Slovenia and discusses the dangers and consequences of human trafficking in the future. The authors conclude with a positive perspective, in which Slovenia is considered a positive example it is approach and assistance to victims of THB.

Chapter "How Organized is Labour Trafficking? On the Involvement of Organized Criminal Groups in Labour Exploitation" is authored by Masja van Meeteren and Joanne van der Leun who wrote about labour exploitation in THB as a form of organised crime. This chapter discusses human trafficking that takes place outside of the realm of sex work and focuses on labour trafficking. Starting by reviewing empirical research literature on labour exploitation, human trafficking and organised crime, the authors show that in the field of labour exploitation, there is probably less involvement in criminal syndicates or criminal networks that maintain contacts with other criminal networks. Examples from the Netherlands of perpetrators within labour trafficking were used, illustrating the practice of THB crimes by individuals or family business and not only, as most commonly, from the perspective of transnational organised crime, taking into account the need to clarify definitions on organised crime. Literature by various researchers is analysed, leading the authors to conclude that there appears to be little empirical evidence for the involvement of criminal syndicates in labour exploitation, although they highlight that there is nothing conclusive about the extent to which organised crime is active in the field of labour exploitation.

Chapter "Human Trafficking in Brazilian Law: The New Legal Definition" is authored by Artur Gueiros and it analyses THB both as a phenomenon on a global scale as well as the specific situation in Brazil. The legal evolution of this crime is analysed taking into consideration the period from the Brazilian Empire to perceptions of the country as part of the globalised world. Furthermore, this chapter questions the controversy involving the new legal definition of THB crime, which was brought in by a new law from 2016, providing details on the different meanings and new forms of human trafficking. This does not mean that the seriousness of this crime has not been recognised, but that the different forms of exploitation that human trafficking may entail (such as sexual exploitation, organ removal or the illegal adoption of minors) may have been previously defined in different ways. The author concludes that, paradoxically, instead of decreasing in intensity, THB has increased exponentially and Brazilian lawmakers have realised the need to amend the legislation to deal with the new forms of exploitation.

The last chapter is authored by Felipe Chiarello de Souza Pinto and Ana Cláudia Ruy Cardia Atchabahian and it aims to study THB based on a protective perspective of the Regional Human Rights Protection Systems, notably through a critical analysis of the decision made by the Inter-American Court of Human Rights in the case 'Fazenda Brasil Verde vs. Brazil'. This chapter focuses mainly on the exploitation of labour as one of the main and most serious undercurrents in Brazil's invisible forms of exploitation. The authors try to obtain grounds for comprehension of the subject in the international landscape and invoke the applicability of its conclusions to the national doctrine and jurisprudence.

To end this short introduction, we would like to highlight article 18 of Directive 2011/36/EU which draws attention to the measures that EU Member States should take to increase education and awareness among the population to reduce the number of victims or potential ones. Paragraph 2 of this article refers to the possibility of organising campaigns, research and educational programmes to raise awareness of this crime and reduce the risk of victims, including children, suffering from this type of exploitation. The University of Coimbra Centre for Legal Research is committed to this and has been organising seminars, conferences and other activities. This book is one of the initiatives we would like to present to the academic community and hope its serves as a tool to help practitioners increase their knowledge, in addition to enabling justice system operators to apply measures against this serious violation of fundamental rights better.

We hope that this book will encourage more research on this topic and raise more questions leading us to reflect upon new answers, contributing to a wider perspective on the needs of victims and the action of the state in the preventing and combating against this crime.

We cannot end this introductory chapter without expressing our heartfelt gratitude to the authors who contributed to this joint production and to the Centre for

Legal Research of the University of Coimbra, where both of us are researchers, for supporting our project.

Disclaimer The information and views set out in this book are those of the authors and do not necessarily reflect the official opinion of any institution.

Anabela Miranda Rodrigues (anarod@fd.uc.pt) is currently a full professor in penal law of the Faculty of Law at the University of Coimbra, Portugal. She is also the president of the European, Economic and Penal Law Institute (IDPEE) and the vice president of the International Society of Social Defence (ISSD/SIDS) and a researcher at the University of Coimbra Centre for Legal Research (IJ). She is also the president of the Portuguese Group of the International Penal Law Association (IPLA/AIDP-PT) and a member of the International Penal Law Association (IPLA/AIDP). She is a voting member of the International Penal and Penitentiary Foundation (IPPF/FIPP) and she is a member of the National Council for Legal Medicine.

Maria João Guia (maria.joao.guia@ij.uc.pt) holds a PhD in Law, Justice and Citizenship in the twenty-first century, by the University of Coimbra, Portugal and four Master Degrees (Law, Sociology, Translation and Strategic Border Management). She has been a European Commission external expert in the area of 'Security, Liberty and Justice (2014)' after being an alternate member of the Group of Experts on Trafficking in Human Beings. She has been working professionally in criminal investigation, borders, and document control in the area of migration. She is Invited Assistant Professor of Criminology and Researcher of Ratio Legis—Center of Research and Development of Legal Sciences of the Universidade Autónoma de Lisboa [Project: *Corpus Delicti*—Studies in Transnational Organized Criminality], Researcher in the Centre for Legal Research, University of Coimbra and Researcher of *Ius Gentium Conimbrigae*/Centre for Human Rights of the Faculty of Law, University of Coimbra. She lectures on the intersection of sociology, law, and criminology in Post-PhD, PhD, master, postgraduation, degree, and training courses of various areas of knowledge. Maria João Guia is a national expert and researcher in several European and national projects, namely in the areas of the rights of victims of crimes, human trafficking, and the rights of immigrants.

From the Social Condemnation of Prostitution to the Criminalisation of Sexual Exploitation: Pimping and Human Trafficking in the Portuguese Penal Code

Anabela Miranda Rodrigues and Maria João Guia

Abstract Prostitution practices have undergone several changes over time and have been viewed more recently from three angles: (1) as morally reprehensible; (2) with freedom of action; (3) laden with protectionism over women. Even so, on European agreement, each EU Member State has adopted a different policy, criminalising either the sexual exploitation of others or the client (Nordic model), or criminalising human trafficking in terms of sexual exploitation, depending on the legal description of the crime and the legal assets to be protected. In Portugal, prostitution has gone through moments of legalisation and prohibition, and has remained decriminalised since 1982, despite successive intersections with the statute relating to the crime of pimping. Considering how understanding about prostitution has evolved and the blurred boundaries between the different types of pimping and human trafficking crimes, the present chapter aims to question the current configuration of para 1 of Article 169 of the Penal Code, which incriminates only pimping.

1 Introduction

The history of prostitution shows that this practice dates back many centuries, initially conceived completely differently than it is today. In fact, the moralisation of this secular practice was only introduced along with Christianity and the Church adopting supervision of societal morals over the years. However, the dividends that could be gained from prostitution were soon discovered to hold a hidden potential that would allow the state to finance military management, as Solón had come to

A. M. Rodrigues
Faculty of Law, University of Coimbra, Coimbra, Portugal
e-mail: anarod@fd.uc.pt

M. J. Guia (✉)
Centre for Legal Research of Faculty of Law, University of Coimbra, Coimbra, Portugal
e-mail: maria.joao.guia@ij.uc.pt

A. M. Rodrigues, M. J. Guia (eds.), *New Forms of Human Trafficking*,
https://doi.org/10.1007/978-3-031-39732-5_2

realise, and so it became a desirable practice for those looking for an easy profit. However, the morals instilled by the Catholic Church in the Middle Ages implied a change in the exploitation of this activity, despite records of frequent brothel attendance by the clergy. Failing to impose a prohibitionist moral upon this activity, the Portuguese State decided to regulate prostitution houses between the years 1836 and 1962, enforcing regular and mandatory sanitary control over prostitutes, who had to be accompanied and show a records booklet that allowed tight control of their activity. With the spread of syphilis, tuberculosis, leprosy and other venereal and infectious diseases (Oliveira 2013) and according to a medical study[1] by Francisco Ignacio dos Santos Cruz, vice president of the Public Health Council created in 1837, prostitution was prohibited by Decree-Law No. 44579 of 19 September (Moreira 2009, pp. 18–22).

Twenty years later, and taking into account the abolitionist movement initiated in 1875, defended by Ricardo Jorge (Decree-Law No. 44579), an eminent Portuguese professor of hygiene at that time and appointed Director-General of Public Health, as well as the regulatory system being abandoned by France (in 1946), Belgium (in 1948), Romania (in 1949), Hungary (in 1950), Italy (in 1955) and Spain (in 1956) (Decree-Law No. 44579), the practice of prostitution was prohibited in 1963. Following the review of the 1982 penal code, prostitution was decriminalised. Successive revisions of the Portuguese Penal Code were made, particularly the crimes of pimping and human trafficking, in 1995, 1998, 2001, 2007, 2013 and 2015, conferring specifics that made them unique and independent, differentiating them in most of their elements. Both crimes still bear a strong resemblance to prostitution and its eventual criminalisation, with overlapping definitions that make it difficult to define their legal boundaries clearly. We will present here some reflections, questioning the current way in which these crimes appear in the Penal Code, mainly from three aspects: (1) the removal of any substance from the simple pimping crime and the permanence of para 1 of Article 169; (2) the approach towards the serious way in which victims of pimping and trafficking in persons are sexually exploited; (3) the revival of possible legal morality.

2 From 'Sacred Prostitution' to the Criminalisation of Pimping and Human Trafficking

Around 250 years ago, a woman, her body and spirit were regarded with a reverence that elevated her to the role of goddess within the matriarchal society of that time. Roberts (1996) quotes the research of Evelyn Reed who describes women as the 'earthly incarnation of divinity', central to prehistoric nomadic society (Moreira 2009, p. 11) and imbued with an interconnection between the group's social balance trilogy where culture, religion and sexuality were inseparable.

[1] Study entitled 'Prostitution in the City of Lisbon', published in 1841, Lisbon.

Fifteen centuries later, with societies becoming more sedentary, this woman-goddess was integrated as a central figure in temples, assuming the role of priestess, endowed with the power to administer and manage her society. At this time, the relationship between sexuality and religion became even more pronounced, especially considering that the rituals in those temples were filled with a sacred sexual charge that energised all members of the group.

Matriarchal power was soon disputed by man, leader of nomadic tribes, who became aware of his reproductive role and introduced the figure of the male gods, dethroning the role that woman had assumed until then and relegating her to a secondary role, her social existence justified only by marriage to a man. It was during the second century BC that the figure Moreira calls 'sacred prostitution' (Moreira 2009, p. 12) was introduced, in which the priestesses of the temples assumed an ambivalent and simultaneous role of 'sacred and prostitute', with the goddess Ishtar symbolically representing the first prostitute in history, and by which they assumed a highly sacred status.

The Babylonians even documented the different degrees that these sacred women achieved, earning income in the form of 'offerings in the name of the goddess Ishtar' who, in a brief pyramid of power, called themselves 'enthu' and 'naditu' (those who assumed the highest level), 'qadishtu' (sacred women), 'ishtaritu' (devout women serving the goddess Ishtar), down to the 'harimtu' (first street prostitutes to exercise inside and outside the temple, independently) (Moreira 2009, p. 12).

Consequently, women were classified as legitimate or prostitutes, depending on whether they were married 'virtuous wives' and therefore obligatorily devoted to their 'owner', deprived of liberty and dependent on their husband, or otherwise independent of the male sex, integrated in a group of lower esteem in fifth-century BC Athenian society, which included the poor, foreigners and slaves. At that time, Sólon, governor of Athens, became the first to regulate and exploit official brothels (dicterion) (Prado 2002, apud Bezé and Câmara 2014) run by the Athenian State, in the form of a 'semi-private company', taking such huge profits from exploiting the activity that they managed to finance the military apparatus. Payment for sexual acts performed by prostitutes was made directly to the brothel manager, the 'pronobosceion' (Roberts 1998, p. 36 apud Montreozol 2006), and taxes were also paid on this amount. Prostitutes were classified as 'deikteriades', public women available to anyone (while men and youngsters were also found prostituting themselves in the streets), 'hetairae', elite prostitutes and 'auletrides', women who played music and performed sensual banquet dances (Fisbane 2007, p. 91; Moreira 2009, p. 13).

Emperor Caligula and later Constantine (the first emperor after the birth of Christ) also imposed on prostitutes the payment of a tax on which they made a substantial profit, maintaining full, widespread acceptance of the exploitation of prostitution by the state also during the Ancient Roman Empire, exempting this activity from any imposition of sin. Prostitution was therefore fully accepted and integrated into society as a social and economic activity, without any negative moral judgements of prostitutes nor those who exploited them. But the state would lose its monopoly in this area from the moment the religious domain was installed, with the implementation of Christianity and the moralisation of customs, installing the first prohibitionist era, when a prostitute was considered 'a criminal, outside the law, deserving persecution' (Cadaval 2002 apud Moreira 2009, p. 15). In effect, Charlemagne 'the Great', crowned Emperor of the Romans by Pope Leo III, sealing the connection of religious power with military power, imposed the first moralistic laws, highlighting 3 sins that were linked with 'adultery, fornication and prostitution', followed by the imposition by his successor that prostitutes should be 'thrown naked in cold water and spectators should scoff' (Moreira 2009, p. 15 and following). The Church prohibited sexual relations outside of marriage (instituting the practices of infibulation and the use of chastity belts), accepting them only for the purpose of procreation, and consequently prostitutes and their clients were socially condemned. That said, the great university cities-maintained prostitution throughout the centuries (Moreira 2009), with nobility and even the clergy identified as frequenters of the brothels. However, in modern times, with the increase in male prostitution, penalties were also increased, including 'pecuniary penalties, nose and ears cut', during the reign of Louis XIV (Cadaval 2002 apud Moreira 2009). The French post-revolution saw an increase in male and child prostitution, and the Victorian era was marked by the search to end this practice, considered a 'social evil' (Moreira 2009). Movements of support and prostitution censorship sprang up all over Europe, largely dominated by religious morality. Considering the different ways in which the exploitation of sexual practices came to be seen by different countries, some decided to criminalise the conduct of female prostitutes, others that of clients, while others embarked on the criminalisation of human trafficking and others still decided to criminalise anyone who obtained profits from the sexual practices of others. The choice of model was split, one focused on an approach towards prostitution as a violation of women's rights in the form of sexual slavery, seen as a way to perpetuate gender inequality. The second model, on the other hand, focused mainly on prostitution as the promoting gender equality and a woman's right to decide regarding their own body (Report on sexual exploitation and prostitution and its impact on equality (2013/2013 (INI); Fundação Scelles 2012). Pimping was not criminalised for a period in Germany, the Netherlands, Austria, Denmark, in some cantons of Switzerland and in several of the states of Australia (prostitution being legal Greece), while the United Kingdom, France, the Republic of Ireland, Croatia and some of the states of the United States of America criminalised prostitutes, and a third way, known as the 'Nordic model', that criminalised the client seeking sexual services, was implemented in Sweden (1999), Norway (2008 and including demand for sexual services outside Norway), Iceland (2009) and Finland, and in the latter country it only constitutes a crime to benefit from sexual services from persons who are victims of human trafficking (Report on sexual exploitation and prostitution and its impact on gender equality (2013/2013 (INI) and Patto 2013).

We will now analyse the evolution of this phenomenon in the light of state legislative intervention.

3 From the (De)Criminalisation of Prostitution to the Delimitation of the Crimes of Pimping and Human Trafficking

Briefly, summarising what Portugal has done in the area of prostitution, we can point out five fundamental moments: the first that was in force until 1836 under prohibitionism. A second, until 1858, with the regulation of prostitution. A third that followed until 1962, with the neo-prohibitionism of prostitution (due to the abolitionist movement that was asserting itself against the previous regulation). A fourth moment, marked by the publication of the 1982 Penal Code, noted the decriminalisation of prostitution and the delimitation of three phenomena within the context of sexual crimes: pimping (Art. 215), aggravated pimping (Art. 216) and human trafficking (Art. 217). A fifth and final moment, marked by the revision of the 2007 Penal Code, redefined the crime of trafficking in persons (Art. 160), which is now included in crimes against personal freedom and the crime of pimping (Art. 169), and maintained in crimes against sexual freedom (but integrated in crimes against sexual freedom and self-determination). There have been other notable moments amongst these milestones, especially considering the revision of the Penal Code of 1995, for example, when the crime of pimping was first integrated in a sole article (Article 170), leaving sexual crimes outside the 'social ethical foundations of social life', to be integrated as crimes against people (Figueiredo Dias 2012, p. 708). But before we start to reflect on the texts of the law and its amendments, we will present a brief historical overview of the evolution of prostitution and the two crime acts of human trafficking and pimping.

During the thirteenth century, during the reign of D. Afonso III, it was common for nobles to be accompanied by prostitutes on trips to court, a tradition that continued under the reign of D. Dinis, given the opinion that it would be immoral to tax prostitutes on follow-up work (Alberto 2012, p. 21). As of 1481, under the reign of D. Afonso IV, it was decided that prostitutes should live in separate neighbourhoods from the rest of the population, obliged to use a currency that distinguished them from other women.

3.1 The Administrative Offence (Prohibition)

During the Manueline Orders (between 1512 and 1605), persecution of prostitutes and pimps worsened until 1836, when the repression of prostitution was included in the Administrative Code:

> To curb public debauchery, and the scandal caused by immorality, and the dissolution of the custodians of Women Prostitutes, inhibiting, as long as the Government does not publish special regulations, that they remain with the Temples, Public walks, Squares, Main streets, establishments of 'Public Instruction, Gatherings. & similar.; and making those who are not subject to this rule to be punished in court; as well as those that their hands examples, vices,

> and shamelessness become scandalous, and unworthy of coming together with honest and modest families.

Paragraph 6 or Article 109, Title II, Chap. I, 'Do Administrador Geral'.

3.2 Regulation

In 1853, the first regulation of prostitution in Portugal was published, the Health Regulations of Harlots in Porto,[2] motivated by the spread of syphilis, with blame attributed to prostitutes and never to clients (Tavares 2008, p. 437; Fontinha; 2006). In 1858, another more general regulation was published,[3] which obliged prostitutes to be registered at the Police or Civil Government office, a regulation that persisted until 1962.

3.3 The Prohibition of Criminal Offences

In that year, Decree-Law No. 44579 of 19 September 1962 (in force since 1 January 1963) was published, prohibiting prostitution, based on the publication of health studies on the spread of contagious diseases and their serious threat to public health (subheading XV of Law No. 2036 of 9 August 1949). Prostitutes were, as stipulated in Article 1(3)[4] of this law, 'equated to strays',[5] with 'imprisonment up to one year and a corresponding fine for all individuals who consciously encourage, favour or in any way facilitate the exercise of prostitution or intervene in it for profit'. In any case, it is important to mention that the crime of 'pimping' had already been established in Articles 405 and 406[6] of the Penal Code of 1852, as follows:

---

[2] Health Regulations for Harlots in Porto, created in 1853. It was there that the prostitutes were subject to periodic health inspections.

[3] Police Regulation of Whores and Tolerated Houses in the city of Lisbon, created in 1958 (Alberto 2012).

[4] 'Prostitutes are equated with strayers, for the purpose of applying security measures. Children under 16 will be subject to the protection, assistance or education measures provided for in Decree-Law 44288 of 20 April 1962'.

[5] Recalling what is stipulated in Article 256, Section 1, Chap. IX 'Strays, and beggars, and associations of evildoers', of Title 3 'Crimes against order and public tranquility', of December 10, 1852: 'Strays - article 256. That person, who has no certain domicile in which he lives, nor more than a few suspects, nor habitually exercises any profession, or officio, or other profession, in which he earns his life; not proving the need for force majeure, which justifies him to find himself in these circumstances, he will be competently tried and declared to be a stray, and punished with correctional imprisonment up to six months, and handed over to the Government, to provide him with work for as long as it seems convenient'.

[6] Article 406 had the following wording: 'Anyone who habitually excites, favours, or facilitates the debauchery, or corruption of any child under the age of twenty-five, in order to satisfy the dishon-

'If, in order to satisfy the dishonest wishes of another, the ascendant excites, favours, or facilitates prostitution, or corruption of any person of his descendants, he will be sentenced to imprisonment from one to three years, and a corresponding fine, being suspended from political rights for twelve years.

1. The husband, who commits the same crime regarding his wife, will be sentenced to a maximum of exile, and a fine of three months to three years of his income, being suspended from political rights for twelve years.

2. The guardian, or any other person in charge of education, or direction, or custody of any child under twenty-five, who commits the same crime with respect to that child, will be punished with a prison term of six months to two years, and a corresponding fine., and suspension for twelve years of the right to be a guardian, or a member of a family council, and to teach, or direct, or run in the direction of any educational establishment'.

Text (in an outdated version) of Article 405, crime of pimping (introduced by the Penal Code of 1852)

4 The New Era of Pseudo-Abandonment of Morality Concerning Prostitution and Its Transfer to the Text of Pimping

The revision of this article, which was maintained as Article 405 in the Penal Code by the decree of 16 September 1886, only shortened the maximum sentence provided for in para 1, which now provided for imprisonment of one to two years (instead of 1 year, 3 years ago). Prohibitionism persisted until Decree-Law No. 400/82, of 23 September, came into force (the Penal Code, which had the effect of revoking the prohibition of prostitution—Art. 1 of Decree-Law No. 44579)[7] and reformulated the crime of pimping, with Article 215,[8] which first appeared in Chap. I, 'Crimes against the ethical-social foundations of social life', of Title III, 'Crimes against the values and interests of life in society'.

The text of pimping as a crime was therefore replaced by the following:

'1 - Anyone who promotes, favours or facilitates the practice of acts contrary to the person or sexual morality, or prostitution in relation to: a) The minor or person with a psychic anomaly; b) Any person, exploiting a situation of abandonment or extreme economic need; will be punished with imprisonment up to 2 years and fine up to 100 days.

2 - The same penalty applies to those who exploit the immoral gain of a prostitute, living, totally or partially, at their own expense'

Text (in an outdated version) of Article 215, crime of pimping (introduced by Decree-Law No. 400/1982, of 23 September)

The Penal Code also introduced Article 216, aggravated pimping, which provided for higher penalties for those who engaged in such practice with a view to

est wishes of another, shall be punished with imprisonment of three months one year, and a corresponding fine, and suspension of political rights for five years'.

[7]Article 1–1. The exercise of prostitution from 1 January 1963 onwards is prohibited.

[8]At this time, it was also enacted in Article 216 the aggravated pimping and in Article 217 the crime of human trafficking.

making a profit (para A), professionally (para B), by fraud, violence or serious threat (para c) or if the victim was 'the agent's spouse, ascendant, descendant, adopted son, stepson or guardian' (para d). The crime of trafficking in persons appears in the following Article (217), inserted in the same Sect. II, Chap. I and Title III, worded as follows:

> '1 - Anyone who traffics in people, enticing, seducing or diverting someone, even with their consent, for the practice, in another country, of prostitution or of acts contrary to modesty or sexual morality, shall be punished with imprisonment from 2 to 8 years and fine up to 200 days.
>
> 2 - If the agent practices the conduct referred to in the previous number with a profit intention, professionally or uses violence or serious threat, the penalty of one third will be increased in its minimum and maximum limits.
>
> 3 - If the victim is a spouse, ascendant, descendant, adopted son, stepson or guardian of the agent, or has been handed over in view of his education, direction, assistance, custody or care, the penalty will be increased by half, within its minimum limits and maximum'.
>
> *Text (in an outdated version) of Article 217, crime of trafficking in persons (introduced by Decree-Law No. 400/1982, of 23 September)*

5 The Definitive Abandonment of Moralisation on Social Ethics and the Path of Defending Freedom and Sexual Self-Determination

With the revision of the Penal Code and the publication of Decree-Law No. 48/95, of 15 March, both the crime of pimping and that of human trafficking have been included in Sect. I 'Crimes against sexual freedom', in Chap. V, 'On crimes against sexual freedom and self-determination' and Title I, 'On crimes against people'. This constitutes a paradigm shift on the definitive abandonment of the issue of sexual moralism that was inherent to its formulation[9] when prostitution itself (and later pimping) became 'a social evil', seen as an essentially personal 'value', riddled with freedom and self-determination—freedom negatively speaking, in resistance to unwanted impositions, and positively, in the freedom for sexual interaction between consenting adults, without restrictions (Andrade, 1991; Figueiredo Dias, 2012; Patto, 2001; Sousa, 2015). In the words of Maria João Antunes (2010), 'sexual criminal law has evolved in the sense of ceasing to be a tutelary right to "honesty", "customs" or "good customs"—and where the punishment of sexual practices that, in the light of the "general feelings of sexual morality", should be considered (...) in a word "immoral" (...) prostitution included [...]'.

The two articles were merged into one (Art. 170), and simple pimping appears in para 1 of Article 170 and most seriously in para 2:

[9] Paragraph 7 of the preamble to Decree-Law No. 48/95, of 15 March, objectively mentions the decision to abandon the 'moralistic conception ("general feelings of morality") in favour of sexual freedom and self-determination, eminently personal assets'.

> '1 - Anyone who professionally or for profit intends to promote, favour or facilitate the exercise by another person of prostitution or the practice of significant sexual acts, exploring situations of abandonment or economic need, is punished with a prison sentence of 6 months to 5 years.
> 2 - If the agent uses violence, a serious threat, deception or fraudulent manoeuvre, or takes advantage of the victim's mental incapacity, he is punished with a prison sentence of 1 to 8 years'
> *Text (in an outdated version) of Article 170 crime of pimping (introduced by Law No. 48/1995, of 15 March)*

In turn, the crime of trafficking in persons was also reformulated, first appearing in Article 169, with the following text:

> 'Anyone who, through violence, a serious threat, deception or fraudulent manoeuvre, leads another person to practice prostitution or major sexual acts in a foreign country, exploiting their situation of abandonment or need, is punished with a prison sentence of 2 to 8 years'.
> *Text (in an outdated version) of Article 165, crime of trafficking in persons (introduced by Law No. 48/1995, of 15 March)*

6 The Removal of Substance from Simple Pimping and the Progressive Convergence of Pimping in Its Serious Form and Trafficking in Persons

The revision of the Penal Code introduced by Law No. 65/98, of September 2, removed the mention of the exploitation of 'situations of abandonment or economic need' from the crime of pimping in its simple form (no. 1), allegedly due to great difficulty in the production of evidence at trial. We understand, however, that such an amendment hollowed out the implicit justification of the formulation of the legal text of para 1, with no actual exploitation of any condition of the alleged victim that could justify prosecution and its respective punishment by imprisonment of between 6 months and 5 years. This caused a setback to moralistic values, based only on the moral censorship of someone professionally exercising the sexual exploitation of others. This issue has been widely debated (see Miranda Rodrigues 1999, 2012),[10] with para 1 so far unchanged in its form (see, for example, Constitutional Court Judgement no. 396/07, on the possible unconstitutionality of Article 170(1) of the Penal Code, largely from the elimination of the 'typical requirement' of 'exploiting a situation of abandonment or need' (see Costa Andrade's losing vote in case no. 401/16[11] of the Constitutional Court of 21 November, 2016).[12]

[10] Miranda Rodrigues (1999); Miranda Rodrigues and Fidalgo (2012); Figueiredo Dias and Antunes (2019).

[11] Retrieved from https://blook.pt/caselaw/PT/TC/511745/?q=relator:%20Fernando%20%20 Ventura.

[12] As mentioned, the matter has been debated and para 1 has always been considered constitutional (see Constitutional Court Judgments no. 144/04, 196/04, no. 303/04, no. 170/06, no. 396/07, no. 522/07 and no. 591/07 - all available at www.tribunalconstitucional.pt/tc/acordaos/), cf., however,

On the other hand, with the publication of Law No. 99/2001, of 25 August, the crime of pimping underwent a significant change in the provisions of para 2, with the addition that the agent be incriminated and convicted in the event of use, in addition to the forms of coercion already foreseen, 'abuse of authority resulting from a hierarchical, economic or labour dependency relationship' and 'any other situation of special vulnerability'. Number 1 kept its simple form, due to the previous change:

> '1 - Anyone, professionally or with a profitable intention, to encourage, favour or facilitate the exercise by another person of prostitution or the practice of significant sexual acts is punished with a prison sentence of 6 months to 5 years'.
>
> *Text (in outdated version) of no. 1 of Article 170 crime of pimping (introduced by Law No. 99/2001, of 25 August)*

It is interesting to note that the crime of trafficking in persons, provided for in Article 169 of this law, mentions exactly the same 'abuse of authority resulting from a hierarchical, economic or labour dependency relationship', with the addition of taking advantage of a particular vulnerability (among additions that distinguished it from the crime of pimping). This, however, made pimping and trafficking in persons converge in diametric opposition to the simple article 170(1) (Pimping). Therefore, the text of trafficking in persons came into force with the following wording:

> 'Whoever, by means of violence, serious threat, deception or fraudulent manoeuvre, abuse of authority resulting from a relationship of hierarchical, economic or work dependence or taking advantage of any situation of special vulnerability, enticing, transporting, accommodating or welcoming a person, or providing the conditions for the practice by that person, in a foreign country, of prostitution or of relevant sexual acts, is punished with a prison sentence of 2 to 8 years'.
>
> *Text (in an outdated version) of Article 169 crime of trafficking in persons (introduced by Law No. 99/2001, of 25 August)*

7 The Specifics of Trafficking in Persons and the Return of Simple Pimping to a New Penal Morality

The revision of the Penal Code, introduced with the wording given by Law No. 59/2007, of 4 September, materialised in the separation and distinction between the crimes of pimping and human trafficking: the first continued to appear in Article 169, Section I, 'Crimes against sexual freedom', within Chap. V, 'On crimes against sexual freedom and self-determination', while the second first appeared in Article 160, Chap. IV, 'On crimes against personal freedom', despite both being found in Title I, 'On crimes against People'. We consider this to have been a remarkable milestone in the final cut (insofar as it shifted the crime of human trafficking from sexual crimes to crimes against personal freedom), moving towards the moral

---

the recent Constitutional Court judgment that went against this guideline and found the rule in Article 169/1 of the Penal Code unconstitutional: Constitucional Court Judgment n°134/2020. On this ruling, see Figueiredo Dias and Antunes (2019).

judgement of certain interrelated behaviours, due to their historical reminiscences summarised in this article, and endorsed by item 7 of the preamble to Law No. 59/2007, of 4 September:

'... it is worth noting the shift from sexual crimes from the chapter on crimes against the values and interests of life in society to the title of crimes against people, where they constitute an autonomous chapter, under the heading "On crimes against sexual freedom and self-determination", abandoning the moralistic conception ("general feelings of morality"), in favour of sexual freedom and self-determination, eminently personal assets'.

The texts of both the crimes of pimping and trafficking in persons acquired a new paragraph layout, with new points introduced in the latter's text. It should be noted, however, that the text of para 1 of the crime of pimping remained the same (having even removed the provision for the 'practice of important sexual acts'). Emptied of its foundation, with no change to consent, nor threats, offences, violence, ruses, remaining a formulation for criminalising the fact that someone can professionally, or with the intention of making a profit, 'foment, favour or facilitate' another person's exercise of prostitution, which leads us to question whether the legislator's intention was based on a return to moral condemnation of the practice of prostitution, as a secular tradition instituted before Christianity. This is because the exploitation of prostitution is not included in the crime's description, only the promotion, favouring and facilitation of the practice of prostitution by a prostitute's free will. According to Figueiredo Dias (2004), 'under no circumstances is sexual activity considered a crime if carried out privately by adults who consent to it' (apud Antunes 2010). The fact that it has no value worthy of protection under criminal law—a most serious form of limiting people's rights—leads us to question the incrimination of the act of profiting from prostitution other than the eventual moralistic reprobation and condemnation of such activity. This leads us to question the legislator's decision reflected in para 1 of Article 169 of the Penal Code.

Paragraph 2 of the pimping article is presented in a clearer way, the items appearing neatly[13] with each of the conducts that constitute that aggravated form of crime, still today written as follows:

> 'Article 169 – Pimping - 2 - If the agent commits the crime provided for in the preceding paragraph: a) Through violence or serious threat; b) Through trickery or fraudulent manoeuvre; c) With abuse of authority resulting from a family relationship, guardianship or custody, or from hierarchical, economic or work dependence; or d) Taking advantage of the victim's mental disability or situation of special vulnerability; is punished with imprisonment from one to eight years'.
>
> *Current text of the crime of pimping, Article 169 CP (introduced by Law No. 59/2007, of 4 September)*

[13] Note the preamble of Law No. 59/2007, of 4 September, point 27: 'Another point that should be highlighted—it has already been mentioned—is the rigor with which each legal type of crime was defined. For each of the incriminating prescriptions, meticulous care was taken to always trace the elements of the type in the clearest and most immediately understandable way, because only then, it is repeated, and it will never be too much to say, if the principle is honoured in all lines. of typicality, one of the bulwarks of the citizen's constitutional guarantees'.

On trafficking in persons, substantial change was made, with specifications also listed at all levels: both in action conduct, in means, and in intentions.[14]

Law No. 60/2013 of 23 August again brought a reformulation of the crime of trafficking in persons by transposing part of what was recommended in Directive 2011/36/EU, by the European Parliament and Council, of 5 April 2011, extending the forms of exploitation, in addition to sexual exploitation, labour exploitation or organ harvesting, as well as introducing levels of severity of the crime, the commission of the crime against a minor, and the question of the irrelevance of the victim's consent (to name but a few). This new wording was the last one introduced to the crime of trafficking in persons to date, written as follows:

> 'Article 160 – Trafficking in Persons - 1 - Anyone offering, delivering, recruiting, enticing, accepting, transporting, accommodating or hosting a person for the purpose of exploitation, including sexual exploitation, labour exploitation, begging, slavery, the harvesting of organs or the exploitation of other criminal activities: a) Through violence, abduction or serious threat; b) Through trickery or fraudulent manoeuvre; c) Abuse of authority resulting from a hierarchical, economic, labour or family relationship; d) Taking advantage of the victim's mental disability or situation of special vulnerability; or e) Upon obtaining the consent of the person who has control over the victim, he is punished with a prison sentence of three to ten years. 2 - The same penalty is applied to anyone who, by any means, recruits, entices, transports, accommodates or welcomes minors, or delivers, offers or accepts them for purposes of exploitation, including sexual exploitation, exploitation of work, begging, slavery, organ harvesting, the adoption or exploitation of other criminal activities. 3 - In the case provided for in the preceding paragraph, if the agent uses any of the means provided for in paragraph 1, paragraphs or acts professionally or with a profit intention, he shall be punished with a prison sentence of three to twelve years. 4 - The penalties provided for in the preceding paragraphs are increased by one third, in their minimum and maximum limits, if the conduct referred to therein: a) Has endangered the victim's life; b) Has been committed with particular violence or has caused the victim particularly serious damage; c) Has been committed by an official in the performance of his duties; d) It was committed in the

[14]Version of Article 160, Law No. 59/2007, of 4 September—'Trafficking in persons - 1 - Anyone offering, delivering, enticing, accepting, transporting, accommodating or accommodating a person for purposes of sexual exploitation, labour exploitation or organ harvesting: a) Through violence, abduction or serious threat; b) Through trickery or fraudulent manoeuvre; c) Abuse of authority resulting from a hierarchical, economic, labour or family relationship; d) Taking advantage of the victim's mental disability or situation of special vulnerability; or e) By obtaining the consent of the person who has control over the victim; he is punished with a prison sentence of three to ten years. 2 - The same penalty is applied to anyone who, by any means, entices, transports, accommodates or welcomes minors, or delivers, offers or accepts them for purposes of sexual exploitation, labour exploitation or organ harvesting. 3 - In the case provided for in the preceding paragraph, if the agent uses any of the means provided for in paragraph 1, paragraphs, or acts professionally or for profit, he shall be punished with a prison sentence of three to twelve years. 4 - Anyone who, by means of payment or other consideration, offers, delivers, requests or accepts a minor, or obtains or provides consent for their adoption, is punished with a prison sentence of one to five years. 5 - Whoever, having knowledge of the crime referred to in paragraphs 1 and 2, who uses the victim's services or organs is punished with a prison sentence of one to five years, if a more serious sentence does not fit under another provision. Cool. 6 - Anyone who retains, hides, damages or destroys identification or travel documents of a person who is the victim of a crime provided for in paragraphs 1 and 2 shall be punished with a prison sentence of up to three years, if a more serious sentence is not imposed by virtue of another legal provision'.

framework of a criminal association; or e) results in the victim's suicide. 5 - Anyone who, by means of payment or other consideration, offers, delivers, requests or accepts a minor, or obtains or provides consent for their adoption, is punished with a prison sentence of one to five years. 6 - Anyone who, having knowledge of the crime referred to in paragraphs 1 and 2, who uses the victim's services or organs is punished with a prison sentence of one to five years, if a more serious sentence does not fall under another provision. cool; 7 - Anyone who retains, hides, damages or destroys identification or travel documents of a person who is the victim of a crime provided for in paragraphs 1 and 2 shall be punished with a prison sentence of up to three years, if a more serious sentence does not fit under another legal provision. 8 - The consent of the victim of the crimes provided for in the preceding paragraphs does not under any circumstances exclude the illegality of the fact'.

Current text of the crime of trafficking in persons, Article 160 CP (introduced by Law No. 60/2013, of 23 August)

In short, both the crime of pimping, in its no. 2, and the crime of trafficking in persons, especially for the purpose of sexual exploitation, evolved alongside each other, albeit for different reasons, leading to overlaps that were legally handled and analysed by the courts, once the degree of 'reification' of victims had been identified as the distinguishing element of both criminal behaviours. Trafficking in persons was considered the prime example of that same sexual exploitation of others. As an example thereof, we highlight the judgement of the Court of Appeal of Porto, of 07/08/2015, related to case 1480/07.9PCSNT.G1.P1, in which both crimes are at stake and referred to, therefore in point I their distinctive elements are iterated: 'the criterion of distinction between the crime of trafficking in persons, article 160, paragraph 1, d) of the Penal Code and the crime of aggravated pimping, article 169 (2) (d) of the same Code is linked to the victim's degree of instrumentalisation (objectification); human trafficking approaches the peak of instrumentalisation of the person who represents slavery and goes beyond what is already inherent in the exploitation of prostitution, in the deprivation of liberty and in the offence to the dignity of the person'.

Further on, in para 6 of the judgement's appeal, it says 'It is tenuous, we recognise, the border line that separates human trafficking from pimping'. Subsequently, considerations are made (based on Patto, 2008) that present an attempt to delimit these differences:

'To affirm that human trafficking is distinguished from aggravated pimping by approaching the peak of instrumentalisation of the person who represents slavery does not mean that all situations of trafficking constitute quasi-slavery (...). To consider that we are facing a situation of human trafficking (in this case, taking advantage of the situation of the victim's special vulnerability), in the confrontation with aggravated pimping, it is enough that the conditions of the exercise of prostitution go beyond, in the deprivation of freedom of victim and in the offence to the dignity of the victim's person, of those who are already part of the exploitation of prostitution (in this case, taking advantage of the situation of special vulnerability of the victim)'.

8 Conclusions

The moralisation of conduct related to the exploitation of prostitution dates back several centuries. Christianity marked a turning point in the way in which sacred rituals involving prostitution as common practice (without any pejorative connotation) became a focus of sin, and prostitution was later to be banned and criminalised.

In Portugal, prostitution practices were regulated for a certain period, through a prohibitionist era, followed by decriminalisation and several reformulations of the texts of the crimes of pimping and human trafficking.

The successive revisions to which the Penal Code of 1982 was subjected raised three questions: (1) simple pimping is currently presented, as far as we know, void of any typical requirement for fostering, favouring or facilitating the exercise of the prostitution of others (without even mentioning the exploitation of prostitution), for profit or professional purposes. The question arises whether we are witnessing a return to moralistic censorship of whether one can enrich or exercise the profession of 'promoting, favouring or facilitating' the prostitution of others. Either it should be explained what the legal good in question actually is,[15] adding its typical elements to para 1, or its appearance makes no sense (as defended by Anabela Miranda Rodrigues), unless the purpose is indeed to return to the moralisation and condemnation of prostitution; (2) the possible overlap, in certain cases, of the crime of aggravated pimping and that of human trafficking, especially for the purpose of sexual exploitation, may bring different perspectives in specific cases, revealing the need for further reflection, since the degree of 'reification' (presented in the aforementioned judgement) is not sufficient to settle the border between one crime and the other, which seriously undermines the justice process; (3) the approach taken by Portuguese Criminal Law regarding a minimum intervention of criminal law in the delimitation of citizens' moral and social life, in favour of the defence of citizens' right to freedom, does not seem to have been recorded completely specifically regarding prostitution and the crimes involved therein, so further debate and reflection on the political-criminal options adopted (and the reasons why these choices are made) is needed urgently.

We end with a reflection by Maria João Antunes (2010), 'with the certainty that the legitimacy of criminal intervention in a democratic state of law cannot be based on the "little secular" legal good of public morality or good customs or target a certain type-of-author, to which "war is declared"'.

---

[15] Anabela Miranda Rodrigues presents the conception without any doubts (apud Silva 2013, p. 24) According to Roxin, 'legal assets are the essential assumptions for a common existence, which are materialized in a series of valuable situations, such as, for example, life, physical integrity, freedom of action or property'.

References

Alberto JM (2012) Dos crimes sexuais: do crime de lenocínio em especial. O Novo paradigma da criminalidade sexual. Dissertação de Mestrado em Ciências Jurídico-Criminais. Universidade Autónoma de Lisboa

Andrade M d C (1991) Consentimento e Acordo em Direito Penal: contributo para a fundamentação de um paradigma dualista. Coimbra Editora, Coimbra

Antunes MJ (2010) Crimes Contra a Liberdade e a Autodeterminação Sexual dos Menores. Texto apresentado nas Jornadas de Direito Penal – Crimes no seio da família e sobre os menores. Ponta Delgada, 7–8 Maio 2010

Bezé P, Câmara J (2014) Uma Visão Constitucional da casa de Prostituição. Revista Eletrônica de Direito Penal AIDP-GB. Ano 2, vol 2, N° 2

Cadaval C (2002) Contributo para o Estudo do Auto-Conceito em Prostitutas de Rua Toxicodependentes e Não Toxicodependentes (Concelho e Braga). Tese de Mestrado em Toxicodependências e Patologias Psico-Sociais, Coimbra

Figueiredo Dias J (2004) Direito Penal. Parte Geral. Questões Fundamentais. A Doutrina Geral do crime. Coimbra Editora

Figueiredo Dias J (2012) Nótula antes do art. 163°. In: de Figueiredo Dias J (ed) Comentário Conimbricense do Código Penal, Parte Especial, Tomo I. Coimbra Editora, Coimbra, pp 708–713

Figueiredo Dias J, Antunes MJ (2019) Da inconstitucionalidade da tipificação do lenocínio como crime de perigo abstrato. In: Estudos em Homenagem ao Conselheiro Presidente Joaquim de Sousa Ribeiro, vol I. Almedina, p 984s

Fishbane S (2007) Early rabbinic literature. A collection of socio-anthropological essays. Brill, Leiden. ISBN 97890 04 15 833 7

Fontinha MI (2006) Para a Compreensão (Social) da Prostituição. Seara Nova, no 1965, Lisboa

Miranda Rodrigues A (1999) Anotação ao art. 171°. In: Comentário Conimbricense do Código Penal - Parte Especial Tomo I, Artigos 131° a 201°, 2nd edn. Coimbra Editoria

Miranda Rodrigues A, Fidalgo S (2012) Comentário ao artigo 170°. In: de Figueiredo Dias J (ed) Comentário Conimbricense do Código Penal, Parte Especial, vol I, 2nd edn. Coimbra Editora

Montreozol J (2006) O sentido subjetivo do trabalho para a profissional do sexo. Dissertação de Mestrado da Universidade Federal de Mato Grosso do Sul – UFMS, Centro de Ciências Humanas e Sociais, Campo Grande

Moreira RA (2009) Prostituição de Rua: Um problema de saúde pública? Contributos para o seu estudo. http://repositorio-aberto.up.pt/handle/10216/7205

Oliveira A (2013) Prostituição feminina, feminismos e diversidade de trajectórias. Ex-aequo 28:17–30

Patto PV (2001) Direito Penal e Ética Sexual. In: Revista Direito e Justiça, vol XV. UCP Editora, Lisboa

Patto PV (2008) O crime de tráfico de Pessoas no Código Penal revisto – análise de algumas questões. In: Revista do CEJ, n° 8 (especial), 1° semestre de 2008, p 179

Prado LR (2002) Curso de direito penal brasileiro, volume 3: parte especial: arts. 184 a 288, 2nd edn. Editora Revista dos Tribunais, São Paulo

Patto PV (2013) O Quadro Legal da Prostituição e a Dignidade Humana. http://www.oninho.pt/ficheiros/documentacao/O_QUADRO_LEGAL_DA_PROSTITUICAO_E_A_DIGNIDADE_HUMANA.pdf

Roberts N (1996) A prostituição através dos tempos na sociedade ocidental.. Editorial Presença

Roberts N (1998) As Prostitutas na História. Record. Rosa dos Tempos, Rio de Janeiro

Silva L (2013) O Tráfico Internacional de Crianças para Exploração Sexual. Mestrado em Direito Criminal. Universidade Católica do Porto

Sousa AP (2015) O crime de Abuso Sexual de Menores dependentes. Uma análise crítica. Dissertação de Mestrado em Direito Criminal. Universidade Católica Portuguesa, Porto

Tavares MM (2008) Feminismos em Portugal (1947–2007). Tese de Doutoramento. Universidade Aberta

Anabela Miranda Rodrigues (anarod@fd.uc.pt) is currently a full professor in penal law of the Faculty of Law at the University of Coimbra, Portugal. She is also the president of the European, Economic and Penal Law Institute (IDPEE) and the vice president of the International Society of Social Defence (ISSD/SIDS) and a researcher at the University of Coimbra Centre for Legal Research (IJ). She is also the president of the Portuguese Group of the International Penal Law Association (IPLA/AIDP-PT) and a member of the International Penal Law Association (IPLA/AIDP). She is a voting member of the International Penal and Penitentiary Foundation (IPPF/FIPP) and she is a member of the National Council for Legal Medicine (e-mail address: anarod@fd.uc.pt).

Maria João Guia (maria.joao.guia@ij.uc.pt) holds a PhD in Law, Justice and Citizenship in the twenty-first century, by the University of Coimbra, Portugal and four Master Degrees (Law, Sociology, Translation and Strategic Border Management). She has been a European Commission external expert in the area of 'Security, Liberty and Justice (2014)' after being an alternate member of the Group of Experts on Trafficking in Human Beings. She has been working professionally in criminal investigation, borders, and document control in the area of migration. She is Invited Assistant Professor of Criminology and Researcher of Ratio Legis—Center of Research and Development of Legal Sciences of the Universidade Autónoma de Lisboa [Project: *Corpus Delicti*—Studies in Transnational Organized Criminality], Researcher in the Centre for Legal Research, University of Coimbra and Researcher of *Ius Gentium Conimbrigae*/Centre for Human Rights of the Faculty of Law, University of Coimbra. She lectures on the intersection of sociology, law, and criminology in Post-PhD, PhD, master, postgraduation, degree, and training courses of various areas of knowledge. Maria João Guia is a national expert and researcher in several European and national projects, namely in the areas of the rights of victims of crimes, human trafficking, and the rights of immigrants.

Cross-Border Organized Crime and Human Rights: The Awfulness of Trafficking in Human Beings

Laura Zúñiga Rodríguez

Abstract This chapter intends to highlight the difficulties of the legal treatment of the crime of trafficking in human beings, especially because it is an invisible phenomenon and, in many cases, it takes place behind legal businesses, such as bars, clubs, etc. The problem of its criminal treatment is that it is a phenomenon full of ambivalences, conflicting interests, and generalisations that prevent seeing individualities, since it is concealed by other phenomena such as prostitution, sexual exploitation and illegal immigration. This has led to contradictory criminal policies that violate the rights of victims. The analysis focuses on the case of abusive trafficking for the purpose of sexual exploitation due to the vulnerability of the victim, considering that it is in those cases where the difficulty of differentiating between free prostitution and coercive prostitution arises, since the victim due to being in a situation of need, does not have full autonomy of her will. In accordance with international conventions, human dignity, as a human right is protected, which is intangible, in disregard of the personal will, when there are objective conditions of sexual exploitation.

1 Introduction

In Spain, the crime of trafficking in persons was introduced into the Penal Code in Article 177 *bis* during the 2010 reform, these changes being supplemented during the 2015 reform. Therefore, not many years have passed since it was expressly criminalised in our country, and according to CITCO (Intelligence Center for Counter-Terrorism and Organized Crime) information, it allowed police forces to intervene and rescue 5600 people from slavery in 2012–2016: 4430 human trafficking and sexual exploitation victims, from 2012 to 2016. If we add victims of labour exploitation, which has been pursued with greater effort since 2015, the number

L. Zúñiga Rodríguez (✉)
University of Salamanca, Law Faculty, Salamanca, Spain
e-mail: lzr@usal.es

A. M. Rodrigues, M. J. Guia (eds.), *New Forms of Human Trafficking*,
https://doi.org/10.1007/978-3-031-39732-5_3

reaches 5675 people (Domínguez and Gálvez 2017). This first approach to the problem presents the following questions: has this phenomenon not existed before? What role has the criminal law played in its visibility? Is penal regulation effective? It also presents some answers: it can be clearly demonstrated that out of different forms of trafficking, trafficking in persons with the purpose of sexual exploitation is significantly more prevalent.

Evidently, this work of penal and legal approach does not claim to provide answers to the questions mentioned. However, its objective is to draw attention to different aspects which indicate that we are facing a complex and multi-faceted phenomenon with recurrent ambiguities and opposing interests which hinder our ability to confront or pursue it. Legal definitions, bound to set generalisations and abstractions, seem to neglect specific situations and personal choices. Nonetheless, criminal law force has allowed pursuing unsustainable situations of human rights violations, especially in cases of women and children. We encounter many assumptions of borderline cases, in which it is not easy to know the willingness of the trafficked person—and no less important, the interpreter's view on prostitution (trafficking in persons with the purpose of sexual exploitation backdrop) conditions human trafficking treatment, overall, when it refers to the use of criminal prosecution. 'The world's oldest trade is not prostitution; it is looking the other way'[1] (Domínguez and Gálvez 2017).

Out of this combination of problems which arise from the approach to trafficking in persons, I will focus on *abusive trafficking with the aim of sexual exploitation*, as it is impossible to exhaust the immense dimensions of this phenomenon in one chapter. My choice is due to the fact that human trafficking with the aim of sexual exploitation is, as it has been observed, the one which appears in outrageous numbers worldwide. In the social scenario, there is an amalgam of behaviours that are associated with what is called *the sex industry* or *the sex business*, where frontiers between what is wanted and what is imposed are not clear, or where the prohibited and the permitted conducts are separated by a thin red line. A famous Spanish case, Torbe case, exemplifies it. The person who is known as *the King of Spanish porno* was charged with child pornography crimes, child abuse, trafficking in human beings, money laundering and crimes against the Public Treasury in April 2016. A few months later he was released from jail on bail of 100,000 Euros (the case is not closed yet). His Ukrainian partner, Boris, with whom he had started a business in Spain to film *Bukkakes* (a collective sexual practice, with women hired in Boris's country of origin) was also arrested. The accusations were based on the testimonies of three protected witnesses, including a minor, who later retracted their first testimonies, claiming that sexual practices took place with their consent. In the case of the minor, she declared that she had been given a false ID (sic) and therefore Torbe did not know her real age. However, the three witnesses' original declarations which appear in an article published in *El País*, are absolutely heartbreaking and plausible.

[1] English translation of the original in Spanish: El oficio más viejo del mundo no es la prostitución, sino mirar para otro lado.

They explain how the three were forced into exaggerated sexual practices without safety controls (with false medical test results), which made them vomit and cry (Verdú 2016), and in which humiliating treatment is obvious. We ask ourselves why these girls are in this situation, doing this work, as presumably nobody obliges them to do it and the difficulties to understand that we are dealing with voluntary actions are evident. Obviously, there are cases when women willingly decide to engage in such behaviour. However, the objective of law is to protect the people who are suppressed by others and forced to engage in behaviours they would never choose—and specifically, in the case of trafficking in persons, it is to prevent objectification of people when they become a source of financial gain for the dealer. As Ferrajoli argues, the purpose of the law is to offer protection to the weakest and thus I find it interesting to delve into the controversial concept of *victim's vulnerability*, which has been regarded both positively and negatively by the doctrine (Ferrajoli 1999). All this will lead us to addressing *dignity as a legally protected good* and, over all, its *availability* (another controversial issue) which will have an impact on criminal prosecution, being even linked to evidence aspects.

If states commit themselves to prevent and prosecute crimes and protect victims of trafficking in persons (the three Ps) at an international level, as it is deduced from the Palermo Protocol 2000 and the Directive 2011/36/EU, on preventing and combating trafficking in human beings and protecting victims, it is essential to understand the scope of these concepts, as the fact whether criminal prosecution takes place, certain borderline behaviours are penalised and certain situations are interpreted in favour of victims of trafficking in persons strongly depends on it. It is because cases of coercion, violence or deception are usually more evident than alleged abuses or victim's vulnerability, especially in such a field as sexual exploitation in which clear limits do not exist, in contrast to cases of labour exploitation with labour laws, which establish minimum thresholds of protection.

To approach these issues, I will start by focusing on some data of trafficking in persons in a global context and particularly in Spain. These data show us that we are unfortunately facing a significant phenomenon of the present. Different numbers indicate that we are dealing with an illicit business which competes with arms trafficking for the second position on the global scale[2] of illicit trades, yielding only to drug trafficking. Thus, we find ourselves before an illicit trade which involves a great amount of money. According to the information from the United Nations Office on Drugs and Crime (UNODC) it reaches around 32 trillion dollars. According to the United Nations Global Initiative to Fight Human Trafficking (UNGIFT), out of the global profit from the illicit market of trafficking in persons, 1.3 trillion dollars, which equate to 4.1%, are generated in Latin America. Forty-nine percent of human trafficking is originated by developed countries which are the main destinations for victims of Latin American origin (UNODC 2011, p. 2). It

[2] Truly, these numbers usually consider the mixture between illicit trades of people and trafficking in persons which, despite being different phenomena, are actually intertwined in many cases, as it will be seen further.

demonstrates that at a global level in human trafficking business, victims come from poor countries, and is directed to consumers, in rich countries.

2 Trafficking in Human Beings in the Global Context

Trafficking in human beings is a phenomenon, which expresses all the complexities of globalisation. According to the professor from Palermo, Militello, trafficking in human beings is one of the most common manifestations of contemporary crime: it is a criminality of benefits, it is a gender criminality and it is a transnational crime (Militello 2018, p. 87 [author's translation]). In the same way as it occurs in other illicit trades, traffickers' logics is the same: to find low risk areas with a relative control of the institutional environment while searching for preferential markets in areas of a richer demand to charge higher prices (Castells 2001, p. 201).[3] On a global scale, sexual, labour and other forms of human exploitation follow the same pattern of illicit markets behaviour: supply and demand from poor areas to rich areas, based on abuse of countries with institutional weakness, caused by wars, famine, natural catastrophes or a Failed State. Transnational organised crime is manifested in the development of these illicit trafficking exchange networks, using the routes of other types of traffic, subcontracting and exchanging information, exchanging illicit businesses, in what Castells names *global crime*, 'Global crime, the interconnection of powerful criminal organisations and their partners in joint activities all over the world is a new phenomenon which deeply affects the economy, politics and national and international safety' (Castells 2001, p. 199 [author's translation]).

First, it should be noticed that in the global context trafficking in persons is linked to another criminal phenomenon, migrants smuggling, as traffickers take advantage of migration flows (which are in fact networks used for people's movements) to conduct a trade of humans (Pérez Cepeda 2004). Therefore, it originates from the same sources: poverty, marginalisation, lack of expectations, social and political conflicts, wars, diseases on the side of supply. On the side of demand are found opulent societies with demographic growth deficit, in which natives are unwilling to do certain jobs and in which sexual gratification appears to be complicated due to people's isolation and selfishness, typical of the welfare understood as material wealth. For Pérez Cepeda, there is a tendency to demand workforce for low-skilled jobs, sexual pleasures at low price, etc. in developed countries (Pérez Cepeda 2004, p. 33 [author's translation]).

The majority of trafficked people come from the world's poorest countries, and inside those countries (domestic trafficking) movements take place following the same pattern, from poor to rich areas. It is noteworthy that the majority of victims are from Sub-Saharan Africa and from Eastern Asia, according to UNODC latest

[3] More extensively, see Chap. 3, *La conexión perversa: la economía criminal global*, where it is emphasised that over the last decades criminal organisations have carried out their operations at an international level with more frequency.

Report (UNODC 2016, p. 5). A total of 69 countries reported victims from sub-Saharan Africa.

Obviously, these connections are linked to criminal organisation features on the global scale, that is, to transnational organised crime which possesses a flexible network system to associate itself with or dissociate itself from different forms of crime according to particular interests. This is why criminal groups at international level engage in various types of crime, the most interrelated of which are people smuggling and trafficking in human beings. According to European Union-Serious and Organised Crime Threat Assessment (EU-SOCTA) 2017 Report, 45% of the reported organised crime groups are involved in more than one criminal activity. The share of these polycriminal groups has increased sharply compared to 2013. Organised crime groups also often engage in more than one criminal activity to mitigate risks, reduce operational costs and increase profit margins. Many organised crime groups are highly flexible and able to shift from one criminal activity to another or to add new criminal activities to their crime portfolio. In many cases, organised crime groups operate on an on-demand basis and only become active once new profit opportunities emerge (EU-SOCTA 2017, p. 15).

Indeed, one of the problems of the transnational criminal policy approach to trafficking in persons is its connection with migrant smuggling networks or migratory flows. It is evident that the immense business of people smuggling, in which international criminal organisations take advantage of migratory flows caused by wars, poverty, or natural disasters, also conceals trafficking in persons, as in the process of forced migration people are exposed to fraud, abuse, violence and death, being a vulnerable prey to traffickers. Especially when the political-criminal approach is against the perpetrators of trafficking, the solution is usually repressive, focusing on the prosecution of criminal organisations that are carrying out illegal trafficking in migrants, and covering up sexual or labour exploitation, or other types of behaviour, becoming a real trafficking in human beings.[4]

All the reports on trafficking in human beings have mentioned this proximity between the two phenomena, which have influenced contradictory criminal policy features. EU-SOCTA 2017 report indicates that criminal organisations involved in trafficking in persons often exploit immigrants, especially victims of migration inside the EU. Irregular migrants represent a large pool of potential victims susceptible to promises of work even if this entails exploitation (EU-SOCTA 2017, p. 53). Indeed, labour exploitation, which UNODC report has manifested as a rising phenomenon, is related mostly to irregular migration. Immigrants, both men and women, may be a target for mafias and unscrupulous businessmen who take advantage of their irregular situation to subject field, service and illegal workshop workers to semi-slavery conditions. In November 2015, a joint operation between Spanish and Polish police and European authorities, coordinated by Europol, dismantled smuggling networks which exploited irregular immigrants of Pakistani origin in

[4] On the difficulties in delimiting both phenomena when trying to achieve a comprehensive approach to trafficking, see Professor Militelo's article (Militello 2018).

Spanish restaurants. The irregular immigrants were forced to work long hours in completely illegal working conditions, without money, holidays or any work safety to pay their debts to smugglers, which consisted in expenses on transportation and identity documents forgery. The profits obtained by criminals would be invested into new restaurants, where irregular immigrants' exploitation was used again. It all made it a successful and immensely profitable business.

It is important to delve into the causes that explain why we are facing a rising criminal phenomenon to obtain a clear analysis when making suggestions of criminal policy and, over all, when considering a possible impact of criminal legislation on this subject.

At the international level, trafficking in human beings with the purpose of sexual exploitation continues to be the widest segment. However, over the last 10 years human trafficking for forced labour has increased, according to UNODC latest report. It changes the victim profile from exclusively feminine to the one with a higher number of males. The data indicating that about four in ten victims detected between 2012 and 2014 were trafficked for forced labour, and out of these victims, 63% were men, is significant (UNODC 2016, p. 6). On children, in 2014 they represented 28% of detected victims, comprising approximately a quarter of trafficked people. Nonetheless, although there has been an increase of male victims, women still represent a majority of victimised people. The percentage is the following: 51% of adult women, 21% of adult men, 20% of female children and 8% of male children (UNODC 2016, p. 11). Therefore, human trafficking remains a criminal sector with mainly female victims, who reach 71% despite the significant increase of male victims over the last years due to forced labour.

As Castells remembers, the key to global crime success and expansion in the 1990s is the flexibility and versatility of its organisation. Interconnection is the form in which it operates both internally, inside every criminal organisation, and externally, in relation with other criminal organisations. Distribution networks act through autonomous local groups to which goods and services are supplied. They have a safety system, but the most worrying issue is the network of law enforcement agents, judges and politicians who form part of their payroll (Castells 2001, p. 213 [author's translation]). It is important to draw attention to this fact: the existence of these organised crime networks, as well as those of human trafficking, greatly depends on nationals, professionals and authorities' participation in and collaboration with criminal organisations. In Palma de Mallorca in 2016, a network of police officers and authorities was arrested and charged with extortion of entrepreneurs and workers of brothels which they attended free of charge in exchange for not carrying out inspections and closing complaint reports (Bohórquez 2016). This corrupt police conspiracy (28 police officers were investigated) would even implicate the PP president in Palma, the Superintendent in Palma and one of the so-called *night businessmen* (Penalva 2016). The *night businessmen*, Bartolomé Cursach, was imprisoned in March 2017 for the alleged parties with free sex, alcohol and drugs for 28 officials and officers of the Local Police of Palma which took place in the night club Tito's. He is charged with five crimes: bribery, influence peddling, drug trafficking, perversion of justice and criminal organisation (Armendáriz 2017). For the same reason the president of Trade and Tourist Services Association in Mallorca was also arrested in May 2017 (Mestre 2017). Later he was released in June 2017. This case of authorities and professionals' involvement in illicit practices, typical of organised crime, is reinforced with profile analyses of this type of criminal phenomenon authors.[5] As shown, behind the trafficking in human beings phenomenon we found white collar criminal, with all the specific problematic of this kind of criminality. Additionally, in many cases the trafficking takes place inside legal business establishments (bars, restaurants, clubs, etc.), which makes even harder the criminal investigations.

Undoubtedly, it is very difficult to provide true numbers of trafficking in persons as it is an invisible phenomenon which is hidden behind socially acceptable practices such as prostitution or procuring. However, it may be calculated approximately. In 2015, the Secretary-General of the United Nations estimated that 2.5 million people are trapped in the networks of modern slavery (Burgo 2015 [author's translation]). Thus, the expansion of this phenomenon is plausible in a globalised and commercialised society, where market rules seem to establish social rules and therefore, lead to people's objectification which appears to be normal.[6]

3 Human Trafficking in Spain

As Giménez-Salinas Framis and De La Corte Ibáñez affirm, over the last decades, Spain has consolidated itself as a place of cocaine and hashish storage and distribution in Europe, an area of clandestine immigration transit originating from nearby and remote countries; an area of African route for vehicle theft, a refuge for powerful foreign criminals, a propitious area for systematic assaults, money-laundering operations and sexual and labour exploitation practices (Giménez-Salinas Framis and De La Corte Ibáñez 2010, p. 368 [author's translation]).

To sum up, trafficking in persons in Spain, like in other countries, is expressed in a harsh way often taking advantage of different illicit traffics, which became easier due to globalisation. Spain's geographical location as a point of intersection between Latin America and Europe, and as an entrance from Africa to Europe, its climate

[5] A study on criminal profiles in the Spanish organised crime shows that almost 60% of people under investigation for organised crime maintain their legal activity in parallel with their illegal activity. It shows us that the world of organised crime is not only compound of professional criminals, but also of collaborators of different professions who provide all kinds of support to criminal organisations. This information is relevant to deduce how many people are on the periphery of criminal organisations, being those who nurture and reinforce them. On the other hand, these data are worrying as they denote the complicity of the so-called *White collar crime*, of people with a good social and economic status who provide institutional support and also profit from illegal activity, in this case, from sexual exploitation (Giménez-Salinas et al. 2011, p. 28).

[6] In 2015 Doctors of the World reported that human trafficking with the aim of sexual exploitation is one of the most widespread and, unfortunately, most normalised forms of trafficking in persons (Burgo 2015 [author'stranslation]).

which fosters exaltation of feelings, its economy dedicated to tourism and as a consequence, to service sector (bars, night clubs, brothels, etc.) are the elements which help to understand the relevance of diverse illicit trades, and especially those related to trafficking in persons and sexual exploitation.

Evidently, it is impossible to identify prostitution with trafficking in human beings, as the former is understood as a voluntary exchange, while the latter is a forced behaviour. However, it is clear that behind the drop scene of sex business there exist many situations of undeclared sexual exploitation, rendered invisible or forgotten. Over all, exploitation of the prostitution of others truly presents cases of forced behaviours and abuse, according to testimonies of trafficked women and specialists who have approached the phenomenon of trafficking in persons. As it may be clearly seen from the example provided at the beginning, in pornography business, it is sometimes impossible to identify if we deal with voluntary or forced actions, or where the limits of exploitation are.

According to UNODC data, it is estimated that about 350,000 women practice prostitution in Spain, out of whom 80% are foreigners in situation of irregular migration, who come from Brazil, Colombia, Nigeria, Romania, Russia and Ukraine (UNODC 2016, p. 6). The percentage of foreigners engaged in prostitution is noteworthy. It shows that it is not a very attractive trade for nationals, being more common among women who come from poorer countries.

On the other hand, other relevant data to understand sexual exploitation in Spain is that our country is ranked first in Europe for prostitution demand (Domínguez and Gálvez 2017) and third at the international level. Indubitably, tourism, being the main source of the country's income, also hides relevant sex tourism, to which analysts have drawn attention for a long time (De La Cuesta 1999). We have to mention anew that, obviously, there exists a legal, voluntary and consensual supply of sex tourism, by adults. However, it is also evident that behind this situation there coexist many forms of trafficking in persons, as the supply of the mentioned services is mainly provided by foreign women, many of whom are irregular immigrants,[7] who are even more vulnerable to become prey of body commercialisation. As Beatriz Sánchez, the prosecutor who managed to obtain evidence to sentence the Romanian capo Ioan Clamparu, *Pig's Head,* (considered to be the main procurer of human trafficking in Europe[8] and sentenced to 30 years of prison), explains, It is absurd to

---

[7] A report by Surt Foundations indicates that out of 1428 victims of human trafficking in Spain 98.7% are women. The majority of them is under the age of 25 and has been captured in consequence of an *affectionate relationship* with the exploiter and with the collaboration of their family. Out of these victims, 34% are of Romanian origin (Iborra 2016).

[8] The case of this Romanian trafficker is impressive. He is considered to be the responsible of women trafficking network which, forced more than one hundred Romanian girls to engage in prostitution in Spain, between 2000 and 2004, however, the number may be even greater. The *modus operandi* was almost always the same, almost out of a manual: in Romania, women were captured with offers of a normal job in Spain, and, once here, were obliged to exercise prostitution like slaves, with the *excuse* that they had to repay their debt with the organisation. Although the destination was Spain, he also had contacts in Italy, Ireland, France and Great Britain. He was sentenced in Romania and took refuge in Spain. One of the women was courageous enough to

think that a woman who works 24h and at the end of a year does not have either a bank account, or money, or property or a rent, or can reject a client, is free (Domínguez and Gálvez 2017 [author's translation]).

Certainly, many women arrive in Spain to engage in prostitution consciously and voluntarily as in their country of origin there is no better alternative for them to survive. However, it does not mean that sometimes they do not find themselves in situations of unexpected deception or exploitation. According to Doctors of the World, Spain is the country of transit and destination for trafficked women and female children. The president of the organisation, Yolanda Rondríguez, warns that the conditions in which these women are forced to exercise prostitution and the physical and mental consequences which this exercise presents for them are against people's fundamental rights: the right to life, right to freedom, to physical and moral integrity, sexual freedom, health, privacy and human dignity (Burgo 2015 [author's translation]).

As we lack true information on trafficking in persons, it is appropriate to use other evidence, and therefore all these analysis, journalist reports, studies, and news oblige us to recognise that the human trafficking problem in Spain is a serious question both with reference to numbers and its depth. The invisibility which characterises this criminal phenomenon redounds to the necessity of using all the possible sources to understand the impact of human trafficking in our country.[9]

4 Difficulties of the Approach to Criminal Policy Against Trafficking in Persons

As it could be seen until now, we are facing a scantily visible criminal phenomenon in our society, which on many occasions does not seem to recognise the dimensions of the damage and pain inflicted on its most vulnerable members, mainly poor women and children. Statistics are either scarce or made by diverse institutions with different results,[10] and sentences for these crimes do not abound either.[11] Therefore

---

report on him, and when she escaped he sent some killers to her home in Romania to threaten her family. The methods he used to threaten women were terrifying. One of those was showing them a photo of a woman tied to a palm tree and devoured by dogs (Alsedo 2012).

[9] While District Attorney's Office of Immigrant Affairs provides information on detection of between 1300 and 1400 victims of human trafficking, the Plan against Human Trafficking of the Ministry of Health estimates that these women represent the third part of all those who exercise prostitution, 40,000 people, according to their estimation ('Las cifras' 2016).

[10] In this way for example, the Report presented to the OEA by *Women's Link Worldwide* in May 2017 reveals that none of the five countries which have been studied (Colombia, Ecuador, Mexico, Paraguay and Peru) have neither unified nor reliable date, which would measure the magnitude and the dynamics of the crime (Women's Link Worldwide 2017, pp. 22–23).

[11] Actually, the figures of prison sentences for this crime are derisory compared to the figures which show the reality in the news and studies on the topic. According to *Women's Link Worldwide,* in Colombia the authorities do not have protocol to identify possible cases. From January 2011 to

it is easy to discern the existence of a great dark figure of crime in this field. According to the Report presented to the OEA by the NGO *Women's Link WorldWide*, indifference is what most severely affects victims of trafficking in persons in Latin America. Victims are defenceless on this Continent as plans of protection and social support are non-existent and prison sentences are scarce. Besides, the punitive approach often revictimises the victims leaving them at the mercy of their captors when the former report the facts.[12] Evidently, this phenomenon is similar to gender violence: if the perpetrator is punished before the victim is offered protection, the perpetrator will eventually turn against her.

However, to develop a criminal policy that can confront trafficking in persons with regard to prevention and repression, it is essential to have clear objectives, which is not easy in this criminal phenomenon hidden behind various contradictions, opposing interests and ambiguities. Criminal law, expressed in crimes which carry out a series of generalisations about punishable offences, does not allow grasping some nuances which may take place in reality. We can observe a series of presumptions made on Congress pulpit, which often forget about personal feelings behind this phenomenon. My objective is to highlight these contradictions to refine criminal protection of the weakest people's rights.

4.1 Trafficking in Persons and People Smuggling

One of the main problems which criminal prosecution for trafficking in persons has faced, especially in Europe, is the confusion over the phenomena of trafficking in persons and people smuggling. Certainly, in many cases they are coincident, inasmuch as irregular immigrants become vulnerable victims of trafficking in persons. However, in reality these phenomena are very different and even require opposite political and criminal approaches in some situations. Without going into details about the differences, it should primarily be remembered that while trafficking in persons is a coercive phenomenon, in which free will does not exist, either as a consequence of violence, or deception, or a situation of necessity or vulnerability;

April 2016 there have only been passed 52 prison sentences out of 908 investigations. In Ecuador, 26 sentences have been pronounced out of 742 crime reports. They are barely identified, which impedes victims' rights protection. Mexico, with 152 prison sentences, is the only country which is considered to be *proactive* on domestic human trafficking situations. In Paraguay, between 2010 and 2013 the Public Ministry reported 145 investigations of this crime and there have been imposed 19 sentences. The victims have not been indemnified either. In Peru, for this crime to be recognised, legal proceedings should take place. Out of 908 cases between 2011 and 2016 only 52 sentences have been passed (Palomino 2017). In Spain, sentences for the crime of trafficking in persons may be found starting from 2015 as it was introduced in 2010 and there are still few sentences, according to the country, transit and destiny consideration.

[12] A Venezuelan minor, 13 years old, sold by her father for a brothel of a border city in Colombia, was returned to Venezuela despite her fears as she had received death threats from her father (Palomino 2017).

in the phenomenon of people smuggling the migrant crosses the border voluntarily, aspiring to a better life. Besides, this identification excludes the phenomenon of domestic trafficking, which is important in some countries where people move from poor to rich areas, or to specific places, as it happens in case of illegal mining industry in Peru, Brazil or Ecuador. The latest report by UNODC on trafficking in human beings indicates that 42% of victims are an object of domestic trafficking, being this an important figure indeed (UNODC 2016, p. 9).

Effectively, as Pérez Alonso highlights, until recently European policy on trafficking in persons was focused on migratory and *crime-centred* paradigm, forgetting about the obligation of the state to ensure the protection of victims (Pérez Alonso 2013-2015). Recently, with the Council of Europe Convention on Action against Trafficking in Human Beings signed in Warsaw in 2005, a change towards a paradigm of victims' protection, or a *victim-centred* perspective has been promoted. This orientation of the criminal policy towards the recognition of victims' human rights was manifested in the Directive 2011/36/EU on preventing and combating trafficking in human beings. The author emphasises how the so-called three Ps (crime prevention, criminal prosecution and victim protection) have been promoted starting from the Palermo Protocol in 2000, providing appropriate criminal policies to protect victims' human rights.

In Spain, specialists have spoken out against the approach to trafficking in persons centred on *trafficking* and its inherent contradictions, emphasising victims' defencelessness (Daunis 2013). That is to say, favouring EU desire to control irregular immigration through criminal instruments, European countries and especially, the countries of Southern Europe, threatened by immigration, have promulgated a series of criminal laws which virtually left victims of trafficking in persons unprotected, as they could not report on their offenders out of fear to be immediately prosecuted as irregular immigrants for the crimes of trafficking in human beings and clandestine immigration. In our legislation until year 2010, common protection against trafficking in persons and people smuggling was exempt, with the Art. 318 *bis* CP, introduced in 2000 under the heading of *Crimes against foreign nationals*.

As Villacampa claims: with this, the Spanish Government expressed an approximation to the phenomenon of trafficking in persons attached to its origins, in which the aforementioned reality was related to clandestine immigration, linked to the Union policy of Fortress Europe, of citizenship stratification and its *apartheid*. With the former regulation in our country, was disregarded an increasingly stable international tendency to demarcate, as differentiated realities, border controls and judicial boundaries to legal residence of foreign citizens—with criminal relevance which such conduct may involve—from a much crueller reality, the one of transporting people to the first world and their treatment during the transit and upon arrival, as if they were things to be exploited (Villacampa 2011, p. 1099 [author's translation]).

Certainly, the Europe of security and liberties was conceived for its own citizens, while *the others*, the immigrants, would have other rights, not a full citizenship. Inside this frame, victims of trafficking in persons are defenceless subjects, deprived of protection, and it may significantly increase their vulnerability before criminal organisations which use trafficking in persons to obtain profits. As Daunis points out, the governmental control of immigration is precisely that which results in immigrants' vulnerability and/or victimisation (Daunis 2017, pp. 32 y ss. [author's translation]). Besides, it is verified that immigrants' protection or safeguards are used in a perverse way, to actually establish more controls and obstacles for immigration, producing a situation of greater legal defencelessness or vulnerability for the immigrant. This approach from combating illegal immigration and the one of criminogenic nature has mainly contributed to concealing the desire of the states to control migratory flows to Europe from countries with humanitarian problems caused by wars, famine and natural disasters under the pretext of fighting against mafias or organised crime which benefit from trafficking in persons. Therefore, it is evident that the real objective behind foreign citizens protection by Art. 318 *bis* CP was migratory policy protection of the Spanish State, being these completely different legal assets. The use of the term *mafias* by politicians and the press and the references between immigration and organised crime present another counter-productive effect: to consider all immigrant transfers to be coercive conduct similar to slavery, although it is not always true.

These are some observations on the contradictions between the two similar but different phenomena: trafficking in persons and migrants smuggling. The simplifications of linking illegal immigration to organised crime result in two consequences for the subsequent approach to trafficking in persons and prostitution: generalisation of the migrant's situation of vulnerability and the belief that every person (especially female immigrants) who engages in prostitution is (or has been) a victim of trafficking in human beings (Daunis 2017, p. 457).

However, fortunately, over the last years this situation has been changing, over all from the moment when the crime of trafficking in persons was included into the Penal Code in 2010, and, even more, with the Directive 2011/36/EU in which, from the European International arena, a differentiated treatment towards trafficking in persons and migrants smuggling is fostered, promoting the protection of victims' human rights. Conceptual autonomy and regulations of trafficking in persons versus immigration policy of the states and versus the fight against organised crime have been a key issue to implement a real criminal policy to protect victims of sex or labour trade, to which they may be subjected.

4.2 Prostitution and Trafficking in Persons with the Aim of Sexual Exploitation

Another issue with contradictory approaches or opposed interests is related to the regulations on prostitution and the prevention and prosecution of trafficking in persons in different countries. As Lorente-Molina claims, prostitution is a multidimensional phenomenon, which requires a complex approach (Lorente-Molina 2016, p. 305 [author's translation]). Therefore, regulations usually raise important debates, as the view on the phenomenon or the orientation of legislative proposals may be very different and even polemical. Without mentioning diverse approaches and emphasising the fact that in the twenty-first century there are no agreements even in Europe, it is enough to point out two opposing positions existing inside feminism itself: the abolitionist model and the business model. It is evident that the views of both models on prostitution are opposed. For radical feminism which supports the abolitionist model, prostitution is an activity related to gender violence in patriarchy, which is humiliating and objectifies women (who mainly exercise it) and, thus, must be eradicated prosecuting the client.[13] As it may be observed, this approach to prostitution and the exploitation of the prostitution of others considers them to be similar to trafficking in persons, as in this case a person's free will would be conditioned by the socioeconomic situation of inequality which characterises prostitution. Obviously, from this point of view, the attitude to prostitution and trafficking in persons is similar and any form of sexual exploitation is prohibitionist.[14]

On the contrary, specialists who are in favour of the business model, that is to say, who consider voluntary prostitution to be sex work, with social and labour rights, supported by the other sector of feminism, believe that the abolitionist model obliges women to engage in sex services in bad conditions, increasing their vulnerability before clients, and facing more risks in an activity which is usually surrounded by secrecy instead of protecting women who exercise prostitution. Indeed, according to criminal approaches, prohibition conceals problems instead of solving them, sometimes aggravating them, as it happens in activities which are usually surrounded by violence, for example in case of prostitution. Therefore, the abolitionist model leaves women at the mercy of the client, the procurer or criminal organisations, without offering any kind of protection.

It is certain that prohibition may entail lack of legal protection for prostitutes, which may revictimise them instead of providing help. However, it should be admitted that the business model has its limitations. This model is based on the distinction between voluntary and coercive prostitution, the latter being similar to trafficking in human beings. However, the problem is that there are many alleged limits where it is not easy to identify the delineation between voluntary and coercive prostitution, especially in assumed situations of the victim's vulnerability in which there is no deception, violence or intimidation. That is to say, difficulties start when we intend to treat differently two realities which often superimpose or hide behind one another.

[13]The main reference for this model is the Swedish Law, which has prosecuted clients of prostitution since 1999. Following Sweden, criminalisation of clients was adopted in Iceland, Canada, Singapore, South Africa, South Korea, Northern Ireland (from 2015) and France (2016) (Sahuquillo 2016).

[14]According to Boza, regarding the Directive N° 2011/36/UE on preventing and combating trafficking in persons and protecting victims: The policy which European texts follow is of the abolitionist model. Thus, prostitution and sexual exploitation are recognised as gender issues, which contribute to human dignity violation, being against such human right principles as gender equality and being therefore in contradiction with the Charter of Fundamental Rights of the European Union (Boza 2017, p. 74 [author's translation]).

4.3 Vulnerability vs. Liberty to Exercise Prostitution

The crux of the approach to the issue of trafficking in persons with the aim of sexual exploitation is the importance which has been given to the vulnerability of trafficking victims by international instruments and how this has been considered harmful for some sectors which support liberalisation of prostitution.

The emphasis on the protection of trafficking victims' human rights originates in the Preamble of the United Nations Convention against Transnational Organized Crime of 2000. At the Millennium Summit, world leaders proclaimed freedom—from fear and from want—as one of the essential values in the twenty-first century. Yet the right to live in dignity, free from fear and want, is still denied to millions of people around the world. It is denied to the child who is working as an indentured labourer in a sweatshop; to the father who must pay a bribe to get medical care for his son or daughter; to the woman who is condemned to a life of forced prostitution. In the same document, Kofi Annan, United Nations Secretary-General at that time, insists: I believe the trafficking of persons, particularly women and children, for forced and exploitative labour, including for sexual exploitation, is one of the most egregious violations of human rights that the United Nations now confronts. It is widespread and growing. It is rooted in social and economic conditions in the countries from which the victims come, facilitated by practices that discriminate against women and driven by cruel indifference to human suffering on the part of those who exploit the services that the victims are forced to provide. The fate of these most vulnerable people in our world is an affront to human dignity and a challenge to every state, every people and every community.

From that moment, a series of international norms intended to protect human rights of the weakest (De la Cuesta 1999), especially women and children facing sexual or labour exploitation of the strongest, mafias, parents who sell their children, etc. have been adopted. That is to say, having abolished slavery in International Bills of Human Rights in the 1950s, the United Nations commit themselves to abolishing the new forms of slavery, the exploitation of man by man. In their desire to achieve it, the authors of international agreements realise that not only does this behaviour take place with explicit violence, but also, in many cases, there is an abuse of power, as it happens with parents, teachers, authorities, or an abuse of a situation of vulnerability such as poverty, marginality and incapacity to survive. This is something that is leveraged by dealers. In these cases, victims do not have a possibility to choose, neither is there a clear opposition to exploitation, that is, the freedom of choice is limited. This is the case of abusive trafficking in persons, more typical of counties or areas of extreme poverty where female and male children are sold by their parents or forced to leave home so that they *make their own living*.

However, in the doctrine, some authors are critical to the concept of vulnerability. Maqueda, questioning the development of the concept of vulnerability by international legislation, claims: As if following a secret slogan, different regulations started to gradually abandon the old references to voluntary or forced prostitution to replace them by a wrong term which remains vague: sexual exploitation. Trafficking in persons, for its part, would be eventually identified as a coercive reality, but its presupposition, the vice of consent, would not be limited to classical situations of violence, intimidation or deception, instead, it would be dangerously extended to other situations of personal or economic weakness which condition victims' liberty. It was then that the notion of vulnerability appeared (Maqueda 2015, p. 450 [author's translation]).

According to this author, the discourse on vulnerability conceals treating women who engage in prostitution as weak people, with limited abilities to decide for themselves[15] (Maqueda 2015, p. 452). Following this same line of analysis, there would be a presumption of unwillingness in relation to the exercise of prostitution which is difficult to prove (Maqueda 2015, p. 453 [author's translation]).

Again, we come up against difficulties related to willingness to exercise prostitution, something that is defended by supporters of the business model of prostitution regulation. As we have previously mentioned, from the point of view of the sectors which defend liberalisation of prostitution suggesting regulations which would recognise it as sex work with social and labour rights, in international agreements there has been adopted an abolitionist view which compares prostitution to trafficking in persons and sexual exploitation, and therefore, makes it an *evil* destined to eradication. Thus, voluntary prostitution, exercised by an adult woman who gives her express consent, is disregarded.

Undoubtedly, there is voluntary prostitution, accepted by a woman, and without exploitation; or in case of exploitation, it is also accepted. However, situations of sexual exploitation, abuse of situations of necessity, which are used by dealers who subject women to unbearable submission, must not be ignored. In my opinion, we cannot presume that the exercise of prostitution is always coercive; neither can we believe that it is always voluntary. As we have insisted, there exist many situations in which prostitution exercised by an adult woman conceals sexual exploitation, similar to trafficking in persons. There are many nuances and it is difficult to obtain data on the number of women who engage in prostitution voluntarily, without being forced to it by necessity. The situation in European countries, with social protection, is different from the countries of Africa, Asia or Latin America, where poor women do not have another choice in life.[16]

As Mintjas and Molnar, who have carried out a research on sex workers victimisation in the Province of Malaga, explain: During the research, it has been observed how sexuality, immigration, sexual identity, an increasing feminisation of poverty

[15] Moreover, according to this author, it is related to the colonial views of the occidental feminists orientated to perpetuating the presumption of infantilism and helplessness of women from the Third World.

[16] According to what has been said so many times, in the phenomenon of trafficking in persons one reality seems to conceal others, like in the case of Russian dolls. As Women's Link WorldWide Report indicates in relation to five Latin American countries, it is essential to make greater effort to detect domestic trafficking in persons and other means of exploitation, as there is a tendency to identify only victims of sexual exploitation and forced labour, while other modalities, such as begging, servile marriage, domestic servitude or organ trade are rarely detected (Women's Link Worldwid 2017, p. 2 [author's translation]).

and the economic crisis are intertwined, resulting in diverse realities, which we have analysed; complex realities of human beings which cannot be encoded as *victim* or *not victim*. Equally, there exist many situations, which cannot be encoded in a binary way as voluntary or coercive prostitution, especially in cases of a situation of necessity abuse. The same research mentioned previously states that if women admit having engaged in prostitution willingly, it is true that all of them see themselves practicing another profession in the future[17] (Mintjas and Molnar 2016, p. 366 [author's translation]).

Feminisation, poverty and marginality may be associated to the exercise of prostitution, in which autonomy of willingness is not always clear. It is impossible to ignore vulnerability of many women and children, especially those who are mostly affected by poverty in the world. The proof of this situation is that the data on trafficking in persons revealed by international reports indicate that victims usually come from the poorest countries around the globe (Pérez Cepeda 2004), without considering the fact that domestic human trafficking is directed from poor to rich areas inside a country. Recent economic and social instability do not augur that we are following the right way to avoid situations which condemn millions of people to live without dignity, without liberty, free of enslaving poverty. Human Development Report 2016 indicates that despite recent important advances in eradication of poverty, still one person in nine in the world is hungry, and one in three is malnourished. About 15 million girls a year marry before age 18, one every two seconds. Worldwide 18,000 people a day die because of air pollution, and HIV infects two million people a year. Every minute an average of 24 people are displaced from their home. Such basic deprivations are common among various groups. Women and girls, ethnic minorities, indigenous peoples, persons with disabilities, migrants—all are deprived in the basic dimensions of human development (PNUD 2016, p. 5).

People who live in a situation of extreme poverty, without any expectations of social or family support are evidently vulnerable and likely prey of people or criminal organisations who take advantage of such situations to exploit others—and in my view, it is indisputable that criminal law should prosecute offenders to protect victims. However, in the social context or in these situations of extreme poverty, in which such practices take place, it is difficult to identify victims and offenders, consent or coercion; these are binary realities. As it is shown in the field study by Mujica in Peru, sexual exploitation in an area of Amazonia, characterised by extractive industries of wood, petrol, minerals and gas, presents astonishing results (Mujica 2014; Mujica and Cavagnoud 2011). The exploitation cycle (sexual or labour) takes place in a daily practice of organisational logics in a community,

[17] Equally in Spain, the majority of sentences for trafficking in persons reveals that it is related to victims who come from countries without social protection, such as Romania, Nigeria, Morocco, Colombia, etc., with the same modus operandi: victims are deceived in their native countries with promises of jobs in Spain or Europe and later, as they arrive in Spain, they are deprived of their documents and obliged to engage in prostitution to pay for the transportation expenses (transport, passport, permits, etc.). These are the cases of a clear situation of vulnerability abuse. Even some sentences expressly define it.

distributed by age and sex, associated to structural violence, characterised by insecurity, poverty and inequality. Inside this circle, girls from the age of 12 are employed in bars, which also offer sex services, and finish this activity between the age of 19 and 25 when they have their second child. At this time, they usually set up a market stall. They perpetuate this cycle having their small children collect wood and sending their daughters at the age of 12 to do the same work which they did themselves. From this example we clearly see how exploited victims become offenders and that these practices do not take place as part of organised crime, instead, they are part of the vital circle of survival.

It is likely that this example may be applied to other areas of Asia or Africa, places of origin of trafficked women in our European countries. This is defined as situation of vulnerability. According to law, it is when a person does not have another option except prostitution and this is the case of women who are brought from their countries with false promises, as irregular immigrants, having few or no options to escape from the circle of their captors. It is also the case when in the beginning certain conditions are proposed and later those become graver.

From a criminological point of view, in human trafficking there is always an asymmetric reality between the dealer and the victim. As Montoya argues: effective exploitation of a person—exploitation of the prostitution of others, sexual exploitation, servitude, forced labour, slavery, etcetera—also shapes a situation of one person's control over another. However, this form of control results in an expression, which is quantitatively more intense than that initial control expressed in the use of violence, threatening, deception and abuse of a situation of vulnerability with the aim of exploitation (Montoya 2017, p. 491 [author's translation]).

What the author intends to emphasise is that besides the initial means of making the victim follow the dealer's logic, what is truly grave is this permanent control which the offender exercises, using the person for their own purposes, objectifying the person, degrading the autonomy of the person's decisions.

The fact that vulnerability discourse is used to prosecute all types of exercise of prostitution and especially against irregular immigrants, something which has been reported by all specialists, is despicable. Simplifications, reductionism, generalisations in such a delicate field of setting apart prostitution from trafficking in persons and immigration have to be eradicated because, among other reasons, if there is no clarity of concepts, it is even more difficult for police forces to understand them to prosecute offenders and protect victims.

4.4 Voluntary or Coercive Sexual Exploitation

Criminal treatment of people who live off the exploitation of the prostitution of others has also proved to be a difficult issue in criminal policy. The most liberal sectors have been very critical of criminalisation of procuring in cases when it takes place with adult women's consent. However, in the fight against trafficking in human beings with the aim of sexual exploitation, it has been postulated that to effectively deal with this scourge, which mainly affects women and children, it is necessary to prosecute all forms of sexual exploitation, probably in the belief that behind it there are abuses and humiliating situations, similar to trafficking in persons. This last position certainly seems to ignore the liberty of an adult sex worker who, exercising her freedom of choice, decides to offer her partner, friend or any other person the benefits obtained from her services.

Undoubtedly, this position on criminal response to procuring is linked to the view on prostitution and the model which is projected for its regulation. As it has been mentioned, according to the abolitionist model, prostitution, human trafficking and sexual exploitation are evils which have to be eradicated as they constitute forms of violence against women, degrading them as persons and there is no space for voluntary prostitution. Instead, for those who support the business model and the recognition of voluntary prostitution, to penalise procuring is a form of stigmatising a third party who profits from an activity which must be recognised with all its rights.

Again, the debate focuses on abusive sexual exploitation, that is, the one without deception, violence or intimidation (as in these cases it is clearly culpable), but it is due to the abuse of a situation of need. International agreements seem to follow the abolitionist model, suggesting penalty for any cases of sexual exploitation. Joint Action (97/154/JHA) of 24 February 1997 adopted by the Council on the basis of Article K.3 of the Treaty on European Union concerning action to combat trafficking in human beings and sexual exploitation of children, induced national legislations to complement the concept of trafficking in persons with the one of sexual exploitation understood as: a) sexually exploiting a person other than a child for gainful purposes, where use is made of coercion, particularly violence or threats, or where deceit is used, or where there is abuse of authority or other pressure *such that the person has no choice but to submit to the pressure or abuse of authority*. This way the objective to prosecute any form of abusive sexual exploitation is introduced into the European criminal policy.

Finally, the Directive 2011/36/EU on preventing and combating trafficking in human beings, among the infractions which the countries must categorise in their criminal legislations, indicates a concept of exploitation in the Art. 2.3: Exploitation includes as a minimum, sexual exploitation or prostitution, forced labour or services, including begging, slavery, exploitation of criminal activities, or the removal of organs. Whereby may be visible a broad conception of sexual exploitation, of all forms of exploitation of the prostitution of others or other forms of sexual exploitation, such as the ones related to pornography.

The legislator of 2015 went even further in the authentic interpretation of what sexual exploitation is considered to be in the crime of inciting prostitution of the Article 187.1 of the Penal Code, in which any form of procuring is penalised, even despite an adult person's consent. It stipulates: *En todo caso, se entenderá que hay explotación cuando concurra alguna de las siguientes circunstancias: a) Que la víctima se encuentre en una situación de vulnerabilidad personal o económica. b)*

Que se le impongan para su ejercicio condiciones desproporcionadas, gravosas o abusivas.[18]

The legislator intended to penalise the use of other people's difficulties to subject a person to prostitution and obtain profit, when the person is in a situation of personal necessity. Besides, the purpose is *to objectify the conditions of exploitation*, independently of verifying the victim's consent, as in many cases the victim cannot freely declare their situation of defencelessness.

As it has been said, there are many borderline cases in which it is not easy to determine whether we face a behaviour against the victim's choice, imposed by their personal situation and used by the trafficker, or it is a voluntary act (In the same way Pérez Alonso 2013-2015). Besides, the world of prostitution is located inside the so-called *sex business*, with its innumerable forms: brothels, pornography, self-employment, work under contract, massage parlour, service delivery, leaseholds, etc. It is difficult to identify the presence of sexual exploitation, especially because these activities are clandestine according to their characteristics.

However, evidently, not all types of sexual exploitation are crime related to trafficking in persons, as it is the gravest and the most complex crime with a greater level of harmfulness. Trafficking in persons is characterised by a process or phases, such as capture, transportation and exploitation, being the aim of exploitation (sexual, labour, etc.) another crime, which requires its own reproach.[19] Nonetheless, to determine this point, it is necessary to delve in some relevant technical aspects.

5 Criminal Classification of Trafficking in Human Beings: The Protected Legal Good

It is important to mention the decisiveness of the influence of international agreements on national legislations of different countries to classify the crime of trafficking in human beings, make it visible and condemn it. As it was an *invisible crime* or a crime which had not been prosecuted enough, penal codes had to give a name and a concept to the reality which existed in our society, indifferent to this phenomenon. It is very similar to the case of gender violence which had to be classified, meaning, a name and a detailed description had to be given to the unbearable actions which had already existed in our society, to start the prosecution of offenders and to protect

---

[18] English translation: It will be understood that sexual exploitation takes place in one of the following circumstances: (a) when the victim is in a situation of personal or economic vulnerability. (b) when the victim is subjected to disproportionate, burdensome or abusive conditions for its exercise.

[19] See Villacampa: trafficking in persons constitutes a simple mechanism to enslave a person, represents the normative reference to the process of enslavement. It is reflected in criminal legislation, in the Art. 177.8 *bis* CP: In all cases, the penalties foreseen in this article shall be imposed without prejudice to the relevant one, as appropriate, for the offences of Article 318 *bis* of this Code and other offences effectively committed including those related to the relevant exploitation (Villacampa 2012, p. 232 [author's translation]).

victims. The so-called *white slave traffic* is something which has always existed, as well as the exploitation of prostitution, forced labour, and servitude. However, it did not constitute an object of criminal prosecution for legal practitioners. Indeed, as legal practitioners dealing with this type of crime or reports of the previously mentioned international organisations and NGOs indicate, laws often contain technical problems for their use, there are few sentences, the civil servants, whose task is to apply the law, do not recognise situations of trafficking in human beings in the operative reality (it is confused with prostitution), and the prosecution of these crimes is not sufficiently effective.

It is crucial to analyse which are the most controversial dogmatic aspects of criminal legislation, where impunity, and as a consequence, the lack of victims' protection, may lie. I will focus on the protected legal good of trafficking in persons which, as it will be seen, proves to be crucial for the prosecution of this crime.

5.1 What Is the Protected Legal Good? Validity of Consent in These Cases

There is an extremely interesting debate about the protected legal good in this crime, its reach and contents. This debate is worth a close consideration to understand the limits of the harmfulness of these actions. Undoubtedly, determining the object of prosecution helps to centre the criminal wrong of the actions which are intended to include in the crimes and therefore to increase or decrease victims' protection.

There are three positions in respect thereof: (1) personal freedom is protected. (2) human dignity is protected and (3) it is related to a crime, the final purpose of which is the protection of a legal good, object of exploitation (sexual freedom, crimes against workers, etc.). The consequences for victims' rights protection are enormous according to the chosen position. The third option is virtually unfeasible as it would be against all the international agreements which regulate trafficking in persons, focus on gravity and harmful actions for human rights (beyond an individual legal good), the character of the process or phases (its complexity) in which several legal goods are damaged (liberty, sexual freedom, labour rights, etc.) and the substantivity of this criminal process such as criminal wrong with its own reproach, different from exploitation.[20] The different consequences of the choice between liberty and dignity are worth considering.

In Spain, few authors can support the idea that the crime of trafficking in persons protects personal freedom as the crime classification of the Art. 177 *bis* CP, with its own adaptability (its own title) and the Explanatory Memorandum reveal that behind these crimes, there is the protection of liberty and human dignity. The approach from victims' human rights, which is promoted by the Palermo Protocol 2000 and which is followed by International Institutions, shows that personal

[20] See the previous footnote.

freedom, as an attribute of the human being to decide according to his freedom to choose on their own way of life, cannot be the object of protection in the crime of trafficking in persons. Not only is it so because minors are protected under any circumstances, even without coercive means, but also because the introduction of abusive means (abuse of superiority or vulnerability) shows that freedom of choice is not a decision-making element even in case of adults. It is true that in the cases of adults who consent sexual exploitation in a clear and evident way, human trafficking could not exist, as in these cases the subject would not be objectified, instead, they would use a fundamental right to development of their free personality.

However, although it is not common to assume this option of freedom of choice autonomy in the crime of human trafficking, it is interesting to observe the consequences of considering personal freedom to be the protected legal good in comparative law. According to the Supreme Court of Justice in Peru, the Plenary Agreement 3–2011 CJ/116, para 12: *la trata de personas protege la libertad personal entendida como la capacidad de autodeterminación de una persona para desenvolver su proyecto de vida*[21] (Montoya 2017, pp. 485). This interpretation is certainly erroneous as it leaves children unprotected and thus it is against all the international agreements on children and trafficking in persons. It is also erroneous even in case of adults as the legal good is not freedom, it is dignity, being this one the basic human right from which all the other human rights arise. Children's defencelessness is especially painful; even in the situations mentioned above in the Peruvian Amazon, in which family context incites trafficking of girls. However, this perspective of the legal good also permits an inverted approach in the process of evidence collection. In both cases, the result is the level of criminal protection and weak criminal procedures for victims of trafficking in persons (Montoya 2017, p. 482).

Following Villacampa, if human trafficking must be considered a global crime, the crime which incriminates it must be a value which also receives global recognition of the same level, that is to say, reach and contents of a human right (Villacampa 2011, p. 1111 [author's translation]). Thus, human dignity is a protected interest, able to achieve this objective of recognition of a protectable human right in any state. This is because the International Bill of Human Rights recognise human dignity as their base, although in constitutions, as it is the case of the Spanish Constitution, human dignity is not an expressly recognised fundamental right. In the same sense, Militello, for whom, despite of the variety of human trafficking manifestations, there is a common core: the human person is being used instrumentally by another subject to extract any usefulness (Militello 2018, p. 90 [author's translation]).[22] It is related to the recognition of Kantian ideal placed in international instruments, according to

[21] English translation: Human trafficking protects personal liberty, understood as the capability of self-determination of a person to fulfill their life project. Various sentences, in this same line, argue that if a minor (at the age of criminal responsibility, able to consent sexual freedom, age of 14) consents sexual exploitation, there is no harm, and, therefore, several cases brought to court have been absolved.

[22] In all cases, whatever the legally asset protected by the incriminating norm, in the background is human dignity in its minimum conditions (Militello 2018, p. 91 [author's translation]).

which man exists as an end in himself and no person can be used as means to achieve another person's objectives. Human trafficking is exactly this, objectification of a person, use of a person for another person's purposes, negation of a basic condition of a person—and criminal law must protect the weakest, children and defenceless people, in a situation of necessity or vulnerability at all times.[23] As law is erected as a social instrument against abuses and the empire of the law of the strongest.

I consider that in cases of necessity or vulnerability abuse,[24] when a person is subjected to *objective situations of exploitation*, it is not appropriate to carve liberty, as it is not an objective situation for a choice, it is a situation of submission, in which the intangibility of human dignity, as expression of a person's condition, disappears (Alonso 2007, p. 7).[25] As Montoya claims: Both the asymmetric and vertical context which characterises the relation between the active subject and the victim of trafficking in persons, and the aim of exploitation of the victim in this crime (use of a person for another person's purposes) make the victim's consent irrelevant, especially in case of minors trafficking (Montoya 2017, p. 501 [translation mine]). This argument is clearly observed in the case of a minor and it seems irrefutable. However, in relation to adults there may appear doubts, and therefore it is appropriate to delve into the objective situation of exploitation.

In my opinion, it is important to emphasise that *the objective situation of exploitation does not depend on personal freedom of choice* in any case. It may be clearly observed in labour exploitation. If labour conditions degrade below the threshold which is considered inalienable by labour law (salary, vacation, work day length, etc.), it is a case of labour exploitation, without taking into account the consent of the subject (who may accept them because of different reasons, often out of necessity). In these cases, a person's consent, their freedom of choice and age are irrelevant. *The objective conditions indicate the presence of labour exploitation, something which is indisputable and related to human dignity as an intangible human right.* Undoubtedly, it is more difficult to identify this situation in case of sexual exploitation, in which, due to secrecy reasons and the absence of regulations, a possibility to determine the minimum irrefutable threshold does not exist. However, a judge will be able to evaluate, according to the evidence available, if a person has truly been objectified, used by the dealer for personal purposes, affecting the victim's dignity, beyond the statements of consent by the dealer and the victim's freedom of choice. Victims almost always, due to the relation of power which exists

[23] It is expressed this way in the Directive 2011/36/UE on preventing and combating trafficking in human beings. Article 2.4 says: The consent of a victim of trafficking in human beings to the exploitation, whether intended or actual, shall be irrelevant where any of the means set forth in para 1 has been used.

[24] Interesting is Montoya's reflection: In his view, the case of family victims is a type of vulnerable victims, as the situation of vulnerability dwells in a family or domestic context where a relative dominates the victim or abuses the situation of trust (Montoya 2017, p. 487 [author's translation]). In Latin America, Asia and Africa, many female children are sold by their own parents. This phenomenon is also hidden in girls' forced marriages.

[25] Although the author understands human dignity as moral integrity, which is part of a person's condition, inalienable and independent of the freedom of choice.

between the active subject and the victim, will say that sexual exploitation took place with their complete consent, something which may not be true.

As it has been emphasised in this work, in cases of vulnerability or superiority there is no either explicit coercion, or explicit consent, or any evident opposition as many of these cases take place inside hidden practices of exploitation. As Montoya explains correctly, criminological diagnosis previously exposed,[26] which indicates that equally in cases of a crime committed in the context of organised crime or a crime, which is part of domestic criminal complicity or even individual practices, *the crime of human trafficking is always expressed in a previous or triggered situation of an asymmetric relation of one person's control over another* (Montoya 2017, p. 491 [author's translation]). Therefore, in these cases it is important to verify the objective situation of sexual or labour exploitation, in which the freedom of choice is undermined by the created situation of power. It is evident that if there existed a clear and decisive expression of an adult person's consent, the fundamental right of free personal development would go first. Nevertheless, it is important that in situations of objective exploitation testimonies and proofs on the freedom of choice on both sides are not sufficient. Instead, a serious investigation is required to verify the situations previously mentioned, in which the burden of proof would belong to the active subject to confirm whether there has existed any consent, as behind, there is human rights protection and the protection of victims against objectification.

6 Conclusions

1. Trafficking in human beings is a complex and multi-faceted phenomenon with recurrent ambiguities and opposing interests which hinder our ability to affront or pursue it. Legal definitions, that are limited to set general and abstract concepts, seem to neglect specific situations and personal choices. We encounter many assumptions of borderline cases, in which it is not easy to establish the willingness of the trafficked person.
2. It is an invisible phenomenon, where statistics are not found, or they are disparate, with little persecution and minimal punishment. However, since the Palermo Protocol of 2000, states are urged to establish the crime of trafficking in human beings to guaranty the protection of the human rights of the weakest mainly women and children, against the strongest, mafias, parents who sell their children, etc. Thus, criminal law force has allowed pursuing unsustainable situations of human rights violations.
3. The difficulties in the approach made by criminal policies to the trafficking in human beings for the purpose of sexual exploitation are centred on its links with other phenomena such as clandestine immigration, prostitution and sexual

[26] The reference is made to the previously mentioned studies (Pérez Cepeda 2004) about trafficking in persons in the Peruvian Amazon. However they may be perfectly applied to many situations in Africa, Asia, Eastern Europe, poor regions from which trafficked women arrive in Europe.

exploitation, whose licit and illicit status varies from one country to another and where we find clear-dark difficult to elucidate.

4. The political and criminal approach in Europe against the trafficking in human beings was focus on clandestine immigration and the *criminocentric* paradigm until recent, forgetting the states' duties of protection with the victims. Only with Directive 2011/36/EU has there been a political and criminal approach towards the recognition of the human rights of the victims.
5. Conceptual autonomy and regulations of trafficking in human beings versus states immigration policy and versus the fight against organised crime have been a key issue to implement a real criminal policy to protect victims of sex or labour trade, to which they may be subjected.
6. For radical feminism which supports the abolitionist model, prostitution is an activity related to gender violence and patriarchy, which is humiliating and objectifies women (who mainly exercise it) and, thus, must be eradicated prosecuting the client. As it may be observed, this approach to prostitution and the exploitation of the prostitution of others considers them to be similar to trafficking in humans, as in this case a person's free will would be conditioned by the socioeconomic situation of inequality. Certainly, prohibition does not solve problems, but hides them and, in some cases, enlarges them, as can happen with activities that are usually surrounded by certain violence such as prostitution.
7. The business model of prostitution is based on a distinction between free prostitution and coercive prostitution that would be closer to trafficking. However, the problem is that there are many alleged limits where it is not easy to identify the boundaries between voluntary and coercive prostitution, especially in assumed situations of the victim's vulnerability in which there is no scam, violence or intimidation. That is to say, difficulties start when we intend to treat differently two realities which often overlap one another.
8. The concept of vulnerability of the victim of trafficking has been controversial. For a sector of feminism, the discourse of vulnerability hides a treatment of women that practices prostitution as weak persons, without freewill. However, the authors of international agreements realise that not only does this behaviour takes place with explicit violence, but also, in many cases, there is an abuse of power, as it happens with parents, teachers, authorities, or an abuse of a situation of vulnerability such as poverty, marginality and incapacity to survive. This is something that is leveraged by dealers. In these cases, victims do not have the possibility to choose, neither is there a clear opposition to exploitation.
9. We cannot presume that the exercise of prostitution is always coercive; neither can we believe that it is always voluntary. As we have insisted, there are many situations in which by an adult woman concealing sexual exploitation, similar to trafficking in persons, exercised prostitution. Feminisation, poverty and marginality may be associated to the exercise of prostitution, in which autonomy of willingness is not always clear. It is impossible to ignore vulnerability of many women and children, especially those who are mostly affected by poverty in the world. The proof of this situation is that the data on trafficking in persons revealed by international reports indicate that victims usually come from the

poorest countries around the globe, without considering the fact that domestic human trafficking is directed from poor to rich areas inside the same country.

10. On the classification of the different crimes, the discussion must focus on the protected interest and the validity of consent in cases of trafficking. The positions that consider that the protected legal right in the crime of trafficking is personal freedom, as in Peruvian legislation, where there is a total lack of protection of the victims, even of minors that pass the criminal age to consent sexual relations. This interpretation goes against the International Agreements for the protection of minors and against the Palermo Trafficking Protocol.
11. Following Villacampa, if human trafficking must be considered a global crime, the crime which incriminates it must be a value with global recognition of the same level, that means with the scope and content of a human right. Thus, human dignity is a protected interest, able to achieve this objective of recognition of a protectable human right in any state. Human trafficking is exactly this, objectification of a person, a person obtaining profit from another one, negation of a fundamental condition of human—and criminal law must always protect the weakest, children and defenceless people, in a situation of necessity or vulnerability.
12. From a criminological point of view, in human trafficking there is always an asymmetric reality between the dealer and the victim, situations in which it is difficult to perceive the autonomy of the person's decisions. That is, beyond the initial mechanism used by the dealer to get the victim inside his logic what is truly serious is the permanent control over the victim which the offender exercises, using the person for his own profit, using people as objects, degrading the autonomy of their decisions.
13. Therefore, in situations of objective exploitation testimonies and proofs on the freedom of choice on both sides are not sufficient. Instead, a serious investigation is required to verify the situations previously mentioned, in which the burden of proof would belong to the active subject to confirm whether there has existed any consent, because there is human rights protection and the protection of victims against objectification.

References

Alonso M (2007) ¿Protección penal de la dignidad? A propósito de los delitos relativos a la prostitución y a la trata de personas para la explotación sexual. Revista Penal 19:3–20

Alsedo Q (2012) El horror de Cabeza de Cerdo: 'Una mujer atada a un árbol y devorada por perros'. El Mundo. http://www.elmundo.es/elmundo/2012/02/01/madrid/1328126395.html

Armendáriz F (2017) Caso Cursach: El juez imputa cinco delitos a Cursach por las fiestas en Tito's. Diario de Mallorca. http://www.diariodemallorca.es/mallorca/2017/08/22/juez-imputa-cinco-delitos-cursach/1241929.html

Bohórquez L (2016) Sexo, drogas y corrupción en la policía local de Palma. El País. https://politica.elpais.com/politica/2016/07/03/actualidad/1467539442_889012.html

Boza E (2017) Sobre la prostitución. Un análisis desde la política criminal y su necesidad de legalización. Tesis Doctoral. Universidad Pablo de Olavide, Sevilla

Burgo P (2015) La trata de personas con fines de explotación sexual es una de las más extendida y normalizada. El Diario.es. http://www.eldiario.es/norte/euskadi/personas-explotacion-sexual-extendida-normalizada_0_414358873.html

Castells M (2001) La era de la información. Fin de milenio, vol 3. Alianza Editorial, Barcelona

Daunis A (2013) La trata de seres humanos. Tirant lo Blanch, Valencia

Daunis A (2017) La inmigración ante la encrucijada: el tráfico de personas, la trata de seres humanos y la explotación sexual. In: Rodríguez LZ (ed) Criminalidad organizada transnacional: una amenaza a los Estados democráticos. Tirant lo Blanch, Valencia, pp 445–476

De La Cuesta JL (1999) Las nuevas corrientes internacionales en materia de persecución de delitos sexuales a la luz de los documentos de organismos internacionales y europeos. In: Diez Ripollés JL (ed) Delitos contra la libertad sexual. Estudios de Derecho Judicial, Madrid, pp 323–373. Posted on the web: http://www.ehu.eus/documents/1736829/2010409/CLC+45+Las+nuevas+corrientes+internacionales+materia+persecucion.pdf

Domínguez I, Gálvez JJ (2017) 5.660 víctimas de esclavitud afloran tras las reformas de los últimos años. El País. https://politica.elpais.com/politica/2017/04/14/actualidad/1492152357_266303.html?rel=mas

EUROPEAN UNION (EU) Serious and Organised Crime Threat Assessment, Crime in the age of technology (SOCTA) (2017) Report. https://www.europol.europa.eu/activities-services/main-reports/european-union-serious-and-organised-crime-threat-assessment-2017

Ferrajoli L (1999) Derechos y garantías. La ley del más débil. Trotta, Madrid

Giménez-Salinas Framis A, De La Corte L (2010) Crimen.org: evolución y claves de la delincuencia organizada. Ariel, Barcelona

Giménez-Salinas A, Requena L, De La Corte L (2011) ¿Existe un perfil de delincuente organizado?, Exploración a partir de una muestra española. Revista Electrónica de Ciencia Penal y Criminología 13(3):1–32

Iborra YS (2016) El 34% de las víctimas de trata para la explotación sexual en España son de origen rumano. El Diario.es. http://www.eldiario.es/catalunya/victimas-explotacion-Espana-origen-rumano_0_541396538.html

Las cifras de la explotación sexual en España: 40.000 mujeres la sufren (2016) Eco Diario/EuropaPress. http://ecodiario.eleconomista.es/sociedad/noticias/7845621/09/16/Las-cifras-de-la-explotacion-sexual-en-Espana-40000-mujeres-la-sufren-.html

Lorente-Molina B (2016) Otredad, marginación y política en la prostitución. In: Copello PL, Rodriguez AD (eds) Colectivos en los márgenes del Derecho. Tirant lo Blanch, Valencia, pp 329–368

Maqueda M (2015) Cuando el discurso sobre la vulnerabilidad se convierte en un discurso ideológico (A propósito de las "víctimas" de la prostitución y el tráfico sexual de mujeres). In: Pérez Álvarez F (ed) Serta, In memoriam Louk Houlsman. Ediciones Universidad de Salamanca, Salamanca

Mestre JF (2017) El presidente de Acotur ingresa en prisión acusado de varios delitos. Diario de Mallorca. http://www.diariodemallorca.es/mallorca/2017/05/12/presidente-acotur-ingresa-prision-acusado/1214422.html

Mintjas L, Molnar L (2016) Trabajadoras sexuales: víctimas de la exclusión. Estudio sobre la victimización de las trabajadoras sexuales en la provincia de Málaga. In: Copello PL, Rodriguez AD (eds) Colectivos en los márgenes del Derecho. Tirant lo Blanch, Valencia, pp 305–328

Militello V (2018) La tratta di esseri humani: la politica criminale multilivello e la problematica distinzione con il traffico di migrante. Rivista Italiana di Diritto e Procedure Penale LXI(1):86–108

Montoya Y (2017) El delito de trata de personas como delito complejo y sus dificultades en la jurisprudencia peruana. In: Rodríguez LZ (ed) Criminalidad organizada transnacional: una amenaza a los Estados democráticos. Tirant lo Blanch, Valencia, pp 477–506

Mujica J, Cavagnoud R (2011) Mecanismos de explotación sexual de niñas y adolescentes en los alrededores del puerto fluvial de Pucallpa. Anthropologica 29:91–110
Mujica J (2014) Trayectorias y ciclos de explotación sexual y trata para la explotación sexual de mujeres en la Amazonía peruana. Anthropologica 33:163–177
Palomino S (2017) La indiferencia golpea a las víctimas de trata de América Latina. El País. https://elpais.com/internacional/2017/05/23/colombia/1495512913_588284.html
Penalva M (2016) Prisión sin fianza para el comisario de Palma y tres agentes por la trama corrupta de la Policía Local. Ok.Diario. https://okdiario.com/espana/2016/12/14/prision-sin-fianza-comisario-palma-tres-agentes-trama-corrupta-policia-local-598088
Pérez Alonso E (2013-2015) La política europea en materia de trata de seres humanos. Revista de la Facultad de Derecho de la Universidad de Granada, (16-18), 1147–1194
Pérez Cepeda AI (2004) Globalización, tráfico internacional ilícito de personas y derecho penal. Granada, Comares
Programa De Las Naciones Unidas Para El Desarrollo (PNUD) (2016) Informe sobre Desarrollo Humano 2016. http://hdr.undp.org/sites/default/files/HDR2016_SP_Overview_Web.pdf
Sahuquillo MR (2016) Prohibido pagar por sexo en Suecia, Francia y otros seis países. El Pais. https://elpais.com/internacional/2016/04/07/actualidad/1460050306_463588.ht/ml
Villacampa C (2011) Art. 177 bis. In: Olivares GQ (ed) Comentarios al Código Penal español, vol I. Aranzadi, Navarra, pp 1093–1113
Villacampa C (2012) La trata de seres humanos para explotación sexual: relevancia penal y confluencia con la prostitución. In: Estiarte CV, Gomis JRB (eds) Prostitución: ¿hacia la legalización? Tirant lo Blanch, Valencia, pp 221–266
Verdú D (2016) Yo trabajé para Torbe. Tres chicas relatan a EL PAÍS su sórdida experiencia con el rey del porno español imputado y encarcelado por delitos de difusión de pornografía. El País. https://elpais.com/ccaa/2016/06/14/catalunya/1465919624_004283.html
UNODC (2011) Algunos datos relevantes sobre la Trata de Personas. https://www.unodc.org/documents/lpo-brazil/sobre-unodc/Fact_Sheet_Dados_Trafico_de_Pessoas_geral_ESP.pdf
UNODC (2016) Global Report on trafficking in persons 2016. https://www.unodc.org/documents/data-and-analysis/glotip/2016_Global_Report_on_Trafficking_in_Persons.pdf
Women's Link Worldwide (2017) Informe # 7. Víctimas de trata en América Latina. Entre la desprotección y la indiferencia, http://www.womenslinkworldwide.org/files/4d238ebdc3a934ff85ae8398bb390e3a.pdf

Laura Zuñiga Rodriguez (lzr@usal.es) is a Professor of Criminal Law at the University of Salamanca. She has carried out research stays at the universities of Friborg in Switzerland and Friborg in Germany. Her last stay is at the Institute of Economic Criminal Law and Criminology with Prof. Klaus Tiedemann. She has published the following monographs in Spain: 'Personal Liberty and Citizen Security', 'Bases for a Model for the Imputation of Criminal Responsibility of Legal Persons,' 'Criminal Policy' and 'Organized Crime and Criminal Law System'. She has published book chapters in 'Penitentiary Law Manual', 'Introduction to Criminal Law'. She authored various articles published in specialised magazines in Spain, Portugal, Italy, Peru, Colombia, Guatemala, Brazil, Argentina, Mexico and Chile. Her lines of research are: Human Rights and Criminal Law, Criminal Responsibility of Legal Persons, Criminal Policy and Organized Crime. She is currently Director of the Master of Criminal Law at the University of Salamanca (http://masterderechopenal.es/) and Director of the Observatory of Transnational Organized Crime (http://crimtrans.usal.es/).

Combating Human Trafficking in South Africa

Nina Mollema

Abstract South Africa is a fertile ground for the human trafficking crime due to the propensity of southward migration flows, porous borders and coastlines, fragile structures and institutions, serious rates of poverty, and persistent gender inequalities. However, the jurisdiction is currently one of the few nations in Africa that have actively engaged in combating the crime. South Africa has adopted specific and comprehensive anti-trafficking legislation, namely the Prevention and Combating of Trafficking in Persons Act 7 of 2013, essentially based on the UN Protocol of 2000. Before the implementation of this Act on 9 August 2015, the crime of human trafficking was penalised in a fragmented manner by means of diverse common-law crimes such as assault, rape, murder, abduction, kidnapping, and also statutory crimes such as racketeering, money laundering. The introduction of the new all-inclusive legislation covers all aspects of human trafficking by protecting vulnerable persons and victims of trafficking; by preventing the crime by means of awareness raising and reducing the demand, and by punishing traffickers in a commensurate manner. This chapter explores the above-mentioned aspects; elucidate on the root causes and particular types of trafficking as well as the flow patterns of human trafficking in this particular region.

1 Introduction

South Africa, the southernmost country in Africa, is in many ways a unique country. After years of political turmoil, its peaceful transition from apartheid to democracy in 1994, and transformation of the conflict stands out as one of the most significant events in modern history. South Africa is located in the poorest part of the world, yet it is ranked by the World Bank as an upper middle-income country with the second largest economy in Africa, and the 33rd largest in the world (World Bank 2019). The

N. Mollema (✉)
University of South Africa, Law Faculty, Pretoria, South Africa
e-mail: mollen@unisa.ac.za

A. M. Rodrigues, M. J. Guia (eds.), *New Forms of Human Trafficking*,
https://doi.org/10.1007/978-3-031-39732-5_4

country's GDP or GNI is four times greater than some of its Southern African neighbours. The jurisdiction has copious natural resources, its legal and financial communications, transport and energy sectors are well-developed, and its stock exchange ranks amongst the top twenty in the world. Still, similar to many other regions in Southern Africa, the country has also suffered adverse economic, political, and ecological changes that has had serious implications on the institutions shaping the security and livelihood of communities (Truong 2006). These dynamics augment the conceivability of human trafficking in the region.

South Africa has been categorised as one of the most unequal countries in the world (World Bank 2018). The new government of the past 29 years is still confronted by many historical issues, such as educational imbalances caused by apartheid, the unequal distribution of wealth, and dissimilar service delivery. South Africa is mainly a developing country; however, the developmental process is impeded by crime, which damages human, social and cultural capital. Crime destroys society's moral character, accomplished especially through the crime of corruption. Corruption in the public sector, as well as in government, is steadily increasing, resulting in low investment levels from foreign stakeholders. This yet again impacts on the general population by further impoverishing them. As will be seen in this chapter, these are some of the root causes which contribute to the trafficking crisis—a growing problem—in South Africa.

Before the implementation of specific legislation to combat human trafficking, the country's commitment to curb the crime in the region was largely accomplished by adopting several international and regional human-rights instruments. The country became an official party to the primary international anti-trafficking instrument, namely the Protocol to Prevent, Suppress and Punish Trafficking in Persons Especially Women and Children, supplementing the United Nations Convention against Transnational Organized Crime 55/25 of 15 November 2000 (Trafficking Protocol). This instrument was signed by South Africa on 14 December 2000, but only ratified on 20 February 2004. On the African continent, except for the Southern African Development Community's (SADC) 10 Year Strategic Plan of Action on Combating Trafficking in Persons, especially Women and Children (2009–2019), there is no regional or sub-regional instrument that explicitly combat human trafficking, or that contains concrete directives for combating the crime. However, South Africa has concluded many bi- and multilateral cooperation agreements in the sub-region with it closest neighbours as regards human rights, refugees, drugs, education, corruption, gender issues, etcetera. As many of the countries in sub-Saharan Africa do not have applicable legislation or even specific policies to fight trafficking, these agreements are very important as they encompass some of the concerns related to trafficking in persons, and could be utilised to combat the crime.

South Africa was rated by the United States' Department of State as a Tier 2 level-country for seven consecutive years, however, in 2018, the jurisdiction was downgraded to the Tier 2 Watch List where it remained in 2023 (US Department of State 2023). This rating has been allocated to the country as it does not fully comply with the minimum standards provided in the United States' Trafficking Victims Protection Act of 2000 (TVPA), but is making significant efforts to bring themselves into compliance with those standards. The drop in rating was the consequence of the government's failure to indicate any further efforts in combating the crime, as compared to the previous year's results. The jurisdiction does currently comply with international obligations as the Trafficking Protocol's minimum standards have been met, and domestic anti-trafficking legislation, namely the Prevention and Combating of Trafficking in Persons Act 7 of 2013 (Trafficking Act), has been passed. However, the implementing regulations for the Trafficking Act's immigration provisions covered in sections 15, 16, and 31(2)(b)(ii) have not yet been promulgated (US Department of State 2023)

In this chapter, the root causes of human trafficking in South Africa will first be examined. This will involve identifying the distinctive factors which contribute to making the country so susceptible to the offence. There are furthermore unique forms of trafficking in South Africa, many originating from specific cultural beliefs. The chapter intends to clarify the reasons for these particular types of trafficking. South Africa has been identified as a human-trafficking source, transit, and destination country for men, women, and children for mainly labour and sex trafficking (US Department of State 2023). The flows of trafficked persons to, from and within the country will be elucidated. Legislation regulating the crime of trafficking will be explained as to the prevention of the crime, protection of its victims and persons vulnerable to trafficking, and prosecution of the perpetrators of human trafficking. Lastly, the chapter will assess the country's successes and failures in eradicating the crime of human trafficking, and briefly discuss the way forward.

2 Root Causes of Human Trafficking in South Africa

The South African Trafficking Act recognises in its preamble that poor socio-economic circumstances and the demand for the services of trafficking victims contribute to making persons vulnerable to becoming victims of trafficking. However, nowhere in the Act are these root causes specifically addressed, thereby failing to bolster preventative measures. The demands for the services of trafficking victims are only dealt with by criminalising the use of these services. It is essential to consider the core causes of trafficking of the specific country to enable an understanding of trafficking in the jurisdiction. This again facilitates suitable responses towards trafficking, and the development of appropriate anti-trafficking policies.

In South Africa specifically, slavery was already established as an institution during colonialism. This oppression was perpetuated by the apartheid regime, and is presently sustained in the form of modern-day slavery or human trafficking. The root causes of human trafficking in the country are in some aspects very distinct, but in others very similar to the rest of the world, which may include, amongst others, poverty, lack of adequate employment opportunities, increasing economic inequalities, lack of education prospects, and discriminatory gender practices.

In especially the last two decades, South Africa has seen an immense migration of foreigners seeking to escape the impoverished living conditions in their countries of origin, and anxious to find employment in this country (Chichava and Kiremire 2007).[1] These people also flee from war,[2] hunger, political unrest, economic turmoil, deadly diseases, amongst other reasons. Not only do these migrant workers place additional strain on a country already plagued by high unemployment levels,[3] widening economic disparities, wage inequalities for a surplus of low-skilled workers (Bermudez 2008),[4] and a high cost of living, traffickers prey on these desperate migrants for labour exploitation. South Africans in poor rural areas also move to more affluent urban centres because of reduced economic opportunities and loss of traditional livelihoods. These are all factors enhancing susceptibility to human trafficking.

Not only is South Africa a major migrant destination in Africa, the jurisdiction also has the highest number of asylum seekers in the world (Apleni 2012).[5] The jurisdiction moreover accommodates an estimated five million illegal immigrants, including approximately three million Zimbabweans (Crush and Williams 2001). These numbers are confirmed by Solomon (2005), who, however, cautions that accurate numbers are difficult to attain. According to Adepoju (2000), migration has always been endemic in Africa, but the high influx of migrants into South Africa is facilitated by permeable land and sea borders (Delport et al. 2007),[6] as well as the ineffective policing of these boundaries, and poor monitoring of transportation modes. This allows trafficked persons to become an indistinguishable part of these flows.

[1] Adepoju (2000) asserts that: 'At the current growth rate of 2.7% in the labour force, the region now requires 7.5 million new jobs merely to stabilise the employment situation. Beginning from the 1980s, Sub-Saharan Africa (SSA) countries experienced negative economic growth rates; GDP stagnated whilst population increased annually at 3% and average per capita income declined by one quarter. … Today SSA is the world's poorest region, where people were poorer at the end of the eighties than they had been in the beginning of the decade'.

[2] For the past two decades 'Sub-Saharan Africa has been a theatre of internecine warfare' (Adepoju 2000). More than six million people became refugees and another 17 million displaced persons during 1969–1990 when 17 of the world's recorded 43 civil wars occurred in Africa.

[3] According to the World Bank (2019), unemployment is at 27.6%, with youths aged 15–24 accounting for 55.2% of the unemployed population. More females (58.8%) than males (49.2%) are unemployed. See also CIA (2020).

[4] 'Unlike many other emerging economies, South Africa's Apartheid legacy is such that income inequality is amongst the most severe in the world, and a very large proportion of the workforce earns extremely low wages relative to the cost of living' (Altman 2007).

[5] According to the UNHCR, in 2015, there were 586,000 people of concern in South Africa, comprising of 112,192 refugees and an estimate of 463,940 asylum seekers. The refugees are mainly from the Democratic Republic of Congo (30,125), Somalia (40,133), Burundi (3653), Zimbabwe (6217), Cote D'Ivoire (6035), Rwanda (1814), Ethiopia (18,830), and other states in Africa (5385).

[6] South Africa has a total perimeter of 4862 km, with bordering countries consisting of Botswana (1840 km), Lesotho (909 km), Mozambique (491 km), Namibia (967 km), Eswatini (430 km), and Zimbabwe (225 km). It also comprises of 2798 km of unprotected coastline. The land borders are particularly difficult to police due to their length and because local communities share cultural relations with people in adjacent countries. See CIA (2020).

It is especially women and children who migrate to and within South Africa to escape poverty and gender-based violence. In some South African cultures, females are regarded as subordinate in status, and thus have less power than their male counterparts. Their inequality on income and access to resources render them vulnerable to exploitation (Truong 2006).[7] Gender inequality[8] and associated cultural dynamics form part of the main root causes of trafficking in the country because of:

> …the deeply patriarchal ethos which pervades South African society. Rigid social constructions of masculinity and femininity and a profoundly conservative ethos relegates women and children to positions of being 'owned' (and therefore disposable at the whim of the 'owner') and there is limited recognition of even women, and still less of children, as human beings with rights in their own right. There is a sense of entitlement around sex and sexual activity—almost as though that's what women and children are there for, and they shouldn't complain about it (Truong 2006).

As can be seen from the excerpt above, there is a general tolerance of violent behaviour towards women and children in South African society. This culture of patriarchal privilege has resulted in the country having one of the highest rates of rape in the world. South Africa is regarded as the 'world's rape capital' as it has the highest number of confirmed rapes of all countries, with nearly half of the victims younger than 18 years old (AfricaCheck 2019).[9]

Another root cause of trafficking in this region which relates to gender discrimination is the lack of access to education, especially for girl children. Some girls

---

[7] Gettu (2012) asserts that women exercise less power over control of land in sub-Saharan Africa than anywhere else in the world: 'Women in sub-Saharan Africa and elsewhere have less control over productive resources such as assets, land and credit; their time is often devoted to activities that are non-marketed and undervalued; and their access to key institutions such as courts and markets is curtailed'.

[8] There is still much discrimination against women despite a gender-even population (from a population of 50,460, 00 with 25,002, 37 males and females 25,457, 61 females) (2011 census). See CIA (2020). Discrimination against women is especially noticeable in indigenous law as seen in the case of *Bhe and Others v Khayelitsha Magistrate and Others* (CCT 49/03) [2004] ZACC 17; 2005 (1) SA 580 (CC); 2005 (1) BCLR 1 (CC). The South African Constitutional Court held in this case that that the custom that the eldest son inherits his father's property after his father dies is unconstitutional, as it is a violation of women's rights to equality and human dignity. This is the case in most African societies, where cultural structures limit and define 'women's access to credit, land and modes of production thus impinging seriously on women's self-actualisation and autonomy' (Adepoju 2000). For example, a recent Zimbabwean Supreme Court decision held that women 'should never be considered as adults within the family, but only as "junior males"' (Adepoju 2000). In South Africa, sections 8, 24–25 of the Promotion of Equality and Prevention of Unfair Discrimination Act 2000 guarantee that no person be discriminated against on the ground of gender.

[9] According to Interpol's estimates of 1996, a South African woman had a greater chance of being raped in this country than learning how to read. Statistics from the South African Police Service show that in 2019, 41,583 women were raped. This rape rate increased from 70.5% in 2018 to 72% in 2019, i.e. an average of 114 rapes per day. See AfricaCheck (2019). One must keep in mind that less than 1% of rape cases are reported to police.

attend primary schooling but are denied any further education (Delport et al. 2007).[10] This happens especially in rural areas where tradition demands that these girls produce offspring as soon as they are of child-bearing age. It is not unusual to see girls as young as 14 years already being mothers. Children who have ailing HIV/AIDS parents or siblings are also obliged to leave school prematurely to assume the role of caregiver. Lack of education lessens these children's likelihoods of employment in the formal sector, and they are forced to find work in the informal sector with little or no skills, where they become easy prey for traffickers (Delport et al. 2007; Molo Songololo 2000).

In South Africa, health crises such as Covid-19 and the HIV/AIDS pandemic have especially led to the disintegration of family structures. South Africa has the highest ranking of people living with HIV/AIDS (7.7 million) in the world, and the most HIV/AIDS deaths also occur in this country (71,000 persons) (CIA 2020). The prevalence rate of HIV/AIDS amongst adults is the fourth highest in the world with 20.4% of all adults living with the disease in 2108. A direct result of adult AIDS-related deaths is orphan-headed households. It is estimated that 1.2 million children under the age of 18 are the primary caretakers of their families in this jurisdiction (Chichava and Kiremire 2007). As mentioned above, these children become highly susceptible to the ploys of human traffickers. The pervasiveness of HIV/AIDS in the country, as well as fear and/or ignorance on the disease's transmission have again increased the demand for juveniles as sexual partners, as these children are regarded as disease-free. This so-called '*marche du petit vagin*' (literally 'the market of the small vagina') (Allais 2006) is exploited by traffickers who manage the supply to fulfil customers' needs. The belief that HIV/AIDS-infected males who have sex with a child (a virgin) will be cured or cleansed also contributes to the fact that increasingly younger girls or even infants are targeted by human traffickers. This could be one of the contributing factors to the high numbers of infants and children being raped in South Africa (Bermudez 2008; Andersen 2018). These children are also utilised in South Africa's growing sex tourism industry where visitors to the country pursue local sexual encounters as part of their travel experience (Bermudez 2008).[11] These distinctive causes of trafficking in South Africa have led to the country being ranked 133 out of 160 countries in the Global Slavery Index (2023) as to the prevalence of human trafficking, with estimations of as many as 158,000 modern slaves in the country.

[10] Lack in education also results in ignorance about trafficking. Only 33% of people living in South Africa regard trafficking as a serious problem (Adepoju 2005), and 29% had no awareness of the crime (Bermudez 2008).

[11] Adepoju (2005): 'Tourists from Germany, the Netherlands, and the United Kingdom use gifts and cash to lure young boys and girls under the age of 18 who reside at tourists' spots into pornographic sex acts. They later put the films on the Internet with the victims' names and addresses. The victims' parents are deceived with gifts under the pretence that their wards would be assisted with education and jobs abroad. The unsuspecting children who follow the tourists to Europe end up as sex slaves to the traffickers or are distributed into the paedophile network'.

3 Forms of Exploitation in South Africa

Although all people may be trafficked in this jurisdiction, it is a well-known fact that as the most vulnerable in society, females and children are generally targeted for sexual exploitation. Men, women and children may also be trapped in exploitative labour practices, yet in Southern Africa child labour is escalating at a significant rate (Sloth-Nielsen 2016). This is the only region in the world where child labour is increasing. The growth in child labour may be attributed to the influx of juveniles into the country, as it is thought that 'as many as 30,000 young people annually arrive in South Africa from SADC countries' (Chichava and Kiremire 2007). It is estimated that children comprise 60% of all trafficked persons in South Africa, and that approximately 28,000–38,000 children are exploited as prostitutes in South Africa (Molo Songololo 2000). In Cape Town alone, children offer 25% of all prostitution services, even though prostitution is criminalised by the Sexual Offences Act of 1957.

Apart from sex trafficking, women and girls are mostly subjected to domestic servitude and child-minding, whereas boys are forced into criminal activities, forced begging, street hawking, the food service sectors, livestock herding, and mine and farm labour (US Department of State 2019). It seems that even in agricultural child labour in South Africa, girls comprise the majority of the victims—a study established that 55% of all 10–14-year-old-workers were girls; whereas the older age group of 15–17-year-olds consisted of 40% girls. The decline in the number of girls in the older age group may be attributed to them leaving to rear their children, and to deal with accompanying domestic responsibilities (Bosch and Gordon 1996). Trafficked persons are often compelled to commit additional criminal acts such as selling drugs to patrons; however, they may also be coerced into becoming drug mules by their traffickers (Van der Watt 2018).

A unique form of trafficking in this jurisdiction is the abuse of the custom of *ukuthwala* (literally meaning 'to carry' in isiXhosa) or forced marriage. This tradition is practised for the conclusion of a valid customary marriage and comprises a pretend abduction of the female by the male's family to force the female's family into negotiations for a customary marriage. This practice was especially performed for timid males or females who were not yet married by a certain age. Usually, a customary marriage begins with a marriage proposal by the family of the future husband-to-be to the family of the proposed wife-to-be. If the proposal is accepted, the intended bridegroom's family commences with negotiations as to the payment of the bride price (*lobola)* to the intended bride's family. On finalisation of the negotiations and the *lobola* price settled, many rituals and ceremonies follow. To avoid these ceremonials, the practice of *ukuthwala* may be employed. In this practice, both parties' families are involved in the proposal stage, and both the intended bridegroom and bride must give consent to the process. A mock abduction is staged at dusk, where the future bride is abducted by the bridegroom's family (with her consent) and taken to their homestead. The bridegroom's family then informs the bride's family that she is in their custody, and that they wish to begin marriage negotiations. At no stage is sexual intercourse allowed between the couple. After this step, normal customary marriage negotiations follow.

The custom is still practiced in certain rural areas but abused by especially elderly men who pay money to marry a virgin, or an underaged girl (Mwambene and Sloth-Nielsen 2011). The girl usually does not know the prospective husband, and does not consent, but is married off, usually by a family member (commonly the uncle or grandmother). This act amounts to human trafficking as evidenced in *Jezile v S and Others* (2015). In this case, the appellant appealed against his sentence of 22 years' imprisonment for human trafficking, rape, common assault and assault with intent to cause grievous bodily harm. Jezile married a 14-year-old girl according to the *ukuthwala* custom, without her consent. The girl refused to marry him as she wanted to continue with her education, and ran away, but was apprehended and returned to him. She suffered abuse as he not only assaulted her with a belt, but also raped her on several occasions. His appeal was dismissed. Another *ukuthwala* case occurred in 2017, where a 13-year-old mentally disabled orphaned girl from the Eastern Cape was trafficked and forced into a marriage with a 61-year-old man. Her aunt and uncle, who were abusive towards her, organised the marriage. She was frequently raped by her so-called husband, who also forced her to do house labour, such as the daily cooking and cleaning (Sain 2019).

Certain cultures in South Africa still adhere to the practice of virginity testing. It has been submitted that this ceremony may expose these girls to human traffickers who allegedly scrutinise these rituals to find those girls verified as virgins (Allais 2010). The jurisdiction also has an active market for trafficking in body parts, whether domestically or globally. Internationally, it has been revealed in *State v Netcare Kwa-Zulu Natal (Pty) Ltd* (2010) that kidney donors from Brazil travel to South Africa where their organs are transplanted to mainly Israeli recipients (Scheper-Hughes 2000). Locally, organs are harvested to be utilised for traditional medicine (or *muti*) (Bermudez 2008).[12] *Muti* (or rather *umuthi*) is a word from the Nguni languages in South Africa referring to traditional potions made from natural products such as herbs, roots, bark, plants, animal or mineral products. The medicine may be used to cure various ailments such as infertility, erectile dysfunction, cancer, HIV/AIDS, but also to fulfil specific needs such as an increase of wealth and status, succeeding in court cases, and regaining of lost lovers, amongst others. It is believed that the use of human body parts increases the strength of some medicines. This conviction has led to trafficking of body parts becoming a pervasive problem in Southern Africa (Fellows 2008). For example, in Polokwane, the capital of the Limpopo province, 21 young girls had been reported missing from the community since 2004 (Bermudez 2008). Of these 21 girls, seven girls' bodies were discovered in 2008. They all had their wombs removed, probably as cure for others' infertility. As evidenced by the extensive removal of organs from very young children or

[12] According to statistics from the South African Police Services (SAPS), approximately 150–300 *muti* murders occur annually (see Allais 2010). It is highly likely that these estimates are underrated due to poor documentation and lack of evidence of this type of trafficking in the country. Cultural beliefs and fear that a similar fate would befall them forces witnesses to silence.

people suffering from albinism (or both), the potions made from these persons are considered as particularly powerful.[13] The medicine becomes even stronger if the body parts are harvested while the victim is still alive, as seen in a murder case heard in the Alberton Magistrate's Court (Mooki 2012). In this instance, Monde Tokwe, the bishop of the Eden Zionist Church in Katlehong, and his wife, consulted a traditional healer as to their dwindling church congregation. They were told to mix herbs with the human tissue of a girl, and their church will flourish again. They then abducted Yonela Skweyiya, a 9-year-old girl. All her body parts were removed from her body while she was still alive. The bishop's wife sat on top of the child's chest and used a razor blade to cut the girl's vagina from her body, while the bishop removed the girl's eyes, ears and fingers, using the same blade. Such incidences occur quite frequently in the jurisdiction, as further demonstrated in the case of Moses Mokgethi. He was found guilty of murder in the Rand Supreme Court for killing six children and selling their organs to a local businessman who wanted to boost his business with special *muti*. It is clear that the trafficking of body parts generates great sums of money for both traditional healers, as well as those collecting and delivering the organs to the healers.

There are many other customs which contribute to the spread of trafficking in the region (Edmonds 2005). One such traditional practice is child fostering and child placements, where children are placed in the custody of a family member for extended periods of time. It is especially the grandmother who is selected for this purpose, and who must take care of her charge by means of her small government pension. As in many cases, this income is inadequate for large families to subsist on, and the children are sent out to find work. Begging is another form of trafficking in the area, especially at traffic lights, where especially babies and young children are hired out to beggars for as little as ZAR20 per day (Comrie and Wiener 2010). The belief is held that motorists will sympathise and give more money to a beggar with a baby or a small child. Many of these children are drugged to keep quiet or dehydrated because of exposure to the direct sun. Children also risk illegal adoption, and are trafficked for use in ritual sacrifice (Allais 2006), to paedophile rings, and for use in pornographic videos.

4 Human Trafficking Flow Patterns in South Africa

Trafficking in South Africa comprises national and transnational trafficking to, from, and within the country. International trafficking mainly involves organised crime networks from Africa, Asia and Eastern Europe, amongst others. It is widely believed that syndicates from Nigeria control the commercial sex trade within the jurisdiction (US Department of State 2023). Not only do these criminals import

[13] A new trend apparently is harvesting the heads of bald men, which according to witchdoctors in Mozambique contains gold. The heads are used in rituals to advance the wealth of clients. See BBC (2017).

women from Nigeria to South Africa as prostitutes, local South African girls are also kidnapped by them, and held captive as sex slaves. Nigerian syndicates are also involved in the transnational trafficking of South African women to work in African migrant clients' households in Europe and the United States. Other international trafficking rings in South Africa are operated by Chinese, Russian, Bulgarian, and Thai crime cartels (Bermudez 2008). Many females (and LGBTQI+ persons) from overseas countries such as Thailand, Taiwan, China, Russia, Ukraine, Bulgaria, Cambodia, and India are lured to the country with bona fide work propositions, but, on arrival, are coerced into trafficking activities such as forced labour and sex work (Martens et al. 2003). If these trafficked persons resist, they are either gang-raped or killed in transit (Martens et al. 2003).

Many women from Asia or Eastern Europe are trafficked to South Africa via routes such as Lesotho, Botswana and Eswatini (Delport et al. 2007). Eastern European women are mainly exploited as sex workers in brothels and private clubs (US Department of State 2016). Women from the Middle East and Asia are also trafficked into South Africa for use in the commercial sex industry, or shipped further to North America (Delport et al. 2007). Men recruited in the South China region (e.g. from Indonesia and South Korea) for work on commercial fishing vessels owned by mainly Chinese, Taiwanese or Thai captains are underpaid, forced to labour for long hours under appalling conditions, and not allowed to disembark for years. For example, in 2015, an estimated 10–15 victims of forced maritime labour were discovered in Cape Town on almost a monthly basis (US Department of State 2016). Men from China and Taiwan are also trafficked to South Africa, but mainly to be exploited as labourers in Chinese-owned mobile-sweatshop factories. Similarly, Pakistani and Bangladeshi citizens are bonded in forced labour in businesses owned by their fellow nationals in South Africa (US Department of State 2019).

Except for international trafficking to South Africa, regional trafficking to the country is very robust. Trafficked persons are sourced from almost all the SADC countries to be imported into South Africa. African asylum seekers in South Africa traffic family members to the country, as well as other refugees for exploitation in especially the sex trade (Delport et al. 2007). Women from the Democratic Republic of the Congo, Cameroon, Nigeria, Malawi, Mozambique, Eswatini, and Zimbabwe are especially vulnerable for sexual exploitation in South Africa. With offers of legitimate work from mainly female recruiters, girls from Mozambique are transported to Durban and Johannesburg, only to be coerced into prostitution or forced into marrying mine workers on the West Rand (Delport et al. 2007; US Department of State 2023; Adepoju 2005). Women from Central Africa are exploited for forced labour in hair salons in South Africa (US Department of State 2016).

Men and boys from Zimbabwe, Ethiopia, Malawi and Mozambique are also prone to becoming victims of trafficking in South Africa, and are mainly exploited as farm, vineyard, factory and construction labourers. Children from rural areas in Lesotho migrate to Maseru for job opportunities, where they are recruited as farm workers on asparagus farms in the Eastern Free State and Bloemfontein. They work in extremely poor conditions, and are paid either a meagre salary or nothing at all.

If they dare complain, their employers have them arrested as illegal immigrants and deported. Young boys and men from Zimbabwe, Malawi and Mozambique are also forced by gangs to excavate any gold, diamonds or coal remaining in derelict mines (the so-called *zamazamas*) (US Department of State 2016).

Trafficking recruiters are usually women and men from the specific country from which victims are sourced. Often people the trafficking victim trusts are involved such as the parents, family members, friends, or neighbours (Allais 2010). Recruiters are sent to rural towns to snare victims, or fabricated employment opportunities are advertised in local newspapers to entice victims. Women and girls are trafficked by long-distance truck drivers who promise them jobs, proposals of marriage, or assistance with schooling (Adepoju 2005). Similarly, Zimbabwean taxi drivers (so-called *malaichas*) transport trafficked persons across the South African borders, and gangs (*gumagumas*) take advantage of travellers crossing the border on foot (Allais 2010).

Locally, South African children are often recruited from small towns in rural regions (such as Orange Farm, Graaf-Reinet and Beaufort West) and transferred to the major cities (such as Johannesburg, Durban, Cape Town and Pretoria) for exploitation (Iroanya 2018; Bermudez 2008). Although persons from rural as well as urban areas are trafficked, it is primarily poor, unemployed black South Africans residing in rural towns that are the most vulnerable to becoming trafficked victims in this country. Other persons susceptible to trafficking are women and children from impoverished and distressed communities, such as children from the Cape Flats who are allegedly sold to ship's crews (Allais 2006), street children,[14] AIDS orphans, disabled youngsters, and abused children from broken homes. Several South African cities have become established destinations for child sex tourists, and local gangs operate child prostitution rings in the country to supply the demand (Adepoju 2005).

Trafficking victims are also sourced from South Africa for exploitation elsewhere in the world (Delport et al. 2007). South African trafficking victims have been located in Macau (US Department of State 2011), New Zealand, in Bangladesh and in Turkey (US Department of State 2016). South African men are hired to work as taxi drivers in Abu Dhabi, but once in the United Arab Emirates, they are exploited as forced labourers (US Department of State 2016). South Africans are also lured by employment agencies to work in Europe, particularly in England. A group of South African nationals accepted employment at one of the major fruit packers in Britain that offered extraordinarily high wages. After their arrival in England, the vouched salaries did not materialise. From the extremely little payment received, interest for the loan towards their flights and visa was deducted, together with excessive rent monies for small and overcrowded lodgings as well as steep administrative costs for every shift. These workers had hardly anything left for basic subsistence and could not afford to either reimburse their debt or return home (Belser 2005). South African immigrants also recruit their ex-compatriots for exploitation, as was seen in the case

[14] An estimated 10,000–12,000 children are homeless in South Africa. See Heiberg (2005). Moser (1999) claims that 20% of South African children are not living with their parents.

of *US v Johannes du Preez et al.* (2005). Du Preez promised South Africans executive posts at his Atlanta granite and marble company, but had the applicants enter the United States illegally under a special foreign manager visa program. Not only did Du Preez force his fellow ex-citizens to work relentlessly, but their wages were also withheld as payment for their visas and accommodation. Any objection to this treatment was characteristically met with threats of deportation (DeStefano 2007). Such behaviour is typical of bonded labour.

5 Prosecution of Traffickers and Punishment of Human Trafficking

The Constitution of the Republic of South Africa, 1996 is the supreme law of the land, and all other laws are subordinate to the Constitution. The Bill of Rights in the Constitution specifically prohibits all forms of human trafficking in section 13, stipulating that no one may be subjected to slavery, servitude or forced labour. Other constitutional imperatives applicable to human trafficking violations include, amongst others, section 12, which guarantees the freedom and security of the person; section 11, which protects the right to life; section 10, which underscores the right to human dignity; and section 21, which upholds the freedom of movement and residence. Although no human trafficking contravention has yet been considered by the South African Constitutional Court, there are many constitutional provisions that trafficked persons may rely on in defence of any encroachment of their fundamental human rights.

South Africa has always prosecuted the crime of human trafficking under fragmented ancillary laws, which included various common-law and statutory crimes. Under common law, traffickers would have been charged with the crimes of rape, abduction, kidnapping, assault, and similar applicable crimes. For example, in the case of *S v Elizabeth Maswanganye* (2006), the accused attracted young girls with fabricated employment opportunities, apprehended them at her home, and forced them into prostitution. On the charge of kidnapping and keeping a brothel, Maswanganye was sentenced to 5 years' imprisonment. Likewise, in the case of *S v Amien Andrews* (2002), the accused was sentenced to 17 years' imprisonment for kidnapping young females and exploiting these captive girls as sex workers. Andrews branded each girl with a tattoo as his property, and used drugs to keep them submissive.

There are also statutory provisions which can be employed to punish the crime. These are mainly statutes relating to sexual offences, corruption, racketeering, money laundering, organised crime, and so on. Contravening the Sexual Offences Act 1957 as regards the keeping of a brothel, and living off the proceeds of prostitution were the most common infringements applicable to human trafficking scenarios. The appellant in *Phillips and Others v National Director of Public Prosecutions* (2006) was convicted of violating these provisions for procuring 40 undocumented foreign females to have sex with clients at his at 'The Ranch Executive Entertainment Centre'. Sex traffickers were also prosecuted by utilising racketeering legislation as seen in *S v Sayed* (2010). The South African citizen, Basheer Sayed, ran a brothel where he kept Thai females who were recruited in Thailand by Sayed's partner-in-crime, his Thai wife. These women were brought to South Africa to ply their trade as prostitutes; however, they were debt-bonded, and did not receive any remuneration for any sex work performed. Sayed was arrested after seven Thai females escaped from the brothel, and contacted their embassy. Sayed and his wife were convicted but the verdict was overturned because of a technicality. As can be seen from the examples provided above, both common-law crimes and statutes are not comprehensive enough to provide proper sentences for human trafficking perpetrators, and to protect trafficking victims.

More specific interim anti-trafficking legislation was enacted to combat the crime of trafficking in the jurisdiction. These laws comprise of the Criminal Law (Sexual Offences and Related Matters) Amendment Act 32 of 2007 (sections 70–71), and the Children's Act 38 of 2005 (sections 281–291). The 2007 Act established the first statutory crime of human trafficking for this region. However, the offence only protected victims trafficked for sexual exploitation. Other forms of trafficking such as labour exploitation were not covered. This Act has however successfully been utilised by prosecutors to charge and convict human traffickers, as observed in *S v Shembe* (2012), where the accused was sentenced to 23 years' imprisonment for trafficking a girl from Eswatini, and raping her. Also, in *Dos Santos and Another v The State* (2010), Dos Santos was sentenced to life imprisonment for the trafficking of three 14–17-year-old Mozambique girls who were confined in a house in Pretoria East, and forced to prostitute themselves. In *S v Veeran Palan and Another* (2015), Palan received a sentence of 10 years and a fine of R10,000 or 5 months' imprisonment following his conviction on charges relating to human trafficking for sexual exploitation. Also, in 2016, three men were found guilty of human trafficking for sexual purposes and running a prostitution ring, and sent to an effective 85 years in jail. They operated from a Durban hotel and forced girls as young as 12 years old to prostitute themselves.

The Children's Act also contain counter-trafficking provisions, but these only pertain to child trafficking. This Act was utilised to convict a prominent 60-year-old businessman for the sex trafficking of five Mozambican girls in *S v Lloyd Mabuza and Another* (2014). Mabuza and his co-accused, a Mozambique national, lured girls aged between 10 and 16 years with promises of a better life, educational opportunities and a holiday, which never materialised. The girls were kept captive in a secluded compound, and exploited as Mabuza's personal sex slaves for a period of 4 years. Mabuza was sentenced to eight life terms, the most severe punishment pronounced for human trafficking at that time in this country.[15] Since the passing of these two anti-trafficking Acts, the government steadily increased its human

[15] The heaviest sentence to date in a South African trafficking case is 19 life terms, which each of the accused in *S v Seleso* (2019) received for trafficking an orphaned child.

trafficking convictions by sentencing eleven traffickers and initiating the prosecution of five sex traffickers in 2015, a substantial increase to the three convictions and nineteen prosecutions in 2014. The 2014 statistics is again a slight increase compared with the conviction of three offenders and prosecution of 12 suspected sex traffickers in 2013 (US Department of State 2016).

The jurisdiction finally obtained specific and all-inclusive legislation to combat human trafficking in South Africa with the implementation of the South African Trafficking Act in August 2016. This Act defines all applicable trafficking offences, provides suitable punishments for the various offences created, as well as processes for protecting trafficking victims and for preventing the crime of human trafficking. The definition of human trafficking follows that of the Trafficking Protocol, but the scope has been broadened (as indicated by the words in italics):

> '4. (1) Any person who *delivers*, recruits, transports, transfers, harbours, *sells*, *exchanges*, *leases* or receives another person *within or across the borders of the Republic* by means of-
>
> *(a)* a *threat of harm*;
>
> *(b)* the threat or use of force or other forms of coercion;
>
> *(c)* the abuse of vulnerability;
>
> *(d)* fraud;
>
> *(e)* deception;
>
> *(f)* abduction;
>
> *(g) kidnapping*;
>
> *(h)* the abuse of power;
>
> *(i)* the *direct or indirect* giving or receiving of payments or benefits to obtain the consent of a person having control or authority over another person; or
>
> *(j) the direct or indirect giving or receiving of payments, compensation, rewards, benefits or any other advantage,*
>
> *aimed at either the person or an immediate family member of that person or any person in close relationship to that person*, for the purpose of any form or manner of exploitation, is guilty of the offence of trafficking in persons.
>
> (2) Any person who-
>
> *(a) adopts a child, facilitated or secured through legal or illegal means*; or
>
> *(b) concludes a forced marriage with another person,*
>
> *within or across the borders of the Republic, for the purpose of the exploitation of that child or any person in any form or manner*, is guilty of an offence'.

The wide-ranging elements of the definition cover all possible human trafficking conduct, yet it is specifically tailored for local South African realities. The Act further creates various new offences that include, amongst others, utilising the services of trafficked persons, debt bondage, and the possession, destruction, confiscation, concealment of, or tampering with travel documents. The Act imposes suitable sentences for trafficking violations which reflects the severity of the crime in section 13. Anybody found guilty of human trafficking as in section 4(1) and (2) of the Act is liable to a fine not exceeding ZAR100 million or imprisonment, including imprisonment for life, or such imprisonment without the option of a fine or both. Partaking in any conduct that forces a person into bonded labour or debt bondage is penalised by a sentence of up to 15 years' imprisonment. Making use of the services of trafficked persons renders one liable to a fine or imprisonment for a period not exceeding 15 years or both; while facilitating trafficking in persons is penalised with a fine or imprisonment for a period not exceeding 10 years or both. The Act also allows the government to confiscate the assets of traffickers.

The first human trafficking judgment decided under the new Trafficking Act in Gauteng is *S v Eke Ugochukwu* (2017). Ugochukwu, a drug-dealing Nigerian pimp, was found guilty of contravening the Trafficking Act for drugging, raping and trafficking a 15-year-old South African minor girl, and sentenced to 20 years' imprisonment. The first case to be finalised under the new legislation in the KwaZulu Natal region is *S v Makhosini Fakudze* (2017). In this case, a 40-year-old Eswatini national abused the vulnerabilities of a 14-year-old girl, his step-daughter. He started abusing her at the age of 11 years when they were living in Eswatini. Her mother had abandoned her, and the child was defenceless, and completely vulnerable. The accused brought the girl along with him to South Africa, without any identification documents, where he made her his wife, and repeatedly sexually exploited and raped her. He knew that as a stranger in the country, she had no one to turn to for help. She was kept hostage in their house, and lived in constant fear as the accused threatened to kill her if she screamed or told anyone about what was happening. At 14 years old, she fell pregnant and gave birth to a baby. These experiences not only injured her physically but had an immensely harmful psychological effect on her. The accused was sentenced to life imprisonment. In another typical case of human exploitation, *S v Eze* (2017), a 30-year-old Nigerian drug dealer and pimp forced a teenage girl to prostitute herself. He was found guilty of contravening the Prevention and Combating of Trafficking in Persons Act, and sentenced to 20 years' imprisonment. A further two more Nigerian nationals were convicted of human trafficking in 2017. The brothers Obioma Benjamin Abba (32) and Chinedu Justine Obasi (38) forced two women to work as prostitutes. Abba was sentenced to 12 years' imprisonment, while Obasi, the mastermind, was sentenced to 18 years' imprisonment.

There have been very few reported cases involving forced labour in South Africa. Although it is assumed that the majority of trafficking victims are forced labourers in this country (US Department of State 2019), only two labour-related trafficking cases have successfully been prosecuted by 2023, with two forced labour cases still ongoing. It is consequently alleged that the government does not address labour trafficking offences systematically. News bulletins do appear from time to time relating purported cases of labour exploitation, but hardly any of these indictments result in prosecutions or convictions. Reports surfaced in February 2017 about the trafficking of 72 workers from Eswatini, Lesotho and Mozambique for labour exploitation in Newcastle. Four Chinese and one Eswatini national were arrested for alleged forced labour practices, as they paid these bonded workers a pittance to work in their textile factory (Newcastle Advertiser 2017). Many other incidents are initially investigated as cases of suspected human trafficking, only to be charged as another crime. In June 2017, close to 300 young men and women from KwaZulu-Natal were left stranded in a suburb of Pretoria. They paid fees to a man claiming to be a General in the South African National Defence Force (SANDF) and running a military recruitment workshop. He had promised them they would be employed in the SANDF (TimesLive 2017). Although the above incident does encompass elements of human trafficking, this clearly appears more a case of fraud.

As seen from most of the case law provided, all cases which have been successfully prosecuted in South Africa comprise a single perpetrator or small trafficking groups. Although the police have investigated the Nigerian, Thai, Chinese, Russian or Bulgarian trafficking networks, the government has not yet prosecuted or convicted traffickers involved in major international syndicates. These criminal organisations dominate the sex trade in South Africa, and more attention should be given by the government in prosecuting these networks as well as any government officials and law enforcement agencies allegedly complicit in trafficking offences.

6 Protection of Trafficked Persons in South Africa

The Trafficking Act outlines victim protection measures and identification processes in Chaps. 3 and 4. The legislation provides for the protection of all victims of trafficking, including foreign trafficked victims. Foreigners who have been trafficked to South Africa may be granted a recovery and reflection period and, under certain circumstances, temporary as well as permanent residence permits may be issued to them. South African courts are accorded extra-territorial jurisdiction in specific circumstances, as, for instance, where the person trafficked is a South African citizen or where the suspected trafficker is present in the country.

The Act implements a victim-centred approach that prioritises trafficked persons and their welfare before, during and after criminal proceedings. The well-being of trafficked children is especially safeguarded. Any person who knows or reasonably believes that a child has been trafficked is obliged to report this knowledge to the police. Non-reporting constitutes an offence. Discovered child victims of trafficking are referred to a designated social worker for investigation, and placed in temporary safe care. Foreign trafficked children are also assisted to apply for asylum. Further protective measures for victims include access to public health-care services, the prohibition on the prosecution of victims for any illegalities committed as a result of being trafficked, an injunction on any summary deportation of foreign victims[16] and proper processes for repatriating victims of human trafficking to their home countries, where it must be ensured that protective systems are also in place. Victims may also institute a monetary claim against their convicted trafficker for any physical or psychological injuries, or loss of income or property suffered.

The Act further ensures that trafficked persons are assisted by a protective national framework comprising of several multi-sectoral role-players such as the Department of Justice and Constitutional Development, the National Prosecuting Authority (NPA), the South African Police Services (SAPS), the Department of Home Affairs, the Department of Social Development, and civil society. These entities form the National Task Team responsible for developing and implementing a

[16]Regulations to implement the provision providing relief from deportation has not yet been promulgated.

National Action Plan to combat human trafficking in the jurisdiction, as mandated in the Trafficking Act. The main objectives of the National Task Team include developing a strategic framework, enhancing the capacity for coordinated service delivery to and protective measures for victims of trafficking, raising public awareness by means of campaigns, and implementing effective training programmes. Services that must be provided to trafficking victims include medical care, accommodation, counselling, and reintegration into their family units. Victims may also apply for mental health therapy, education and skills development training.

Although there are no dedicated human trafficking refuges offering services to identified victims in South Africa, accredited social service organisations render these services after they have complied with certain minimum standards as prescribed in the Act. For example, multipurpose shelters such as the Thuthuzela Care Centres provide a 24-h, one-stop professional response to victims of sexual abuse. They provide temporary accommodation, and medical, psychological, social assistance without delay. They also serve as referral centres for legal assistance. There is however only one shelter for male victims of trafficking located in the Gauteng province, and two shelters for LGBTQI+ victims, but available space is limited. The Department of Social Development funds and oversees these places of safety for victims of trafficking (US Department of State 2023). These institutions will also assist in the assessment and reporting of trafficked persons. The number of identified victims fluctuate from year to year. In 2017, 399 victims were identified, however, in 2018, only 260 victims were identified (US Department of State 2019). In 2022, 83 victims were identified by the government, but in 2023, the number of identified victims dropped to 74 (US Department of State 2023). Of the victims identified, 42 persons were exploited in forced labour, 23 in sex trafficking, and nine in an unknown type of trafficking. These victims comprised of 31 women, 25 men, 14 children and four unspecified persons. Identified victims are referred to shelters across the provinces, however some voluntarily choose to return to their countries, while a number abscond from care facilities.

7 Prevention

The Trafficking Act requires that the government institute a coordinated program to prevent and combat trafficking. Many people in South Africa are not aware of what the crime of human trafficking comprise of, as well as the magnitude thereof. To correct this predicament, adequate resources must be allocated to provide for counter-trafficking preventative measures, such as information and training sessions. Although the South African government does allocate funds to awareness raising and anti-trafficking campaigns, more can be done. The Act mandates government to develop programs to educate people on the dangers of human trafficking, its causes and different forms, especially as regards forced labour as well as to discourage the demand for trafficked persons. In this regard, government has progressed significantly by conducting several awareness-raising campaigns in schools, on television and radio, and distributing anti-trafficking brochures in vulnerable communities, at transport hubs and road blocks near border crossing points (US Department of State 2023).

Prevention of the crime also involves accurate statistics as regards the trafficking types found in the jurisdiction, and the extent of the crime in the various regions of the country, etcetera. Although the Trafficking Act requires consolidated reporting of trafficking statistics, South Africa does not possess a national human trafficking data base providing integrated and legitimate statistics on trafficking cases in the region. As part of the Crime Administration System (CAS), the SAPS gathers data on human trafficking, but only for sexual purposes (as per section 71 of the Criminal Law (Sexual Offences and Related Matters) Amendment Act 32 of 2007), as well as other sexual offences related to trafficking under this Act (Allais 2010). These reports are difficult to get hold of, and no recent figures are available. The SAPS Annual Crime Report of 2021/2022 contains statistics of sexual offences, but not specifically that of human trafficking. The LexisNexis Human Trafficking Awareness Index provides helpful information as to the incidences of human trafficking in South Africa, and across the African continent (Manyathi-Jele 2015). However, the numbers provided reflect not only prosecuted human trafficking cases, but also alleged instances of trafficking recounted in news reports. There have been other research conducted as to the scope of trafficking in South Africa, such as the studies concluded by the International Organisation for Migration (IOM) (Martens et al. 2003),[17] the United Nations Children's Fund (UNICEF 2005),[18] Molo Songololo[19] and the South African Human Sciences Research Council (HRSC) (Allais 2010). These studies have been criticised as the '[s]ample sizes are small and the findings are based primarily on interviews with governmental and non-governmental stakeholders, as well as a few conveniently chosen individuals with first-hand experience of trafficking' (Pharoah 2006). The research is further limited by the restricted geographical range as only people from selected areas were interviewed. The topics introduced by means of questionnaires are furthermore limited, and the forms of trafficking mentioned dubious (Pharoah 2006). For example, in the Molo Songololo study, the manipulation of girls willing to have sexual intercourse with their teachers in exchange for school fee payments are perceived as human trafficking. Similar sexual abuse is also equated to trafficking in the IOM research—in this instance, it was alleged that businessmen and farmers from South Africa abduct street children

[17] The IOM researchers conducted interviews with 232 persons, however only 25 people were human trafficking victims.

[18] This study conducted no interviews with any human trafficking victims, and the results were based solely on secondary information provided by law enforcement agencies, support organisations and NGOs.

[19] This organisation held interviews with 19 child sex workers; however, only one girl claimed to have been trafficked into sex work when she was a young child. Other information was gathered from two trafficked children's family members, and three adult prostitutes. In another study conducted by this organisation, interviews were held with 44 sex workers of whom only four were trafficked.

from Lesotho, sexually abuse them for a few days where after the men drop them off at the border of Lesotho. It is submitted that studies done on organ trafficking in this region could also be flawed. The HSRC's *Tsireledzani* (2010) report (Allais 2010) was the most recent research conducted on the topic in South Africa until their 2023 publication titled *Human Trafficking in South Africa* (Frankel 2023). The first-mentioned study has also been slated as being neither ample nor useful, and it 'also fails to adequately inform governmental decision-making by failing to provide evidence-based interpretations of key concepts' (Gould et al. 2010). An accurate and consolidated situational analysis of human trafficking on the nature, scale and trafficking routes in the region will assist in the prevention of the crime. Information on trafficking in South Africa remains scant, but no data exists in terms of illegal migration and migrant smuggling, that may also contribute to trafficking of persons.

8 Conclusion: The Way Forward for South Africa

There are still many impediments in eliminating human trafficking in South Africa. A serious lack of capacity and widespread corruption among government officials and law enforcement agencies hinder anti-trafficking efforts (US Department of State 2023). It is submitted that all government employees and other officials who have received anti-trafficking training must apply the training received, and if this is not done, they should be held accountable for their omission. Government officials suspected of complicity in trafficking activities should be investigated and prosecuted.

Statistics on human trafficking in the Southern African region remains deficient, and much information is founded on sheer assumptions (Delport et al. 2007). This was quite evident in the time leading up to the 2010 FIFA World Cup in South Africa where speculations were rife that the human trafficking cases in the region would dramatically increase, although there was no supporting research to back such suppositions. This concern did not materialise at all (IOM 2009). Only five cases of human trafficking could be linked directly to the FIFA event, and only one case led to a conviction: Nigerian national Chinemere Bartholomew Amajouyi—who forced two teenage girls into prostitution during the 2010 FIFA World Cup—was sentenced in the East London Magistrate's Court to 16 years behind bars. Although South Africa has been unable to provide detailed statistics on trafficking in the region, the government is constantly improving on its endeavours to address the crime. It is envisaged that consolidated statistics on investigated and prosecuted trafficking crimes will be made more readily available in the near future.

Notwithstanding a paucity of viable and reliable data concerning the scale, nature and practices of trafficking in South Africa, the diverse and complex culturally-unique trafficking types and many more dilemmas such as the high crime rate in the country, the government has improved in its efforts to address trafficking in persons. This is especially demonstrated in the implementation of comprehensive counter-trafficking legislation for the jurisdiction. The legislation holistically prescribes specifications for accredited organisations to collect information on victims of trafficking, determine the purpose, methods used and extent of the crime to assess and measure the efficacy of the South African anti-trafficking strategies. There is a general increase in the number of investigations and indictments of human trafficking, and more such cases are prosecuted. It is noticeable that punishment for convicted offenders consists in much longer sentences than previously imposed. For example, in 2010, only fines or suspended sentences were imposed on convicted traffickers; such penalties are ineffective for the purposes of deterrence.

Still, legislation alone will not prevent human trafficking. The complex multi-disciplinary crime can only be addressed if attention is also given to the socio-economic causes of human trafficking, patriarchal attitudes towards women and children, and proper border and immigration monitoring, amongst others. A concerted response from all role players in government and civil society is required, as was evidenced in the FIFA World Cup held in South Africa in 2010. The combined efforts of law enforcement agencies who specifically focused on human trafficking concerns, combined with the resources that were made available to inform people of the dangers of human trafficking, resulted in the protection of people and prevention of the crime. Additionally, the strong police presence ahead and during the event deterred criminals from committing the crime, and those who dared contravene the law were summarily arrested and prosecuted. This integrated and constructive approach to combating the crime should serve as a paradigm and underpinning for all counter-trafficking strategies in South Africa.

References

Adepoju A (2000) Issues and recent trends in international migration in sub-Saharan Africa. Int Soc Sci J 52(165):383–394

Adepoju A (2005) Review of research and data on human trafficking in sub-Saharan Africa. Int Migr 43(1):75–98

AfricaCheck (2019) Factsheet: South Africa's crime statistics for 2018/19. https://citizen.co.za/news/south-africa/crime/2178462/factsheet-south-africas-crime-statistics-for-2018-19/

Allais C (2006) An overview of human trafficking in sub-Saharan Africa. Paper presented. https://www.researchgate.net/publication/237769872_AN_OVERVIEW_OF_HUMAN_TRAFFICKING_IN_SUB-SAHARAN_AFRICA

Allais C (ed) (2010) Tsireledzani: understanding the dimensions of human trafficking in Southern Africa. HSRC, Pretoria

Altman M (2007) Low wage work in South Africa. HSRC, Pretoria

Andersen A (2018) Shocking stats reveal 41% of rapes in SA are against children. https://www.thesouthafrican.com/news/rape-statistics-41-children/

Apleni M (2012) Speaking notes for Home Affairs Director-General Mkuseli Apleni following briefing to media. SA Home Affairs, Pretoria

BBC (2017) Mozambique police warn bald men after ritual attack. http://www.bbc.com/news/world-africa-40185359

Belser P (2005) Forced labour and human trafficking: estimating the profits. ILO, Geneva

Bermudez L (2008) 'No experience necessary': the internal trafficking of persons in South Africa. IOM, Pretoria

Bosch D, Gordon A (1996) Child labour in commercial agriculture in South Africa. ILO, Dar-es-Salaam

Chichava M, Kiremire MK (2007) A situational analysis of the abuse and trafficking of children in Southern Africa. SANTAC, Maputo

CIA (2020) Country report: South Africa. https://www.cia.gov/library/publications/resources/the-world-factbook/geos/print_sf.html

Comrie S, Wiener M (2010) Rent-a-baby. Carte Blanche, 23 May 2010. http://beta.mnet.co.za/carteblanche/Article.aspx?Id=3964&ShowId=1

Crush J, Williams W (2001) Making up the numbers: measuring 'illegal immigration' to South Africa. Southern African Migration Project, Pretoria

Delport E, Koen K, Mackay A (2007) Human trafficking in South Africa: root causes and recommendations. UNESCO, Paris

DeStefano AM (2007) The war on human trafficking: US policy assessed. Rutgers University Press, New Jersey

Edmonds EV (2005) Understanding child labour - patterns, types, and causes. Econ Perspect:21–26

Fellows S (2008) Trafficking body parts in Mozambique and South Africa. Human Rights League, Maputo

Frankel P (2023) Human trafficking in South Africa. HSRC, Pretoria

Gettu T (2012) Towards a food secure future. UN, New York

Global Slavery Index (2023) South Africa. https://www.walkfree.org/global-slavery-index/map/#mode=map:country=ZAF:region=2:map=prevalence:year=2023

Gould C, Richter M, Palmery I (2010) Of Nigerians, albinos, Satanists and anecdotes - A critical review of the HSRC report on human trafficking. SA Crime Q 32:37–45

Heiberg T (ed) (2005) Listen and speak out against sexual abuse of girls and boys. International Save the Children Alliance, Norway

Interpol. (1996) International crime statistics. Interpol, Lyon

IOM (2009) Human trafficking and the 2010 Soccer World Cup. Eye on Human Trafficking 21:1–8

Iroanya RO (2018) Human trafficking: the South African experience. In: Iroanya RO (ed) Human trafficking and security in Southern Africa. Palgrave Macmillan, Cham, pp 119–150

Manyathi-Jele N (2015) Analysis of the human trafficking awareness index report. De Rebus 553:9–11

Martens J, Pieczkowski M, Van Vuuren-Smyth B (2003) Seduction, sale and slavery: Trafficking in women and children for sexual exploitation in Southern Africa, 3rd edn. IOM, Pretoria

Molo Songololo (2000) Trafficking in children for the purposes of sexual exploitation. Molo Songololo, Cape Town

Mooki O (2012) Bishop, wife face charges of mutilating young girl. The Star, 7 Aug 2012. http://www.iol.co.za/the-star/bishop-wife-face-charges-of-mutilating-young-girl-1.1357710

Moser CO (1999) Violence and poverty in South Africa: the impact on household relations and social capital. World Bank, Washington DC

Mwambene L, Sloth-Nielsen J (2011) Benign accommodation? *Ukuthwala*, 'forced marriage' and the South African Children's Act. J Fam Law Pract 2(1):5–16

Newcastle Advertiser (2017) 72 victims rescued from human trafficking in Newcastle. http://newcastleadvertiser.co.za/112220/must-read-72-victims-rescued-from-human-trafficking-in-newcastle/

Pharoah R (2006) Getting to grips with trafficking: Reflections on human trafficking research in South Africa. ISS, Pretoria

Sain R (2019) Trial involving forced marriage of mentally disabled girl halted. https://www.iol.co.za/news/south-africa/eastern-cape/trial-involving-forced-marriage-of-mentally-disabled-girl-halted-19806105

Scheper-Hughes N (2000) The global traffic in human organs. Curr Anthropol 41(2):191–224

Sloth-Nielsen J (ed) (2016) Children's rights in Africa: a legal perspective. Routledge, London

Solomon H (2005) Turning back the tide: illegal immigration into South Africa. Mediterr Q 16(4):90–111

TimesLive (2017) Army 'colonel' lures 300 youth from KZN to Gauteng in job scam. https://www.timeslive.co.za/news/south-africa/2017-06-27-army-colonel-lures-300-youth-from-kzn-to-gauteng-in-job-scam/
Truong T (2006) Poverty, gender and human trafficking in sub-Saharan Africa: rethinking best practices in migration management. UNESCO, Paris
UNHCR (2015) South Africa fact sheet. UN, New York
UNICEF (2005) Trafficking in human beings, especially women and children, in Africa, 2nd edn. UNICEF, New York
US Department of State (2011) Trafficking in persons report 2011. US Department of State, Washington DC
US Department of State (2016) Trafficking in persons report 2016. US Department of State, Washington DC
US Department of State (2018) Trafficking in persons report 2018. US Department of State, Washington DC
US Department of State (2019) Trafficking in persons report 2019. US Department of State, Washington DC
US Department of State (2023) Trafficking in persons report 2023. US Department of State, Washington DC
Van der Watt M (2018) The nature and future of human trafficking in South Africa. GIBS Business School, Johannesburg
World Bank (2018) Overcoming poverty and inequality in South Africa: an assessment of drivers, constraints and opportunities. World Bank, Washington DC
World Bank (2019) The World Bank in South Africa. https://www.worldbank.org/en/country/southafrica/overview

Nina Mollema (mollen@unisa.ac.za) is a professor teaching Criminal law and International Criminal law at the University of South Africa. She has attained the following qualifications: BA, BA (Honours), HED (University of Pretoria), MA (Vista University), DLitt et Phil, LLB, LLM, LLD (University of South Africa). Her doctoral thesis in law focuses on human trafficking in South Africa—comparing the South African legal response to combat human trafficking to other jurisdictions as well as to international standards. She is also involved in human trafficking initiatives at the University of South Africa such as the child trafficking and child justice community projects. In this regard, she raises awareness of the crime, and makes available counter-trafficking initiatives by way of publications and training of under- and post-graduate students. She has published in many journals and received the Hugo de Groot award in 2014 for the best contribution in the *Journal for Contemporary Roman Dutch Law* for her article on human trafficking in South Africa. She has presented papers at national and international conferences in South Africa, Botswana, Namibia, Swaziland, Brazil, Cuba, France, Australia, and the US.

Human Trafficking Policies in Scandinavia: What Happens When International Obligations Meet National Problem Definitions?

May-Len Skilbrei

Abstract This chapter presents a demonstration and discussion of various shifts in how Denmark, Norway and Sweden have approached human trafficking since the inception of the UN Trafficking Protocol in 2000. While the policy domain of human trafficking is framed by this international instrument, the formulation and implementation of concrete policies stem from national and local institutions and problem definitions. To investigate the relationship between international obligations and national implementation, this chapter examines how the problem of trafficking appears in presentations of trafficking. The chapter also examines how that definition has changed over time in governmental white papers and statements. The chapter identifies commonalities in the trajectories of the three countries' trafficking policies, all of which have reproduced a bias towards prostitution-related trafficking and female victims. This outlook must be understood both in light of the existence of such biases in international policy frameworks as well as how domestic debates on prostitution have affected the policy domain of trafficking. In all three countries, the policy domain of trafficking is also intermingled with concerns about migration, which has had consequences for the countries' abilities to identify and assist victims.

1 Introduction

The launch of the US Trafficking in Persons (TIP) report attracts a great deal of attention each spring. The report presents a description and evaluation of how countries around the world approach human trafficking, broken down into how well they do on prevention, prosecution and protection, often referred to as the 'three Ps' framework. Countries are divided into tiers 1, 2 or 3, depending on their efforts and progress, where tier 1 is the top ranking of countries. This tier 'fully meets the minimum standards for the elimination of trafficking' set forth in the US Trafficking

M.-L. Skilbrei (✉)
University of Oslo, Faculty of Law, Oslo, Norway
e-mail: m.l.skilbrei@jus.uio.no

A. M. Rodrigues, M. J. Guia (eds.), *New Forms of Human Trafficking*,
https://doi.org/10.1007/978-3-031-39732-5_5

Victims Protection Act (TVPA).[1] What was initially a US framework and criteria for evaluations has become a global trafficking framework. The Scandinavian countries Denmark, Norway and Sweden have consistently received favourable mention in the annual reports and have almost always received a tier 1 ranking, except in 2019, when Denmark was demoted to a tier 2 ranking, with the conclusion that (US State Department 2019, n.p.): 'the Government of Denmark does not fully meets [sic!] the minimum standards for the elimination of trafficking but is making significant efforts to do so'.

The second international trafficking framework important to the Scandinavian countries is the Council of Europe Convention on Action against Trafficking in Human Beings, established in 2005. The Group of Experts on Action against Trafficking in Human Beings (GRETA) is a control body that issues reports on how signatories meet the requirements of the convention (for a description and discussion of GRETA's mandate and work, see Planitzer 2012). GRETA performs rounds of evaluation. Since the convention entered into force in 2008, GRETA has issued three evaluation reports on Denmark (2011, 2016 and 2019), three on Norway (2013, 2017, 2022a) and three on Sweden (2014, 2018, 2022b).

Countries are compared on their performance in combatting trafficking, and the information conveyed in such reports and how countries respond to these assessments are both key factors to understanding human trafficking as a contemporary policy field. The Scandinavian countries share a history and key features and have well-established collaborations on criminal justice, welfare, equality and borders. This cooperation makes it interesting to look at how they have adapted to the two international policy frameworks outlined above. Figures on the identified victims of trafficking are consistently low in the three countries. The figures for Denmark have ranged between 17 and 121, for a total of 827 (Danish Centre against Human Trafficking 2019). The majority of these victims have been from Nigeria. In the period 2007–2016, a total of 2800 potential victims were registered in Norway (US State Department 2017, p. 307).[2] Sweden's National Council on Crime Prevention has reported that the figure of possible victims of trafficking in that country varies but is consistently low, with only ten possible victims identified in 2011, while the number was 62 for 2012 (GRETA 2014, p. 11). Sweden has been criticised by GRETA for only reporting on victims involved in cases reported to the police, not possible victims identified by other agencies than the police (GRETA 2018, p. 14).

This chapter presents a discussion of how Denmark, Norway and Sweden have approached human trafficking since the countries' establishment of their first trafficking policies following the inception of the UN Trafficking Protocol in 2000, often referred to as the Palermo Protocol. While the policy domain of human

[1] More details on these standards are available at https://www.state.gov/j/tip/rls/tiprpt/2013/210553.htm.

[2] Tellingly, the Norwegian authorities no longer issue an annual figure of assumed victims of trafficking, but are instead working on quality assuring their registration systems and on developing a way to report figures that makes it more difficult to misrepresent these as representative of the extent of trafficking in Norway (National Police Directorate 2019).

trafficking is framed by this and other international and broadly appropriated instruments, the content of trafficking policies are drawn from national and local institutions and problem definitions (Marmo et al. 2013). Trafficking as a policy field currently consists of a multitude of obligations, institutions and norms (Wylie 2016). Countries that have ratified the protocol display markedly different policies, which mandates an investigation of the relationship between international instruments and national appropriations.

The fact that Scandinavian countries 'do well' in terms of trafficking policies and figures may be attributable to their strong welfare levels and their emphasis on gender equality and labour rights, but while the three countries share many similarities, their approaches to human trafficking are in no way the same, as I will demonstrate. Instead, they approach the phenomenon in distinctively different ways. This chapter will describe these policies both on paper and in action, as well as contextualising the policies within broader political developments. I ask how the problem of human trafficking is represented within different policies and how that representation has shifted over time. The fact that trafficking is spoken of and acted upon in particular ways produces various types of silence that may stand in the way of effecting trafficking policies. As particular representations become normalised, they authorise certain activities and make others appear irrelevant. At any given time, several problem definitions may be in operation, but governmental policies such as those I examine in this chapter will often constitute an established norm. This situation does not mean that governments and their problem definitions operate in a vacuum, but rather that these definitions have a particular status.

The material for this chapter consists of documents that in different ways present and evaluate trafficking policies in the three countries. I have read and analysed national action plans in the three countries: five in Denmark, five in Norway and two in Sweden. These action plans were examined within the purview of identifying 'policy on paper' in the three countries and developments in that respect, particularly by looking at how the problem of trafficking is presented by examining how the different authorities choose examples, which terms they apply and which are their top priorities. To identify developments in 'policy in action', I have read evaluations from the Council of Europe and the US State Department. All three countries have signed the Council of Europe Convention on Action against Trafficking in Human Beings, and I have looked at the seven of the nine GRETA reports that have been issued to date. As mentioned above, the US State Department issues a report every year that evaluates how countries fare in their efforts to combat human trafficking. I have read and analysed the short reports the three countries have produced in the years 2014–2019.

2 Scandinavian Trafficking Policies on Paper

Human trafficking has come to be an important policy domain in Denmark, Norway and Sweden since the inception of the Palermo Protocol. Although the development has followed different trajectories in the three countries, as welfare-oriented Northern European nation states, they share the main structural frameworks constituted by international conventions and cultural features. The three countries are representative of social democratic welfare regimes (Esping-Andersen 1990). This combination of the strength of welfare solutions, the extensive public sectors and the particular ways of organising state/labour union relations is often referred to as the Nordic model.

The welfare-state framework also has consequences for how punishment and welfare measures are balanced. All three countries have introduced prohibitions against trafficking in their penal codes: Denmark implemented a trafficking act in 2002, Norway in 2003 and Sweden in 2002. The formulations in these acts were designed to meet requirements in the Palermo Protocol, except for the fact that the first version of the Swedish Trafficking Act only criminalised trafficking for the purpose of prostitution and sexual exploitation; the act did not criminalise labour trafficking and other forms of exploitation. Two years later, the act was revised to better reflect the full breadth of the definition found in the Palermo Protocol. In all three countries, the original formulation of the acts has been revised several times, although the driver of these changes has differed. In some instances, the change was a result of concerns about exploitation in new sectors, such as when Norway included 'begging' as a form of exploitation. In other instances, changes have come about because of a critique of the current law.

While penal codes are indeed an important tool for combating trafficking, the policy domain is marked by a complexity of instruments and institutions, which makes the issuing of action plans a key tool to operationalise obligations and link them to existing national institutions.

2.1 *Denmark*

The Danish government has issued five action plans in the period I study, in 2002, 2007, 2011, 2015 and 2018.[3] Evaluations of the government's efforts often explicitly note that the 2002 Danish action plan was the first of its kind in the Nordic region (Danish Government 2010, p. 5). Several policy domains refer to how the other Scandinavian countries are faring. Another Danish action plan was launched in 2007. The first two action plans clearly related the policy domain of trafficking to prostitution (Spanger 2011). In a very literal sense, the policy domain has shifted

[3] Denmark has issued a supplement to the action plan on trafficking especially related to minors, but I have not included these efforts in this chapter.

over time by way of the titles of the action plans. The first action plan bore the title 'Trafficking in Women for Prostitution', while the second was titled 'Human Trafficking'. The second plan broadened the way for concerns to extend beyond trafficking for the purpose of prostitution and also recognised that men and children may be victims of trafficking.

The general bias towards prostitution-related trafficking and female victims has attracted criticism. GRETA's 2011 evaluation of Denmark's efforts concluded that the Danish authorities did not pay sufficient attention to forms of trafficking other than the trafficking of women for prostitution. In the 2016 report, GRETA commended the Danish authorities for improving somewhat upon this situation, but at the same time the report stated that Denmark continued to offer insufficient protection for male victims. The two later action plans, one for the period 2011–2014 and one for 2015–2018, mentioned labour exploitation more explicitly. The 2011–2014 action plan recognised that although very few cases of prostitution-related trafficking had been identified in Denmark at that time, international reports had demonstrated that the exploitation of labour (among other things) was an important form of trafficking. This acknowledgement was not reflected in the Danish government's priorities. While the 2011–2014 action plan stated that the Danish authorities' obligations extended far beyond simply combating trafficking for prostitution and that the official figures did not adequately convey the phenomenon outside the prostitution market, the action plan still stated that the Danish authorities' efforts during the period in question would primarily be directed at the trafficking of women for prostitution (Danish Government 2011, p. 3), because women 'constitute the largest group of registered victims in Denmark'. Among the goals set forth in the action plan was the goal of identifying more victims of trafficking in the prostitution market, not victims generally (p. 5). The action plan for the period 2015–2018 demonstrated more concern about the authorities' responsibilities to combat trafficking beyond prostitution. This action plan presented outreach work in prostitution markets and labour arenas side by side as ways of identifying victims and building trust (Danish Government 2015, p. 22). The policy domain of trafficking thus intersects with prostitution, which, together with other factors, helps to establish trafficking as a problem in which primarily women are victimised—an outlook that GRETA has criticised (2011).

A lack of focus on trafficking for the purposes of forced labour is the case in many countries, as is the tendency to be mostly concerned with female victims (Chuang 2010). Governments in general struggle to take on the whole breadth of the phenomenon of trafficking for a variety of reasons, but in Scandinavia the relationship between the policy domains of trafficking and prostitution is one important reason, which I will elaborate on below.

This bias is not the only one to be read from the framing of the problem of trafficking in the Danish action plans. Marlene Spanger (2011) has argued that the establishment of repatriation and reintegration programmes indicates that human trafficking is defined to be a problem that has to do with involuntary migration (see also Ausserer 2008). The 2007–2010 Danish action plan (Danish Government 2007) listed various efforts directed at female victims of trafficking for prostitution, one of which was to establish more shelters in Denmark, while the general provision for victims was to facilitate their return to their countries of origin. GRETA (2011) warned that the focus on immigration in how Denmark approach identification meant that victims could be prosecuted for immigration-related crimes instead of being treated as possible victims. In the case of resident permits, GRETA (2011) also warned of the danger that the policy at the time emphasised preparation for return more than support for victims. For a period, Denmark was the only EU country to not have a residency scheme in place for the victims of trafficking (US State Department 2014). When Denmark was downgraded to tier 2 status in 2019, among the main reasons the US State Department cited were that the Danish authorities had failed to (1) identify victims due to a prioritisation of detecting status as irregular migrants among prospective victims and (2) offer residence permits, which otherwise could have encouraged victims to collaborate with the police and prosecutors (US State Department 2019). The 2018 TIP report recommended that Denmark strengthen the latter approach (US State Department 2018). The 2019 TIP report (US State Department 2019) further criticised Denmark for a lack of prioritisation in prosecuting traffickers, noting that Denmark had only investigated one case in the past year.

2.2 Norway

The first Norwegian action plan was issued in 2003, under the title 'Action Plan against Trafficking in Women and Children (2003–2005)' (Norwegian Government 2003).[4] As the title shows, a gender perspective is integral to this first action plan. Throughout the text, trafficking was described as something that women and children were primarily the victims of (Norwegian Government 2003, p. 1); as the plan noted, 'Because it is mainly women and children who are exploited, trafficking entails a serious form of sexualised violence that is in conflict with the principle of gender equality'.

According to this description, trafficking primarily happens to women and children and is only related to prostitution. The expression of these two biases was very much the same as in the case of Denmark. The anti-trafficking efforts listed in the plan to protect and assist victims were strongly influenced by this bias. The first page of the plan even stated that 'we have a responsibility for protecting and assisting women and children who are victims of trafficking' (Norwegian Government 2003, p. 1). The plan did not recognise any obligations towards male victims. This bias did not stem from experiences of what trafficking looks like and who is victimised, as this action plan was published before the government had identified any

[4] Norway has approached the trafficking of adults and minors together since the issuing of the first action plan in 2003.

cases. These formulations were therefore more a reflection of the framing of international obligations than expressions of national characteristics.

In the preface to the second plan (Norwegian Government 2005), the Minister of Justice did not describe women as being particularly vulnerable to exploitation or as a particular target group for governmental efforts, and the main goals (which only applied to trafficking that involved women and children in the first plan) were now all gender neutral. Still, the action plan used the fact that the only identified cases to date had involved women who had been trafficked into prostitution as an argument for directing most of the government's efforts towards such trafficking. Since that time, the policy on paper has become more gender neutral, but that does not mean the implementation of the policies has. While the language and obligations described in the subsequent action plans were more gender neutral, a decade later, the 2013 GRETA report criticised Norwegian trafficking policies for maintaining a bias towards female victims of trafficking for the purpose of prostitution. This situation leads to the pertinent question of which characteristics of the Norwegian context produced this outcome.

The third Norwegian action plan (Norwegian Government 2006) was issued in 2006, although the second action plan was established for the period 2005–2008. This action plan explicitly referred to a shift in focus from only prostitution to other purposes of exploitation (Norwegian Government 2006, p. 3). The action plan stated that instead of solely focussing on such trafficking, the Norwegian government would direct more attention to human trafficking for forced labour and organ trafficking. Still, the plan continued to direct measures towards the exploitation of women in prostitution, not least by the fact that it still portrayed outreach work in the prostitution market as the best way to disclose trafficking and identify victims (Norwegian Government 2006, p. 17).

The fourth action plan, 'Together against Trafficking: Governmental Action Plan against Human Trafficking (2011–2014)', was issued in 2010. The plan mentioned prostitution numerous times; one of the initiatives it listed was to evaluate the recent criminalisation of the purchase of sex. But the plan also highlighted trafficking for forced begging and referred to this practice as being a more common phenomenon than before; the plan also referred to a successful trial on such trafficking in Sweden. The fourth action plan specifically focussed on the institutionalisation of protection and collaboration to ensure assistance, and it described the complexity of the various strands of Norway's efforts to combat trafficking. This action plan is thus dedicated to the professionalisation of a system, more than to introducing new angles and policies.

The fifth Norwegian action plan was heavily delayed, which the 2016 TIP report interpreted as a lack of dedication (US State Department 2016). The action plan was introduced late in 2016 and did not indicate which period it applied to. The plan consisted of much less content than the other action plans and thus presented the issue and existing policies in a very simplistic way. The plan mentioned the issue of the trafficking of minors more consistently than was the case in the other action plans. Both the US State Department (such as in the 2018 TIP report) and GRETA have criticised Norway in their more recent assessments for being overzealous in addressing the possible breaches of immigration law among the victims of trafficking.

Together, the five Norwegian action plans demonstrate a development towards more gender neutrality and a broader definition of the problem of prostitution; another development was in how the relationship between trafficking and migration is formulated. The first two action plans presented trafficking as a form of forced migration, while in the third plan, the government acknowledged that some victims had actively sought migration and may not have wanted to return to their country of origin upon identification. The strong emphasis on the repatriation and reintegration of victims in the first few years of Scandinavian trafficking efforts may have stood in the way of revising residence permits and instructing immigration authorities. What characterised the development, particularly in the case of Norway, was that the opportunities to stay in Scandinavia improved in the second half of the 2000s. Norway had also developed a generous and comprehensive residency scheme for the identified victims of trafficking; in theory, residency would be granted with low thresholds and without a prerequisite to cooperate with the Norwegian authorities. All three countries have introduced 'reflection periods' for victims, and while the countries award such periods in very different ways and with different thresholds, at least on paper the three nations have developed in a more generous direction.

2.3 Sweden

The Swedish authorities have issued two action plans on human trafficking (Swedish Government 2008, 2018),[5] 10 years apart, and both deal with both human trafficking and prostitution; the first even addresses only trafficking for the purpose of prostitution, with the title 'Action Plan against Prostitution and Human Trafficking for Sexual Purposes' (Swedish Government 2008). This plan was originally issued for the years 2008–2010 but was later prolonged to include the years 2011–2014 (GRETA 2014). As the title indicates, the plan addressed both prostitution per se and human trafficking for sexual exploitation, including for the purpose of prostitution. The action plan addressed prostitution and trafficking together, and the plan described the exploitation that traffickers subject their victims to side by side with descriptions of the harms of prostitution and the responsibility of the clients of prostitutes. The plan also repeatedly mentioned that these harms mainly befall women and girls. This action plan was thus biased towards female victims and the purpose of prostitution, something GRETA (2014) criticised the plan for, but in a more explicit way than in the Danish and Norwegian cases.

As described above, these early biases in the Danish and Norwegian action plans have become weaker throughout the years. In contrast to the developments in those

[5] Sweden has also issued a separate action plan on the sexual exploitation of minors, which I will not describe and discuss further in this chapter.

two countries, Sweden has maintained a strong association between human trafficking and prostitution. While the country's second action plan broadened the policy domain to encompass other forms of trafficking than for prostitution and sexual exploitation, the text was still filled with references to prostitution and female victims and did not clearly distinguish between efforts designed to combat prostitution and efforts directed at human trafficking (Swedish Government 2018). The plan described human trafficking as a sub-domain of violence against women (Swedish Government 2018, p. 4).

The bias towards female victims and prostitution-related trafficking is not only expressed through action plans: Sweden's national coordinator on trafficking is a coordinator for both prostitution *and* trafficking policies, and both issues are treated together by the National Task Force and the specialised police units, as well as in ongoing research and information-gathering activities (GRETA 2014). The 2014 GRETA report mentioned that the Swedish authorities had stated that 'it is important to recognize that THB [trafficking in human beings] can be a form of violence against women' (2014, p. 13) and that the recurring evaluations of Swedish trafficking policies treated human trafficking, pimping/procurement and the sexual exploitation of minors together (Swedish National Police Board 2014). This situation points to a specific national problem definition that is more explicit in linking trafficking with broader concerns about gendered or sexualised violence than is visible elsewhere. The US State Department (2018) has criticised the Swedish government for prosecuting very few cases of trafficking and for not supporting non-governmental organisation (NGO) victim support. The second GRETA report (2018) noted that as of 2016, the organisation of anti-trafficking efforts under a new Gender Equality Agency may have stood in the way of broad identification practices.

3 Scandinavian Trafficking Policies in Action

While various reports have concluded that trafficking measures in Denmark, Norway and Sweden are comprehensive and generous, it is important to look at whether any biases exist in how these measures are implemented. Because human trafficking is typically framed as an issue in which women in particular are victimised in prostitution, as I described above,[6] it is first important to examine whether this situation means in practice that the needs of male victims are not being met. All three countries often single out women in the countries' trafficking efforts. An important question is which consequences such biases on paper have. To date, most anti-trafficking efforts in many countries (see O'Connell Davidson 2006; Surtees 2008) are directed towards women who are trafficked into prostitution. Some have argued that this focus makes the identification of men difficult and have questioned

[6]An example of this outlook is how women and children are singled out in the full title of the Palermo Protocol: the 'Protocol to Prevent, Suppress and Punish Trafficking in Persons, Especially Women and Children'.

whether the needs of male victims can be satisfactorily met under such circumstances (Lindquist and Piper 2007; Surtees 2008).

One common factor among the three countries is their primary orientation towards identifying and assisting female victims of prostitution-related trafficking, but to different degrees. Within institutions that were established to help female victims of domestic violence, women's shelters have been mandated to offer services to victims in both Denmark and Norway, which means that services to date have been for women only, and with a bias towards victimisation in prostitution. And, in both countries, organisations that already work to provide harm-reduction and exit services for women involved in prostitution have been tasked with central tasks in the anti-trafficking work: the Danish Reden[7] (GRETA 2011) and the Norwegian Pro Centre.[8] Also in Sweden, identified victims are housed in women's shelters that were originally established to meet the needs of victims of domestic violence (US State Department 2017).

While the laws and victim obligations are gender neutral, law enforcers and service providers have been geared towards particular forms of trafficking (i.e. for prostitution) and have looked to identify particular victims (i.e. women), as expressed in the critique offered in the GRETA reports. The 2013 GRETA report on Norway concluded that some of the welfare services were only available to female victims. The report further critiqued the Norwegian authorities for not doing enough to identify the victims of forms of exploitation other than prostitution. The report explicitly stated that this approach meant that victims were prosecuted for immigration-related crimes, although victims should be met with impunity.

The various TIP reports also mention the problem of how the Norwegian authorities have prioritised trafficking for the purpose of prostitution, although the reports do note that improvements have been made. For example, the 2015 report stated that the authorities' 'recognition of labor exploitation increased, although the government continued to dedicate the bulk of resources and attention to sexual exploitation' (US State Department 2015, p. 267). The 2017 TIP report (US State Department 2017) encouraged Sweden to issue an action plan that would encompass the full scope of trafficking, instead of only establishing trafficking policies related to prostitution and other forms of sexual exploitation. Noting that neighbouring Norway and Sweden had identified and prosecuted several cases of trafficking for forced labour, Anders Lisborg (2012) examined the background of why very few such cases had been identified in Denmark. Lisborg contends (2012, p. 7) that the increase in cases after 2009 was probably due to how broader institutions had become more knowledgeable about the phenomenon.

The critique that Denmark's policy in particular does not handle the issue of migration in an optimal way is also reflected in critiques of governmental practices. Various reports have criticised the Danish authorities for being too strict in their

[7] A Danish NGO that offers services to people involved in prostitution in several Danish cities. The name translates to 'the nest'.

[8] The service provider for people involved in prostitution in Oslo and a national resource center on prostitution.

evaluation of applications for residence permits on humanitarian grounds (GRETA 2011) and asylum (US State Department 2015). According to the 2015 TIP report, 'While an asylum process existed to protect victims who face retribution in their countries of origin, only four victims have ever been granted asylum, despite the government officially identifying more than 200 victims in the last 3 years' (US State Department 2015, p. 14). The 2017 TIP report assessed that the Danish authorities had improved the country's ability to offer resident permits for victims, but Denmark 'continued to focus on foreign trafficking victims' illegal immigration status, often incarcerating them while pending review of their status and repatriating non-EU resident victims to their countries of origin without proper screening' (US State Department 2015, p. 151). GRETA (2016) contended that the reflection period was heavily under-utilised, and the group argued that the Danish authorities should look to revise this policy.

Norway has several residency-permit schemes for assumed victims: an initial 6-month-long reflection period that is not contingent upon cooperation with the police and a 1-year renewable residency permit for victims who have reported a crime and whose presence is deemed necessary for further investigation of their cases. Upon bearing witness in a trafficking or pimping/procurement court case, victims may be afforded a permanent-residence permit in Norway (Brunovskis and Skilbrei 2016). The reflection period in Sweden consists of a 30-day period to reflect and recover (US State Department 2017). The period is given a higher threshold than in Denmark and Norway, as it hinges on police recognition and an evaluation of whether the described experiences equal the legal definition. The 2017 TIP report (US State Department 2017, p. 377) critiqued this practice and urged Sweden to award social workers the authority to grant the status of 'identified victim', while GRETA (2014) urged Sweden to not make assistance contingent on working with the police and prosecutors.

In Denmark and Norway, the immigration authorities are the ones who award residence permits on the basis of human trafficking; they also evaluate whether a particular person meets the requirements of being counted as a victim, based on information from the police, but also public and NGO-run welfare services. In Sweden, in contrast, at least until 2017, the police were the ones to grant such permits and to evaluate eligibility. According to the 2017 TIP report, the 'authorities stated that because only an investigating police officer or prosecutor could file this application [for the 30-day reflection period], such temporary visas were in practice primarily available to victims already in contact with law enforcement' (US State Department 2017, p. 377).

As described above, Denmark, Norway and Sweden exhibit several differences in their policies and institutionalisation methods; as a result, ascertaining which way of approaching trafficking works best is very difficult. While the way of addressing the relationship between trafficking and migration is less generous on paper in Denmark than it is in Norway, in practice, many of the same problems in obtaining a residence permit for victims are visible in both countries (for information about Norway, see Brunovskis 2016). And while on paper the lack of recognition of trafficking for labour exploitation is problematic, since such a practice could stand in the way of the identification and protection of victims (Ollus 2015), the case of Sweden demonstrates that the relationship between policies on paper and policies in action is complex. Although the policies and trajectory of the policy domain in Sweden strongly links it with the phenomenon of prostitution on paper and in what policies it provides, e.g. by only training judges on sex trafficking, the Swedish authorities have actually identified a larger share of labour trafficking than in Denmark and Norway. In 2016, the Swedish police investigated 114 cases of labour trafficking (US State Department 2017, p. 377), and ever since 2010, such cases have constituted the majority of reported trafficking offences in Sweden (Marmo et al. 2013).

One way of evaluating this scenario would be to compare victim counts across countries, but doing so is complicated by how countries define, count and report victims differently. Even within Scandinavia, the various countries exhibit major differences in registration. Judging by the victim data issued by EUROSTAT (European Union 2018), Sweden has fewer victims than Denmark and Sweden, but an examination of how these figures are compiled shows that the data cannot be used to compare the effectiveness of the trafficking policies in the three countries. In Sweden, those who are counted as trafficking victims are people who are registered in relation to a case of trafficking reported to the police (European Union 2018, p. 39), while in Denmark, the Danish Immigration Service and the Danish Centre against Human Trafficking are the bodies that grant someone the status of a victim of trafficking (European Union 2018, p. 38). The higher victim count in Norway must also be understood in light of the low threshold for victims to receive services, which is the basis for the count.

4 Scandinavian Trafficking Policies in Context

What the three countries share is that the impetus to act to criminalise and prevent trafficking at the beginning of the 2000s did not come from domestic developments but from international obligations and discourses. Due to how international obligations were framed, particularly in the case of the Palermo Protocol, trafficking and prostitution were discursively and practically linked at the outset. But domestic debates on prostitution have also informed the development and implementation of trafficking policies to a great extent. In the case of Denmark, Spanger (2011) has argued that human trafficking as a policy domain became entangled with the issue of prostitution and that the emergence of the trafficking framework thoroughly shifted domestic policy debates on prostitution. In Norway, this conflation served to promote the criminalisation of the purchasing of sex (Skilbrei 2012).

The linking of trafficking and gender equality more generally is more a result of national understandings than stemming from the international frameworks and trends. As described above, human trafficking is typically formulated as a gendered issue in the region, both on paper and in practice. This outlook is caused by the heightened importance of gender equality and the interpretation of prostitution as a gendered institution. While this is the case in many countries, one could argue that the 'gender lens' directed at social problems is particularly strong in these countries, and that NGOs and others that wish to change policies find it particularly productive to argue that the problem is related to gender. Scandinavia is widely considered to be marked by strong ideals of social and gender equality (Sümer 2009). Particularly in Norway and Sweden, the governments have taken up feminist agendas to such an extent that the term 'state feminism' has been used to describe their approach (Hernes 1987). Discussions of what are public and what are private problems have been a strong part of this outlook, and problems related to gender and sexuality have to a great extent been included in state agendas, both by welfare-oriented preventive measures and criminal justice.

Janie Chuang (2010) argues that the conflation of human trafficking and prostitution and the adjacent bias towards the trafficking of women for the purpose of prostitution not only means that male victims remain unidentified and lack services and protection, but also that women's mobility is prevented in the name of protection. Because of the way in which female victims are construed to be victims of forced migration, refusing them at the border or deporting them both seem like appropriate responses. Both Denmark and Sweden have a provision in their respective aliens acts to prevent non-citizens from selling sex, which the authorities use to both stop people at the border and to expel non-citizens identified in prostitution markets (Skilbrei and Holmström 2013). No such provision exists in Norway, but there as well, the authorities use the need to fight trafficking as an argument for applying various provisions in the country's aliens act in a way that affects non-citizens involved in prostitution negatively and prevents entrance to Norway for people suspected of becoming victims of trafficking (Jahnsen and Skilbrei 2018).

As described above, the Danish authorities appear to apply a strong migration lens to the issue of trafficking. Danish immigration policies and general sentiments towards migrants have hardened in the same period (for a discussion of this development, see Mouritsen and Olsen 2013), more so than in neighbouring Norway and Sweden. Therefore, it does not seem random that Danish trafficking policies seem to have this bias. Denmark has moved in a direction of stricter immigration policies generally, often as a way to keep high levels of welfare and inclusion for those who already live in the region (Smith 2012). Not only do immigration policies and anti-immigrant sentiments affect how trafficking policies are implemented, but there is also the possibility that fears of trafficking will serve as a lever for stricter immigration control and the demonisation and exotification of particular groups of migrants (Wylie 2016). The Norwegian and Swedish police have been criticised for prioritising deportation before the protection of victims (GRETA 2013, 2014). The emphasis on equality, solidarity and universalism is widely considered to be the backbone of the region's inclusionary and equal citizenship (Lister 2009), but one could argue that the strength of the internal equality, solidarity and universalism comes at the cost of a high threshold of inclusion (for a discussion of this topic see Bech et al. 2017).

5 Conclusion

In this chapter I have set out to describe, compare and discuss how the Scandinavian countries Denmark, Norway and Sweden have approached human trafficking since they established trafficking policies in the early 2000s. While countries all over the world have signed the Palermo Protocol and are obliged to define and approach human trafficking in a particular way, the framework that the protocol has created can be filled and transformed by domestic agendas. Several important differences are notable in the institutionalisation of anti-trafficking efforts, the prioritisation of policies and the thresholds for identification and protection. In all three countries, human trafficking as a policy domain has interacted with that of prostitution. For this and other reasons, female victims of human trafficking for the purpose of prostitution have received the bulk of attention and thus have received more and better protection than male victims and victims of other forms of trafficking. Gender equality is a much more omnipresent perspective in Swedish society than it is in Denmark and Norway. In all three countries, human-trafficking policies and their implementation are also affected by migration as a perspective. This approach manifests differently in the three countries, but the latest TIP report's criticism that Denmark is unable to look beyond the irregular status of victims (US State Department 2019) could have been directed at Norway and Sweden as well. In many respects, the Scandinavian countries are very similar countries. They are known as prosperous welfare states that balance welfare and exercise punishment differently than many other Western countries, to the extent that they are often taken to be exceptional in how they handle crime and criminals (Pratt and Eriksson 2012). They are also countries where the consideration of and inclusion of victims of crime have been revised and are generally considered generous.

Trafficking as a policy domain has emerged in its contemporary form quite recently and since that time has undergone important structural and normative challenges, both internationally and domestically. This scenario offers scholars the opportunity to observe a policy domain in the making. The tempo and directions of changes mean that scholars should not become locked into their understanding of how a country manages trafficking, since comparisons such as those presented in this chapter demonstrate that policies on paper are not the same as policies in action, and that this relationship may be very different even in empirical contexts that appear similar in many respects, as is the case with the Scandinavian countries.

References

Ausserer C (2008) Control in the name of protection: A critical analysis of the discourse of international human trafficking as a form of forced migration. St Anthony's Int Rev 4(1):96–114

Bech EC, Borevi K, Mouritsen P (2017) A 'civic turn' in Scandinavian family migration policies? Comparing Denmark, Norway and Sweden. Comp Migr Stud 5(7):1–24. https://doi.org/10.1186/s40878-016-0046-7

Brunovskis A (2016) Special rights within universal welfare: assistance to trafficking victims in Norway. J Comp Soc Work 11(1):5–37. http://journal.uia.no/index.php/JCSW/article/view/359
Brunovskis A, Skilbrei M-L (2016) Two birds with one stone? Implications of conditional assistance in victim protection and prosecution of traffickers. Anti-Traffick Rev 6(1):13–30. https://doi.org/10.14197/atr.20121662
Chuang JA (2010) Rescuing trafficking from ideological capture: prostitution reform and anti-trafficking law and policy. Univ Pa Law Rev 158(6):1655–1758
Danish Centre against Human Trafficking (2019) Statistik 2018. Ofre for menneskehandel i Danmark. The National Board of Social Services, Copenhagen
Danish Government (2002) Handlingsplan til bekæmpelse af kvindehandel 2003–2006. Ministry of Social Affairs and Gender Equality, Copenhagen
Danish Government (2007) Handlingsplan til bekæmpelse af menneskehandel 2007–2010. Ministry of Gender Equality; Ministry of Refugees, Immigrants and Integration; Ministry of Foreign Affairs; Ministry of Justice, Copenhagen
Danish Government (2010) Evaluation of the national effort to combat human trafficking 2007–2010. Gender Equality Division, Copenhagen
Danish Government (2011) Handlingsplan til bekæmpelse af menneskehandel 2011–2014. Ministry of Gender Equality; Ministry of Justice; Ministry of Foreign Affairs; Ministry of Refugees, Immigrants and Integration, Copenhagen
Danish Government (2015) Handlingsplan til bekæmpelse af menneskehandel 2015–2018. Ministry for Children, Gender Equality, Integration and Social Affairs, Copenhagen
Danish Government (2018) Handlingsplan til bekæmpelse af menneskehandel 2019–2021. Ministry of Foreign Affairs, Copenhagen
Esping-Andersen G (1990) The three worlds of welfare capitalism. Polity Press, Cambridge
European Union (2018) Data collection on trafficking in human beings in the EU. European Union, Brussels
GRETA (2011) Report concerning the implementation of the Council of Europe Convention on Action against Trafficking in Human Beings by Denmark. First evaluation round. Council of Europe, Strasbourg
GRETA (2013) Report concerning the implementation of the Council of Europe Convention on Action against Trafficking in Human Beings by Norway. First evaluation round. Council of Europe, Strasbourg
GRETA (2014) Report concerning the implementation of the Council of Europe Convention on Action against Trafficking in Human Beings by Sweden. First evaluation round. Council of Europe, Strasbourg
GRETA (2016) Report concerning the implementation of the Council of Europe Convention on Action against Trafficking in Human Beings by Denmark. Second evaluation round. Council of Europe, Strasbourg
GRETA (2017) Report concerning the implementation of the Council of Europe Convention on Action against Trafficking in Human Beings by Norway. Second evaluation round. Council of Europe, Strasbourg
GRETA (2018) Report concerning the implementation of the Council of Europe Convention on Action against Trafficking in Human Beings by Sweden. Second evaluation round. Council of Europe, Strasbourg
GRETA (2019) Report concerning the implementation of the Council of Europe Convention on Action against Trafficking in Human Beings by Denmark. Third evaluation round. Council of Europe, Strasbourg
GRETA (2022a) Report concerning til implementtaion of the Council of Europe Convention on Action agains Trafficking in Human Beings by Norway. Third evaluation round, Council of Europe, Strasbourg
GRETA (2022b) Report concerning til implementtaion of the Council of Europe Convention on Action agains Trafficking in Human Beings by Sweden. Third evaluation round, Council of Europe, Strasbourg

Hernes H (1987) Welfare state and woman power: Essays in state feminism. Norwegian University Press, Oslo
Jahnsen S, Skilbrei M-L (2018) Leaving no stone unturned: the borders and orders of transnational prostitution. Br J Criminol 58(2):255–272. https://doi.org/10.1093/bjc/azx028
Lindquist J, Piper N (2007) From HIV prevention to counter-trafficking: discursive shifts and institutional continuities in South-East Asia. In: Lee M (ed) Human trafficking. Willan Publishing, Cullompton, pp 138–158
Lisborg A (2012) Human trafficking for forced labour in Denmark? National Board of Social Services, Odense
Lister R (2009) A Nordic Nirvana? Gender, Citizenship, and Social Jusitice in the Nordic Welfare States. Social Politics 16(2):242–278
Marmo M, Aird E, Åström K (2013) Victims of labour trafficking: a comparative study between Sweden and Australia. Int Perspect Victimol 7(2):25–35
Mouritsen P, Olsen TV (2013) Denmark between liberalism and nationalism. Ethn Racial Stud 36(4):691–710. https://doi.org/10.1080/01419870.2011.598233
National Police Directorate (2019) Rapport fra Koorineringsenheten for ofre for menneskehandel. National Police Directorate, Oslo
Norwegian Government (2003) Regjeringens handlingsplan mot handel med kvinner og barn (2003–2005) [Governmental action plan against trade in women and children]. Norwegian Ministry of Justice and the Police, Oslo
Norwegian Government (2005) Regjeringens handlingsplan mot menneskehandel (2005–2008). Norwegian Ministry of Justice and the Police, Oslo
Norwegian Government (2006) Regjeringens handlingsplan mot menneskehandel (2006–2009): Stopp menneskehandelen. Norwegian Ministry of Justice and the Police, Oslo
O'Connell Davidson J (2006) Will the real sex slave please stand up? Fem Rev 83(1):4–23
Ollus N (2015) Regulating forced labour and combating human trafficking: the relevance of historical definitions in a contemporary perspective. J Crime Law Soc Change 63(5):221–246
Planitzer J (2012) GRETA's first years of work: Review of the monitoring of implementation of the Council of Europe Convention on Action against Trafficking in Human Beings. Anti-Traffick Rev 1(1):212. https://doi.org/10.14197/atr.201212
Pratt J, Eriksson A (2012) In defence of Scandinavian exceptionalism. In: Ugelvik T, Dullum J (eds) Penal exceptionalism? Nordic prison policy and practice. Routledge, London, pp 235–260
Skilbrei M-L (2012) The development of Norwegian prostitution policies: A marriage of convenience between pragmatism and principles. Sex Res Soc Policy 9(3):244–257. https://doi.org/10.1007/s13178-012-0096-z
Skilbrei M-L, Holmström C (2013) Prostitution policy in the Nordic region: Ambiguous sympathies. Ashgate, Aldershot
Smith PS (2012) A critical look at Scandinavian exceptionalism: welfare state theories, penal populism and prison conditions in Denmark and Scandinavia. In: Ugelvik T, Dullum J (eds) Penal exceptionalism? Nordic prison policy and practice. Routledge, London, pp 38–57
Spanger M (2011) Human trafficking as a lever for feminist voices? Transformations of the Danish policy field of prostitution. Crit Soc Policy 31(4):517–539
Sümer S (2009) European gender regimes and policies: comparative perspectives. Ashgate, Aldershot
Surtees R (2008) Trafficked men as unwilling victims. St Anthony's Int Rev 4(1):16–36
Swedish Government (2008) Handlingsplan mot prostitution och människohandel för sexuella ändamål. Ministry of Integration and Gender Equality, Stockholm
Swedish Government (2018) Handlingsplan mot prostitution och människohandel. Ministry of Social Affairs, Stockholm
Swedish National Police Board (2014) Människohandel för sexuella och andra ändamål. Lägesrapport 14. Swedish National Police Board, Stockholm
US State Department (2014) Trafficking in persons report. US State Department, Washington, DC
US State Department (2015) Trafficking in persons report. US State Department, Washington, DC

US State Department (2016) Trafficking in persons report. US State Department, Washington, DC
US State Department (2017) Trafficking in persons report. US State Department, Washington, DC
US State Department (2018) Trafficking in persons report. US State Department, Washington, DC
US State Department (2019) Trafficking in persons report. US State Department, Washington, DC
Wylie G (2016) The international politics of human trafficking. Palgrave Macmillan, Basingstoke

May-Len Skilbrei (m.l.skilbrei@jus.uio.no) is a professor in criminology at the University of Oslo, Norway. She has done empirical studies on prostitution and human trafficking, sexual violence, marriage, labour, irregular migration and return migration, and has recent publications in *British Journal of Criminology*, *Anti-trafficking Review* and *Identities: Global Studies in Culture and Power*. She has co-chaired the Working Group 'Immigration, Crime and Citizenship' at the European Society of Criminology, together with Maria João Guia.

Fight Against Human Trafficking in Poland: From Theory to Practice

Joanna Beata Banach-Gutierrez

Abstract Human trafficking is one of the most dangerous phenomena arising in our world. This crime should be taken very seriously because the so-called vulnerable victims are people—women, girls, and children. However, in many recently reported cases the victims are men, searching for work abroad. In all these cases, the fundamental rights of individuals such as life, health, dignity and freedom are seriously endangered by traffickers. Human trafficking is often referred to as modern slavery. The reasons of human trafficking find their roots usually in poverty, lack of education and employment, homelessness, attitudes and norms towards sexuality or gender relations, socio-economical and judicial circumstances.

Poland is a country of origin, a transit country, and a destination country for trafficked victims. This chapter will illustrate the essence of human trafficking, as a serious crime, the adopted legal regulations against it, and some data on the convictions. The findings of the research may indicate that the dominating forms of abuse in human trafficking are sexual exploitation and forced labor. Most of the identified victims in Poland are citizens of Poland, Ukraine, Romania, and Bulgaria. Poles also become victims abroad, mainly in the United Kingdom, the Netherlands, and Germany.

1 Introduction

Trafficking in human beings (THB) is considered to be the modern slavery of twenty-first century. Victims of trafficking are most often brought into conditions in which their fundamental rights are violated. The trapped victims are particularly used for sex work, forced labor, begging, obtaining loans, social benefit fraud, or entering into sham marriages with foreigners. The victims usually feel lonely in their lives, without support or any aid. Even if they fear for their health and lives,

---

J. B. Banach-Gutierrez (✉)
University of UWM in Olsztyn, Law Faculty, Olsztyn, Poland
e-mail: joanna.banach-gutierrez@uwm.edu.pl

A. M. Rodrigues, M. J. Guia (eds.), *New Forms of Human Trafficking*,
https://doi.org/10.1007/978-3-031-39732-5_6

they do not make any complaints or inform the police or judicial authorities about their cases authorities. The problem is that they remain under the severe pressure and control of their "owners". Also, they are in fear of reprisals against themselves and their close relatives. Hence, in the cases of THB, the victims' access to justice can be quite limited due to accompanying factors rooted in their very specific situations.[1]

THB as a widespread phenomenon is often described as a problem that is global in nature. In fact, it is recognized as the most dangerous type of crime. According to the Human Trafficking Glossary: "It is a serious crime and a violation of human rights defined in international law. Human trafficking is a crime against the person; it is non-consensual or without the validated consent of the person involved; it is part of a long-term, exploitative relationship and it may be internal or international" (THB Glossary).

It is also worth recalling the opinion of the European Court of Human Rights (ECtHR) in the case of *Rantsev v. Cyprus and Russia* in which the Court decided that THB could be regarded as violation of Article 4 of the European Convention on Human Rights which deals with the prohibition of slavery and forced labor (Piotrowicz et al. 2019). In fact, the ECtHR obliged the states to prevent THB and to support both victims and potential victims of this crime considering, inter alia, that "*trafficking in human beings, by its very nature and aim of exploitation, is based on the exercise of powers attaching to the right of ownership. It treats human beings as commodities to be bought and sold and put to forced labour, often for little or no payment, usually in the sex industry but also elsewhere*" (Rantsev v. Cyprus and Russia, para 281). Furthermore, in the opinion of the ECtHR "*there can be no doubt that trafficking threatens the human dignity and fundamental freedoms of its victims and cannot be considered compatible with a democratic society and the values expounded in the Convention*" (Rantsev v. Cyprus and Russia, para 282).

Furthermore, the ECtHR also stressed the requirement of establishing certain safeguards in national legislation for effective "*protection of the rights of victims or potential victims of trafficking,*" in addition to introducing the effective "*criminal law measures to punish traffickers*" (Rantsev v. Cyprus and Russia, para 284). Therefore, one on hand, the Member States are obligated to protect victims or potential victims of trafficking, but on the other hand, they must also "*penalise and prosecute effectively any act aimed at maintaining a person in a situation of slavery, servitude or forced or compulsory labour.*" The ECtHR emphasizes three main aspects which should be applied all together for more effective fight against THB: (1) making a direct reference to measures toward the prevention of trafficking; (2) the protection of victims; and (3) the punishment of traffickers (Rantsev v. Cyprus and Russia para 285).

Generally, THB is a very serious problem which requires a comprehensive, interdisciplinary, and multilevel approach, at both a national and international scale. It is closely linked with transnational organized crime all over the world, which is

[1] COM (2020) 661 final.

constantly seeking potential victims to abuse in many forms of modern slavery. This chapter aims to illustrate the fight against THB in Poland placing special attention on the forms of victim exploitation as well as their access to justice in such cases. In this context, the effective penalization of THB under criminal law, and also the available victim support schemes, are of great importance.[2] In Poland, the Ministry of the Interior and Administration produced a few national reports on the scale of this precedent and its current trends. In accordance with the data available in the national reports, Poland is a country of victim origin, a transit country, and is increasingly becoming a destination country for those seeking employment.[3, 4]

2 Forms of Exploitation of Victims of THB: A Polish Experience

Both Poles and foreigners can be trapped by traffickers into doing various kinds of slave work. They are forcibly engaged in such areas of activity as sex work, work in agriculture camps or construction companies, providing services in private homes or in factories, begging, obtaining loans and benefits by deceit, and entering into sham marriages. For many years, sexual exploitation was said to be the most common and socially visible form of victimization. However, in recent years, the trends have been slightly changing, especially starting from the year 2015 in Poland. Other forms of human exploitation can be observed as developing, namely, forced labor and begging. Furthermore, the first cases involving women holding Polish citizenship being forced into marriages with foreigners were revealed.

Foreign victims of THB within Poland are the most often exploited in sex industry, agriculture (including agri-food processing), construction, forced begging, and so-called home help. The victims are usually poorly-educated people, often helpless in life and with difficult family relationships. These are mostly victims originating from Bulgaria, Romania, Ukraine, Belarus, Vietnam, and occasionally from the continents of Africa and South America. In sexual exploitation, victims are mainly women and girls coming from countries such as Bulgaria, Romania, and Ukraine.[5] They are usually forced into prostitution instead of being given the well-paid job they were promised. Another concerning phenomenon which has started to become more visible recently is that of forced labor. In many cases, the victims of forced labor were revealed to be from Ukraine, Belarus, Vietnam, and the Philippines. However, in the majority of cases of forced panhandling, the victims are Romanian

[2] COM (2020) 661 final.

[3] Trafficking in Human Beings in Poland. Reports 2015–2019.

[4] Pekkarinen A.G, Jokkinen A., Patterns of exploitation. Trends and modus operandi in human trafficking in Finland, Latvia, Estonia, Poland and Ukraine. HEUNI Report series np. 103a Helsinki 2023.

[5] Trafficking in Human Beings in Poland. Reports 2015–2019.

citizens (quite often children, women, and persons with visible disabilities, of Roma origin) that are forced to beg in Poland.

In turn, young Polish women are usually forced into the sex industry in Western Europe, such as Germany, Holland, or France. Concerning forced labor, both Poles living abroad (e.g., Great Britain, Germany, Holland, Sweden, Norway) and those living in Poland can be trapped by traffickers for the purposes of exploitation. There are also reported cases of forced begging by Polish citizens. Actually, Poles have the potential to be victims of all kinds and exploited in every form of slave work.[6]

3 Who Are the Victims and Perpetrators of THB in Poland?

In discourse about prevention against THB, protection of victims or potential victims, and effective prosecuting of the perpetrators, certain issues related to the characteristic features of victims and offenders require special attention. In other words, who are the victims or potential victims of THB? And who can be the perpetrators of this crime? Certainly, in the fight against THB, there is a need to identify the potential victims and, at the same time, undertake preventive measures. In this respect, efforts should be particularly focused on the analysis of driving factors that influence the victimization process.

Using the case described below as an example, it is clear that victims are usually first engaged by being offered a well-paid and easy job. The announcements can be often found in the national press and through websites. In one case in 2017, the Krakow District Court sentenced Mr. XY to 6.5 years of imprisonment for running a criminal group that trafficked women. Specifically, there were 15 people in the trial and the court found all of the accused guilty. The indictment dealt with human trafficking and acting in organized crime. The victims were nearly 100 Polish women trapped by traffickers between the years 2004 and 2006. The victims were forced to work in nightclubs for men in Italy and Greece. Six of the other 14 defendants were sentenced to imprisonment for terms of 5 years, 4 years and 2 months, 3 years and 8 months, and 3 years and 6 months. The remaining eight defendants had sentences of suspended imprisonment. In this particular case, Mr. XY used advertisements in the media and online to offer a well-paid hostess job advertising alcohol at reputable restaurants in attractive locations in Italy and Greece. It was not until they reached their final destination that the young girls learned that their role would actually be providing sexual services. The candidate girls were only required to be between 18 and 30 years old and physically attractive. All the girls who passed the competition procedure were further invited by Mr. XY to Warsaw for a 1-day training course during which they were taught some basic Italian or Greek words. They were also instructed to wear elegant evening dresses while advertising high-quality alcohol in reputable restaurants. Also, during this training course for hostess

[6] Trafficking in Human Beings in Poland. Reports 2015–2019.

jobs, it was ensured that the offered work does not have any sexual aspects. At the end of the training, Mr. XY asked the girls to sign work contracts in which he agreed to make his best efforts to obtain well-paid jobs for them and to legalize their stay. Later, those girls were transported at their own expense to Italy or Greece where they were then directed to nightclubs. It was only upon reaching their final destination that they learned that their work would involve providing sexual services. The girls were in difficult situations because they did not have any money, they did not know the language, and they had no legal residence or permission to work. Only few of them, with the help of their families or friends, managed to flee and return to Poland. Among the 15 defendants aged 24–67 years, nine of them were women. Most of the accused had obtained higher education, including one doctor and one actor, as well as an Italian language interpreter. All the victims were recruited by four companies in Poland.[7]

This particular case sheds some light on the issue of who can be the potential victims and traffickers, as well as what kind of job is initially offered. Generally, the victims of THB are young persons, not well educated (having only primary or secondary education), unemployed or without stable employment, as well as those who are searching for any temporary job. While the perpetrators are usually of the same nationality as the victims but acting in organized groups and, in contrast to victims, often better educated. In addition, the recruitment of a victim may also be "for love", whereby a man who deals with this type of recruitment does not raise the suspicion of his potential victim. Another option is using the mechanism of debts, for example, to fund travel abroad or maintenance and then later using this debt to trap the victim and force her or him into obedience. The victims are typically offered manual labor or entry-level jobs not requiring special qualifications, which include services, cleaning, waitressing, farm or field work, dancing, or working as a hostess (Radoniewicz 2011, pp. 134–153; Aromma et al. 2011).

In reference to the risk factors of potential victimization, these include lack of sense of safety, domestic violence, sexual abuse, family reunion, lack of opportunity to take up and continue education, and lack of employment opportunities to cover the family's daily living expenses. In many reported cases, the victims are single mothers or men searching for a job and a better life abroad. Perpetrators often take time to find suitable persons, for example, those which are uneducated or poorly educated, stuck in a difficult life situation and, in some circumstances, with a visible physical disability. Thus, the driving factors of potential victimization are influenced by a set of rather complex factors, of both psychological and material nature.[8] The complex nature of these factors can be demonstrated by the next Polish case, in which underage boys became victims of THB. In this case, three men (citizens of Poland) were accused of trafficking human beings, forcing them into prostitution, and producing child pornography. The apparent leader of the group was a German citizen. The criminal proceeding was conducted by the District Prosecutor's Office

[7] Wyrok w procesie o handel kobietami 2017.

[8] Trafficking in Human Beings in Poland. Report 2019; COM (2020) 661 final.

in Wrocław. The perpetrators were recruiting young boys under the promise of organizing for them legal employment in Germany. This criminal group was active between January 2014 and July 2015. The recruited boys were minors and one of them was even under 15 years old.[9]

The next example is a case of recruiting, transporting, and delivering a group of Poles to the territory of Finland, with the intent to exploit them for begging. This criminal activity took place between the years of 2009 and 2014. The victims were misled about the nature of the work they would have to perform in Finland and their remuneration for this work. After arriving in Finland, they were forced to beg for money claiming to be in poor health in need of treatment, having a disability or other critical life situations, or offering wooden items of small values. There were 76 victims identified in the course of the conducted investigation (Trafficking in Human Beings in Poland. Report 2015).

A common problem in the cases of THB is identifying the victims. This is indeed not easy task because they have limited contact with the outside world. Specifically, they are intimidated and choose to remain hidden from national law enforcement out of fear in their place of staying (police and authorities). Also, quite often they do not know the language of the target country. Hence, the victims of THB are usually kept silent as they may fear acts of revenge by the perpetrators (COM (2020) 661 final).

Victims of THB very often live in fear of perpetrators doing harm to them or their immediate family, especially to their children in the cases of single mothers. Their mental and health conditions may also prevent them from making any reports against their traffickers. Lastly, there is a separate group of disobedient victims who were therefore deprived of their lives. In the majority of revealed cases, the victims of THB were seriously beaten, as well as deprived of their liberty. As a result, they started to suffer from mental disorders and other health problems. To conclude, the research indicates that women, young persons (especially minors), and disabled persons are especially as risk of being targeted by traffickers. Finally, all victims of human trafficking need very careful and special treatment that should be offered by authorities (National Reports 2014–2019; Lasocik 2014; Lasocik et al. 2014).

4 Human Trafficking Under the Polish Criminal Law

It said that Polish legislators are taking responsibility for the fight against THB and pushing for national criminal laws related to the issue. The actions taken by Polish governmental and non-governmental institutions do, to an extent, reflect the international and European approach towards this global scale problem. Poland is a party of many international and European legal instruments on counteracting THB. A few of note include: (1) Convention for the Suppression of the Traffic in Persons and of

[9] Trafficking in Human Beings in Poland. Report 2015.

the Exploitation of the Prostitution of Others, 1950; (2) United Nations Convention against Transnational Organized Crime and the Protocol to Prevent, Suppress and Punish Trafficking in Persons, Especially Women and Children, Supplementing the United Nations Convention against Transnational Organized Crime, 2000; (3) Council of Europe Convention on Action against Trafficking in Human Beings, 2005.[10]

THB is penalized under the Polish criminal law (Article 189a PPC). Accordingly, both the legal definitions of human trafficking (Article 115§22 PPC) and slavery (Article 115§ 23 PPC) are reflected in the Polish Penal Code. Such an approach is the result of Poland's activity in both international and European fora. Not only is human trafficking punishable by law, but also the preparation of trafficking activities (Article 189a § 2). In addition, specific acts closely related to human trafficking are also punishable, such as deprivation of freedom (Article 189 PCC), forcing to carry out a specific action, omission, and endurance (Article 191 PCC), pornography (Article 202), forced prostitution (Article 203) as well as procurement or pimping (Article 204). It is also considered THB to have intent to use another person to obtain cells, tissues, or organs contrary to the provisions of the Act of 1 July 2005 on the collection, storage, and transplantation of cells, tissues, and organs.[11]

However, the total number of valid convictions under Article 189a PCC on human trafficking is relatively low in comparison to the other provisions linked with this offense. For instance, in the year 2018, there were nine offenders officially given prison sentences (one person of 1 year, three persons over 1–3 years, and five persons over 3–15 years) while there were 146 sentenced under Article 202 PCC for publicly presenting or producing pornographic content (three persons up to 3 months, eight persons to 4 and 5 months, 23 persons to 6 months, 28 persons over 6 months below 1 year, 42 persons to 1 year, 38 persons over 1–3 years, and four persons over 3–15 years). In addition, there were in total 16 offenders officially sentenced for forcing into prostitution (Article 203 PCC): three persons to 1 year, 13 persons over 1–3 years. Finally, there were 117 sentenced for procurement or pimping (Article 204 § 1–3 PCC): three persons to up to 3 months, six persons to 4 and 5 months, 13 persons to 6 months, 29 persons over 6 months below 1 year, 31 to 1 year, 35 over 1–3 years. A similar trend is observed in the previous years when highest number of sentences given by criminal courts was for forcing into prostitution and for procurement or pimping, for a total of 488 and 430, respectively, between the years of 2015 and 2017.[12]

An important aspect of discourse around THB is the question of victims' rights. More specifically, attention should be given to their treatment in criminal proceedings as well as their legal status within target countries. With this in mind, Poland implemented such European Union legal acts as the Directive 2012/29/EU, which establishes minimum standards for the rights, support, and protection of victims of

[10] Trafficking in Human Beings in Poland. Reports 2015–2019.

[11] Journal of Laws, No. 169, item 1411 as amended.

[12] Statistical Yearbook of the Republic of Poland 2019, Opracowania wieloletnie 2010–2018.

crime, the Directive 2011/36/UE, which prevents and combats trafficking in human beings and protects its victims, and the Directive 2011/99/EU on the European Protection Order. It is worth mentioning the Act on victim and witness protection and support of 2015, and the amendments introduced into the Polish Code of Criminal Procedure. Particularly, there are specific rules provided for giving testimony for victims of crimes under the criminal procedure. Victims who are minors are to be interviewed in so-called "friendly questioning rooms" (Articles 185a–185d Code of Criminal Procedure.) In addition, Polish legislator introduced a possibility of hearing victims via video-link (Article 177§1a Code of Criminal Procedure).

5 The National Strategy in the Fight Against THB in Poland

Above all, the national strategy in the fight against THB in Poland aims to eliminate this dangerous phenomenon. The elaborate system of multilevel coordination functions on the basis of three main components: legal regulations, national policy, and institutions and organizations. One of the major facets of the national strategy is to develop a highly effective program for THB prevention. For this reason, many information campaigns have been established in Poland, as well as closer international cooperation with specialized agendas. For the last few years, Polish national policy has been primarily directed at combating the trafficking and sexual exploitation of women, both in Poland and abroad. However, now there are much more intensified efforts made towards preventing and combating the growing number of victims recruited for the purpose of exploitation by slave labor. By being aware of the present forms of "modern slavery" and the methods used by perpetrators, Poland is consequently taking many initiatives aimed at preventing, combating, and detecting such activities (Wieczorek 2017; Lasocik 2016; Lasocik et al. 2015; Lasocik et al. 2014).

Additionally, schemes are gradually being developed that give the necessary legal aid and assistance or support to victims of THB. One of the key documents is the National Action Plan against Trafficking in Human Beings for years 2020–2021 ("NAP 2020–2021"), which specifies the major tasks toward preventing this precedent. The first document, known as "National Program for Combating and Preventing Trafficking in Human Beings", was adopted by the Council of Ministers in September 2003. In 2009 the document's name was changed to the "National Action Plan against Trafficking in Human Beings". In accordance with the NAP 2020–2021, there is a need to intensify prevention, information, and educational measures, especially due to the increasing number of people searching for employment in Poland. The role of the Voivodship/Regional Teams for Counteracting Trafficking in Human Beings has also grown in importance as they are engaged in providing assistance and support to all victims of THB.[13]

[13] Krajowy Plan Działań Przeciwko Handlowi Ludźmi na lata 2020–2021.

The aforementioned activity is organized in coordination with the National Consulting and Intervention Centre for Victims of Trafficking in Human Beings (NCIC). The specific tasks of NCIC are to provide aid to victims of THB within the framework of crisis intervention by ensuring them accommodation in a safe center, food, basic medical care, psychological support, legal consultations, assistance in contact with law enforcement agencies, and the help of an interpreter. The Center also runs shelters, ensures the realization of victims' rights, supports state and local government institutions in identifying victims of THB and working with them, and provides preventive counseling for private individuals, as well as consultations for those institutions which are responsible for providing victim assistance. The home page of NCIC has launched in six languages (Polish, English, French, Ukrainian, Russian). The centre offers a 24/7 hotline for victims and witnesses of THB (National Consulting and Intervention Centre for Victims of Trafficking).

The activities undertaken under the NAP 2020–2021 should be, inter alia, to improve the prevention, support, and protection of victims, to prosecute perpetrators of THB, and also to further strengthen international cooperation at various levels. It is directly stated that Poland is obligated to regularly submit progress reports on the implementation of international anti-trafficking policies and strategies. The main goal of the NAP 2020–2021 is to establish the conditions necessary to effectively combat THB in Poland and support its victims. In this context, the specific objectives of the NAP 2020–2021 refer to such issues as: raising social awareness of human trafficking; improving the standard of support offered to human trafficking victims (including minors); increasing effectiveness of the institutions responsible for prosecuting human traffickers through improvement of legal tools, structures, and implementation of best practices; improving qualifications of institutional and organizational representatives involved in the fight against THB and support of its victims; enhancing the knowledge of human trafficking as well as the effectiveness of the actions taken, especially in the context of forced labor; and consolidating international cooperation. The tasks envisaged for realization under the NAP 2020–2021 are nationwide, meaning, they relate to the activities of central institutions that create commonly-implemented legal regulations or model practices as well as some activities undertaken in all regions through the relevant units. Particularly, these are Voivodeship Teams for Counteracting THB.[14]

NAP is the main document that concerns the process of combating and preventing trafficking in human beings in Poland. This is a government document adopted by the Council of Ministers obligating its addressees to perform specific tasks in the fight against trafficking in human beings. NAP is addressed to individual central administration units as well as other institutions and non-governmental organizations voluntarily involved in the activities against trafficking in human beings in Poland. The established system of implementation and monitoring activities consists of the following elements: (1) Team for counteracting THB, chaired by the Minister of the Interior and Administration; (2) Working group for NAP monitoring

[14] Krajowy Plan Działań Przeciwko Handlowi Ludźmi na lata 2020–2021.

and realization/implementation, composed of experts representing participating institutions; (3) Working group for the support of victims of THB, composed of experts representing participating institutions; (4) Ad hoc working group on a handbook for judiciary and law enforcement authorities as well as other bodies engaged in the fight against THB in the scope of case proceedings related to THB.

At the institutional level, actions are undertaken by the Ministry of the Interior and Administration which functions as the national coordinator, Office for Foreigners, Police, Border Guard, Public Prosecutor's Office, Ministry of Family, Labor and Social Policy, National Labor Inspectorate, and Ministry of Investment and Development. The contribution of Voivodeship Teams for Counteracting Trafficking in Human Beings at the regional level is also important. Those Teams are composed of representatives from various public institutions, law enforcement agencies, and non-governmental organizations at the regional level. Moreover, the critical role of non-governmental organizations should be emphasized. Non-governmental organizations provide strong support for the state bodies and institutions in terms of activities aimed at preventing and combating THB, assisting victims, and educating the public. Here a crucial role is especially played by Foundation Against Trafficking in Human Beings and Slavery "La Strada", Association "Po-MOC" for Women and Children named after Mary Immaculate. It is worth mentioning the activity of National Office of the International Organization for Migration in Warsaw which is implementing a voluntary return assistance program for victims of trafficking. This means that if they decide to leave Poland, they have the right to get help organizing a safe return to their country of origin.[15]

Concerning international cooperation, it is important to note that Ministry of the Interior and Administration joined the Council of the Baltic Sea States (CBSS), Task Force against Trafficking in Human Beings (TF-THB), a transnational project "*Paving the Way for the Harmonized Operational Framework in the Baltic Sea Region*" (HOF-BSR), financed by the Government Offices of Sweden and the Swedish Institute (2018–2019). In November 2019, the international conference was organized in Warsaw as the final event of this project. One of the project's primary achievements is the Transnational Referral Mechanism of the Baltic Sea Region, Bulgaria, Romania, and Ukraine as well as "Human Trafficking Glossary". Information is available online at the home page of Council of the Baltic Sea States and Harmonized Operational Network (CBSS, HOF-BSR).

[15] Krajowy Plan Działań Przeciwko Handlowi Ludźmi na lata 2020–2021, Together Against Trafficking in Human Beings, Poland.

6 Conclusions

The phenomenon of human trafficking is linked with the activities of transnational organized crime. Well-organized criminal groups are able to make high profits with a relatively low risk of prosecution. The perpetrators are usually in search vulnerable individuals, or people currently experiencing difficult life situations. There are such vulnerable individuals present in each society, regardless of the level of its developments. The objective factors actively contributing to this sort of victimization are, for example: gender inequality, violence against women, lack of employment, discrimination, child labor, poverty, lack of opportunities and education, and conflict or post-conflict situations. Even if human trafficking is most often the result of specific social, economic, and cultural determinants, there still exists a real danger that each person has the potential to become a victim. This is because of the demands of the market and the methods used by perpetrators.

Poland is an active party in many international and European legal instruments that have been adopted to fight against human trafficking. Poland has undertaken some actions as part of its response to human trafficking that penalizes it under the Polish criminal law. In practice, Poland is focused on both legal and non-legal measures of preventing, combating, and detecting human trafficking. The national strategy tends toward effective elimination of human trafficking by the use of such tools as trainings and workshops for police officers, border guards, labor inspectorate, public prosecutors, and judicial authorities. Significant attention is also placed on the public campaigns to bring awareness to potential victims about the threat of trafficking and also about their rights. Another important aspect is the increased financing for victims' assistance. The victims have access to medical care, legal advice, and safe shelter, among other resources. They should be offered the necessary support and protection.

The dominant forms of human trafficking in Poland are forced labor, sexual exploitation, and begging, with a noticeable recent increase in sham marriages. Upward trends in the use of people for forced labor results from the fact that forced labor has become more profitable than prostitution. Hence, there is still a need for closer multilevel coordination among the existing anti-trafficking activities. Also, the importance of the interdisciplinary approach should be emphasized. In such cases as those of forced labor, Poland is not only a country of victims' origin or a transit country, but even a destination country for trafficking victims. Despite all efforts made by Polish institutions and organizations, criticism of the national policy exists. Specifically, there are some difficulties in identifying potential victims, especially in cases of forced labor. Furthermore, public prosecutors usually classify human trafficking as lesser offense, and there are too few convictions in which traffickers are sentenced to significant prison terms (2020 Trafficking in Persons Report: Poland).

References

Act of 1 July 2005 on the collection, storage and transplantation of cells, tissues and organs. Journal of Laws, No. 169, item 1411 as amended

Aromma K, Jokinen A, Ollus N (eds) (2011) Trafficking for forced labour and labour exploitation in Finland, Poland and Estonia. European Institute for Crime Prevention and Control (HEUNI), Helsinki

CBSS. Council of the Baltic Sea States. https://cbss.org/2019/08/23/a-glossary-to-help-navigate-through-the-complexities-of-human-trafficking/

CBSS. Council of the Baltic Sea States. https://bsr-trm.com/wp-content/uploads/2019/10/Response-of-Poland-to-the-Questionnaire-regarding-cooperation-in-transnational-cases-of-trafficking-in-human-beings-in-Polish.pdf

HOF-BSR. Harmonized Operational Framework in the Baltic Sea Region. https://bsr-trm.com/countries/poland/

Krajowy Plan. Działań Przeciwko Handlowi Ludźmi na lata 2020-2021. https://handelludzmi.eu/hl/baza-wiedzy/krajowy-plan-dzialan/6958,Krajowy-Plan-Dzialan-Przeciwko-Handlowi-Ludzmi-na-lata-2020-2021.html

Lasocik Z (2014) Human trafficking in Poland – evolution of the devil. In: Sullivan LE (ed) Criminal justice and law enforcement annual. Global perspectives. AMS Press, Inc, New York, pp 223–275

Lasocik Z (2016) Study on reduction measures to combat trafficking in human beings for the purpose of labour exploitation through engagement of the private sector. Project PL15 – Schengen Cooperation and Combating Cross-border and Organized Crime, including Trafficking and Itinerant Criminal Groups, Norway Grants Financial Mechanism 2009–2014, Strasbourg 2016. Council of Europe, p 32

Lasocik Z, Rekosz-Cebula E, Wieczorek Ł (2014) Human trafficking for forced labour in Poland -effective prevention and diagnostics of mechanisms. Human Trafficking Studies Center University of Warsaw

Lasocik Z, Boćko P, Buchowska S et al (2015) Filling the gap in the system of combating human trafficking in Poland – research report. Human Trafficking Studies Center University of Warsaw, Warsaw

National Consulting. and Intervention Centre for Victims of Trafficking. https://kcik.pl/k2/about-u/14567,What-is-the-National-Centre.html

Opracowania wieloletnie 2010–2018. https://isws.ms.gov.pl/pl/baza-statystyczna/opracowania-wieloletnie/

Piotrowicz R, Rijken C, Uhl BH (eds) (2019) Routledge handbook of human trafficking. Routledge, London

Radoniewicz F (2011) Przestępstwo handlu ludźmi. Prokuratura i Prawo 10(2011):134–153

Rantsev v Cyprus and Russia, Application No. 25965/04. European Court of Human Rights (2010). https://rm.coe.int/16806ebd5e

Report from the Commission to the European Parliament and the Council. Third report on the progress made in the fight against trafficking in human beings (2020) as required under Article 20 of Directive 2011/36/EU on preventing and combating trafficking in human beings and protecting its victims. (COM (2020) 661 final). https://eur-lex.europa.eu/legal-content/EN/TXT/?uri=CELEX%3A52020DC0661

Statistical Yearbook of the Republic of Poland, Table 33, pp 180–181, Warsaw 2019., https://isws.ms.gov.pl/pl/baza-statystyczna/roczniki-statystyczne-gus/

THB Glossary. https://cbss.org/wp-content/uploads/2020/03/TF-THB_Glossary.pdf

Together Against Trafficking. in Human Beings, Poland, https://ec.europa.eu/anti-trafficking/member-states/poland_en

Trafficking in human beings in Poland. Report 2015. Ministry of Interior and Administration, Warszawa (2016). https://www.gov.pl/web/handel-ludzmi/handel-ludzmi-w-polsce-raport-2015

Trafficking in human beings in Poland. Report 2016. Ministry of Interior and Administration, Warszawa (2017). https://www.gov.pl/web/handel-ludzmi/handel-ludzmi-w-polsce-raport-2016
Trafficking in human beings in Poland. Report 2017. Ministry of Interior and Administration, Warszawa (2018). https://www.gov.pl/web/handel-ludzmi/handel-ludzmi-w-polsce-raport-2017
Trafficking in human beings in Poland. Report 2018. Ministry of Interior and Administration, Warszawa (2019). https://www.gov.pl/web/handel-ludzmi/handel-ludzmi-w-polsce-raport-2018
Trafficking in human beings in Poland. Report 2019. Ministry of Interior and Administration, Warszawa (2020). https://www.gov.pl/web/handel-ludzmi/raporty-i-analizy-dotyczace-polski
Trafficking in Persons Report: Poland (2020). https://www.state.gov/reports/2020-trafficking-in-persons-report/poland/
Wieczorek Ł (2017) Praca przymusowa – zagadnienia prawne i kryminologiczne. Ośrodek Badań Handlu Ludźmi Uniwersytet Warszawski, Warszawa
Wyrok w procesie o handel kobietami 2017. https://www.polsatnews.pl/wiadomosc/2017-06-13/wyrok-w-procesie-o-handel-kobietami-konrad-d-skazany-na-65-roku/

Joanna Beata Banach-Gutierrez (joanna.banach-gutierrez@uwm.edu.pl) is a professor of Criminal Law and Procedure. She has been working as a lawyer in Poland and abroad, for international organizations, among others. Joanna Beata Banach-Gutierrez is engaged in several research projects dealing especially with EU criminal justice. Her current research is mostly focused on the project "*Cultures of Victimology: Understanding processes of victimization across Europe*"—COST Action 18121. The above-mentioned victimological research project is launched by the Working Group on Victimology at the European Society of Criminology. She is a member of the Management Committee in this COST Action.

The Silenced Coercion of Voodoo over Nigerian Women Trafficked from West Africa to Europe

Maria João Guia and Sandra Dumitrescu

Abstract More than one of the most frequent forms of coercion into trafficking in human beings in Nigeria, voodoo is a practice often not so familiar to both academia and practitioners. The way in which victims are introduced into a form of complete psychologic dominance is difficult to understand by the justice officers. Nevertheless, this is a current problem to the European Union, since the identification of several thousands of Nigerian women exploited in prostitution over different Member States, in the last years, obliged justice to understand how this crime is committed under the specific case of voodoo coercion. This chapter provides the reader with an in-depth analysis of how voodoo pushes women into the hands of traffickers and points out the relative inadequacy of control and deterrence measures promoted and financed by the European Union. The externalization of European Union's border control measures is chosen as the most adequate theoretical framework for this analysis, given the multitude of programs financed by the EU in Nigeria, our case study for THB practices through voodoo coercion.

1 Introduction

The importance of this analysis is directly related with the European (EU) border security and the effective application of fundamental rights when identifying and rescuing victims of trafficking in human beings (THB), by taking into account the many implications of this phenomenon—such as psychological trauma, stigmatization of victims and, last but not least, coercion of victims through mystical practices (the very focus of this chapter). Thus, it is the authors' view, to be further explored throughout the chapter, that border control applied to third country nationals may

M. J. Guia (✉)
Centre for Legal Research of Faculty of Law, University of Coimbra, Coimbra, Portugal
e-mail: maria.joao.guia@ij.uc.pt

S. Dumitrescu
Police Academy in Bucharest, Alexandru Ioan Cuza Police Academy, Bucharest, Romania

A. M. Rodrigues, M. J. Guia (eds.), *New Forms of Human Trafficking*,
https://doi.org/10.1007/978-3-031-39732-5_7

and should increasingly work as prevention and repression to this lucrative crime through possible recognition and support of its victims.

Beyond the narrow scope of border checks at EU's external borders, the chapter looks at the externalization of EU's border control practices in countries of origin and transit, through the European Union Trust Fund (EUTF) funded projects focused on border checks at the departure point of potential THB victims.

In this context, some theories over human trafficking will be presented to frame the topic, specifically touching the current situation, aiming to analyze the spiritual/ritual/religious coercion techniques used by traffickers to oblige women to submit to sexual exploitation. Some other legal issues will also be problematized. The importance of increasingly gathering knowledge on specific forms of coercion will be highlighted to present proper recommendations on how to improve the recognition of new (or refined) trends that victimize yearly thousands of female victims on sexual exploitation and other forms of exploitation.

2 The EU and Externalization of Border Management in West Africa: The Nigerian Case

Quoting Rijpma and Cremona, Balzacq (2008) defines externalization as the inclusion of Justice and Home Affairs (JHA) provisions in the European Union (EU)'s external policies, deriving from the European Council's note to COREPER[1] on the "European Union priorities and policy objectives for external relations in the field of justice and home affairs." The note of the European Council states that "external JHA action is not fundamentally different from other aspects of the Union's external policy, it should be consistent with the latter"—hence, external policies and actions can be inserted into the JHA domain to safeguard EU's internal security. In this context, the external actions of the EU fulfill specific JHA-related goals, aiming to, inter alia, strengthen the border management capacities in third countries to prevent irregular migration/organized crime/smuggling/trafficking in human beings, etc. to reach EU's external borders. Balzacq concludes by stating that, in this specific context, "the results of cooperation rarely coincide with the planned objectives and might, on different occasions, yield considerable indirect effects." In the following sub-sections, this statement will be further framed into the analysis of externalization practices in the context of the EUTF.

Savino (2018) refers to externalization as a compensatory measure for the inability of MS to properly manage return of irregular migrants and *sans-papiers* on their territory. Thus, by externalizing border and migration management measures to third countries in exchange for financial incentives, the EU hopes to "curb" migration before reaching its own territory—without however being able to efficiently

[1] Committee of the Permanent Representatives of the Governments of the Member States to the European Union.

monitor the compliance of externalization measures beyond its territory with the Charter of Fundamental Rights of the EU or any other legal instruments in the area of international protection. It is thus rightfully concluded that the EU Member States' obligations under international refugee law become symbolic and Member States "de facto regain sovereign control over admission at the expenses of asylum seekers without formally withdrawing from refugee law." The same derogation from international obligations applies to the principle of *non-refoulement*—although EU Member States are bound to respect this principle in the context of the Geneva Convention on Refugees. Now, the externalization of the protection obligations and the respect of the *non-refoulement* principles rely on the third country of origin/transit in which the migrant is contained.

As an illustrative example of the statements above, Papagianni (2013) describes EU's external migration policy as characterized by:

> the irrefutable close interconnection between the internal and the external dimension, not only in terms of competence but also in terms of objectives. It has been rightly argued that it is an internally-driven external policy.

This section investigates the tools applied by the EU to outsource its border control and migration management framework into third countries, of origin and transit for irregular migration and THB towards the EU. It aims to provide the reader with sufficient background to better understand the complex dynamics of West Africa and the actual impact of EU's attempts to externalize its border control model and to better protect borders against practices such as THB.

The externalization of EU's migration and border management strategy in West Africa is hereby analyzed from the perspective of streamlining fundamental rights into concrete EU-financed projects. The implementation of the EU's external policy on migration management in West Africa has been studied by Dumitrescu (2019), and this particular chapter shall draw on her findings, and extrapolate conclusions to better understand the impact of these policies on THB in the region, including coercion through voodoo of Nigerian women.

More specifically, this section focuses on EU-funded projects aimed at improving border and migration management capacities of Nigerian border authorities. Amongst a multitude of financial types of support available to the Nigerian authorities, the research specifically analyzed projects funded by the EU Trust Fund for Africa, one of the funding channels supporting the Migration Partnership Framework. By analyzing the potential externalization of EU's model of border and migration management in Nigeria via the financing of the EUTF, the section thus concludes on the links between controlling migration in third countries of origin and transit and EU's declared goals on sustainable development aid via the EUTF.

The externalization of EU's migration management model to third countries began with the Treaty of Amsterdam, providing the EU competences in the field of managing migration (Adam and Trauner 2019). Going through a series of policy instruments from this date onwards (e.g., the adoption of EU's Global Approach to Migration), this trend continues with the adoption of increasingly complex instruments, such as the Global Approach to Migration and Mobility (GAMM) in 2012.

To the externalization trend described by a variety of sources, authors such as Santos Vara add the "informalization of EU migration relations with third countries" (Santos Vara 2019), which only reinforces the complexity and lack of transparency of the cooperation mechanisms.

From the early onset, a number of EU initiatives only reinforced the trend of externalization (such as the Migration Partnership Framework)—which led to international protection concerns expressed by a variety of NGOs and UN bodies (Carrera 2020). Available academic literature, to be further on reviewed in detail, shows that externalization is profoundly impacted not only by diverging positions of EU institutions, but also by contrasting interests from EU Member States (Kipp 2018). All these varying perspectives have left their marks on EU's international relations with third countries of origin / transit for irregular migration, leaving third country nationals with limited options for legally accessing Europe, and limited protection opportunities when faced with practices such as THB, forced labor, sexual exploitation, and abuse, etc.

Focusing on the EU-Africa relations, the European Union and a selected number of African countries have launched in 2016 the Migration Partnership Framework, with the declared aim of fighting irregular migration and smuggling of migrants/ trafficking in human beings, and thus to ultimately decrease the number of irregular arrivals in Europe.

The Migration Partnership Framework (MPF) was put forward as part of EU's comprehensive approach to irregular migration and its root causes, in complementarity with regional initiatives such as the Rabat and Khartoum Processes, as well as the Valletta Action Plan. Part of EU's Global Strategy for Foreign and Security Policy, the MPF intends not only to address "illegal" (exact wording of the MFP) migration towards the EU but also to encourage return and readmission in the third countries of origin.[2] The MPF is implemented with priority countries of origin and transit, amongst them Mali and Nigeria—the subject of this research and its case study. Describing the MPF, Santos Vara states that "it seems as though the MPF would be replacing previous instruments governing external relations of the EU and its Member States in the area of migration" (Santos Vara 2019), and the applicability of this statement to the particular case study trafficked Nigerian women is analyzed onwards.

Amongst other authors, Castillejo invites us to reconsider the externalization of EU's actions on migration (Castillejo 2017), and specifically assesses the impact of the MPF in the five priority countries, amongst them Mali, Niger, and Nigeria. She concludes by stating the obvious planning flaws of the programs implemented under the MPF and their limited operational added-value. In the context of the intrinsic links between development aid and migration, Castillejo also interestingly points

[2] So far, the EU has signed Migration Partnership Frameworks with five countries of origin for migratory flows: Mali, Nigeria, Niger, Senegal and Ethiopia (source: European Union External Action Service, *Partnership Framework on Migration, One year on: Lessons learned, challenges and way forward*, https://eeas.europa.eu/sites/eeas/files/factsheet_partnership_framework_on_migration.pdf.

out to the EU's reluctance to withdraw aid to particularly fragile third countries, even if they do not comply with the expected approach to irregular migration and THB, because of obvious fears that this might further jeopardize the security context. Although well-considered from a conflict perspective, this approach reinforces the obvious push for externalization of EU's migration management policies and the overall aid conditionality it implies.

The implicit obligation placed by EU's external policy on third countries as regards readmission of own nationals found in irregular stay is debated by a series of scholars. In the wider context of the European Agenda on Migration and its EU Partnership Framework with third countries, a series of third countries were identified as priorities for the adoption of Readmission Agreements—amongst them, Nigeria. The formal signature of these agreements was delayed, was defined as ineffectual or never took place in many of the priority countries, and was replaced by less formal "readmission arrangements"—or "policy ghosts" (Carrera 2020). Carrera further engages in a critical reflection on the efficiency and effectiveness of the aforementioned arrangements. Nigeria did not yet sign a readmission arrangement with the EU, having begun negotiations in 2016 (Slagter 2019). After having critically assessed the negotiation process and its outcomes with each of the priority countries, Carrera concludes on the lack of willingness of African countries to engage in such a dialogue.

Whilst frustration of Nigerian authorities regarding the added-value of investments under the MFP is referred to by various authors (amongst them, Castillejo 2017), this section shall take a closer look at the specific funding via the EU Emergency Trust Fund for Africa, earmarked in Nigeria for border management, fight against THB and management of irregular migration.

According to the available information (European Commission 2020), the EU has committed 2.023 MEUR to financing of EUTF in the Sahel/Lake Chad area (also including Nigeria). These activities, to be locally carried out by a variety of implementing entities (including UN and other humanitarian agencies, NGOs, local agencies, etc.) have a relatively balanced approach amongst the political priorities of the EU in the area:

- 21% for improved governance and conflict prevention;
- 31% for improved migration management;
- 21% for greater economic and employment opportunities;
- 24% for strengthening resilience of communities.

In addition to these initially stated very broad and generic principles, according to the same source the EUTF Board for Africa has further specified priority areas, as of 2018: return and reintegration, refugee management, securitization of travel documents and civil registry (thus further enabling border checks and identification/return of potential irregular migrants), anti-trafficking measures, stabilization and supporting migration dialogue.

Out of the total amount of funding for the Lake Chad/Sahel area, Nigeria (as the primary source of irregular migration towards Europe, according to the same source) benefits of 128,523,633 MEUR, for the implementation of eights projects. Of this amount, 73,400,000 MEUR are earmarked for improved governance and conflict prevention, 15,500,000 MEUR for migration management, and 39,623,633 for strengthening resilience.

However, should we take a closer look at the specific implementation scope of each of the quoted projects, it can be easily noted that the scope is always closer linked to one of the main priorities of the EU, namely migration management and control. A detailed analysis of the projects is carried out in the following paragraphs, further outlining this theory.

(a) The first project, "*Linking relief, rehabilitation and development and promoting the stability and safety of communities in displacement in North Eastern Nigeria*" focuses on stabilization of conflict-displaced communities (mainly conflict between Boko Haram and Nigerian armed forces), and reducing the risk of radicalization / engagement in criminality amongst the local youth. Interestingly, the expected results and main outcomes list, inter alia, that "Young IDPs are more resilient to negative influences and manipulation such as criminality, irregular migration and radicalization and have alternative, legitimate opportunities." Although the Nigerian states scoped by the project (Borno, Yobe, and Adamawa) are facing dire insecurity, extreme poverty and recurrent terror attacks led by Boko Haram, displaced persons from these states are seen as potential irregular migrants to the EU, with limited to no concern about their specific plight or need for international protection. Irregular migration is quoted in the project action fiche amongst other "negative influence" such as criminality and radicalization. And the alternative, legitimate opportunities left to IDPs facing extremely adverse conditions are not at all detailed. It can be thus concluded that, amongst the perfectly valid envisaged outcomes of the project (such as improving access to water, health and sanitation facilities, fight against malnutrition), the project nevertheless has a strong dimension of discouraging migration towards the EU, without any concern for the individual plight of persons who may be in need of international protection—amongst them, women victimized and trafficked.
(b) "*Investing in the safety and security of Nigerian girls*" project targets adolescent girls in Borno, Adamawa and Gombe states, and aims to improve financial literacy, reproductive health, and livelihood skills. Adolescent girls are identified as one of the main categories at risk following protracted conflict in the area, being targeted by sexual violence and abuse, exploitation, and abduction by extremist militants. Although the project action fiche rightly identifies a wide variety of concrete threats faced by young women and girls (including THB), unfortunately it does not foresee any concrete action to reduce the risk of occurrence (e.g., building up coping strategies with the main categories of risks affecting this community), and chooses to focus instead on extremely generic actions such as traditional gender roles, understanding access to livelihood through drama and role playing, etc.
(c) The third project, "*Enhancing state and community level conflict management capability in North eastern Nigeria*" mainly deals with reinforcement of stabil-

ity in those communities mostly affected by displacement, with a sub-focus on the involvement of women and girls in peace-building. Although "addressing the impact of violence on women and girls" is also mentioned by the project fiche, it is assessed that, in its entirety, this project is not related to the THB focus of our study.

(d) "*Strengthening the management and governance of migration and the sustainable reintegration of returning migrants in Nigeria*" mainly focuses on safe return and reintegration of migrants, including through the provisioning of "comprehensive and developmental packages for safe return and reintegration," as per the project's action fiche. Although one of the project's sub-objectives is to "prevent irregular migration," the focus in the context of THB efforts is mainly centered on return and reinsertion of THB victims, and to a much lesser extent in actually countering the trafficker's narrative or dissuading potential victims from engaging in such journeys.

(e) The EUTF website lists a fifth project, TAN (acronym not explained) with a budget of 2,400,000 EUR and implemented by the Cordoba Foundation of Geneva. The project fiche is not available on the EUTF website, and no additional information could be found on the objectives of this project and its potential links with THB-related topics.

(f) "*Strengthening psychosocial support, mental health, reintegration and protection services for children in Borno, including children associated with Boko Haram*" is mainly focused on preventing radicalization and violent extremism, and as such does not list THB amongst its intervention objectives.

(g) "*EU support to Response, Recovery and Resilience in Borno State*" is, as in the case of the previous project, focused on different intervention topics and does not relate to THB.

(h) The final EUTF project in Niger, and by far the most substantially funded with a budget of 50,000,000 EUR, relates to funding the response to COVID-19.

From the brief analysis above, it can be safely concluded that prevention of THB in Nigeria is not one of the primary intervention areas of the EUTF. Although Nigeria is one of the countries most affected by this phenomenon, and as demonstrated in the following pages of this chapter coercion into THB by means of practices such as voodoo is an endemic situation, the EU chooses to focus its intervention rather on return and reinsertion of migrants and reducing the risk of radicalization / violent extremism.

As demonstrated by research on the externalization of EU's border management model to West Africa by targeted projects funded via the European Emergency Trust Fund for Africa (Dumitrescu 2019), it can be argued that the European Union is offering financial incentives for the migrants to leave its territory and return to their countries of origin however without an equally mindful focus on the perils that migrants may face alongside the migratory routes—amongst them, THB and associated practices. Few authors (Trauner 2013; Dunnewald 2011) argue that stranded migrants are often reduced to various forms of economic modern slavery to be able to pay the fees to the smugglers and continue their journey. This can be also a result of targeted reinforcement of security capacities in selected border areas, which forces migrants to choose alternate (and more dangerous routes), and thus turn to smugglers or become prey to traffickers to be able to continue their journey.

The result of the externalization of the EU's border checks can thus be, as previously shown, an increased degree of difficulty added to the journey of migrants (notwithstanding the various categories they belong to, e.g., forced migrants, refugees, economic migrants)—which leads to the search for alternative routes and possibly turn to smugglers or becoming THB victims. Thanks to the same funding instrument—the EUTF, the migrants (or at least some of them) receive emergency assistance alongside the migratory routes. Thus being said, it is quite obvious that the provisioning of emergency assistance to migrants is conditioned to the accessibility of the sites to the aid providers.

Without questioning the operational added-value of the emergency aid provided by humanitarian agencies and financed by the EUTF, physical limitations (such as insecurity limiting access to migrants and victims of trafficking, or limited knowledge of the implementing agencies in the social and religious practices of the concerned country) have to be acknowledged and weighed against the implications of the same EUTF-funded projects securing borders without fully integrating either a fundamental rights dimension, or the historical traditions of the countries arbitrarily separated by post-colonial border. The same EUTF thereafter funds voluntary return of migrants stranded in countries of transit towards the Western Mediterranean route, although no legal access pathways towards Europe are in place and migrants have no choice BUT to migrate and become stranded, or rather become victims of traffickers and finish their journeys in Europe, exploited through the loopholes of a border guarding system not fully ready to face this challenge.

3 The Voodoo

According to the UNODC 2022 report, it is estimated that 38.8% of the detected victims are exploited in forced labor and 38.7% are exploited sexually, after the collection and treatment of data has differentiated its focus (UNODC 2022, p. 25). This report shows regional trends in victims' exploitation, as well as a key element showing that "women and children suffer greater violence at the hands of traffickers" (UNODC 2022, p. 22). Another finding shows a decrease on of 11% of the number of detected trafficked victims (comparing data collected for 2019 and 2020), mostly because of the quick adaptation to COVID-19 situation, turning to an increased invisibility of the exploitation, especially concerning the sexual forms (24% of decrease, UNODC 2022, p. 26, 37). The EUROSTAT report highlights the five largest countries of origin in terms of victims identified in Europe: Nigeria, Brazil, China, Vietnam, and Russia (EUROSTAT 2015), as well as countries of origin where the largest number of traffickers from third countries has been identified in Europe: Nigeria, Turkey, Albania, Brazil, and Morocco (EUROSTAT 2015). It is therefore clear that Nigeria and Brazil stood out as the countries that "exported" most both victims and agents of trafficking in persons. The 2022 UNODC report, for example, refers that the "Sub-Saharan African victims [are] increasingly detected in transnational trafficking flows" (UNODC 2022, p. 42).

The estimates done by ILO (ILO 2017a, b) amounted to "40.3 million people in modern slavery and 15.4 million in force marriage." From these, 24.9 million have been detected in forced labor, and from these figures, 4.8 million in forced sexual exploitation. From this sexual exploitation, females represent 99% of the sex industry, from the signalized in forced labor (while EUROSTAT 2015, counts 85%). Data published by UNODC (UNODC 2016) confirms "more than 500 different trafficking flows" between 2012 and 2014 and "137 different citizenship of victims." Trends in this report also show an increase in convicted women for this grievous crime: in 2014, women represented 37% of convictions (among 6800 persons, in the period between 2012–2014 (UNODC 2016, p. 34)—UNODC. Eurostat (EUROSTAT 2015, p. 12) reports that non-EU suspected traffickers were mainly identified coming from Nigeria, Turkey, Albania, Brazil, and Morocco.

It is thus clearly understood that (1) human trafficking constitutes a big problem and a priority to prevent and repress in EU; (2) sexual exploitation is still the highest form of exploitation, where female and children (every year, around one million children are forced into prostitution, amounting a total of more than 10 million currently) (Willis and Levy 2002, p. 1417) victims are disproportionate affected; (3) Nigeria and Brazil are the higher representing country of non-EU victims and suspected traffickers; (4) human trafficking is a fast-changing-crime, with constant new forms of exploitation, routes and coercion over its victims getting the international community engaged in increasing knowledge to better act; and (5) border control and police agents and institutions may have a crucial role in the early detection, prevention and repression of human trafficking.

After some years of joint international and European work to prevent and repress human trafficking, with improvement and harmonization in legislation and with a higher cooperation at investigation and operationalization of justice, Member States still realize there are forms of recruitment and coercion over vulnerable victims that need to be tackled. In this scope, this topic has been elected to research, aiming to focus, on the women exploitation form, on the case of Nigerian women sexually exploited through voodoo coercion.

4 Modern Practices of Human Trafficking: New Coercion Forms in Different European Countries

When researching on human trafficking, one realizes that forms of exploitation differ from the gender, age (and other characteristics) of the victims and also of its exploiters. Just as an example, Kara refers to different identified forms: "Men are regularly trafficked for forced construction, children for forced begging, and women for forced prostitution at the hands of their fellow Turks in Turkey" (Kara 2009, p.

123). Nevertheless, new forms of exploitation arise (such as trafficking for the purpose of terrorism, forced and lured jihadi marriage (Binetti 2015), child forced to pick cotton (OSCE 2019, p. 31), recruited and forced to become child soldiers [Bhabha (2016) identifies around 300,000 children serving as soldiers in armed conflicts worldwide] to be forced to work on cocoa harvest, mines, traditional religious shrines, and the homes of rich urban dwellers (Mbaku 2019, pp. 287, 294) due to an amount of factors, such as legal, political (Lobasz 2019) and social changes, ethnic and economic knowledge of the criminal networks and organized crime interaction (Finckenauer 2018), pull and push factors of the illegal market and many others. The more recent UNODC report (2022, XI), also highlights the "increasing proportions of identified victims (…) trafficked for the purpose of forced criminality and mixed forms of exploitation" counting men and boys in higher numbers. After having previously analyzed the EU Internal Security Strategy concerning specifically vulnerable victims of human trafficking detection at borders (Guia 2017), new threats on this issue have been identified in this research. These are new current trends that are still in need of more information and investigation because there is still a lot to know about the functioning of this social media recruitment of victims (UNODC 2016) ("We do not have an accurate picture of the scope and nature of [the misuse of technology] and cannot act as effectively as we should. Knowledge is essential for evidence-based policy, and we must fill the information gap") and the threats it may be posing to children: "Serious offences are being committed—often right under a parent's nose," said Yury Fedotov, Executive Director of UNODC, in his opening remarks. "The Web literally opens a portal into your home and your children may be letting criminals in" (UNODC 2016).[3] On women, two trends have been identified in Europe to recruit them from abroad and exploit them inside the EU MS: through social networks and through spiritual domination. Taking the first trend, the use of social networks, one should be aware that Internet and new technologies have changed the landscape of relationships, where the online world, according to Arnaboldi et al. (2015, p. 9), has become currently the privileged laboratory to investigate human beings. Facebook and other social networks became a place where people meet and may faint intimate relations, known as "lover boys" (being a preferred *modus operandi* of the East European rings to attract female victims to exploit them through violence later on (Kleemans and Smit 2014, p. 386) with a previous criminal intention of recruiting them to exploit them further on, after establishing an emotional tie.

On the second trend, women in vulnerability, mainly from Ghana, Nigeria and other countries from the Occidental Africa are being dominated by through spiritual voodoo rituals or through other powerful ethical/religious/psychological domination (such as NXIVM sect, headed by Keith Raniere,[4] suspected of having recruited 16,000 women for sexual exploitation/servitude in the USA).

---

[3] Retrieved at https://www.unodc.org/unodc/en/frontpage/2011/April/crime-commission-to-address-the-protection-of-children-from-exploitation-on-the-web.html.

[4] As written in "Information" collected in the webpage https://veja.abril.com.br/entretenimento/nxivm-o-que-e-e-como-se-comportava-a-seita-do-sexo-de-alisson-mack/.

These forms of recruitment and exploitation have been lately more and more reported and vote vulnerable victims to an highest level of invisibility, increasing the level of vulnerability of these victims. These *modus operandi* challenge the EU MS, since they vote victims to a highest level of invisibility and vulnerability entailing a risk to EU MS positive obligations on the rescuing of these victims and on the prevention and repression of this crime.

The first referred new threat concerns victims crossing borders with a supposed partner, a so-called loverboy, after being recruited, coerced, and manipulated through emotional ties, especially after the use of new technologies and social networks (Merodio et al. 2020), such as Facebook, Twoo, Instagram, Snapchat, WhatsApp, among others. "Loverboys" are agents who approach attractive and vulnerable young girls, offering them undying love, treating them to extravagant gifts, and seducing them to migrate to a rich country where they can build a life together"[5] (Kara 2009, p. 7). "News reports have similarly connected Myspace and Facebook to cases of human trafficking, as traffickers use social networking sites to target victims and advertise their sexual services (Latonero 2011)." These new *modus operandi* make victims women even more invisible, as already mentioned, especially when introduced in European countries as wives or partners of a supposed national citizen (even if the origin of this trafficker is the same as the victim). Other similar invisible coercion forms include the use of voodoo. People from different regions practice Voodoo, such as the Ewe, Kabye, Mina, Fon, and the Yorubas people (with some different designation) of southern and central Benin, southern and central Togo, southeastern Ghana, and southwestern Nigeria. Two different types of Voodoo may be identified: one called Black magic, or Petro in which it is common to use sacrifices, including also invocations to the devil, or made for evil. It is compulsory to promise to keep secrecy every time a ceremony is made. If for any reason the promise is broken, there will be a penalty (or a curse) over the person who broke it (Montgomery and Vannier 2017). These terror-inducing rituals, putting victims into a huge and permanent debt (IOM 2023, p. 11) and at the same time completely controlled (Packham 2012). Several victims of human trafficking reported that traffickers show them funeral videos of people who have been subjected to voodoo, stating that this is their destination or their families, aiming to coerce them, but when they are back to life they are still under the "crisis stage" (Surtees et al. 2022). Many victims, whose parents died after they escape, are convinced that their death was the result of the trafficking threat. They say that the dolls used by a wizard facilitate the direction of the magic, thus making the person feel everything that is done with the doll. Voodoo coerced victims will never run away, terrorized their relatives will be hurt or ultimately fearing her own self (Baarda 2016, p. 259), avoiding therefore the early action at crossing borders and putting new challenges to Border Guards when controlling entries into the EU from third country. According to Van Dijk et al. (2006, p. 259), voodoo in Nigerian human trafficking, connected to old West African religious traditions, is practiced by a priest who gets the power

[5] It is very common to find this coercion form of human trafficking in Central and Eastern Europe.

to "manipulate outcomes in people's lives" getting its victims completely, physically, and emotionally, dependent while they believe the spell is over them.

A new threat on this topic was elected concerning the emergence of new recruitment forms and aims on human trafficking victims' exploitation, involving the emotional tie provoked in victims, especially through a faint romantic story, started and maintained in social networks or through spiritual/religious rituals, such as voodoo that aims to involve the victim into a complete dependence of the traffickers. Both forms constitute a threat to EU states and a challenge to the EU strategy since new forms of comprehension of this crime and these new *modi operandi* must be put into force so that an early detection of victims at border crossing may be successfully implemented and effective. In fact, and according to Baarda (2016, p. 269), "voodoo as a coercion mechanism certainly emerges from the data as a main category; it forms the core of the modus operandi of the organization."

5 Human Trafficking Victims: The Case of Nigerian Women and Voodoo Coercion

The aim of this sub topic is to explore one specific form of coercion of female victims recruited into human trafficking for sexual exploitation in Europe. The increased knowledge on these issues may allow state positive measures on preventive detection of victims at borders or within investigation field on the implementation of justice, one of the core jobs of border guards and immigration police forces. The main highlighted goal is the effective application of human rights, on a positive approach (Guia 2017). Questions, such as the following, were raised:

1. How difficult is to detect a potential victim of human trafficking at the airports?
2. Are women being given the due attention, as vulnerable victims, as potentially being coerced through voodoo? How are they recognized/detected as victims at the airports?
3. Is Organized Crime connected to human trafficking crossing airports a real threat to the EU?

To these ones, an extra specific concern has been raised. It is related to the main origin and exploitation form of detected victims. And it has been raised to trying to find out how are Nigerian women being coerced into sexual exploitation into the EU, being at the first place of the non-EU citizenship detected victims.

The United Nations "Transforming our world: 2030 Agenda for Sustainable Development UN, 2015" remarks, as objectives, in several points of the report the eradication of human trafficking and forced labor from our societies. Point 27 on the "New Agenda" refers specifically to it: "We will eradicate forced labour and human trafficking and end child labour in all its forms." In this scope, goal 5 (point 5.2.) mentions the need to eradicate forms of sexual exploitation over women and children ("5.2 Eliminate all forms of violence against all women and girls in the public and private spheres, including trafficking and sexual and other types of exploitation"), goal 8 (point 8.7) refers to the need to take measures to eradicate forced labor, modern slavery and human trafficking ("8.7. Take immediate and effective measures to eradicate forced labour, end modern slavery and human trafficking (…"), goal 16 (point 16.2) reinforces the need to protect children from trafficking—"16.2 End abuse, exploitation, trafficking and all forms of violence against and torture of children."

Global estimates on modern slavery (where trafficking in human beings can be included) illustrate an estimated 49.6 million people as victims of modern slavery in 2021,[6] with an increase of 2.7 million in forced labor identifications between 2016 and 2021. Furthermore, Africa was the reported place where victims are cheaper (Uchikova 2014), costing 3.9 k/victim, on an estimated number of 3.7 million victims (ILO 2014). According to the estimated proportion of population in modern slavery by country, Nigeria is listed on the ten countries "with the largest estimate absolute numbers of people in modern slavery." Crossing this data with numbers collected on the report from Nigerian National Agency for the Prohibition of Trafficking in Persons (NAPTIP),[7] the highest amount of reported cases of human trafficking were "foreign travels which promotes prostitution" (23.1%) and "employment of children as domestic workers and inflicting grievous harm" (22.2%). It is also reported that 21.7% of the arrested suspects of human trafficking were arrested in connection with offense of "foreign travels which promote prostitution" (Aniagoh 2018). This report also highlights the highest number of cases charged to court of procurement of persons for sexual exploitation, where rescued female-victims were in higher number (72.1%). Furthermore, the regional problems suffered by these populations also puts them into an extreme fragile situation. According to IOM (2022), "in North-East Nigeria, for example, during 1 week in August 2022, more than 1,500 individuals were recorded as newly displaced because of military operations in Adamawa and Borno States."

What is important to retain from this is the way in which these female-victims are recruited into human trafficking by criminal organizations. It is common that criminal networks know perfectly the language, culture, religion (Case 2016),[8] behaviors, difficulties, vulnerabilities of victims, therefore targeting those victims who might seem easier to coerce into sexual exploitation. One of the most common ways within Nigerian female-victims in through the imposition of high debts,

[6] The highest rate of modern slavery reported in 2018 was in Africa, with 7.6 victims for every 1000 persons. Information retrieved from https://www.alliance87.org/2017ge/modernslavery#!section=0.

[7] Data collected in different reports published at the NAPTIP, accessed at https://www.naptip.gov.ng/?page_id=120.

[8] Voodoo or Vodun is a traditional African monotechism religion, applied to the branches of an ancestral theistic-based religious tradition, which has its primary roots among the Ewe-Fon peoples of West Africa, in the country now called Benin, formerly Kingdom of Dahomey. Nowadays, voodoo is the national religion of more than seven million people (similar to Cadomble Jeje from Brazil). In voodoo religion, spirits are central. Case (2016).

promising them the possibility of entering Europe and having a better future. But to be sure that debts will be paid and that female-victims will not charge traffickers to the police or justice services, traffickers insure to bring female-Nigerian women to voodoo priests to make rituals with them, cursing their future, or the health of their relatives, or their owns, or other threatens related to the spiritual-religious beliefs in case they show a will to escape from paying her debts.

According to a study (Neves and Pedra 2012), analyzing mainly qualitative information collected among victims of human trafficking in southern EU, between 2010 and 2012, mainly Nigerian women were coerced through voodoo for sexual exploitation purposes. It reports cases where Nigerian and Ghana females were coerced through voodoo (Fandrich 2007)[9] but with a substantial low visible control of victims, since this control was done mainly through intelligent and objective psychological domination through voodoo and threats over their families. At the same time, criminal groups sent regularly (monthly) a small amount of money to their relatives in their origin countries to expressly create the illusion that their migration process was successful and subsequently rendering possible to continuously recruiting new victims, in the circle of life of the victim. Normally the invitation done by the female-victim already being exploited, coerced by the criminal network to call other female relatives or friends, works well, since the proof of the success of the migration process of the first one, can guarantee a success in further displacement of people. Another phenomenon reported in this study stresses that many female-victims, later on assume different posts in organized crime groups ruling and coercing other victims after being victims of sexual exploitation during many years. For this reason, the number of Nigerian women suspected traffickers have been rising. Victims and NGO/lawyers involved in the support of victims interviewed on this research reported being integrated in transnational criminal networks operating mainly in southern Europe (Italy, France, Spain, Portugal). Four identified routes clearly related these four countries: route 1 Nigeria-Spain-Portugal; route 2 Nigeria-France-Spain-Portugal; route 3 Nigeria-Italy-Spain-Portugal, and route 4 Nigeria-Spain-Italy-Spain-Portugal.

In such cases, it is difficult to collect this information during criminal investigation. go even back to the early detection of these victims on crossing European borders. What can and should the European border management do? It is essential to remember that Article 4 of the ECHR, the right not to be subject to slavery, servitude and forced labor, should be respected, not only when detection is visible, but in such a positive obligation to identify and support the potential victims of human trafficking, even if they did not apply for that. Recalling the case of *Siliadin v.*

[9] The term voodoo comes from the word vodun, which means "divinity" or "god" (Mawu is the Supreme Being of the Ewe (Eʋeawo) and Fon peoples), who created the earth and living beings and begat the voduns, deities that (Mawu is female) would second in command of the Universe. It is associated with Lissah, male, and also co-responsible for Creation, and voodles are children and descendants of both. The dual deity Mawu-Lissá is titled Dadá Segbô (Great Father Vital Spirit) in the ewe-gen-aja-fon dialectal group of the Gulf of Guinea (Matory 1999, 61)—west of the contemporary location of the yorùbá (Fandrich 2007).

France (2005)[10] where the applicant claimed through Article 4 that the state "did not afford her sufficient and effective protection against the 'servitude' in which she had been held," being granted the certitude that state should have taken positive measures to protect her from the servitude she was being exploited for (*Siliadin* case, 2005).[11] It is crucial to be aware that these victims dominated through voodoo spiritual coercion are completely convinced that some harm will reach them or their relatives, in case they do not accomplish everything promised during the rituals done before the departure to a destiny of sexual exploitation and states should be aware of entailing specific measures to protect them from exploitation. Recently,[12] mass media have been showing evidence on an arrested woman in Manchester, suspect of maintaining the recruitment of female from Benin and Nigeria to Spain, through voodoo coercion rituals, threatening to kill their families if they did not pay their debts. These rituals would involve forcing victims to eat raw chicken hearts, drink whisky and "had their fingernails and pubic hair pulled out," or "superficial cutting of the body with razors, and the beheading of goats."

It is not always simple to recognize or early detect signs of human trafficking in someone. Surely actions should be developed to protect identified victims of this crime, such as claimed in the case *L.E. v. Greece* where the applicant, a Nigerian women found to be sexually exploited into prostitution through voodoo coercion, only after 10 years of requests, brought to ECHR (Van Dijk 2001),[13] the case was delivered and she got the due protection (after all her efforts to request further investigation on the facts, since it was not clearly detected the guilt of her traffickers) It has been pointed out the importance of the entry and exit checks to prevent, detect and identify, interview and collect information for investigations in situations appearing to be dubious. Acting in the needed time may entail the difference to what is a success case and what is not.

To elaborate over the main question and sub-questions, some of the most recent documents were analyzed on the raised question, such as the United Nations "The 2030 Agenda for Sustainable Development" (2015), the Communication from The Commission to the European Parliament and The Council entitled "Reporting on the follow-up to the EU Strategy towards the Eradication of trafficking in human beings and identifying further concrete actions," (2017), the Global Plan of Action to Combat Trafficking in Persons (resolution 64/293) and other relevant documents for this topic such as the EUROSTAT reports (2013, 2015), the ILO and UNODC reports, a report published by the Nigerian Research and Programme Development Department, and a ECHR case (*L.E. v. Greece*), among other sources. The aim was

[10] (Application No. 73316/01), judgement of the 26 July 2005, final judgement 26/10/2005.

[11] For more details, see the resume here (https://sherloc.unodc.org/cld/case-law-doc/traffickingpersonscrimetype/_irb/2005/siliadin_v._france.html) or the complete case here https://sherloc.unodc.org/res/cld/case-law/fra/2005/siliadin_v__france_html/Siliadin_v_France_en.pdf.

[12] Recently means around 21/02/2018, Information collected in the webpage http://www.nationalcrimeagency.gov.uk/news/1295-suspected-member-of-european-slavery-network-arrested-in-manchester.

[13] See Affaire L.E. c. Grèce, Strasbourg 21 janvier 2016 Définitif (21/04/2016).

to analyze collected data to check if there is evidence voodoo practices as potential increasing risk factor on the rise on human trafficking women from Nigeria into the EU and how to act towards reinforcing services on the European border management on the early detection of potential victims or suspects.

6 The Need of Boosting Fundamental Rights on THB Through Judicial Training

Nigeria was listed 32nd on the Global Slavery Index[14] among 167 countries. The Nigerian National Agency for the Prohibition of Trafficking in Persons (NAPTIT 2018) reports that the highest number of victims identified in THB cases were related to sexual exploitation abroad[15] and also to children trafficked for forced domestic work.[16] At the same time, this agency reported the highest number of criminal agents arrested for THB were coincidently by offenses related to "foreign travels which promote prostitution."[17] At the same time, this report also highlights the highest number of cases charged to court of procurement of persons for sexual exploitation, where rescued female-victims were in higher number (72.1%).

Van Dijk et al. (2006, p. 259) refers that voodoo in Nigerian human trafficking is connected to old West African religious traditions. These authors describe that these rituals are practiced by a priest, considered public leaders or religious figures by Nigerian society, who gets the power to "manipulate outcomes in people's lives" getting its victims under a complete physically and emotionally dependence while they fully believe the spell is over them. According to Baarda (2016, p. 270), "voodoo as a coercion mechanism certainly emerges from the data as a main category; it forms the core of the modus operandi of the organization." In fact, these priests are often connected to traffickers and its seems they cooperate with them conscious of its further consequence of exploiting the victims, so abusing its vulnerable position at the moment of the ritual, although Baarda (2016, p. 269) refers to them as assuming an important role in those societies, namely by "punish[ing] thieves, settle disputes between neighbors and enforce criminal contracts" acting as judicial regulators. But the goal of obliging the recruited victims, mainly female, to go under this ritual is indeed to impose them an unbreakable emotional tie with its recruiters and further exploiters so that they feel obliged to pay them. They are mostly exploited sexually

[14] There are already some slight signs of positive changes: Nigeria was listed 23rd on the Global Slavery Index of 167 countries with the highest number of slaves, according to the estimate proportion of population in modern slavery by country (ILO 2017a, b).

[15] NAPTIT 2018: 23.1% of the THB Nigerian victims were under the classification of "foreign travels which promotes prostitution."

[16] NAPTIT 2018: 22.2% of the THB Nigerian victims were under the classification of "employment of children as domestic workers and inflicting grievous harm" (22.2%).

[17] Aniagoh (2018).

in different EU MS, and after the ritual and a curse thrown to their future life and of their relatives, victims do not dear to denounce, escape or ask for help, or even to speak about, such is the strong spiritual-religious belief with a strong cultural root. For the justice system, and for the police officers in the field, if not aware of this cultural practice, very well known, by the criminal agents of the networks according to Anagioh (2018) that mostly know perfectly the language, religion, behaviors and vulnerabilities, invisibility led to the impossibility of identifying the crime.

As we have apperceived, this form of coercion is mostly hidden and not familiar to most of the European Member States justice systems. Directive 2011/36/EU recommends in point 25 of its preamble that Member States should boost the THB prevention policies and the Article 18 of the mentioned directive highlights the obligation of Member States to promote a regular training to agents and officers that may contact with victims, focusing on the police officers in the field so that they may be able to identify and deal with victims of potential victims, hence those who have been invisible to the justice system.

In this sense, all institutions, universities, NGO's and civil society in EU MS and also European institutions charged with conceiving, preparing, and delivering training about THB should deep-in their knowledge and raise awareness of this invisible coercion that moves thousands of victims to a silenced exploitation life.

7 Conclusions

The externalization of EU's border management practices to third countries of origin / transit for THB victims, via its funding programs in a conflict-sensitive environment (such as the EUTF), may have serious side effects—only some of which intentional, whilst the other rather as unintended results of capacity-building projects designed with little understanding of local realities.

Moreover, and as demonstrated by the referenced studies, the EU engages in externalization of its border control and migration management policies with third countries far from having a pristine record regarding human rights and respect for the rights of refugees / forced migrants. This externalization policy is aligned to the "informalization" trend noted by Carrera as regards relations between the EU and countries of origin/transit for irregular migration and THB victims. To a progressive informalization in EU external relations, Santos Vara (2019) adds the fact that the use of soft mechanisms "can lead in practice to disregard the legal framework established by the Treaties in EU external relations. By means of providing a very limited support to actual THB victims throughout EUTF projects, the EU choses to focus on controlling borders instead of countering traffickers" narratives or boosting investigative capacities of local authorities. In fact, if a higher attention would be given to certain new alarming phenomena on THB, especially increasing awareness and training to those involved in the operationalization of justice, a surely growth in the detection of victims would be a reality and fundamental rights would therefore be effectively put in place, enforcing the Directive 2011/36/EU.

The research on this chapter has previously alluded to the migratory tradition of West African countries, including Nigeria. Indeed, Nigeria has a longstanding history of migration, not only towards Europe but also in the sub-region. However, nowadays migration goes beyond history and tradition—it has become a resilience strategy not only for the migrant but also for his/her family in the country of origin. For Nigerian nationals, migration can no longer be defined as "economic migration", but rather a form of subsistence facilitating access to basic social services and commodities which are lacking in the country of origin. In this context, one cannot help but notice the unilateral approach of externalization instruments such as the EUTF projects. Return of migrants in irregularity and reinsertion of THB victims are encouraged and financed, in an attempt to contain migratory flows as far from the EU as possible. However, what are the viable alternatives—not only for prospective migrants affected by these measures, but also for former trafficking victims now turned into traffickers because of either coercion or lack of economic alternatives? The EUTF projects analyzed in this research do not provide a realistic answer to this complex issue, and by exclusively focusing on reinsertion of migrants/victims of traffic or basic support to migrants during their journey they demonstrate a need for further improving their integrated approach to security and development.

References

Adam I, Trauner F (2019) Ghana and EU migration policy: studying an African response to the EU externalization agenda. In: Carrera S, Vara S (eds) Constitutionalising the external dimensions of EU migration policies in times of crisis: legality, rule of law and fundamental rights reconsidered. Edward Elgar Publishing

Aniagoh N (2018) NAPTIP, Court jails two for human trafficking. Available at https://www.naptip.gov.ng/?p=1838

Arnaboldi V, Valeiro P, Andrea C, Dunbar R (2015) Online social networks: human cognitive constraints in Facebook and Twitter personal graphs. Elsevier. ISBN 978-0-12-803023-3

Baarda CS (2016) Human trafficking for sexual exploitation from Nigeria into Western Europe: the role of voodoo rituals in the functioning of a criminal network. Eur J Criminol 13(2):257–227

BALZACQ T (2008) The policy tools of securitization: information exchange, EU foreign and interior policies. JCMS: J Common Mark Stud, 46: 75–100. https://doi.org/10.1111/j.1468-5965.2007.00768.x

Bhabha J (2016) Child migration and human rights in a global age. Princeton University Press; V. Mlambo et al., 'Armed conflict and the increasing use of child soldiers in the Central African Republic, Democratic Republic of Congo, and South Sudan: Implications for regional security', 2019, https://onlinelibrary.wiley.com/doi/pdf/10.1002/pa.1896

Binetti A (2015) A new frontier: human trafficking and ISIS's recruitment of women from the west. INFORMATION2ACTION A publication of the Georgetown Institute for Women, Peace & Security. http://giwps.georgetown.edu/wp-content/uploads/2017/10/Human-Trafficking-and-ISISs-Recruitment-of-Women-from-the-West.pdf

Carrera S (2020) On policy ghosts: EU readmission arrangements as intersecting policy universes. In: Guild E, Mitsilegas V (eds) EU external migration policies in an era of global mobilities: intersecting policy universes

Case M (2016) Yoruba culture, religion, and gender. In: The Wiley Blackwell Encyclopedia of Gender and Sexuality Studies. https://doi.org/10.1002/9781118663219.wbegss729

Castillejo C (2017) The EU migration partnership framework: time for a rethink? Discussion paper. Deutsches Institut für Entwicklungspolitik, Bonn

Dumitrescu S (2019) EU's Migration Partnership with Africa: Friends or Foes?: The EUTF – an externalization instrument of migration policies. Master Dissertation. European Joint Master in Strategic Border Management, promoted by Frontex

Dűnnwald S (2011) On Migration and Security: Europe managing migration from Sub-Saharan Africa, Cadernos de Estudios Africanos, 22/2011. Centro de Estudos Internacionais, pp 103–128

Fandrich I (2007) Yorùbá influences on Haitian Vodou and New Orleans Voodo. J Black Stud 37(5):2007

Finckenauer J (2018) Human trafficking, modern day slavery and organized crime. In: Clark J, Poucki S (eds) The SAGE handbook of human trafficking and modern day slavery. Sage. https://books.google.pt/books?hl=pt-PT&lr=&id=fQJ6DwAAQBAJ&oi=fnd&pg=PA215&dq=organized+crime+and+human+trafficking&ots=zTZZK5K7D7&sig=MurdXNKZYb6P9whxPXawxm72BQk&redir_esc=y#v=onepage&q=organized%20crime%20and%20human%20trafficking&f=false

Guia MJ (2017) European migration and human trafficking measures: how the European border and coast guard agency is enhancing the protection of vulnerable victims of human trafficking. In: Rodrigues AM, Guia MJ (eds) Livro de Atas. Conferência Internacional 18 De Outubro - Dia Europeu Contra o Tráfico de Seres Humanos. Instituto Jurídico da Faculdade de Direito da Universidade de Coimbra

Kara S (2009) Sex trafficking. Inside the business of modern slavery. Columbia University Press

Kipp D (2018) From exception to rule – the EU trust fund for Africa. SWP Research Paper 13. German Institute for International and Security Affairs

Kleemans ER, Smit M (2014) Human smuggling, human trafficking, and exploitation in the sex industry. In: Paoli L (ed) The Oxford handbook of organized crime. Oxford University Press, Oxford, pp 381–401

Latonero M (2011) Human trafficking online: the role of social networking sites and online classifieds. https://ssrn.com/abstract=2045851 or https://doi.org/10.2139/ssrn.2045851

Lobasz J (2019) Contemporary approaches to human trafficking. In: Constructing human trafficking. Human rights interventions. Palgrave Macmillan, Cham

Mbaku J (2019) The rule of law and the exploitation of children in Africa. Hastings Int Comp Law Rev 42:287. https://repository.uchastings.edu/cgi/viewcontent.cgi?article=1835&context=hastings_international_comparative_law_review

Merodio G, Duque E, Axt Peña JC (2020) They are not Romeo pimps, they are traffickers: overcoming the socially dominant discourse to prevent the sex trafficking of youth. Qual Inq 26(8–9):1010–1018. https://doi.org/10.1177/1077800420938881

Montgomery E, Vannier C (2017) An ethnography of a Vodu Shrine in southern Togo. Of spirit, slave and sea. In: Studies of Religion in Africa, vol 46

Neves M, Pedra C (eds) (2012) A proteção dos direitos humanos e as vítimas de tráfico de pessoas [Documento electrónico]: rotas, métodos, tipos de tráfico e setores de atividade em Portugal. Instituto de Estudos Estratégicos e Internacionais- IEEI

Packham J (2012) Voodoo. The encyclopedia of the gothic. https://doi.org/10.1002/9781118398500.wbeotgv004

Papagianni G (2013) Forging an external EU migration policy: from externalization of border management to a comprehensive policy? European Journal of Migration and Law 15(3):283–299

Santos Vara J (2019) Soft international agreements on migration cooperation with third countries: a challenge to democratic and judicial controls in the EU. In: Carrera S, Vara S (eds) Constitutionalising the external dimensions of EU migration policies in times of crisis: legality, rule of law and fundamental rights reconsidered. Edward Elgar Publishing

Savino M (2018) Refashioning resettlement: from border externalization to legal pathways for asylum. In: Guild E, Mitsilegas V (eds) Immigration and asylum law and policy in Europe, vol 44. Brill Nijhof

Slagter J (2019) An "informal" turn in the European Union's migrant returns policy towards Sub-Saharan Africa. Migration Information Source. https://reliefweb.int/sites/reliefweb.int/files/resources/An%20%E2%80%9CInformal%E2%80%9D%20Turn%20in%20the%20European%20Union%E2%80%99s%20Migrant%20Returns%20Policy%20towards%20Sub-Saharan%20Africa%20_%20migrationpolicy.org_.pdf
Surtees R, Meshi M, Tanellari S, Lila A, Hinaj O (2022) Stages of recovery and reintegration of trafficking victims. A reintegration guide for practitioners. In: Different and Equal (D&E). NEXUS Institute, Tiranë
Trauner F, Deimel S (2013) The impact of EU migration policies on African countries: the case of Mali. Int Migr 51(4):2013
Uchikova M (2014) OECD and modern slavery: how much aid money is spent to tackle the issue? Anti Traffick Rev 3:133–150
Van Dijk R (2001) 'Voodoo' on the doorstep: young Nigerian prostitutes and magic policing in the Netherlands. Afr J Int Afr Instit 71(4):558–586
Van Dijk R, Rasing T, Tellegen N, Van Binsbergen NW (2006) Een Schijn van Voodoo. African Study Centre, Leiden
Willis B, Levy B (2002) Child prostitution: global health burden, research needs, and interventions. Lancet 359(9315):1417

Reports and Legislation

Communication from the Commission to the European Parliament, the Council, the European Economic and Social Committee and the Committee of the Regions, *The Global Approach to Migration and Mobility* (COM 2011/0743 final), https://eur-lex.europa.eu/legal-content/EN/ALL/?uri=CELEX:52011DC0743
Communication from the Commission to the European Parliament, the European Council, the Council and the European Investment Bank on *Establishing a New Partnership Framework with Third Countries under the European Agenda on Migration*, (COM(2016) 385 final), https://ec.europa.eu/home-affairs/sites/homeaffairs/files/what-we-do/policies/european-agenda-migration/proposal-implementation-package/docs/20160607/communication_external_aspects_eam_towards_new_migration_ompact_en.pdf
Communication from the Commission to the European Parliament, the Council, the European Economic and Social Committee and the Committee of the Regions, *A European Agenda on Migration*, COM(2015) 240 final, https://ec.europa.eu/home-affairs/sites/homeaffairs/files/what-we-do/policies/european-agenda-migration/background-information/docs/communication_on_the_european_agenda_on_migration_en.pdf
Council of the European Union, Global Approach to Migration : Priority Actions focusing on Africa and the Mediterranean (doc. 15744/05, of 13 December 2005) http://register.consilium.europa.eu/doc/srv?l=EN&f=ST%2015744%202005%20INIT
European Union External Action Service, Shared Vision, Common Action: A Stronger Europe. A Global Strategy for the European Union's Foreign and Security Policy, June 2016., http://eeas.europa.eu/archives/docs/top_stories/pdf/eugs_review_web.pdf
Europol, THE THB FINANCIAL BUSINESS MODEL Assessing the Current State of Knowledge, July 2015., https://www.europol.europa.eu/publications-documents/trafficking-in-human-beings-financial-business-model
Eurostat, European Commission (2015) Trafficking in human beings, 2015 edition. Publications Office of the European Union, Luxembourg. https://ec.europa.eu/anti-trafficking/sites/antitrafficking/files/eurostat_report_on_trafficking_in_human_beings_-_2015_edition.pdf
ILO (2014) Profits and poverty: the economics of forced labour, Geneva. https://www.ilo.org/global/topics/forced-labour/publications/profits-of-forced-labour-2014/lang%2D%2Den/index.htm

ILO. Global estimates of modern slavery: forced labour and forced marriage, Geneva, September 2017a, p 9. Data collected at the webpage http://www.ilo.org/wcmsp5/groups/public/%2D%2D-dgreports/%2D%2D-dcomm/documents/publication/wcms_575479.pdf

ILO, 'The Global Slavery Index - unravelling the numbers', 2017b., https://www.globalslaveryindex.org/findings/

International Organization for Migration (IOM), Displacement Tracking Matrix – Nigeria Emergency Tracking Tool (ETT), 1–7 August 2022

International Organization for Migration (IOM) and Samuel Hall (2023) Monitoring the reintegration of trafficking survivors: study and toolkit. IOM, Geneva

OSCE (2019) Trafficking in human beings: identification of potential and presumed victims, a community policing approach. SPMU Publication Series 10:31. https://www.osce.org/secretariat/78849?download=true

United Nations. Resolution adopted by the General Assembly on 25 September 2015 [without reference to a Main Committee (A/70/L.1)] 70/1. Transforming our world: the 2030 Agenda for Sustainable Development, https://www.un.org/ga/search/view_doc.asp?symbol=A/RES/70/1&Lang=E

United Nations Office on Drugs and Crime (2011) Crime Commission to address protection of children from exploitation on the Web. https://www.unodc.org/unodc/en/frontpage/2011/April/crime-commission-to-address-the-protection-of-children-from-exploitation-on-the-web.html

UNODC (2016) Global report on trafficking in persons. UN publications. Sales No. E.16.IV.6, https://www.unodc.org/documents/data-and-analysis/glotip/2016_Global_Report_on_Trafficking_in_Persons.pdf

UNODC (2022) Global report on trafficking in persons. UN Publications. GLOTiP_22_Special_points_of_interest.pdf (unodc.org)

Valletta Summit on Migration, Action Plan, 2015., https://www.consilium.europa.eu/media/21839/action_plan_en.pdf

Maria João Guia (maria.joao.guia@ij.uc.pt) holds a PhD in Law, Justice, and Citizenship in the twenty-first century, by the University of Coimbra, Portugal and four Master Degrees (in Law, Sociology, Translation and Strategic Border Management). She has been a European Commission external expert in the area of "Security, Liberty and Justice (2014)" after being an alternate member of the Group of Experts on Trafficking in Human Beings. She has been working professionally in criminal investigation, borders, and document control in the area of migration. She is an Invited Assistant Professor of Criminology and Researcher of Ratio Legis – Center of Research and Development of Legal Sciences of the Universidade Autónoma de Lisboa [Project: *Corpus Delicti* – Studies in Transnational Organized Criminality], Researcher at the Centre for Legal Research, University of Coimbra and Researcher of *Ius Gentium Conimbrigae/* Centre for Human Rights of the Faculty of Law, University of Coimbra. She lectures on the intersection of sociology, law, and criminology in Post-PhD, PhD, master, postgraduation, degree, and training courses of various areas of knowledge. Maria João Guia was a national expert and researcher in several European and national projects, namely in the areas of organised crime, the rights of victims of crimes, human trafficking, and the rights of immigrants.

Sandra Dumitrescu (dumitrescu.sandra@gmail.com) is a former Border Police officer. She has a wide expertise in border and migration management, gained not only at the European level but also in conflict environments such as Mali where she currently works in the security area. She is graduate of the University of London's Masters in Forced Migration and Refugee Protection and of the European Joint Master's in Strategic Border Management. Sandra is now a doctoral candidate with the Police Academy in Bucharest, with a doctoral thesis focusing on alternative access paths to Europe for forced migrants in the G5 Sahel area. She has published extensively in various journals, on topics such as externalization of the EU's migration management policies to third countries, fundamental rights principles in technical assistance projects to third countries on migration and border management, among others.

Transvestites and Transwomen in Human Trafficking for Sexual Exploitation: A Study in Brazil

Andreza do Socorro Pantoja de Oliveira Smith

Abstract In the present chapter, I present an analysis about a narrowed studied situation in Brazil: the victimization of *trans*vestites and *trans*women by the trafficking for sexual exploitation. I argue that the major drive of this problem is the discrimination and prejudice that these people suffer because of their sexual orientation, gender identity and the body they construct for the assumed gender. I use the definition of trafficking in persons (or human trafficking) adopted by the Additional Protocol to the United Nations Convention against Transnational Organized Crime Concerning the Prevention, Suppression and Punishment of Trafficking in Humans, Especially Women and Children and the current Brazilian definition inserted by Law 13.344/2016. I intent to raise questions about the studies and research produced so far that point out to women as the main victims of this crime, considering the identification of a lack or even absence of data on the interviewed public. I also affirm that as long as situations of inequality persist, it will not be possible to adequately address the situation in the country.

1 Introduction

Between the years of 2011 and 2016, I developed bibliographical and field research to produce a doctoral thesis in which I argued that the prejudice and discrimination suffered by *trans*vestites and *trans*women serve as the driving force behind the trafficking of persons for sexual exploitation in the city of Belém.

The interest in the issue arose from my inclusion in the Non-Governmental Organization Sodireitos (in Portuguese), which operates in the city of Belém in confronting the human trafficking. Since the emergence of the NGO, in 2005, we have faced various situations of sexual exploitation and human trafficking, mostly of children and adult women.

Andreza do Socorro Pantoja de Oliveira Smith (✉)
Federal University of Pará, Faculty of Law, Pará, Brazil

A. M. Rodrigues, M. J. Guia (eds.), *New Forms of Human Trafficking*,
https://doi.org/10.1007/978-3-031-39732-5_8

At the beginning of 2011, several journalistic reports reported that the civil police of the State of São Paulo, in cooperation with the civil police of the State of Pará, identified several houses where many *trans*vestites were kept under a regime of sexual exploitation, the majority of them coming from the city of Belém, among them several underage persons. The situation, even if not new, since we had heard reports of these types of cases in the NGO, was not identified in the large diagnostic studies on human trafficking in Brazil.

So I decided to go out on the field and listen to the narratives of those who found themselves in that situation. In this sense, I interviewed over 16 *trans*vestites and *trans*women who experienced human trafficking for sexual exploitation, considering the route between the city of Belém and the city of São Paulo, but all of them were heard on their return (temporary or otherwise) to the city of Belém.

I wanted to demonstrate that there are many cases that can be characterized as trafficking, but I also observed the existence of circumstances that indicate sexual exploitation, not necessarily through trafficking in persons, as well as cases of migration to work in prostitution.

I intended to raise questions about the studies and researches produced by the time, in which biologically considered women were pointed out as the main victims of the crime, since I had identified a lack or even the absence of data on the interviewed public.

In the end, it was possible to conclude that, as long as the situations of inequalities involving the research interlocutors continue, it will not be possible to adequately address the situation in the country.

Therefore, the present chapter constitutes a brief presentation of the data that I produced and the results that I achieved with the realization of the doctoral thesis described above.

2 The Categories of Analysis

By conducting this study, I consider it necessary to explain the categories used to analyze the problem raised. The first concept is human trafficking for sexual exploitation.

In Brazil, the definition of human trafficking has been built in the Brazilian Penal Code since 1940 and, in keeping with the international trend, first dealt with trafficking in women. Only in 2006 did it remove the expression "women" from the definition of the crime, which allowed the widening of the analysis of the problem in relation to other people. However, the purpose of the trafficking was centered on the exploitation of prostitution or other forms of sexual exploitation. It should be noted that the expression "another form of sexual exploitation" was not conceptualized in the legislation, which made it difficult to understand and apply it.

In 2004, Brazil ratified the Additional Protocol to the United Nations Convention against Transnational Organized Crime Concerning the Prevention, Suppression and Punishment of Human Trafficking, Especially Women and Children. Despite that, only in 2016 the necessary legislative compatibility of the definition of the crime was accomplished, with the enactment of Law 13.344 of October 6, which provides for the prevention and suppression of internal and international trafficking in persons and measures for the care of the victims. From then on, trafficking in persons became all conduct related to the follow:

> Art. 149-A. To agency, entice, recruit, transport, transfer, buy, lodge or host a person, by serious threat, violence, coercion, fraud or abuse, in order to:
> I - remove organs, tissues, or body parts;
> II - subject them to work under conditions analogous to slavery;
> III - subject them to any type of servitude;
> IV - illegal adoption; or.
> V - sexual exploitation.

Since the research that supports the production of this work was done between 2011 and 2016, the option was to use the definition of the Additional Protocol to the United Nations Convention against Transnational Organized Crime Concerning the Prevention, Suppression and Punishment of Human Trafficking, in Special Women and Children (2000), as I consider it more adequate to face the issue, as below:

> "Trafficking in persons" shall mean the recruitment, transportation, transfer, harbouring or receipt of persons, by means of the threat or use of force or other forms of coercion, of abduction, of fraud, of deception, of the abuse of power or of a position of vulnerability or of the giving or receiving of payments or benefits to achieve the consent of a person having control over another person, for the purpose of exploitation. Exploitation shall include, at a minimum, the exploitation of the prostitution of others or other forms of sexual exploitation, forced labour or services, slavery or practices similar to slavery, servitude or the removal of organs.

Thus, I take as a definition of trafficking in persons that contained in the UN Protocol, since considering it more complete in relation to the prediction of national legislation in the period of the research. From this definition, it is possible to affirm that the referred crime constitutes a violation of human rights, which consists in a criminal conduct that, based on the use of deceptive or violent devices, aims to promote the mobility of people to subject them to exploitation. This exploitation, in its turn, shall include, at a minimum: (1) sexual exploitation, including the exploitation of forced prostitution; (2) exploitation of forced labor or services; (3) placing the person in a condition analogous to that of a slave; (4) servitude; (5) the removal of organs.

I draw attention to the fact that, in Brazil, prostitution itself is not a crime, only its exploitation is criminalized. Therefore, those who freely sell their body are not subject to criminal prosecution by the State, but anyone who benefits from someone else's sexual activity is subject to criminal prosecution, as it violates the freedom of others. The prostitution client also does not suffer any kind of punishment, except in the case of having relations with people under the age of 18.

By the way, when facing cases involving people under the age of 18, state institutions act to remove the young person from this reality by inserting them in care programs and even with the criminalization of any detected exploiters.

Next, it is essential to weave the conceptualization of *trans*vestites and *trans*-women to be able to comprehend who are the interlocutors of the work. The discussion takes place in the context of feminist gender studies, specifically on gender identity. This is so because, in Brazil, there is a plurality of terminologies used to refer to gender identities.

Therefore, I elucidate that the *trans*vestite is the person who, according to Don Kulick (2008), does not identify herself as a woman and does not wish to submit herself to surgery for sexual reassignment, despite highly investing in body modification to acquire features considered more feminine. Such modifications may include industrial silicone applications by the so-called pumpers,[1] the megahair implant, nail care, the use of makeup, women's clothing, shoes and accessories, not to mention the adoption of names and attitudes considered "of women".

Braga informs that the *trans*vestite person is identified based on their attitudes and wills directed towards the construction of a body considered feminine and draws attention to the "relationship that starts to be established with that body…mediated by different possibilities of producing pleasure" (2008, p. 08).

From the analysis, a central question in the collective imagination about *trans*vestite people in Brazil arises: the "disguise" of women adopted by people who are born with bodies considered masculine is the reason they come to be seen as subjects directly related to pleasure, sensuality and sexuality beyond heterosexual standards, shuffling ideas built on a natural and immutable body, so they become dangerous, hateful, criminal people.

At the national level, studies on *trans*vestites have multiplied since the 1990s and it is Benedetti (2005) who—ethnographing *trans*vestites in Porto Alegre—analyzes that there is in the popular imagination the idea that *trans*vestites operate body transformations exclusively because they want to, linked to work in prostitution, make money. However, the author points out that the construction of the *trans*vestite body and gender is too complex and particular to the group to be reduced to such a look.

Thus, the authors reveal the many investments made by *trans*vestites in the transformation of the body, which include the use of female hormones (most often from the indication of other *trans*vestites about brands and dosage), submission to industrial and/or surgical silicone implant, learning to dress and put on makeup to hide any trace of masculinity (including the penis), walking in high heels, producing hair and nails, using various types of body hair removal, everything to build female representation in a style more suited to what they consider accepted (Benedetti 2005; Kulick 2008).

The bibliography produced on *trans*vestites also refers to another dimension of the investment made by them to become feminine: the construction of a way of being more similar to women. This requires incessant training of the voice, so that the speech is performed in a finer tone, and of the look, which must be less straight and more innocent.

---

[1] For more information on the work of the pumper, check out the movie Bombadeira (2007).

Therefore, considering the exposed bibliography and the narratives I collected, I understand that *trans*vestites are people who transit, in the context of the heteronormativity prevailing in Brazilian society, between the female and the male. That is so since they are born with the body assigned as male and perform (Butler 2010) the female body they want to have, adopting postures, languages and even interfering in that body with the possible technologies to feminize it, without, however, intending to have sex reassignment surgery.

On the category of *trans*women, I coined this expression from studies carried out in the social sciences, a field in which *trans*sexuality is identified as a conflict experience in which there is no correspondence between biological sex and the gender assigned at birth. For Arán, *trans*sexuality "is considered a complex phenomenon. In general lines, it is characterized by the intense feeling of not belonging to the anatomical sex" (2006, p. 50).

From the above statement, it is necessary to recognize the existence of what Ávila and Grossi (2010) call "*trans*experience", observing the existing singularities between female *trans*experience (women in men's bodies) and male *trans*experience (men in women's bodies), with due attention to the intersectionalities present in each person's life in relation to the other dimensions that constitute identity, such as skin color, social class, ethnicity, and age, among others.

For Berenice Bento, *trans*sexuality can be understood as "an identity experience, characterized by conflict with gender norms" (2008, p. 15). The adoption of the idea of experience is purposely chosen by the author as opposed to the pathologizing construction of *trans*sexuality made over time by medicine, psychology and psychiatry, these so-called "psi" sciences.

Thus, I use the expression *trans*women since agreeing that *trans*sexuality should not be considered an adjective attributed to people, but should be taken as a characteristic of the subject, hence the term being the most appropriate, as it becomes a noun (Ávila and Grossi 2010). In addition, I use this expression also because in my incursions on the field I watched several discussions between *trans*vestites and *trans*women about the terminologies and how they felt, until one of the interviewees said she was a "*trans*woman".

After explaining the categories used, I go on to detail the methodology used in the research, since the classic format of research in Law did not contribute to the complete development of the understanding of the issue, so the use of multimethods was necessary, as reported below.

3 The Research Methodology

When researching about the relationship between the prejudice and discrimination suffered by *trans*vestites and *trans*women and the issue of human trafficking for sexual exploitation, I identified great difficulty in producing an analysis using only the bibliography available in Brazil, as there are rare studies that address these specific people as trafficked.

Thereby, I decided to go out to the field to hear the narratives of those who found themselves in that situation. I built, from my circle of personal and professional relationships, a network of 16 interlocutors who offered me, at different times and contexts, their accounts of the experience of entering the trafficking for sexual exploitation from the city of Belém, capital of the State of Pará, located in the Northern region of Brazil.

As a counterpoint, I conducted an interview with a police officer who investigated the situation. I also sought information from the justice organs in Belém to identify possible legal proceedings that dealt with the issue, but I was unsuccessful, since the few existing cases involved people under the age of 18 and were, consequently, under secrecy of justice, according to national legislation.

Therefore, the study I present below is the result of the interviews I conducted, as well as of information collected in journalistic articles published in Brazil, and based on the few studies that I found.

4 Trafficking of *Trans*vestites and *Trans*women in the City of Belém–Pará–Brazil

Based on the interviews carried out, I was able to infer that the reasons that lead *trans*vestites and *trans*women in the city of Belém to insert themselves in the routes of sexual exploitation, sometimes by means of human trafficking, are very different. Nevertheless, they go through the same question: the difficulty for families to understand the "difference" of their son, still very young, as to his sexual orientation.

*Trans*vestites and *trans*women, still at the beginning of their youth, when they start to leave childhood, realize the desire they have for boys and not for girls. In addition, they become aware that they do not feel with the adequate body they understand as such. Thus, when they meet other people like them, they seek information on how to begin the process of body modification, which they do slowly, from adopting more feminine postures, using clothes and accessories considered to be women's, until they reach the point of using hormones, silicone implant and other surgeries that they deem necessary.

As in the vast majority of times, they do not find family support to carry out such changes and, at the same time, they begin to suffer discrimination and psychological and physical aggressions in the domestic and school environment, they run away from this discriminatory system in search of becoming who they wish to be, building the appropriate body to the gender identity they have adopted.

Here it is worth reflecting on the role of families in face of the non-conforming gender presented by their children, which demonstrates family prejudice and discrimination regarding the multiple gender identities. This context causes disrespect for the sexual rights of children and adolescents (Smith 2019) and drives victims still too young for human trafficking, in total disregard for the principle of comprehensive or integral protection of children and adolescents (Pamponet Sá and Smith 2017).

At that moment, very young and without money, they find someone who "helps" them with information, shelter, and money. It is the female pimp. In Brazil, that figure is related to the person who subjects *trans*vestites and *trans*women to sexual exploitation, through daily payments of part of the earnings from the sexual programs carried out. It is worth mentioning that the female pimp does not always arrange the meetings, but she manages the money, the access to body modification technologies, and the home of *trans*vestites and *trans*women who are under her roof (Smith 2017).

For the *trans*vestites and *trans*women interviewed, ending up in the pimp's house is a rule, because there is no other space in which they find, after being expelled or running away from home, housing, food, and insertion in the sexual market that will enable them to raise financial resources to modify their body and acquire the desired products and goods. For this reason, I often heard the interviewees referring to the pimp as "mother", after all they welcomed them, which is why they conquered the position of using the necessary moral and physical reprimands when dealing with their "daughters".

It is interesting to note that the enticement of young *trans*vestites and *trans*women occurs in a very different way when compared to the other studied cases of human trafficking in Brazil. There is no mistake about the destination here, everyone knows that they will be taken to São Paulo, by bus or plane, to work in prostitution. Nevertheless, the invitation is made in such a way as to deceive the young women, as they are offered possibilities for high earnings, which will allow them to do whatever they want, go to Europe, save money for the acquisition of goods.

It is true that the interviewees report that they knew they would have to pay back the pimp what she had spent with the ticket from Belém to São Paulo, a route that most of them did alone, without any companion, being received in the destination city by a person designated by the pimp.

However, all of them reported feeling exploited when they learned that they should pay two or three times more than the real value of the ticket, always with fines imposed by the pimp whenever she considered pertinent, under the excuse of "maintaining order" among those staying in her house.

Thus, there was a fine when they fought, when they left the house messy, when they did not pay the daily accommodation fees, when they wore clothes considered inappropriate, among other things. The values were not displayed in a table; it was always a surprise, defined at the time, according to the "mood" of the pimp.

Despite the interviewees affirming that they did not feel trapped by the exploitation network, in all reports, debt appears as a condition that prevents them from being free from the pimp, who always threatened to have them beaten or killed.

In fact, the pimp does not act alone; she has the service of men to carry out the threats, and the cases of murder of young *trans*vestites and *trans*women who did not pay the pimp, whether for the travel ticket, the daily fees, or the financing of plastic surgery, are prevalent.

The young women who managed to get rid of the exploitation network, in many cases, either fled or managed to pay their debts. Many of them say that they left no problems behind and that, if they want and need, they can contact the networks and travel again.

These are possibilities when, after returning to Belém, they do not get formal work and activities in prostitution do not yield the profits they generated in São Paulo or in cities in Europe. Thus, reintegrating themselves into trafficking networks for sexual exploitation is always a possibility. However, many learn how the sex market works, which allows them to migrate to that job without insertion into trafficking networks. But this usually only happens the second or third time they decide to travel.

Despite reports of violence, physical and verbal aggressions, both by pimps and by men who circulate at night in search of sexual favors, *trans*vestites and *trans*women do not show regret. They claim that they chose to follow this path, as it was the only one available for them to become who they wanted to be, although this comes at a high cost and creates even more difficulties in relation with families. In fact, I heard many cases in which, when they returned with money, mothers, fathers, and siblings accepted them in their new condition.

Therefore, I was able to ascertain that, in the city of Belém, the trafficking of *trans*vestites and *trans*women for sexual exploitation is a verifiable reality, which follows its own rules of enticement, displacement and exploitation, counting on other *trans*vestites and *trans*women in the position of traffickers and trafficked. That is different from what has already been verified in relation to biological women and children, as the victims know they will work in prostitution, but do not know the complete reality of what they will face in the place of destination. That includes rules that have a quite arbitrary system of fines that keeps them under exploitation, fueled by the discrimination suffered due to gender identity and sexual orientation within the surrounding family and social context.

5 Conclusions

At the end of this chapter, I can affirm that the studies and researches produced in Brazil report that, in most of the times, women (biologically considered) and children are the main victims of human trafficking for sexual exploitation (Global Alliance Against Traffic in Women 2006; International Labour Organization 2005; Leal and Leal 2002; United Nations Office on Drugs and Crime 2009).

I believe that the situation is due to the influence of national legislation that, in line with international regulations, for a long time criminalized only the trafficking of women for sexual exploitation.

But I also see the possibility of this situation occurring due to the social invisibility that *trans*vestites and *trans*women suffer, since the researches I read (National Secretariat of Justice and United Nations Office on Drugs and Crime and Brazilian Association for the Defense of Women, Children and Youth n.d., Vasconcelos 2009) suggest that criminal networks do not find a great reaction from society, as the existing discrimination forms the basis for the tolerance of the violence committed against non-heterosexual people (Varandas 2011). This conclusion is also possible to ascertain from the narratives I heard, because in neither case was there any type of investigation (official or required by relatives) about what happened to *trans*vestites and *trans*women when they left their family home, still very young.

Hence, the confirmation of the thesis I raised, that *trans*vestites and *trans*women are driven to human trafficking networks for sexual exploitation due to the discrimination they suffer, in face of their gender identity and/or sexual orientation, within the family and social context in which they are inserted.

The situation is quite serious, considering that many begin the most significant body modifications only in adolescence, usually after leaving the family home, which occurs from the rupture of the most basic relationships, often through verbal and physical violence, practiced by mothers, fathers, siblings and other guardians.

It is at this moment that the human trafficking network acts, as it knows this reality in the city of Belém and as it does not face great resistance, it increases and remains functioning without major inconveniences by the competent authorities to face the issue. I can make this statement because I interviewed a *trans*vestite who made the Belém-São Paulo route in the 1980s and the others made the same trip after that. And they keep doing it.

Nevertheless, I emphasize the need to understand that there are many cases that do not constitute trafficking for sexual exploitation, as the stage of enticement or displacement has not been proven. These routes were made, by some *trans*vestites and *trans*women, autonomously, through the migration to sex work, individually.

Nonetheless, it is possible to say that some of them found themselves sexually exploited in their destination, as they had to enter the labor market on the street, which is known to have pimps (male and female) in action. However, this reality is not always configured, as many *trans*vestites and *trans*women travel and return without difficulties, after they have learned how and where to go.

Considering the above, it is evident that the great knot to be untied is the recognition of and respect for gender identity, the fight against prejudice and discrimination due to gender identity and sexual orientation, through educational and criminalizing actions of these hateful attitudes that push developing young people away from their families and into the arms of criminal sexual exploitation networks.

This is not an easy task, as it requires an effort from families, society and the State, and investment in public policies to promote differentiated human rights. But I believe that the dissemination of the present research constitutes an important step in this matter, at least in its knowledge, providing reflections that are not only within the scope of criminal justice, but that allows us to infer that the tide to confront human trafficking must be much bigger.

References

Arán M (2006) A *trans*exualidade e a gramática normativa do sistema sexo-gênero. Ágora: Estudos em Teoria Psicanalítica 9(1):49–63

Ávila S, Grossi MP (2010) Maria, Maria João, João: reflexões sobre a *trans*experiências masculina. Resource document. Fazendo Gênero 9: Diásporas, Diversidades, Deslocamentos. http://www.fg2010.wwc2017.eventos.dype.com.br/resources/anais/1278255349_ARQUIVO_Maria,MariaJoao,Joao040721010.pdf

Benedetti M (2005) Toda Feita: o corpo e o gênero das travestis. Garamond, Rio de Janeiro

Bento B (2008) O que é transexualidade. Brasiliense, São Paulo

BOMBADEIRA (2007) Direção: Luis Carlos de Alencar. Produtora: Cely Leal. Singra Produções. Salvador, 1h16min, color, Mini DV

Braga S (2008) Escritas do eu do outro: dois modos de escrever o corpo travesti. Resource document. Anais do CELSUL 2008. http://www.leffa.pro.br/tela4/Textos/Textos/Anais/CELSUL_VIII/escrita_de_si.pdf

Brazil (2004) Decreto n° 5.017, de 12 de março de 2004. Promulga o Protocolo Adicional à Convenção das Nações Unidas contra o Crime Organizado Transnacional Relativo à Prevenção, Repressão e Punição do Tráfico de Pessoas, em Especial Mulheres e Crianças. Resource document. http://www.planalto.gov.br/ccivil_03/_Ato2004-2006/2004/Decreto/D5017.htm

Brazil (2016) Lei n° 13.444, de 06 de outubro de 2016. Dispõe sobre prevenção e repressão ao tráfico interno e internacional de pessoas e sobre medidas de atenção às vítimas; altera a Lei nº 6.815, de 19 de agosto de 1980, o Decreto-Lei nº 3.689, de 3 de outubro de 1941 (Código de Processo Penal), e o Decreto-Lei nº 2.848, de 7 de dezembro de 1940 (Código Penal); e revoga dispositivos do Decreto-Lei nº 2.848, de 7 de dezembro de 1940 (Código Penal). Resource document. http://www.planalto.gov.br/ccivil_03/_Ato2015-2018/2016/Lei/L13344.htm

Butler J (2010) Problemas de gênero: feminismo e subversão da identidade. Civilização Brasileira, Rio de Janeiro

Global Alliance Against Traffic in Women (2006) Direitos Humanos e tráfico de pessoas: um manual. Aliança Global Contra Tráfico de Mulheres, Rio de Janeiro

International Labour Organization (2005) Uma Aliança Global contra o Trabalho Forçado - Relatório Global do Seguimento da Declaração da OIT sobre Princípios e Direitos Fundamentais no Trabalho 2005. Resource document. International Labour Organization. https://www.ilo.org/wcmsp5/groups/public/%2D%2D-americas/%2D%2D-ro-lima/%2D%2D-ilo-brasilia/documents/publication/wcms_227553.pdf

Kulick D (2008) Travesti: prostituição, sexo, gênero e cultura no Brasil. Editora Fiocruz, Rio de Janeiro

Leal ML, Leal F (eds) (2002) Pesquisa sobre tráfico de mulheres, crianças e adolescentes para fins de exploração sexual comercial no Brasil. Cecria, Brasília

National Secretariat of Justice, United Nations Office on Drugs and Crime, Brazilian Association for the Defense of Women, Children and Youth (n.d.) Posto de Atendimento Humanizado aos Migrantes: metodologia de recepção e atendimento a mulheres e "trans" possíveis vítimas de tráfico de pessoas no universo de deportados e inadmitidos recebidos pelo posto de atendimento humanizado aos (às) migrantes. Secretaria Nacional de Justiça/ Escritório das Nações Unidas contra Drogas e Crime/Associação Brasileira de Defesa da Mulher, da Infância e da Juventude, São Paulo

Pamponet Sá Y, Smith ASPO (2017) Tráfico de Pessoas *Trans*exuais na Adolescência para Fins de Exploração Sexual no Brasil:enfrentamentos a partir da doutrina da proteção integral. Resource document. Seminário Internacional América Latina: Políticas e Conflitos Contemporâneos. https://sialat2017.com/wp-content/uploads/2018/02/GT-08-COMPLETO.pdf

Smith ASPO (2017) Tráfico de pessoas para exploração sexual. Lumen Juris, Rio de Janeiro

Smith ASPO (2019) Diversidade Sexual e Proteção Integral à Infância e Juventude no Direito Internacional. Revista Direito e Práxis 10(2):1317–1334

United Nations (2000) Protocol to prevent, suppress and punish trafficking in persons especially women and children, supplementing the United Nations Convention against Transnational Organized Crime. Resource document. United Nations. https://www.ohchr.org/en/professionalinterest/pages/protocoltraffickinginpersons.aspx

United Nations Office on Drugs and Crime (2009) Global report on trafficking in persons. Resource document. http://www.unodc.org/documents/Global_Report_on_TIP.pdf

Varandas E (2011) Travestis. Resource document. Jornal da Paraíba. In Oliveira A (ed) Viver e morrer travesti no jornalismo policial: uma análise sobre a desconstrução da identidade trans em Portais Paraibanos. Resource document Repositório Institucional da UFPB: Viver e morrer travesti no jornalismo policial: uma análise sobre a desconstrução da identidade trans em Portais Paraibanos

Vasconcelos KN (ed) (2009) Tráfico de Pessoas: pesquisa e diagnóstico do tráfico de pessoas para fins de exploração sexual e de trabalho no Estado de Pernambuco. SNJ/SENASP/UNODC/ Governo do Estado de Pernambuco, Recife

Andreza do Socorro Pantoja de Oliveira Smith (andrezapantoja@gmail.com) holds a Bachelor of Law from the University of Amazonia (2002), Master (2010) and PhD (2016) in Law from the Federal University of Pará, Brazil (UFPA). She is a post-doctor at the Center for Studies on Democracy, Citizenship and Law of the Center for Social Studies of the University of Coimbra, Portugal. She is a lawyer, Adjunct Professor at the Faculty of Law, Colaborattor Professor of the Postgraduate Program in Law and Permanent Professor of the Postgraduate Program in Law and Development in the Amazon at the Federal University of Pará, Brazil. She is the General Director of the Superior School of Law of the Brazilian Bar Association in Pará (Ordem dos Advogados do Brasil—OAB/PA; member of the Empirical Research Network in Law (Rede de Pesquisa Empírica em Direito—REED), of the National Association of Human Rights—Research and Postgraduate Studies (ANDHEP), of the National Council for Research and Postgraduate Law Studies (CONPEDI) and of the CINETS—Crimmigration Control International Net of Studies; member of the Research Group City, Village & Heritage and of the Research Group Center of Interdisciplinary Studies on Violence in the Amazon (NEIVA). She has experience in the area of law, acting on the following subjects: International Law, Constitutional Law, Human Rights, Child and Youth Law, Human Displacement, Human Trafficking and Gender.

Romania: Trendstetter in European Human Trafficking?

Rafaela Pascoal and Adina Schwartz

Abstract While most of the national, European, and international reports are often contradictory, mainly due to the hidden nature of the phenomenon, on the numbers of human trafficking victims, they usually have one common conclusion: Romanian victims lead the European statistics. This tendency is identified regardless of the form of exploitation, be it sexual exploitation, labor exploitation, forced begging, forced criminal activities or in cases of rather "unconventional" forms of exploitation, raising a series of barriers to law enforcement agents. After 20 years since the ratification of the Palermo Protocol, Europe has embraced positive developments on collaborative prevention, victim support, and combatting measures. However, its effects were not always as productive as estimated. The authors have analyzed the way Romania, its organized crime groups, and victims have contributed, during the past 20 years, to the European legislative framework development in the prevention and the consequences on behalf of the victim support service which had to constantly retailor the assistance mechanisms to avoid the risk of secondary victimization. The chapter leads the readers through a series of unperceived trends and effects of Romanian human trafficking within Europe.

Adina Schwartz is the author of the paragraphs 3, 4, 5 and 6.
Rafaela Pascoal is the author of the paragraphs 1 and 2.

R. Pascoal
West University of Timisoara, Doctoral School of Sociology, Timisoara, Romania
e-mail: rafaeladaconceicao.hilariopascoal@unipa.it

A. Schwartz (✉)
University of Palermo, Palermo, Italy

A. M. Rodrigues, M. J. Guia (eds.), *New Forms of Human Trafficking*,
https://doi.org/10.1007/978-3-031-39732-5_9

1 Research Methodology

As the year 2020 marks 20 years since the Protocol to Prevent, Suppress and Punish Trafficking in Persons, Especially Women and Children ("the Palermo Protocol") to the United Nations Convention against Transnational Organized Crime was adopted and transposed by the member states, the authors have intended to analyze the developments within Europe, during these years, on the fight against human trafficking, focusing particularly on the role Romania and Romanian citizens have played within the European human trafficking chain and in the fight against this crime.

Therefore, the research question raised by the authors was: *Is Romania a trend setter within the European human trafficking?*

The research objectives were as follows:

1. Identification of the exploitation methods used by the Romanian organized crime groups which were "out of the box" and thus raised investigative challenges.

   With this objective, the authors aimed to identify and examine the "modern" forms of human trafficking which have raised a series of investigative challenges due to the methods used by the organized crime groups to:

   - coerce the victims (mainly through psychological threats rather than through physical threats to avoid leaving visible wounds on the bodies of the victims);
   - exploit foreign legislative or administrative procedures to raise financial benefits, hide the proceeds of crimes, and erase possible evidence left behind;
   - exploit the victims through complex methods which were not clearly stated in the legislations of the destination countries or in such a way that there was no precedent before for such methods of exploitation being used and thus lowering significantly the likelihood for the grassroot law enforcement agents to identify the main indicators of victimization.
   - exploit the slow and bureaucratic response of the law enforcement in cases of international criminal procedures;

2. Identification of social weaknesses which have given place to the increase and diversification of Romanian human trafficking within the Western destination countries.

   The authors aimed to identify the way traffickers exploited the naivety and lack of information of the "host communities" and thus have increased the time span spent through exploitation in the "host communities" and have diversified the sphere of crimes in which they were involved from human trafficking to drug trafficking, thefts, or robberies.
3. Identification of legislative and procedural changes within the territory of the main destination countries in response to the Romanian human trafficking, particularly those made after Romania's entrance into the European Union.

   Here, the authors aimed to analyze the responses taken by the authorities or the civil society which address the harms that human trafficking is carrying along, which, depending on its magnitude, is not only affecting the victim but the whole community and state from a public health perspective, migration perspective, employment perspective, public security perspective, etc.

Also, the authors aimed to identify in which way, from a policy or legal perspective, have the states changed their internal approaches based on such strong external influences. The period of reference was taken the entrance of Romanian into the European Union as this has literally raised the migration barriers and enabled traffickers to work on an international level more actively than before.

4. Identification of current referral, prevention and combating of human trafficking procedures introduced in Romania as a response to the high number of human trafficking cases.

   For this objective, the authors aimed to examine which were the measurable results of the existing policies and which was the international impact of the responses taken by the authorities and NGOs from Romania.

The research has combined sociological research methods with legal research methods to address all the four objectives of the research. The authors have split the research in two main stages, corroborating eventually the research outcomes, which were then analyzed, interpreted, and presented in the following subchapters.

The first stage was a *desk research* stage. For this, the authors have analyzed a series of national, European, and international reports on human trafficking and organized crime followed by an analysis of the Romanian and European legal framework on the subject. An extensive academic literature review was further considered to refine the critical socio and legal approach of the chapter. After this, to identify untypical human trafficking cases, the authors have conducted case studies, with a particular attention to the outcomes of European financed joint investigation teams targeting Romanian criminal networks ("Operation Golf" in the UK, the "Clamparu Case" in Spain, and the "Wasp Nest" in Denmark).

The second stage was a *field research* stage. For this, the authors have conducted 23 interviews with specialists in preventing, combatting and victim support services from Romania, Germany, Italy, the UK, and Holland, using a semi-structured interview guide. The interviews were divided into three parts. The first part aimed mainly to identify the overlap between the coercive methods and the proximity ties used by the exploiters to camouflage their purpose to the victims and, consequently, to the law enforcement actors to be able to understand how the traffickers have managed to overcome the national legal frameworks. The second part of the interview was dedicated to identify the nodes regarding the responses of the community and the civil society to the new exploitative forms, especially after the entrance of Romania in the European Union.

2 Overview of the Romanian Human Trafficking Within Europe

Romania is "a primary source country for sex trafficking and labor trafficking victims in Europe. Traffickers subject Romanian men, women, and children to labor trafficking in agriculture, construction, hotels, manufacturing, and domestic service, as well as forced begging and theft in Romania and other European countries."[1]

The research conducted reveals that Romanian organized crime groups are present in almost all the European countries (see Fig. 1), adjusting their modus operandi to the national legislative gaps of the host countries, developing their tentacles where law enforcement agencies are lacking access and, by it, generating, on behalf of the authorities, reasons to always diverse and adapt their investigation methods to the new trends they have developed to flourish their million euros human trade.

With such large scale organized crime groups Romania has, throughout the years, consistently and consequently influenced the legislative responses of the destination countries, which were pushed towards reshaping the definition of human trafficking in such a way that they meet the currently identified elements of "action", "means", and "purpose" and the set of indicators for human trafficking so that the grassroot level police officers would identify the victims and persons at risk in a shorter time span.

According to Arnowitz (2015, p. 9), "For a number of years, police officers in in the Netherlands had encountered young men from Romania working in prostitution servicing homosexual customers and had simply assumed that they were freelance sex workers. Upon closer investigation, the Dutch police discovered that these young men were brought to the Netherlands and had been trafficked into prostitution." In this text, Arnowitz is highlighting that the adaptability of the Romanian organized crime groups specialized in human trafficking to overcome law enforcement barriers, and their ability to exploit legislative gaps which have not been previously identified as "gaps" have raised a series of challenges in the field of combatting human trafficking.

When asked during the research interviews, a former police chief[2] explained: "I remain astounded at the consistency of Romanians being criminally trafficked throughout Europe. Traffickers continue in a near decade long unbroken trend in keeping Romanian nationals as the most trafficked residents of Europe. Such an unbroken record is, of course, according only to relatively recent tracking.[3] The

---

[1] US Department of State, *Trafficking in Persons Report* June 2019, p. 393. https://www.state.gov/wp-content/uploads/2019/06/2019-Trafficking-in-Persons-Report.pdf.

[2] Doctoral research "*The Incidence of Drug Use Among the Sexually Exploited Victims of Human Trafficking*"—carried out by PhD Adina Schwartz. The present subchapter contains only some extracts of the research conducted. The extensive data has not been made public yet.

[3] See statistics throughout the following: Eurostat, Statistical Working Papers, Trafficking in Human Beings, 2015 edition, ISSN 2315-0807, http://ec.europa.eu/anti-trafficking/sites/antitrafficking/files/eurostat_report_on_trafficking_in_human_beings_-_2015_edition.pdf (and previous years' reports); Trafficking in Human Beings in the EU. "Europol. Situation Report Trafficking in

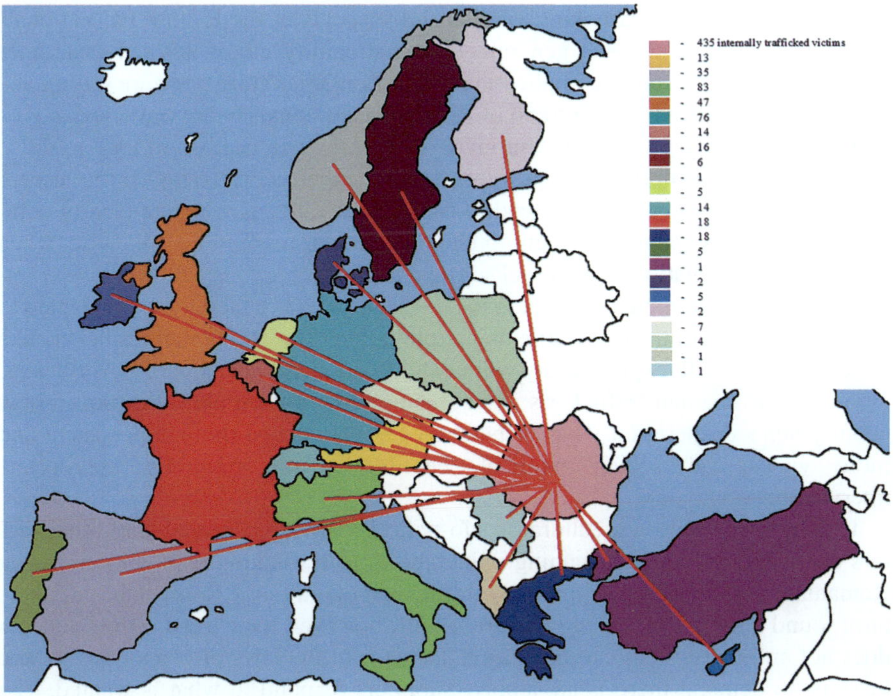

Fig. 1 Human trafficking destination countries of Romanian victims (The map was created by the authors based on the outcomes of the research conducted, corroborated with the data provided through the official 2016 statistics provided by the Romanian National Agency Against Human Trafficking, issued through the Annual Report in March 2017 http://www.anitp.mai.gov.ro/analiza-succinta-privind-traficul-de-persoane-in-2016-perspectiva-victimologica/)

broader history of Romanian trafficking exploitation likely parallels historical patterns among similar countries in the region. That parallel is lost to history. Presently, Romanians set a trend that has only gradually increased in prevalence and pleads the question of how the traffickers maintain their criminal success.

Numerous reports are available documenting the actual trafficking of Romanians in large numbers throughout Europe and the world at-large. The reports do not make it as clear who is at the core of sustaining the trend. Are the perpetrators Romanians trafficking Romanians; or, are the perpetrators among the other top tier traffickers operating in Europe such as the Bulgarians, Albanians, Turks, and Nigerians? A key finding in a Europol 2016 Situation Report on Trafficking in Human Beings is that

Human Beings," 2016. https://www.europol.europa.eu/publications-documents/trafficking-in-human-beings-in-eu; Commission Staff Working Document Accompanying the Document "Report From the Commission to the European Parliament and the Council," http://ec.europa.eu/antitrafficking/sites/.../files/commission_staff_working_document.pdf; United Nations Office on Drugs and Crime, Human Trafficking. https://www.unodc.org/documents/data-and-analysis/glotip/2016_Global_Report_on_Trafficking_in_Persons.pdf.

70% of the identified trafficking victims and suspects in the EU are EU nationals and that victims and suspects generally share nationality, ethnic ties and sometimes kinship links.[4] A reasonable implication is that Romanian traffickers are setting and sustaining this overwhelming trend of Romanians nationals being trafficked.

Persons seeking to overcome survival or crucial basic needs will tend to do so wherever it appears opportune. The more desperate the needs, the higher the susceptibility to exploitation. Citizens tend to trust fellow citizens who can clearly communicate with them and who seem to understand their misfortune. Likewise, when abroad, a foreign national often seeks refuge and safety among fellow native countrymen. This is a tremendous asset to the trafficker who is generally well-adapted to the destination countries of trafficking exploitation. The Romanian trafficker, like all traffickers, will exploit every vulnerability to their advantage; nevertheless, among the Romanian trafficker's assets seems to be a keen ability exploit fellow countrymen's desperation. That desperation can be reduced through persistent and more widespread social, political, economic, and culturally appropriate interventions.

Undoubtedly there are cultural, socio-political, socio-economic, and other factors contributing to and sustaining vulnerability to trafficking exploitation among Romanian and among other routinely trafficked populations.[5] Romanian traffickers have found a key to exploiting vulnerabilities; however, their trend setting success does not end there. They are meeting a demand. In the laws of economics, where there is no demand there is no supply. Suppliers respond to what is wanted. The European destinations of trafficking of Romanians are the greatest asset to the trafficker. To break the proverbial 'chain' of trafficking of Romanians it is key to understand where to strike the blow. In as much as persistent and more widespread and appropriate intervention should occur in Romania, partnerships must occur to reduce demand through widespread social, political, economic and justice system interventions in destination countries."

In the European context, Romania has a long history as a top source country in human trafficking, even if the statistics report a significant decrease of identified human trafficking victims in the last years.

To support the fight against human trafficking (both internally and externally), the Romanian legislator has created in 2006 the institution of the National Agency Against Trafficking in Persons, under the umbrella of the Ministry of Internal Affairs.

The National Agency against Trafficking in Persons (NATIP) has a conceptual, unique approach, among Romanian institutions, which is based on a multidisciplinary team, built to answer the specific challenges of fighting trafficking in human beings.

---

[4] Trafficking in Human Beings in the EU. "Europol. Situation Report Trafficking in Human Beings," 2016. https://www.europol.europa.eu/publications-documents/trafficking-in-human-beings-in-eu, https://www.europol.europa.eu/sites/default/files/documents/thb_situational_report_-_europol.pdf.

[5] National Rapporteur on Trafficking in Human Beings and Sexual Violence against Children (2016).

NATIP is empowered to bind the efforts of different governmental institutions competent in this field and is open to an extended cooperation with civil society representatives involved in the prevention of trafficking and assistance of victims. It further synergizes the common action of these actors, with increased results in reducing trafficking in human beings. NATIP is a specialized structure responsible for coordinating, evaluating, and monitoring at national level the implementation of anti-trafficking and victims' protection and assistance policies by public institutions. The agency cooperates with Romanian and foreign non-governmental and inter-governmental organizations to raise public awareness on human trafficking and its consequences.

NATIP is the national contact point for transnational referral of victims. NATIP also provides support for transnational referral of victims conducted by other entities. The representatives of all 15 Regional Centers (in Alba Iulia, Bacau, Brasov, Bucharest, Constanta, Craiova, Cluj-Napoca, Galati, Iasi, Oradea, Pitesti, Ploiesti, Suceava, Timisoara and Targu Mures) conduct the early evaluation to identify the victim's needs for specialized assistance and ensure the immediate referral to social service providers. Once referred, they monitor the victim's assistance and maintain constant contact to facilitate her/his access to justice. The victims' coordination program during criminal proceedings is available for those victims willing to participate in the trial. It provides emotional support, security, and legal guidance for an informed decision in legal matters.[6]

Based on the annual reports of the NATIP,[7] the number of identified Romanians trafficked both internally and externally are as follows (Fig. 2):

2007—1780, **2008**—1240, **2009**—780, **2010**—1154, **2011**—1048, **2012**—1041, **2013**—896, **2014**—757, **2015**—880, **2016**—756, **2017**—662, **2018**—497, **2019**—698.

Not only do the national figures change year by year but also does the distribution of the victims on Romanian territory, which proves that the organized crime groups are in a continuous move, thus refining the recruitment methods, reconsidering the targeted victims, developing their organized crime networks, and avoiding being caught up.

Nevertheless, Romania also brings about positive examples to the European countries as best practices in the field of combatting and preventing human trafficking and, in the current trend in which, at global level, the number of human trafficking investigations, trials and convictions increase yearly, Romania manages to keep up with the tendencies, reporting yearly hundreds of investigations and trials, thus being a top country also according to the number of convictions not only according to the number of victims.

[6] National Agency Against Trafficking in Persons, "*Identification, Assistance and Voluntary Return of victims of trafficking in human beings between Switzerland and Romania,*" http://www.anitp.mai.gov.ro/ro/docs/Proiecte/PIP/3597_ANITP_Brosura_A5_ENGLEZA_10_OCTOMBRIE.pdf.

[7] Romanian National Agency Against Human Trafficking, http://anitp.mai.gov.ro/categoria/cercetare/analize/.

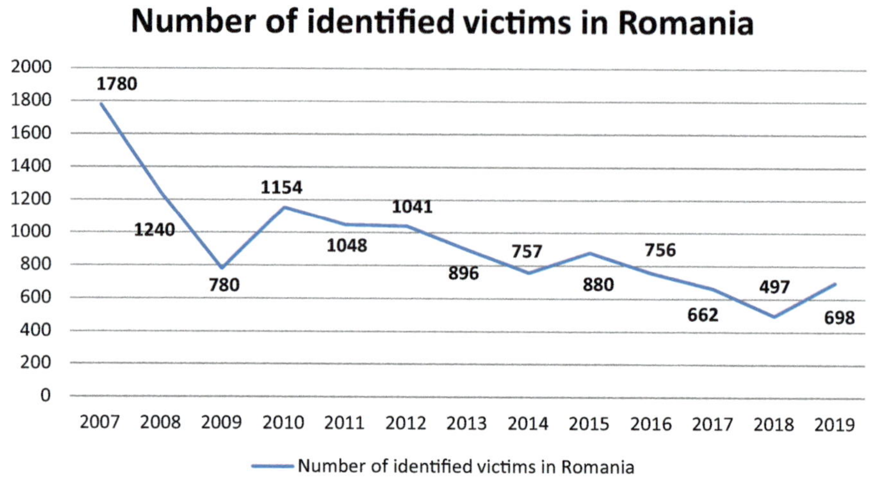

Fig. 2 Romanian human trafficking statistics, 2007–2019 (Elaborated by the authors based on the reports made public by NATIP)

Furthermore, Romania has lead the way through with several other aspects such as being among the first states of Europe to adopt in 2001 a legislation to prevent and combat human trafficking (Law 678/2001 on preventing and combatting trafficking in persons); setting up the National Agency Against Human Trafficking which enables specialists to be updated with the current tendencies identified; initiating several Joint Investigation Teams with different destination countries and, nevertheless, being among the partnering countries within the Southeast European Law Enforcement Center. Recognizing the utility of the law enforcement center, a Chief Prosecutor[8] has mentioned during the interviews that "additionally to the agency with competencies in preventing human trafficking another important organism has powered up the investigations both in Eastern Europe and Romania in the field of organized crime generally, and human trafficking specifically—SELEC, based in Bucharest."

> The objective of SELEC, within the framework of cooperation among Competent Authorities, is to provide support for Member States and enhance coordination in preventing and combating crime, including serious and organized crime, where such crime involves or appears to involve an element of transborder activity. It reunites 12 Member States: Republic of Albania, Bosnia and Herzegovina, Republic of Bulgaria, Republic of Croatia, the Former Yugoslav Republic of Macedonia, Hellenic Republic, Hungary, Republic of Moldova, Montenegro, Romania, Republic of Serbia and Republic of Turkey.

Also, Romania has signed and ratified specific protocols and has adapted its internal procedures to the requirements of European and International Agencies such as

[8] Doctoral research "*The Incidence of Drug Use Among the Sexually Exploited Victims of Human Trafficking*"—carried out by PhD Adina Schwartz. The present subchapter contains only some extracts of the research conducted. The extensive data has not been made public yet.

Frontex, Interpol, and Europol, and thus has actively participated in a series of high impact common actions.

Such common endeavors have led to the participation of several airports from Romania, in collaboration with Frontex and the other relevant institutions, in actions involving interviews and passenger controls at the entrance, transit or exit to, through and from Romanian territory to reduce potential victimization and prevent crimes from happening. "Such measures implemented in Romania in a relatively short time span have proved to be very successful and to have the potential of being replicated throughout Europe" as referred by a Chief Border Police in Romania.[9]

Eventually, Romania has adopted a series of measures, both from a legislative and practical perspective by means of strengthening the collaboration between the relevant state institutions and the civil society represented through specialized NGOs active in assisting the victims of human trafficking and in preventing human trafficking by creating regional inter-institutional and multi-disciplinary task forces.

3 Human Trafficking Legislative Challenges Raised by the Romanian Organized Crime

Romania's entrance into the European Union has brought about a series of positive aspects, both from a social perspective and an economical perspective, alongside with the specific freedoms—free movement of persons, of goods, of services, of labor and of capital.

The free movement of persons and of labor has, however, also lead to a significant migration flow from Romanian, underdeveloped rural areas to the Western countries, in the hope for a better life. For such migration flows were unfortunately neither the Romanian nor the Western institutions well equipped.

In January 2007 Romania joined the EU. Within 3 months, the crime in London committed by Romanian nationals went up to 786%. Analysis showed the offenses to be predominantly theft committed by children from within the Romanian Roma community. Bernie Gravett who led the first and the greatest joint investigation team between Romania and the UK generically known as "Operation Golf" will be described in the following pages.

Such a context has given rise to security concerns and the immediate need of adopting answers, both from law enforcement and the civil society, which would address the specifically identified gaps and needs.

An expert in international relationships and security studies has highlighted throughout the interview that "the European security agenda analyses migration taking into account present and potential consequences of a high number of

[9] Doctoral research "*The Incidence of Drug Use Among the Sexually Exploited Victims of Human Trafficking*"—carried out by PhD Adina Schwartz. The present subchapter contains only some extracts of the research conducted. The extensive data has not been made public yet.

immigrants in European Union's countries. Almost 15% of all citizens of Romania live outside their country, especially in Italy, Spain, Germany, and Hungary. Romanian migrants are generally grouped into homogeneous communities, fact which creates them barriers to integration in the host countries. She has further added that "international migration can be understood as a problem of security. According to the Copenhagen School, represented by Barry Buzan and Ole Waever, societal security is a dimension of the state security, being concerned about threats to a society' identity. From this point of view, Romanian migrants in the EU's countries are often perceived as economic, social and cultural problems. On the other hand, human security concept, developed by the United Nations Development Programme, supports, among others: economic security (access to employment and resources), health security (access to medical treatment), personal security (individual security from violence), community and political security (living in a society that guarantees basic human rights and freedom of expression). In this sense, social security and inclusion of all EU's citizens should no longer be sources of tension among the EU's Member States."[10]

A research conducted on Romanian migrants in Greece has revealed that the Romanians who migrated in another country are, from certain perspectives, seen and they also do "feel as superiors in comparison with those who stayed in Romania" (Stefenel 2013, p. 128). Such an attitude only adds up to the already vast list of push factors which can be identified within the Romanian vulnerable population.

It is a well-known fact that human trafficking is a highly profitable criminal activity, which is acting as a catalyst towards the diversification of other crimes from the sphere of organized crime. During the interview conducted, a police officer from Romania[11] confirmed this by explaining that "the sexual exploitation of Romanian women produces, only at a first glance, a minimum of 1500 euros per week which goes in the pockets of the traffickers. Such a calculation is very simple if we take into account that a simple lap dance with a cocktail costs about 23 euros, not to go further and start evaluating the values of different forms of sexual relationships. Naturally the illegally obtained money needs to be 'washed and whitened'. For this you need to find a proper 'washing-machine' which ends up in being another crime."

Besides the security challenges of migration flows from Romania, the criminal investigations have revealed new and up to then unknown and hardly understood human trafficking cases. The forms of exploitation which the investigators discovered were not only challenging to investigate, given the multiple transit and destination countries, but it was also difficult even to fit the actions identified into the inflexible frame of human trafficking definition and legislation.

---

[10] Doctoral research "*The Incidence of Drug Use Among the Sexually Exploited Victims of Human Trafficking*"—carried out by PhD Adina Schwartz. The present subchapter contains only some extracts of the research conducted. The extensive data has not been made public yet.

[11] Doctoral research "*The Incidence of Drug Use Among the Sexually Exploited Victims of Human Trafficking*"—carried out by PhD Adina Schwartz. The present subchapter contains only some extracts of the research conducted. The extensive data has not been made public yet.

3.1 *Defining the Purpose in the Human Trafficking International Legal Framework*

Human trafficking, being mainly characterized by its dynamic feature, is in continuous transformation. While the main recognized forms of exploitation—labor exploitation, sex exploitation and organ harvesting—remain the same, Romanian traffickers adapt and camouflage as the modalities as the new exploitative forms to the legal and social-cultural context (Pascoal and Schwartz 2016).

Therefore, the concept of human trafficking has suffered a continuous evolution since its application on the International Agreement for the Suppression of the White Slave Traffic in 1904, where human trafficking was mainly referring to women and minors subjected to "an immoral life."[12] In fact, the limitation of the concept of human trafficking has been kept through the twentieth century, following International Agreements[13] that have kept the "purpose" limited to prostitution. The 1991 Recommendation of the Committee of Ministers to Member States concerning sexual exploitation, pornography and prostitution of trafficking in children and young adults[14] has first introduced the concept of exploitation together with other concepts linked to the sex industry, such as sexual exploitation, sexual abuse pornography and prostitution. The Recommendation, despite neglecting a concise definition of "trafficking", "children", and "young adults", mentions trafficking in children as one of the forms of abuse, separated from the other forms previously mentioned.

The concept of "exploitation" is first conceived outside the sex industry in the A4–0326/95 Resolution approved by the European Parliament on the "need to protect human beings against any exploitation of their precarious social and economic

[12] International Agreement for the Suppression of the White Slave Traffic concluded the 18th May, 1904 and came into force on 18 July 1905, ratified by a total of 26 states that had colonies: His Majesty the King of the United Kingdom of Great Britain and Ireland and of the British Dominions beyond the Seas, Emperor of India; His Majesty the German Emperor, King of Prussia, in the name of the German Empire; His Majesty the King of the Belgians; His Majesty the King of Denmark; His Majesty the King of Spain; the President of the French Republic; His Majesty the King of Italy; Her Majesty the Queen of the Netherlands; His Majesty the King of Portugal and of the Algarves; His Majesty the Emperor of all the Russias; His Majesty the King of Sweden and Norway; and the Swiss Federal Council. Five years after the treaty was re-negotiated in Paris and concluded on 4 May 1910.

[13] International Convention for the Suppression of the "White Slave Traffic", May 4, 1910, 211 Consol. T.S. 45, 1912 GR. Brit. T.S. No. 20, as amended by Protocol Amending the International Agreement for the Suppression of the White Slave Traffic; International Convention of 30 September 1921 for the Suppression of the Traffic in Women and Children, as amended by the Protocol approved by the General Assembly of the United Nations on 20 October 1947; International Convention of 11 October 1933 for the Suppression of the Traffic in Women of Full Age, as amended by the aforesaid Protocol, and Amending the International Convention for the Suppression of the White Slave Traffic, May 4, 1949.

[14] Adopted by the Committee of Ministers on 9 September 1991 at the 461st meeting of the Ministers' Deputies.

circumstances or their inexperience for the purposes of clandestine employment in conditions of slavery, prostitution, pornography, any other form of sexual abuse or the trade in human organs."

Despite that exploitation was limited to human organs harvesting as well as labor exploitation, the concept of exploitation seems to be highly redundant without concise elements that can characterize precisely its definition.

The concept of exploitation is enlarged by the "purpose",[15] the third element of the definition of human trafficking under Art. 3[16] of the United Nations, Protocol to Prevent, Suppress and Punish Trafficking in Persons Especially Women and Children supplementing the United Nations Convention against Transnational Organized Crime[17] which, for the first time, applies an open-ended definition. According to the Travaux Préparatoires (UNODC 2006), the introduction of "at minimum" was achieved after a long path. In fact, at the Second Session of the Ad Hoc Committee, a number of countries have supported a broader definition of the initial proposed terms "sexual exploitation" and "forced labour" so it could also cover other types of exploitation, being specifically suggested the inclusion of "forced marriage" or "marriage of convenience" and "domestic work". In the Fifth Session of the Ad Hoc Committee, it was generally agreed on a wider notion of "purpose" with the suggestion of the word "particularly" to include other forms of exploitation rather than "sexual exploitation" and "forced labor". Furthermore, the Netherlands presented a proposal submitted by the United States (A/AC.254/L.54), suggesting to replace the term "sexual exploitation" with the term "slavery", which should mean "the status or condition of a person over whom any or all of the powers attaching to the right of ownership are exercised, including forced prostitution and servitude and other practices similar to slavery as defined in Article 1 of the 1956 Supplementary Convention on the Abolition of Slavery, the Slave Trade, and Institutions and Practices Similar to Slavery." It was in the Seventh Session, taking place between January 17 to 28, 2000[18] that a delegation proposed to insert the words "at a minimum" with the scope to comprehend different types of purposes such as illegal adoption and harvesting of organs (UNODC 2006).

At the Ninth Session of the Ad Hoc Committee, Argentina has defined exploitation as "(...) reduction to servitude, subjection to prostitution, slavery, forced labor or child pornography." There was a debate if the Ad Hoc Committee should do an

[15] The definition of trafficking is composed of three elements, namely, "Act", the "Means, and the "Purpose", which are related to the exploitation.

[16] Article 3, "Trafficking in persons shall mean the recruitment, transportation, transfer, harbouring or receipt of persons, by means of the threat or use of force or other forms of coercion, of abduction, of fraud, of deception, of the abuse of power or of a position of vulnerability or of the giving or receiving of payments or benefits to achieve the consent of a person having control over another person, for the purpose of exploitation. Exploitation shall include, at a minimum, the exploitation of the prostitution of others or other forms of sexual exploitation, forced labour or services, slavery or practices similar to slavery, servitude or the removal of organs."

[17] Adopted and opened for signature, ratification, and accession by the General Assembly Resolution 55/25 of 15 November 2000.

[18] Rolling text (A/AC.254/4/Add.3/Rev.6).

attempt of a list of types of exploitation that included the illicit removal of organs or other body parts or tissues, forced marriage, forced adoption, the purchase or sale of children and the making or distribution of child pornography. To highlight these types of exploitation and at the same time not be limited to them, some delegations have favored the "at a minimum" to ensure that unnamed or new forms of exploitation would not be excluded by implication (UNODC 2006). Therefore, at this point, states are allowed to add types of exploitation and interpret the undefined concepts used in the protocol according to their cultural and country context (Gallagher 2015).

3.2 How to Delimit Exploitation?

The seemingly limitless characteristic of the definition of exploitation provides the Member States with the possibility to expand or limit its interpretation of undefined concepts in the national context (Chuang 1998). Therefore, despite that in some cases "type of exploitation" can be well defined, especially in sexual exploitation and labor exploitation, the nature of the work as well as family ties can camouflage exploitative conditions. In fact, the concept of exploitation is not hegemonically applied at an international level, being defined normally according to the domestic laws (Gallagher 2015). Therefore, if, on one hand, the undefined concept of exploitation gives the possibility to the states to broad the trafficking definition, on another hand, it provides a very unequal and misunderstood application of the concept that can confuse the crime of human trafficking with other typologies of crimes (Gallagher 2015).

Thus, to confirm the "purpose", it is often necessary to analyze it by confronting it with the means, such as "the abuse of position of vulnerability." For instance, in a case judged by the Dutch High Court that included labor exploitation of Chinese workers in a restaurant, the mean of "abuse of position of vulnerability" enhanced the presence of exploitative conditions such as the reduced salary of the workers, that was half of the minimum wage in Netherlands, the extensive working hours, the lack of free days and the living conditions of the workers (Gallagher 2012). In fact, Korvinus's (2007) definition of exploitation describes it as the endeavor to obtain the maximum gain possible by means of abuse and specifically in relation to a person working in unfavorable conditions.

As mentioned by the International Labor Organisation, exploitation should therefore be considered when working conditions largely trespass the worker's normal conditions and earnings as stated in their contract (ILO 2009).

As a solution to provide a mathematic definition of the term exploitation, as well as to attribute a fair sum of compensation to the victim, the researcher Fabrizio Sarrica (2015) suggests an equation that can determine the mathematic equation of exploitation. The equation is composed of four elements including: the desired salary and the obtained salary, corroborated with the desired working hours and the actual worked hours. According to Sarrica (2015), the price of exploitation can be obtained by calculating the difference between the desired wage and the received wage multiplied by the difference between the desired worked hours of the worker for the received wage and the actual worked hours.

3.3 The Element of Trust and the False Consciousness of Exploitation

As previously presented within this chapter, the number of Romanian *identified* victims of human trafficking have significantly decreased in the last years. It seems that this decrease could be related to the use of subtle strategies used by Romanian traffickers to avoid the rebellion of the victims, and consequently, their denounce claim (Baldoni et al. 2012). Therefore, should we consider this decrease to be related to the increase of tutorship and access to rights in the European territory? According to the OHCHR (2010), the increase of tutorship through the European Union citizenship led to the abandonment of blatant force and physical violence and the introduction of blurry coercive methods, usually enhanced by emotional ties.

To gain an in-depth understanding towards the "proper" answer, it is important to analyze the paramount transnational operational cases, such as the "Operation Golf" in the UK, the "Clamparu Case" in Spain, and the "Wasp Nest" in Denmark. If we look closely, the cases are mostly based on proximity ties, acutely grounded in the element of trust (Europol 2016, 2018). In the "Operation Golf", it was identified that many victims were exploited by their own relatives or at least community members (Beddoe 2018) that "act rationally, premeditated, build an image of benefactors, leading the victims to beg them for help; they pursue the recruitment of victims that can be easily manipulated" (GRETA 2019, p. 42). The shared socio-cultural context between the victims and the perpetrators are enhanced by the emotional ties that camouflage the exploitative conditions (Gallagher 2010), not only towards the victims, but also towards the authorities, especially when the perpetrators declare their parenthood in relation to the exploited children (Anti-trafficking Monitoring Group 2010). The use of symbolic violence (Bourdieu 1998) and proximity violence (Bartholini 2013) are often not identified as indicators of trafficking by the civil society or by the court in the way that physical violence is. In fact, these elements hinder also the self-identification of injustice and determinate the dominance consciousness of the social being, consequently delaying the element of "deception".

The perpetrators induce the victims a false consciousness, through the dissimulation of their "exploitative purpose". Therefore, while the victims perceive the ties with the offenders as a Weberian value-rational relationship, the traffickers, in a dominant position, actually implement an instrumental relationship to obtain their surplus. The traffickers turn to the use of "soft means" such as threats, emotional manipulation, verbal insults and humiliation or psychological threats. These coercion elements are also identified on several Romanian cases reported on the human trafficking knowledge portal of the UNODC, where the loverboy method and kinship ties tend to mark the confidence of the victims, and thus, achieve their scope.

Also, through the division of earnings that despite of its unfairness, is presented to the victim as a symbol of equality and balance of power.[19] The sociologist Francesco Carchedi (2003), based on an equation between coercion and autonomy, would nominate this relationship as being semi-autonomous, since it is not based on a hor-roristic violence (Cavarero 2007), but a partial and gradual submission of the victim.

In the four structural forms of coercive exploitation—tribute, serfdom, chattel slavery, and wage labor - , Romanian victims can be identified as object of tribute of their exploiter. Therefore, coercion is based on the dependence that is strategically structured by the perpetrator, through the implementation of the context conditions, as well in the public as in the private sphere that permit the victim's exploitation. As refrained by the scholar Michael (2012), "accept my power, for I will protect you from worse violence," thus, the tribute is established under labor conditions, despite the lack of a legal bound, the victims accept the fairness of the tribute as a contract they could not refuse.

According to the sociologist Francesco Carchedì et al. (2003), there are different levels of coercion, since appropriating and taking an ID card from the victim is differently perceived compared with mobility constriction. For instance, in the case of "Wasp Nest" in 2015, the traffickers obtained the consent to have the victims' documents under the justification of establishing a legal work contract. The trafficker escorted the victims to the Municipality and with the presentation of the victims' ID cards and with false employment contracts they were able to get a Danish ID. The Danish identification permits the traffickers to open bank accounts and have access to money loaning. The traffickers persuaded the victims in buying consumer goods such as luxury cars and electronic devices. The trust of the victims in the traffickers is also based on "the abuse of position of vulnerability" by the traffickers, since the dislocation of the victims from their frame of reference, to an unknown socio-cultural context enhances the victims' vulnerability on the lack of knowledge of the Danish language and bureaucratic procedures. Furthermore, the victims came from impoverish rural areas, which accentuates their vulnerability regarding their familiarity to the structural modalities involved in the creation of an enterprise, as the nature of the crime committed in their name.

Finally, the fabricated attribution of power transferred to the victims, for instance, one of the group was entitled as the CEO of the company, not only results in the false consciousness of agency by the victim, accentuating a *sine diem* exploitation, but it also ascribes to the victim a false conscious of power that can be manipulated by the trafficker, once the victim is aware about the nature of the crime, based on the principle of group oppression, guilt and state punishment.

[19] https://sherloc.unodc.org/cld/en/v3/htms/index.html.

4 Romanian Human Trafficking Cases Which Constituted European Landmarks

Be it sexual exploitation or labor exploitation, for years the Romanian organized crime groups have led the statistics of human trafficking in the majority of the well-developed European countries (Eurostat 2018). Examples of "typical" human trafficking cases based on the "lover boy" method or on the "false promises" method corroborated, later on, with psychical harms and sexual assaults as methods of coercion constitute also nowadays the majority of the *identified* cases.

Kevin Hyland has given two of such examples by attempting to illustrate the human trafficking situation in the UK: "The <<Romanian Cinderella>>, as the media named her, who at the age of four was taken from her mother in Romania, believing her daughter was destined for a better life in the United Kingdom, including a good education. How wrong she was. For the next 3 years, this small and defenseless child was kept as a servant, forced to cook and clean, and never allowed to attend school. Her only possessions were the clothes on her back, and her health deteriorated dramatically" (Hyland 2016, p. 55); "And the 57-year-old Romanian man, who expected to be given work as an electrician. Instead he was forced to commit crimes for the criminals that controlled him, kept in a shed and rarely fed. On one occasion when he asked for food he was instead assaulted and raped" (Hyland 2016, p. 56).

However, a very important aspect is what lies behind the identified cases, which, in the vast majority are the "typical cases" identified rather reactively than proactively. Are the "typical" human trafficking cases constituting the majority of 2020 human trafficking cases or are they jut the peak of the iceberg, being identified in comparison with the thick layer of "out of the box" cases for which many law enforcement agencies still lack the necessary tools to work on?

Within this subchapter, the authors are going to illustrate some "out-of-the-box" cases which have marked the European perception and fight against human trafficking.

4.1 Human Trafficking, Petty Crimes, and Begging: "Operation Golf" UK-Romania

The "Operation Golf", financed by the European Commission[20] with a budget of 998.000€ through the ISEC financing line, with the reference number ISEC/2007/FPA/C1/034 is still one of the most ambitious European operations in the sphere of human trafficking. It was set up based on intelligence that a high number of

[20] European Commission, https://ec.europa.eu/anti-trafficking/eu-projects/operation-golf-%E2%80%93-uk-and-romanian-joint-investigation-tackling-romanian-organised-crime_en.

Romanian children would be exploited through human trafficking in the UK.[21] Back in 2007, these particular forms of exploitation—begging and petty crimes—were not a common method of exploitation. In fact, at that time, there was no precedent at EU level for such a magnitude of criminal behavior where children were used to beg on the street and to commit a series of petty crimes such as stealing. The amounts of money obtained illegally were sent back to Romania where the traffickers were living luxurious lives. Furthermore, the organized crime group has forged official documents to illegally obtain social security numbers to claim benefits on behalf of inexistent or trafficked children.

In an article written for the UK parliament's magazine, "*Operation Golf - A UK and Romania Joint Investigation Tackling Romanian Organised Crime and Child Trafficking*" Bernie Gravett, one of the initiators and leaders of Operation Golf, highlights that: "Operation Golf was a Joint Investigation Team (JIT) between the MPS and the Romanian National Police. The full JIT partnership in Operation Golf was made up of the Romanian National Police, D.I.I.C.O.T. (Romanian Prosecutors Office), the United Kingdom Human Trafficking Centre (UKHTC), Crown Prosecution Service, Europol, and Eurojust. The strategic objectives of the JIT were to successfully investigate and prosecute OCN members both in the UK and Romania, disrupt their activities, identify, restrain and confiscate criminal assets,

[21] The Romanian legislation prohibits child trafficking through Article 211 of the New Criminal Code as follows:

"Trafficking in underage persons

(1) Recruitment, transportation, transfer, harboring or receipt of a juvenile for the purpose of their exploitation shall be punishable by no less than 3 and no more than 10 years of imprisonment and a ban on the exercise of certain rights.

(2) If such act was committed under the terms of Art. 210 par. (1) or by a public servant while in the exercise of their professional duties and prerogatives, it shall be punishable by no less than 5 and no more than 12 years of imprisonment and a ban on the exercise of certain rights.

(3) The consent expressed by an individual who is a victim of trafficking does not represent an acceptable defense".

Also, the exploitation of beggary through human trafficking is foreseen in the Criminal Code under Article 214 "*Exploitation of beggary*"

(1) An act of an individual who causes a juvenile or a person having physical or psychic disabilities to resort repeatedly to the public's pity in order to ask for material help or benefits from financial benefits from such activity shall be punishable by no less than 6 months and no more than 3 years of imprisonment or by a fine.

(2) If such act is committed in the following situations:

(a) by a parent, guardian, curator or by the person under whose care the begging person is;

(b) by means of coercion,

it shall be punishable by no less than 1 and no more than 5 years of imprisonment.

Moreover, the Romanian legislation also punishes under Art. 215 the "*Use of underage persons for mendicancy*", stating that "the action of a person who is of age and has the capacity to work, who resorts repeatedly to the public's pity in order to ask for material help, by using the presence of a juvenile for this purpose, shall be punishable by no less than 3 months and no more than 2 years of imprisonment or by a fine."

reduce criminality, minimise the exploitation of victims, improve victim identification and response to child trafficking by police and partners."

> The UK investigation has led to the arrest of 87 persons for trafficking, money laundering, child neglect and perverting the course of justice. 272 victims trafficked by the gangs were recovered.

While the UK investigation has led to a series of arrest and unique convictions as above mentioned, the same situation cannot, unfortunately, be stated on the Romanian side. With the support of the UK police, during 2010 several homes were raided in Tandarei (Romania) and 26 suspects were arrested and sent to criminal trial, including the suspected head of the organized crime group. The accusations were several, among which child trafficking, money laundering, and the creation of an organized crime group. During 2019, the Romanian Court of Appeal has spoken free all the 26 accused persons, invoking the fact that for some of the crimes, after 10 years, the criminal prescription had already set it in, therefore, the suspects could no longer be held responsible from a criminal perspective. For other crimes, such as child trafficking, the judge has not found enough evidence against the accused as most of the witnesses have not identified themselves as victims during the court hearings. Therefore, all of the 26 accused were set free under Art. 396 (5) and (7) and Art. 16 (c) of the Romanian Criminal Procedure Code and the seized goods which, based on the prosecutors statements, were proceeds of crimes have been returned to the accused ones.

Although the outcomes in Romania have not reached the expectations of the investigators, "Operation Golf" is considered a landmark operation not only for the two countries involved, respectively the UK and Romania but also for the rest of the EU Member States, as it has set a precedent for European cooperation, in the form of joint investigation teams, in cases of human trafficking. It has reaffirmed the importance and benefits of proactive investigation methods, redesigned predictive policing, and led to a major legislative change during 2011 by introducing into the EU Directive 2011/36/EU on preventing and combating trafficking in human beings and protecting its victims the two new forms of exploitation identified within the operation, namely, exploitation of forced begging[22] and forced criminal activities.[23]

---

[22] DIRECTIVE 2011/36/EU OF THE EUROPEAN PARLIAMENT AND OF THE COUNCIL of 5 April 2011 on preventing and combating trafficking in human beings and protecting its victims, and replacing Council Framework Decision 2002/629/JHA: (11)—forced begging should be understood as a form of forced labour or services as defined in the 1930 ILO Convention No 29 concerning Forced or Compulsory Labour. Therefore, the exploitation of begging, including the use of a trafficked dependent person for begging, falls within the scope of the definition of trafficking in human beings only when all the elements of forced labour or services occur. In the light of the relevant case-law, the validity of any possible consent to perform such labour or services should be evaluated on a case-by-case basis. However, when a child is concerned, no possible consent should ever be considered valid.

[23] Ibid. (11)—exploitation of criminal activities should be understood as the exploitation of a person to commit, inter alia, pick-pocketing, shop-lifting, drug trafficking and other similar activities which are subject to penalties and imply financial gain.

4.2 *Human Trafficking, Harvesting of Human Origin Cells: "*Sabyc*" Case*

Year 2009 came with another challenge to the Romanian law enforcement agencies respectively with the first human cells trafficking case, which was notoriously known as the "*Sabyc*" case, taking the name of the Bucharest Clinique SC "SABYC" SRL where such illegal operations with the support of doctors from Israel were performed.

Essentially, the organized crime group has recruited young women to donate ovules and has recruited from abroad women who cannot have children for embryo transfer. All the medical operations were performed illegally and even with doctors who had no authorization to work on the Romanian territory.

In 2014, through the final criminal sentence No. 2848/21.10.2014 of the Supreme Court of Justice, the perpetrators involved have been convicted for:

- M.H.—constituting an organized crime network and trafficking of human origin cells. This person has coordinated the criminal network and the medical procedures as a group leader and thus has introduced on the territory of Romania, fraudulently, genetic material. Further, M.H. was holding the evidence of the donors, of the targeted persons for recruitment from abroad and of the used medication. Also, he was the one who was directly or indirectly financially rewarding the donors and the recruiters.
- L.N.—besides having been found guilty for similar crimes as M.H. he was also found guilty for illegally practicing medicine in Romania, as he was the doctor who, after recruiting patients from abroad, has examined and treated the patients.
- S.G.—the charges were similar ad for L.N. but being a professional in embryology, he has realized the illegal embryo transfers.
- B.C.—was essentially acting as a recruiter, recruiting directly or indirectly young women aged 18–30 who, for financial benefits, have agreed to donate ovules.

In Romania, Law 95/2006 regarding the health reform[24] defines the main operational concepts of organ harvesting and sets the national legislative framework for such procedures. Under Art. 142, they are defined as follows:

> s) *Sampling* - harvesting organs and/or tissues and/or cells of healthy, morphological and functional human origin for the purpose of transplantation procedures;
>
> u) *Transplantation* - that medical activity by which an organ, tissue or cell drawn/taken from another person, called a donor, is implanted or grafted into a patient's body, for therapeutic purposes. The regulations contained in this law also cover in vitro fertilization techniques.

The same law also foresees the sanctions in case the provisions are not respected.

---

[24] Law 95/2006 regarding the health reform, published in the Romanian Official Journal No. 652 in 2015.

Article 154 states that "(1) The taking or transplantation of organs, tissues or cells of human origin from living donors without consent under the law constitutes an offense and shall be punished by imprisonment from 2 to 7 years and the prohibition of certain rights."

Article 156 foresees sanctions for those who donate willingly but for the purpose of obtaining benefits: "(1) A person's act of donating organs, tissues or cells of human origin for the purpose of obtaining material benefits for himself or for another constitutes an offense and is punished by imprisonment from 3 months to 2 years or by fine."

It is also prohibited under the same law to introduce into the country fraudulently organs, cells, or tissues, based on the provisions of Article 158: "(1) The introduction or removal from the country of organs, tissues or cells of human origin without the special authorization issued by the National Transplant Agency constitutes a criminal offense and shall be punished by imprisonment from 2 to 7 years and the prohibition of certain rights."

Therefore, the case has set a precedent for further convictions not only for the illegal trafficking of organs but also of human cells.

4.3 Human Trafficking, Deceit, Financial Fraud: The "Wasps Nest" Operation

In February 2015, the Romanian and the Danish authorities have signed a Joint Investigation Agreement having as subject the investigation of a criminal organized crime group from Romania, exploiting approximately 100 victims of human trafficking in Denmark.

In the case 72 D/P/2014[25] of the Romanian Directorate to Investigate Organized Crime and Terrorism, Arad Service, 20 suspects have been investigated for committing, during 2012–2015 a series of crimes: association in an organized crime group, human trafficking, and the commitment of body injuries. The suspects were accused for recruiting victims from poor families, for transporting and harboring them on the territory on Denmark by means of using false promises of a well-paid job in the destination country.

Once they arrived in Denmark, with the pretext of starting the necessary employment formalities, the suspects have accompanied the victims to the authorities to obtain the identification numbers with which they could have been entitled to work on the Danish territory legally. After this, the suspects have, without the approval of the victims, created false companies, opened bank accounts, and obtained credit cards under the name of the victims. Then they used these instruments to commit several financial frauds using the name of the victims by buying valuable assets on credits from different economical agents.

[25] http://infodosar.ro/d.php?dosar=1885/108/2016&submit=Cauta.

Furthermore, the organized crime group has exploited the victims' positions of vulnerability and thus forced them to stay enslaved. As the victims were threatened, did not have any financial means to return home, did not know the language of the destination country, and they had no identity papers to be able to find a job on their own, they were not aware of the crimes committed on their behalf; they eventually did not understand why exactly they were brought to Denmark.

Through the "Wasp Nest" Operation in Romania in 2016, 20 houses were searched and several suspects have been arrested from different counties.

In Denmark, with the help of 387 police officers, 64 houses were searched, 98 persons were arrested, and 76 victims have been identified.

The prejudice created through the crimes committed was estimated by the investigators to be of seven million euros.

This case is outstanding in the sphere of human trafficking as it is an unprecedented example of exploitation in the Romanian jurisprudence and a very rare example in the European jurisprudence too. It is one of the best examples of how modern forms of exploitation, which do not rely on physical force or physical threats, produce comparable benefits to labor exploitation or sexual exploitation.

However, the challenging part for the authorities is to first recognize such cases as human trafficking and not just financial fraud cases, thus, to not hold the victims responsible for the crimes committed under his/her identity and to prove subjective elements such as the exploitation of the position of vulnerability or the lack of consent of the victim. The next challenging aspect is to build efficient bridges of communication between the source and destination countries to identify the roots of the crimes. As one of the investigators involved in the case revealed during the interview "in the nowadays globalized world Joint Investigation Teams are very important assets as without them our international investigations would be even more challenging!"

5 Tendencies: The Nexus Between Illegal Drugs and Sexually Exploited Victims of Human Trafficking

The scientific research[26] carried out between the period 2015–2019 in Romania, Italy, Germany, and the UK was intended to *identify whether sexual exploitation is a factor which determines the start of illicit drug use and if it can be per se stated that there is a general nexus between sexual exploitation and the illegal drug trafficking.*

[26] Doctoral research entitled "*The Incidence of Drug Use Among the Sexually Exploited Victims of Human Trafficking*"—carried out by PhD. (c) Adina Schwartz under the coordination of Prof. Mihaela Tomita, PhD, Doctoral School of Sociology, West University of Timisoara (Romania). The present subchapter contains only some extracts of the research conducted. The extensive data has not been made public yet.

Table 1 Gender

		Frequency	Percent	Valid percent	Cumulative percent
Valid	Masculine	121	31.5	31.5	31.5
	Feminine	263	68.5	68.5	100
	Total	384	100	100	

The research has combined qualitative (interviews and focus groups) and quantitative (questionnaires) research methods.

To ensure the highest possible level of representation in the quantitative stage of the research, the population of human trafficking victims in Europe was considered to be above 10,000. Thus, for a probability of 95% and a margin of error of 5%, the sample size was calculated at 384 persons.

The 384 persons were selected in such a way that the number of male and female victims to be surveyed was directly proportional to the number of male and female victims officially identified in the countries where the research was conducted, the reference year being 2016. The statistics considered were the national ones, published by each country, for the period 2016–2017.

Following the analysis of the statistics, it was identified that, on average, in each country, more than 60% of the victims were female and more than 30% were male. In the research conducted, as shown in Table 1, this proportionality has been respected.

The same criteria were taken into consideration while selecting the number of participants from the participating countries. Therefore, 70.02% of the respondents were identified in the UK, 11.76% in Romania, 11.58% in Italy, and 6.64% in Germany.

The distribution of the source countries of the respondents identified in the four destination countries is shown in Table 2.

To the research question "Have you used illegal drugs prior, during or after the exploitation," as presented in Table 3, most of the respondents have responded positively. Therefore, 261 victims out of 384 have used illegal drugs, and 142 of them have started using drugs during the exploitation phase. The cross tabulation presented in Table 3 reveals that the majority of the persons who use drugs were those who have been sexually exploited.

A quite surprising aspect during the research was that out of the 92 Romanian respondents, the vast majority (almost 70) have used drugs during the exploitation phase. This has brought the Romanian victims into the top of the analyzed population of human trafficking victims.

The research has also had an extensive qualitative part, including 73 interviews with specialist from the participating countries.

Based on the corroboration between the data obtained through the qualitative research and that obtained through the quantitative one the following preliminary conclusions could be drawn:

(a) Traffickers often recruit persons who are already drug users and then exploit the sexually.

Table 2 Source country

		Frequency	Percent	Valid percent	Cumulative percent
Valid	Albania	15	3.9	3.9	3.9
	Bulgaria	**73**	**19.0**	**19.0**	**22.9**
	Eritrea	22	5.7	5.7	28.6
	Germany	3	0.8	0.8	29.4
	Ghana	23	6.0	6.0	35.4
	Italy	2	0.5	0.5	35.9
	UK	6	1.6	1.6	37.5
	Nigeria	**57**	**14.8**	**14.8**	**52.3**
	Poland	18	4.7	4.7	57.0
	Romania	**92**	**24.0**	**24.0**	**81.0**
	Turkey	35	9.1	9.1	90.1
	Hungary	12	3.1	3.1	93.2
	Vietnam	26	6.8	6.8	100
	Total	384	100	100	

Table 3 Cross tabulation * Form of exploitation * Use of drugs

		Have you used illegal drugs prior, during or after the exploitation?		
Count		No	Yes	Total
Which was the form of exploitation?	**Sexual**	**45**	**161**	**206**
	Labor	68	77	145
	Forced bagging	1	4	5
	Forced to commit crimes	9	19	28
Total		123	261	384

(b) Traffickers tend to control the victims by means of exploiting their addiction.
(c) Often the use of drugs constitutes a coping mechanism for the sexually exploited victims of human trafficking.
(d) A significant percentage of the sexually exploited, drug using victims of human trafficking from Europe are Romanians.

From the data obtained through the project, a series of measures have been proposed to more efficiently prevent the population at risk against human trafficking. Additionally, a series of integrated assistance measures have been proposed to facilitate the rehabilitation process of the Romanian victims to prevent them from the risk of secondary victimization.

6 Conclusions

The dynamic feature of human trafficking as well as its continuous metamorphosis have been recognized through the expression "at minimum", inserted in the definition of the "purpose", stated by Art. 3 of the Palermo Protocol. However, despite the seemingly limitless definition, new forms of exploitation have been representing a legal challenge in fitting them into the national legislative framework. Romania is characterized, on the issue of human trafficking, as being the top source country for victims in the European context (Hall et al. 2017). For the last two decades, annual reports on human trafficking released by the European or international agencies and governmental institutions (Europol 2016; EUROSTAT 2018; GRETA 2019) highlight the fact that Romanian organized crime groups are active in the field of sexual exploitation, labor exploitation, forced begging, or forced criminal activities. These normally fall into the catalogue, legally defined, exploitation types, consequence of the era of "fast profit", where multiple-exploitation has represented a surplus for the trafficker in a period of economic crisis (Anti-trafficking Coordinator 2018).

According to Europol (2016), Romanian organized crime groups are present in almost all the European countries, adjusting their modus operandi to the national legislative gaps of the host countries, developing their tentacles where law enforcement agencies are lacking access and, by it, generating, on behalf of the authorities, reasons to always diverse and adapt their investigation methods to the new trends they have developed to flourish their million euros human trade. One small but very practical example was also highlighted during one of the interviews with a UK police officer working in the field of combatting human trafficking:[27] "It is difficult to find Romanian translators at any time of the day and when we conduct searches the first operational minutes are very valuable but the fact that we do not understand Romanian was a communication barrier. Therefore, we started to wear cameras on us and after the search we give the materials to a translator to see what the traffickers spoke between themselves after we have entered."

Through the desk research and the field research conducted in Romania, Germany, Italy, the UK, and Holland, the authors have examined the way Romanian organized crime groups have influenced the legislative and procedural courses in particular EU Member States and within the European Union as a whole, aiming to come up with an answer to the research question "*Is Romania a trend setter within the European human trafficking?*"

The research outcomes have revealed that compared with the years 2004–2008, many of the Romanian organized crime groups have changed their main modus operandi to exploit legislative or procedural aspects foreseen in the countries of destination. Therefore, currently, there is an ongoing tendency identifiable within the "world of trafficking" to work and think "out of the box". While physical

[27] Doctoral research "*The Incidence of Drug Use Among the Sexually Exploited Victims of Human Trafficking*"—carried out by PhD Adina Schwartz. The present subchapter contains only some extracts of the research conducted. The extensive data has not been made public yet.

coercion can still be identified, especially in sexual exploitation cases, often "softer", less visible, less tangible and, most importantly, less provable coercion methods are used such as psychological threats. Further, currently, complex recruitment and exploitation methods are being used especially by the Romanian traffickers, which were not clearly stated in the legislations of the destination countries. Often, like in the case studies illustrated, the traffickers have worked in such a way that there was no precedent before for the methods of exploitation used and thus, they have/are significantly lowered/lowering the likelihood for the grassroot law enforcement agents to identify the main indicators of victimization.

The socio-cultural differences between Romania, the main source country for EU human trafficking and that of the main destination countries UK, Germany, Italy, Holland are often quite prominent. Thus, as easily identifiable from "Operation Golf" and the "Wasps Nest", the traffickers have exploited the naivety and lack of information of the "host communities" and thus have increased the time span spent through exploitation within the "host communities" and have diversified the sphere of crimes in which they were involved from human trafficking to benefit fraud, money laundering, financial frauds, thefts, or robberies.

The responses of both the destination countries and of the European institutions were not particularly prompt but they did come at some point and the effects have weakened the organized crime ties. The existing European tools support cross border, proactive investigations and can lead to the identification and rescue of hundreds of victims. As illustrated in the case studies Romania has been involved in two of the greatest investigations conducted at European level. The effects of such investigations cannot only be felt at an individual level but also at a collective level, leading, in case of "Operation Golf", to European legislative changes to open the doors for investigators to investigate and for victims to be recognized as such and to receive the victims support services needed.

Since 2001 when Romania has introduced its first law against human trafficking—Law 678/2001, yearly a bunch of new challenges are added to the already long "to do" list of researchers, investigators, legislators, and NGO workers. On the Romanian territory the responses were also strong towards preventing human trafficking and combatting this crime. The regional multidisciplinary task forces, coordinated by the Romanian National Agency Against Human Trafficking are constantly developing tailored prevention and information campaigns to lower the power of the push and pull factors exercised over the population at risk. This has also taken place through a multitude of EU-funded projects which have allowed the partnering countries to exchange know-hows and best practice models and, in a next stage, to transpose adapted models into the national practices.

Given the core characteristic of human trafficking is dynamics, the specialists working in the field (be it social workers, law enforcement, or criminologists) can be assured of one aspect they will never lack: surprise.

References

Anti-trafficking Coordinator (2018) Commission Staff Working Document. Accompanying the document Report from the Commission to the European Parliament and the Council. Second report on the progress made in the fight against trafficking in human beings (2018) as required under Article 20 of Directive 2011/36/EU on preventing and combating trafficking in human beings and protecting its victims. European Commission, DG HOME, Brussels

Anti-Trafficking Monitoring Group (2010) Wrong kind of victim: one year on, an analysis of UK measures to protect trafficked persons. The Anti-Trafficking Monitoring Group, London

Aronowitz A (2015) Victims of human trafficking: a complex issue. Universidad de los Andes, Facultad de Ciencias Sociales, Centro de Estudios Internacionales – CEI

Baldoni E, Castelli V, László É, Stoian G, Ulrich L, Aminosanu L (2012) Speranze in vendita: Ricerca qualitativa relativa alla tratta a scopo di sfruttamento sessuale in Romania e Italia, nel periodo 2007–2011. Anima Nova

Bartholini I (2013) Violenza di prossimità. La vittima, il carnefice, lo spettatore e il "grande occhio". FrancoAngeli, Milano

Beddoe C (2018) Children in the shadows. Child trafficking in the UK. In: Rosemary S, Helen R, Stanley N (eds) Vulnerable children and the Law. International evidence for improving child welfare, child protection and children's rights. Jessica Kingsley Publishers, London

Bourdieu P (1998) La domination masculine. Edition di Seul, Paris

Carchedi F, Mottura G, Pugliese E (2003) Il Lavoro Servile e le nuove schiavitù. FrancoAngeli, Milan

Cavarero A (2007) Orrorismo ovvero della violenza sull'inerme. Feltrinelli, Milan

Chuang J (1998) Redirecting the debate over trafficking in women: definitions, paradigms, and contexts. Harv Hum Rights J 11:67–107

Europol (2016) Situation report trafficking in human beings in the EU. Europol, Hague

Europol (2018) Child Trafficking: who are the victims and the criminal networks trafficking them in and into the EU. Europol, Hague

EUROSTAT (2018) Data collection on trafficking 2018 in human beings in the EU. Publications Office of the European Union, Luxembourg

Gallagher A (2010) The international law of human trafficking. Cambridge University Press, Cambridge

Gallagher A (2012) Issue Paper on Abuse of position of vulnerability and other "means" within of definition of Trafficking in Persons. UNODC, Vienna

Gallagher A (2015) The concept of exploitation in the trafficking in persons protocol. UNODC, Vienna

GRETA (2019) Reply from Romania to the Questionnaire for the evaluation of the implementation of the Council of Europe Convention on Action against Trafficking in Human Beings by the Parties. Third evaluation round Thematic focus: access to justice and effective remedies for victims of trafficking in human beings. European Council, Strasbourg

Hall S, Tomita M, Schwartz A (2017) Social protection of the human trafficking victims from Romania. Agora Psycho Pragm Semest J 11:173–182

Hyland K (2016) The limitations of necessary criminalisation: developing a comprehensive and holistic response to modern slavery. In: Arher MS (ed) Human trafficking:issues beyond criminalization. The proceedings of the 20th plenary session 17–21 April 2015. Libreria Editrice Vaticana, Vatican, pp 54–67

ILO (2009) Training manual to fight trafficking in children for labour, sexual and other forms of exploitation. ILO

Korvinus D, Koster D, Heleen E (2007) Trafficking in human beings: the concept of exploitation in the Dutch trafficking provision

OHCHR (2010) Recommended principles and guidelines on human trafficking. OHCHR. https://www.ohchr.org/Documents/Publications/Traffickingen.pdf

Michael M (2012) The sources of social power, vol 1: A history of power from the beginning to AD 1760 (4 vols), 2nd edn. Cambridge University Press, New York

National Rapporteur on Trafficking in Human Beings and Sexual Violence against Children (2016) Vulnerability up close: an exploratory study into the vulnerability of children to human trafficking. National Rapporteur 2016, The Hague. https://ec.europa.eu/antitrafficking/sites/antitrafficking/files/vulnerability_up_close_interactive_national_rapporteur_on_trafficking_in_human_beings_and_sexual_violence_against_children_tcm24-128353.pdf
Pascoal R, Schwartz A (2016) How family and emotional ties are used as coercive instruments by the exploiters on the Romanian feminine migration. The study case of Italy. In: Ducu V, Csetri A (eds) Managing difference in Eastern-European transnational families. Peter Lang, Frankfurt am Main, pp 43–62
Sarrica F (2015) Stealing labour: an economic analysis of forced labour and human trafficking. In: Forum on crime and society, vol 8. UNODC, Vienna, pp 137–154
Stefenel D (2013) "I feel like having no country": ethno-cultural identity constructs in the Romanian Diaspora in Greece. Polis, Revista de Stiinte Politice, European Institute, Iasi, pp 110–130
UNODC (2006) Travaux Préparatoires of the negotiations for the elaboration of the United Nations Convention Against Organized Crime and the Protocols thereto. UNODC, Vienna

Rafaela Pascoal (rafaeladaconceicao.hilariopascoal@unipa.it) is a Research Fellow in the Department of Culture and Societies at the University of Palermo. Rafaela is the author of the book *Motherhood in the Context of Human Trafficking and Sexual Exploitation. Studies on Nigerian and Romanian Women.* She has published several articles on Human Trafficking, Migration and Gender in Romanian, Portuguese, and Italian Academic journals, as well as several book chapters. She has also presented several conferences in the United Kingdom, the Netherlands, France, Romania, Lithuania, and Italy.

Adina Schwartz (nicoleta.schwartz@gmail.com) is a PhD (c) at the West University of Timisoara, Doctoral School of Sociology, having conducted her doctoral research on human trafficking within Romania, Italy, Germany and the U.K. She has graduated law school at the West University of Timisoara in 2010, and Master in Criminal Law and Criminal Procedure in 2011. From 2011 to 2018, she was the head of the "Justice" Department of Pro Prietenia Arad Foundation (Romania) where she coordinated prevention campaigns against human trafficking, research projects on criminality and was directly involved in the assistance of human trafficking victims. She is now a researcher within various EU-funded projects on restorative justice and victim support and continues to be involved in offerring victim centered and trauma informed support to survivals of human trafficking.

Individuals Treated as Nonpersons and the Challenge to Criminal Justice: The Specific Problems Facing Victims of Trafficking in Human Beings

Cláudia Cruz Santos

Abstract Victims of human trafficking, as especially vulnerable victims of violent and organised crime, require a multitude of measures from the state, some of which are criminal in nature and others related to protection and assistance. They all need to be interlinked. The specific nature of the crime of trafficking in persons and the damage it causes, however, trigger difficulties that the penal system must address to achieve an answer that is both fair and supportive.

1 Introduction

The crime of human trafficking is certainly one of the most damaging criminal offences for victims because in their DNA—in the DNA of the crime—there is the people's objectification clearly expressed in para 1 of Article 160 of the Penal Code to 'offer' or 'deliver' person. Here we have people being treated as things because their individual freedom is limited in order to make a profit, particularly through 'sexual exploitation, exploitation of work, begging, slavery [and] organ harvesting', among others.[1]

[1] On the situations detected in Portugal, 'there is still a clear representativeness of (presumed) trafficking records for purposes of labor exploitation (152), of which 108 confirmed victims, 101 (93%) were victims of this type of exploitation mainly in the agricultural sector (examples: olive picking, raspberry, blueberries, blackberry, pumpkin, orange melon, cherry, tomato, among others'; 'Most of the (presumed) flagged victims are male. Crossing the variables Sex and Type of Exploration there is a clear gender dimension: for records of trafficking for the purpose of labor exploitation (presumed) male victims prevail, and for trafficking records for of sexual exploitation (presumed) female victims prevail'. But also, with regard to Portuguese victims of human trafficking abroad, there is a predominance of labour exploitation of men, in the hypotheses detected

C. C. Santos (✉)
Faculty of Law, University of Coimbra, Coimbra, Portugal
e-mail: claudias@fd.uc.pt

A. M. Rodrigues, M. J. Guia (eds.), *New Forms of Human Trafficking*,
https://doi.org/10.1007/978-3-031-39732-5_10

Using individuals as goods gives this crime a highly profitable nature[2] and therefore enhances its agents' quasi-corporate performance, by creating structures that obey internal rules of hierarchy and discipline, calling for perpetuation over time[3] and with the possibility of resorting to corruption or violence when necessary to achieve their ends. Trafficking in persons is therefore already classified in Article 1 (m) of our Code of Criminal Procedure as highly organised crime, and as the result of Article 1 (l), subsumed under the category of especially violent crime.[4] Hence the conclusion that victims of trafficking in persons are particularly vulnerable (Article 67A (3) of the Criminal Procedure Code), with their rights described in Article 20 of the Victim Statute introduced by Law No. 130/2015, of 4 September (the specific status of especially vulnerable victims).

By combining these elements, criminal justice problems have contributed to defining the concrete ways in which these victims should be protected, ensuring political-criminal commitment to its prevention and repression because of its inclusion in the Criminal Policy Law for the biennium 2015–2017 in the catalogue of priority crimes for prevention.[5]

However, we wish to emphasise that the answer that criminal justice must provide for these victims must be in line with other more protective forms of assistance, as we are confronted by people who, before being victims of a crime, have often been victims of other forms of exclusion or inequality. The 'situation of

mainly in Spain and in the scope of agricultural work (Report 2016 on Human Trafficking, pp. 31 and 40).

[2] 2012 data provided by UNODC already referred to a 'market with an annual profit of more than 32 million dollars' and that 'moves about 2.4 million people' as victims.

[3] The fact that we are frequently confronted with '*continued victimisation*' is underlined in the 2016 Report on Trafficking in Human Beings, of the Ministry of Administration Internal (Observatory of Trafficking in Human Beings), p. 34. In this context, the 'account of a November 2016 Spanish operation, supported by Europol' on an organisation that trafficked young women and then forced them into pickpocket activities in several European Union countries to get them into Spain, where they provided them with false documents and the necessary training for those illicit acts. It refers to the existence of family ties within the organisation (whose members are mainly from Bosnia and Herzegovina) and a hierarchical structure.

[4] Human trafficking is classified as a particularly violent crime by Article 67-A of the Criminal Procedure Code, always considering its victims to be especially vulnerable: '1—It is considered: (a) "Victim": (i) The natural person who has suffered a damage, namely an attack on your physical or mental integrity, an emotional or moral damage, or a damage to property, directly caused by an action or inaction, within the scope of the commission of a crime; relatives of a person whose death was directly caused by a crime and damage as a result of that death; (b) "Especially vulnerable victim", the victim whose special weakness result, in particular, from your age, your state of health or disability, as well as the fact that the type, the degree and duration of victimization resulted in injuries with serious consequences on their balance psychological or in the conditions of their social integration; (...) 3—Victims of violent crime and especially violent crime are always considered to be especially vulnerable victims for the purposes of the provisions of paragraph b) of paragraph 1'.

[5] See Art. 2, point g) of Law No. 72/2015, of 20 July.

vulnerability'[6] of these victims and the abuse of this situation by the trafficking agents cannot be disregarded.

The exclusively criminal solution is unlikely to be entirely fair, if it is the only one, that is to say that it is not enough to guarantee victims of trafficking in persons the possibility of the agents' conviction accompanied by their procedurally dignified treatment, avoiding secondary victimisation.[7] On the other hand, protective measures or assistance cannot be conditional on the victims' interest or willingness to collaborate with the criminal prosecution of their attackers—as seems to have been recognised in the special regime of the residence permit concession to victims of trafficking in persons in para 4 of Article 109 of Law No. 23/2007, of 4 July, as well as in the Decree-Law n° 368/2007, of 5 November.

2 Defining the Subject of Victimology and the Appropriateness of Victims of Human Trafficking in Either the Strictest or Broadest Terms

One of the greatest challenges facing victimology is that of justifying its subject as a branch of knowledge that studies the problems posed by the victims of crimes, or rather by the victims of the most diverse forms of suffering, from illness to unemployment, keeping in mind other disadvantages such as those caused by war, weather and migration.

The understanding that victimology deals only with victims of crimes presupposes an understanding of the specificity of criminal victimisation. What differentiates the suffering of someone robbed while waiting for the bus from a terminally ill person, or someone whose home is destroyed by war, leaving them homeless and without any means of support? One possible answer is that, in the first case, it is possible to assign responsibility to another, concrete person for what happened, which is not the case for those suffering from an illness, a natural disaster or war.

The overvaluation of criminal victimisation to the detriment of other forms of victimisation—that is, the predominance of concern for victims of crime—is criticised by several authors, who see it as a way of legitimising security policies (any means available should preferably be channelled towards punishing the guilty party), to the detriment of assistance policies (any means available should preferably be channelled towards helping those in need).[8]

---

[6] On the 'abuse of a situation of vulnerability' as a core element of trafficking in people, see Euclides Dâmaso, 2009, p. 6 ss.

[7] At the presentation of the recent June 2017 Trafficking in Persons Report of the United States Department of State, Secretary of State Rex Tillerson first states the commitment to seeking justice for victims and only afterwards in making agents accountable, what this primacy means concretely, especially in cases of conflict between the two purposes.

[8] See CARIO (2006). Based on the affirmation of the relevance that societies today attribute to *insecurity*, the author questions his perhaps too frequent association with criminality and considers

It is also possible that a victim of human trafficking does not see herself as the victim of a crime, but rather a victim of disgrace. Caitlin Kelly Lawrence, trafficked for the purpose of sexual exploitation, said: 'I didn't know I was a victim of anything, except of the circumstances'.[9]

There is therefore reasonable doubt concerning the possibility and convenience of finding sufficient criteria for delimiting boundaries between the victim of the crime and someone who considers themselves a victim of any other event.[10] It is believed, however, that there may be something *different* in causing harm that can be attributed to a more or less responsible human action. There is something specific to *being the victim of someone else's behaviour*, insofar as that victimisation undermines our understanding of the meaning of coexistence, as if questioning each one's notion of autonomy and their role in the world.

This damage caused by a typical offence, which can be attributed to another person, tends to be perceived differently by the victim to, for example, the damage associated with a natural phenomenon. Simply put, it could be said that being the victim of a crime is 'especially traumatic', in the words of Howard ZEHR in *Changing Lenses*. Further, in response to the question why the crime is so 'traumatic' and 'devastating', the author views this as explained by the innate 'violation of the self'. The crime is a kind of 'desecration' of the victim, of what she is and what she believes in, of her personal space. ZEHR also adds that crime calls into question two basic beliefs on which people base their lives: the conviction that the world is an orderly place and that it 'makes sense'; and the belief in personal autonomy (Zehr 2005, p. 24).

Specific to the crime of trafficking in persons is that their victims, while they are indeed now victims of a crime, would already in many cases—in most cases—be victims of other forms of suffering associated with situations of social, economic, cultural, political or familial vulnerability. First victims of various forms of societal injustice or exclusion, then victims of a crime. This results in a spiralling enhancement of the damage associated with victimisation, or a snowball effect, in which

---

that 'criminal insecurity is far from being the exclusive source of malaise individual and social development of many of our fellow citizens'. It further affirms the relative disinterest with which we face other factors of insecurity, such as occupational risks, illness, disasters or ecological disaster, and proposes that overvaluation of the criminal factor aims to mask the others. Hence, he concludes with the need to 'relativise' the importance of criminal victimisation (pp. 12–13). That says, we cannot dispense of the need for a movement to discover the criminal victim that triggers the guarantee of their 'legal, psychological and social monitoring', because 'it is important to guarantee the victim and/or a fair process, respecting the dignity owed to all people, in order to ensure offering them the most global and comprehensive recovery possible' (ob. cit., p. 297).

[9] See 2017 Trafficking in Persons Report—US Department of State, June 2017, p. 31.

[10] Frederick McClintock addresses this difficulty, stating that 'it is important to recognize that there are victims not only of crime, but also of other disasters or events not related to the crime' (in Prologue: 1998, p. 13). He adds that, despite being a criminologist, he chose to study the victims of crimes, as it cannot be ignored that 'criminal policy cannot be divorced from social policy' as well as 'issues relating to victims of crime cannot be totally separated other forms of victimization'.

each type of victimisation facilitates the next. This also creates difficulties in defining state policies for repairing the damage caused to these victims, and its diversity and depth. What if today there were a relative consensus on expanding the protection requirements for victims in general, which are currently not enough with the punitive reaction of the state against the accused? Imagine the victim being handled with dignity during the process as they seek amends for the damage they have suffered. It is for a variety of reasons that the answers to human trafficking must be plural and diverse.

In other words: their disadvantaged situation makes these victims worthy of assistance responses in the light of the principle of solidarity that shapes the social state; their situation as victims of crime makes them worthy of criminal responses in light of the principle of justice that shapes the rule of law.

The concrete meaning of such responses can, however, only be questioned and defined after assessing the challenges involved in detecting and protecting victims of trafficking in persons.

3 Challenges in Detecting and Protecting Victims of the Crime of Trafficking in Persons

The fact that human trafficking is based on victimisation, coupled with its enduring nature (or the temporal duration of victimisation) and frequent recourse to violence and/or intimidation deepens the harm suffered by victims.[11]

The extent of such damage is, therefore, the *second challenge* for a criminal response that is not only concerned with the punishment of the agent, but also sufficient amends for the victim's damages. However, to begin making such amends, victimisation must first be stopped, which presupposes the discovery of the crime and the removal of the victim from the situation in question. The first *challenge* in the crime of human trafficking is becoming aware of formal instances of control for the existence of said crime, revealing both agents and victims. There may still be a prior challenge: helping the victim to understand that they are indeed a victim, since one's initial consent is irrelevant whenever unclear or it associated with exploitation. For example, a woman from Latin America who agrees to come to Portugal to dedicate herself to prostitution is unaware of the Palermo Protocol, as well as the section of Article 160 of the Penal Code according to which 'the consent of the victim of crimes provided for in the preceding paragraphs does not under any

[11] The 2016 Report on Human Trafficking, from the Ministry of Administration Intern (Human Trafficking Observatory) quotes a 2014 study on p. 28 with the conclusion that 'These groups have the capacity to deal with a large number of victims and to establish logistical bases and contacts in countries of origin, transit and destination. Highly flexible in nature they conduct operations with active cells in several [member states] (...), easily transferring victims from one country to another. In some cases, victims are used to control others (victim controls victim), complex distribution of functions within these criminal networks' (Morgado 2014: 41–42).

circumstances exclude the illegality of the fact'. And so, this woman does not know that she is the victim of a crime because she is being exploited when forced to work as a prostitute in different conditions than she had imagined, or being forced to pay fabricated, ongoing debt.

Let us consider the words of one such victim, a Brazilian woman who came to Portugal:

> One day, when we arrived, we discovered that it was a strip house, all throughout, that it was for sex. He hadn't told us that, he'd said it was for us to take turns. When we got there, there was a full strip catwalk every 10 minutes, with rather ordinary clothes. And it was a maze, even to drink champagne, another just to do this, do that, and we discovered some rooms and the owner of the house immediately asked, "who's doing the table dance?". Nobody did it in my class. He looked, laughed, always aggressive: "Are you coming to a business like this, thinking you are a saint?" (Boaventura de Sousa 2008, p. 121).

The horrifying nature of human trafficking has been emphasised over recent years, and yet the number of victims recognised as such and the number of agents convicted is comparatively minimal.[12]

The discovery of human trafficking by the authorities is especially problematic for several reasons: the victim's lack of understanding of their own victimisation, the disadvantage of victims in economic, social or cultural terms or age; the complex bonds, for example affective, that often exist between agent and victim; the permanent control or surveillance to which the victims are subjected by agents; threats made to victims or their neighbours, intimidation exploiting those pre-existing weaknesses; the relocation of victims, which often makes them undocumented foreigners in a place where they have no knowledge of the language or the assistance that they might receive; the conviction that reporting the crime of which they are victims may lead to prosecution either by human trafficking officers or by local authorities committed to applying measures that restrict freedom, or even expulsion from the territory.

Knowing that the penal process continues to be more reactive than proactive (that is, most cases are based on a report, which gives the victim an essential role in triggering the state's reaction to crime), failure to cooperate with victims of trafficking in persons can contribute greatly to low statistics.

Criminal justice requires the trust of victims of human trafficking for effective protection and amends. Victims must seek justice and collaborate with formal control bodies. However, such trust is only possible upon resolution of a long-ingrained aporia which has been used widely by traffickers against their victims. That aporia of the state response to human trafficking has oscillated between viewing trafficked persons as real victims or rather as criminals, perhaps responsible for less serious crimes, but crimes nonetheless.

This is illustrated by the example of *Teresa*, a young woman whose story is summarised by Susan COPPEDGE in her introduction to the Trafficking in Persons

[12] See JOVANOVIC, 2017, vol. 1, p. 44, who underlines the fact that very few victims of trafficking in persons see this role to be formally assigned to them, despite extensive research and the great attention devoted to this over the last decade.

Report released by the United States Department of State in June 2017. Teresa was raised by her grandmother in Central America and was deceived at a young age with promises of love and a better life by a man whom she thought cared about her. She was taken by the man to the United States, where he forced her into prostitution, taking all the money and threatening that she would be deported and humiliated before her family. But the point that we wish to highlight here is this: 'his threats not only instilled fear in *Teresa* and coerced her to be exploited; they also convinced her that she was a criminal for violating federal immigration laws and local laws against prostitution. There are people like *Teresa* caught in forced services around the world who fear that justice systems will punish them instead of condemning and arresting their traffickers—and in reality their fears are often justified'. Susan COPPEDGE's conclusion is unambiguous, demanding that 'the criminal justice system does not penalise victims of human trafficking when they are forced to commit crimes as a direct result of their exploitation. When forced crime occurs as part of the scheme, victims of trafficking in persons cannot be punished by the same system that must protect them: and if they are, their penalties must be removed and they must receive the support and ample help'.[13]

4 What Should Criminal Justice Offer Victims of the Crime of Trafficking in Persons?

The starting point for consideration is that victims of crime have no subjective right to punish the agent, and the *objections that in the penal doctrine have deserved precisely the affirmation of this right.*[14]

[13] In the United States Department of State's June 2017 Report on Trafficking People (pp. 329 and 330), although recognising that 'the Government of Portugal fully complies with minimum standards for the elimination of trafficking', it is recommended that the laws are changed to include 'specific measures to protect victims from prosecution for illicit acts committed as a result of having subject to trafficking'. It also adds that 'the lack of specific rules in Portuguese law on the protection of victims against prosecution for acts they were forced to commit can leave victims vulnerable to individual decisions of prosecutors on the making of charges'. Implementing this principle of non-punishment of victims of the crime of human trafficking is complicated, however, when it becomes necessary to specify what it, in the name of protecting human rights, represents. As explained by Jovanovic (2017, vol. 1, p. 41 ss), we know what the objective is—victim protection—but we need to define 'what kind of infringements apply, what are the necessary requirements for their application, what is their legal effect'.

[14] This question earned the critical attention of Silva Sanchéz (2008, p. 149 ss), which associates the 'old ideology of *nullum crimen sine poena*' (with disrespect for fundamental rights and guaranteeing rules in the name of needing to punish all criminals) to the most modern 'doctrine of the *fight against impunity*' and 'doctrine of the *victim's right to punishment of the agent*'. As for these last two lines of thought, he states that, despite their non-coincidence, the first has sought to justify itself through the second: impunity should not be granted *because* the victim would have the right to condemn their aggressor. Silva Sánchez relates the proclamation of this right above all to 'international criminal power' and 'state crime', but affirms the tendency for its expansion to 'serious

In a very succinct way, current doctrine rejects defending the agent's punishment requirement (therefore, the refusal of his impunity) based on the subjective right that victims would have to see their *dignity* reaffirmed through penalty.[15]

The agreement with Silva Sánchez on the absence of this subjective right of victims to punish the agent does not equate to affirming the absence of the offended party's legitimate and proper interest in the criminal process. It is this interest that justifies participation in the process, which should culminate in deciding a specific legal-penal solution that can be considered fair. It was, moreover, recognition of this interest that rooted understanding as to the assistant's legitimacy to appeal, unaccompanied by the Public Prosecutor's Office, regarding the measure or type of penalty in the event of a condemnatory decision. However, the affirmation of this specific interest of the offended person in a decision that is in accordance with the law and, to that extent, just, does not mean the affirmation of any right to *punish* the agent, first because neither criminal law nor criminal procedural law leads to even those whose criminal responsibility has been indicted or proven being sentenced to a penalty. But, above all, because the affirmation of that subjective right is not consistent with what should be considered the function of criminal law: the subsidiary protection of legal assets.

Therefore, it seems necessary to emphasise that the recognition of the offended party's rights (and, in our system, especially those of the victim's assistant) to certain ways of participating in the process in the interest of a fair decision does not, of

---

crime', particularly terrorism and crimes against life. The Author concludes that victims having such a subjective right to punish the agent is unacceptable, considering that 'the core of such a theory should be constituted by the expressive-symbolic (immaterial) responses: declaration of guilt and disapproval. The additional infliction of a "criminal pain" to the agent would only be justified when, after all, there were preventive reasons for doing so (…). In effect, the imposition and execution of a sentence disconnected from such reasons, and justified by the victim's needs, would be nothing but institutionalized revenge under a cloak of supposed rationality' (ob. Cit., P. 171). With mixed opinion, George P. Fletcher considers that the new perception of *justice* results in the victims' right to punishment of the agent, which may imply a derogation from *fair trial* rules ('Fletcher 2005, pp. 547 ff). Similarly, see the author's previous study, 'The place of victims in the theory of retribution', *Buffalo Criminal Law Review*, 3, 1999–2000, p. 51 ff. Note, however, that Fletcher himself does not fail to recognise that it is an 'interesting challenge to integrate the victim in the justification of punishment', because 'the crime of homicide protects life—not the life of a particular person, but the right to live in the abstract (…). The abstract nature of protected interests explains the minimal relevance of the views of the specific victim with regard to the conviction of the aggressor' (last. Ob. Cit., p. 52).

[15] Prittwitz (1999), pp. 109 ff traces the emergence of this concern with the victim in criminal doctrine contemporary to the well-known 'Reemtsma episode'. To summarise, Jean Philipp Reemtsma, a wealthy German businessman connected to the *Hamburg Institute for Social Research,* published a work of his own—after his forced deprivation of liberty for 33 days, in which he remained in a 'small, dark cell' and was threatened with death, which ended with his family's payment of a very large sum to crime agents – in which he defended that punishment shows the community's solidarity with the victim. In Reemtsma's opinion, this punishment means a certain exclusion of the agent and a welcome statement towards the victim, who thus returns to the group.

course, amount to the affirmation of any subjective right to punish the agent.[16] For example, considering criminal law and Portuguese criminal procedural law, it seems unequivocally concluded that the victim should have their rights recognised, conditioning the state's function ius puniendi. Consider, by way of illustration, the impossibility of unofficial criminal procedural promotion (and, consequently, the impossibility of conviction) when a particular crime is involved, and the offended person does not present their complaint; what are the chances of dropping a complaint? Remember the assistant's need for agreement to the provisional suspension of the process; consider the assistant's right to request initiation or to appeal and how it can condition the outcome of that process.

However, when analysing these various hypotheses, it appears that none of them implies the right of the victim or their assistant to the aggressor's effective condemnation. On the contrary, two main forms of accepting the relevance of the victims will seem to be affirmed, both in such a way that does not coincide with that subjective right to punish the agent. There is one group of cases in which the will of the victim is relevant; only, however, when this triggers non-punishment due to the inexistence or limitation of the process in the specific case of private crimes. For all other cases, in which the victim's procedural contribution may favour either the conviction or a more severe conviction of the accused—particularly via the request to open an investigation or the appeal of a decision, whether absolute or not—the victim's own will (admittedly associated with an interest in the realisation of justice for that specific case) is not in itself sufficient for this effective punishment to occur. On the contrary, after taking a position relating to the victim of crime, it will be (or

[16] If interested in pursuing this further, bear in mind that, in the general affirmation of the '"victims" right to punish the agent', various kinds of rights are often implied. As such, Silva Sánchez (last ob. Cit., p. 160), to make the criticism of each segment of thought more precise, assigns autonomy to a 'right to the truth', a 'right to the process', a 'right to justice' and a 'right to punishment'. For the first, he states that 'it is difficult to deny the existence of a right for victims and their families to know the truth. The problem is to maintain that such a right can (and should) be satisfied through criminal proceedings. In fact, the procedural reconstruction of the historical fact is not intended to declare the truth of what happened, but simply to lay the groundwork for an attribution of responsibility'. As for the 'right to justice', the indefinitions are greater, due to the very indeterminacy that underlies it; despite this, Silva Sanchéz seems to associate this right with showing disapproval of the aggressor's conduct (general rule associated with the process, which is why it deals with both the 'right to the process' and the 'right to justice'), this disapproval of the aggressor's behaviour through which 'the one affected by his action is considered a "victim", restoring his dignity and equality'. Now, even if, the proclamation of these rights of the victim is admissible, from the perspective of the Spanish penalist, such is not necessarily the case concerning the 'right to punishment', related to the 'infliction of harm'. This therefore brings into question 'the expressive value that the agent's suffering of pain can have for the restoration of the victim's original position (...)'. Silva Sánchez underscores this by questioning whether 'the realization of justice for the victim requires, in any case, the effective punishment of the agent' and concluding that the victim is entitled to the 'restoration of their dignity'. Now, this reinstatement does not presuppose that punishment, since 'it is inherent to the agent's declaration of guilt (and the corresponding declaration of the victim's character affected by him). Insofar as it is possible to restore the victim's dignity—to show the recognition that he deserves—causing the least possible damage to the agent, it seems that the criminal law system should be oriented towards that' (ob. Cit., pp. 163–4).

not) supported in the judicial decision, which will always be conditioned by the specific criminal and procedural purposes.

Therefore, to a certain extent, recognising the victim's right to effective judicial protection cannot be confused with any subjective right to punishment of the agent.

Victims of crime have the right, in criminal justice, to procedural treatment that does not cause secondary victimisation, and are entitled to protection and reparation of damage.

Yet victims of trafficking in persons are also entitled to protection and assistance measures that go far beyond exclusively criminal responses, and which are based on solidarity from the social state. The Report on Human Trafficking for 2016, from the Ministry of Internal Administration (Observatory on Human Trafficking) identifies the essential vectors of Protection and Assistance measures:[17] 'Reception in CAP or in another structure; psychological and/or medical assistance; legal assistance; Education and training; insertion in the labour market; compensation request; reflection period; residence permits; assisted return to the country of origin'.

5 Conclusions

The abolition of slavery, seen as heritage acquired from contemporary western societies, is perhaps less acquired than we imagined. And trafficking in persons, if not to be confused with slavery itself,[18] is often a tool thereof. We have removed the

---

[17] According to the report (p. 44): 'During 2016 and based on the records of victims "Confirmed", "Pending/Under investigation" and "Flagged by NGOs/other entities"', 92 (presumed) victims received protection and assistance. Separated by type, they appear as follows: During 2016, 69 (presumed) victims were hosted at the 3 Shelter and Protection Centers for Victims of TSH (CAP). Seventy-nine (presumed) victims received psychological and/or medical assistance. Legal assistance was provided to 33 (presumed) victims. Nine (presumed) victims received education/professional training. Twenty-three (presumed) victims were placed in the labour market. During 2016, 38 (presumed) victims were notified of the right to the 'Reflection Term' (under Article 111—'Reflection Period', according to which authorization for residence for foreign citizens who are or have been the victims of criminal offences related to trafficking in persons or assisting illegal immigration, even if they have entered the country illegally or do not fulfill the conditions for granting a residence permit). In 2016, 31 marketing authorisations were granted residence under Article 109. Twenty-five (presumed) victims of foreign and Portuguese nationality returned to their country of origin or another country where close family was located.

[18] The distinction between the crime of slavery (under Article 159 of the Portuguese Penal Code) and the crime of trafficking in persons (under Article 160 of the Portuguese Penal Code) is unambiguous but tends to blur in some reflective and decisive contexts. This would have been the case, and improperly for some perpetrators, in the decision of the European Court of Human Rights in the Rantsev v. Cyprus and Russia, insofar as the application of Article 4 of the ECHR was extended to human trafficking, captioned 'Prohibition of slavery and forced labor'. Such assimilation of trafficking in persons to slavery is questionable, as trafficking, unlike slavery, does not require the actual exploitation of a person, but it is also problematic to require that such exploitation has already taken place to benefit from the protection granted by that Article 4. In any case, whether (or not) Article 4 of the ECHR can be applied to human trafficking depends on the existence of

acceptance of slavery from our laws, but we have not yet managed to remove it from our reality.

The International Labor Organisation and the International Organisation for Migrations announced at the UN General Assembly in 2017 that 40 million people were victims of modern slavery and that 152 million children were subjected to child labour. Many of these slavery victims (although not all) will have been trafficked beforehand. The numbers are so staggering that we run the risk of losing them, accepting them as a banality of evil close to that depicted by Hannah Arendt in her Eichmann work in Jerusalem.

It is this trivialisation that we must resist, as it would also imply a form of objectification of the other. We cannot let such large numbers make us forget the solidarity deserved by each of the victims of human trafficking, because each of these victims experiences their own personal tragedy as if they were the only one. And in one sense, they are. Each of these people lives their personal tragedy by begging on the streets of our cities, working from sunrise to sunset in the fields where the fruit we eat is harvested, prostituting themselves in apartments advertised in the newspapers we read or choose not to read. The victims of crimes of trafficking in persons are among us and therefore depend on us to be treated as what they are: people.

References

Cario R (2006) Victimologie: de l'effraction du lien intersubjectif à la restauration sociale, vol I, 3rd edn. L'Harmattan, Paris

Dâmaso E (2009) Tráfico de seres humanos: prevenção e repressão à luz do protocolo adicional à Convenção de Palermo. Julgar on line

Fletcher GP (2005) Justice and fairness in the protection of crime victims. Lewis Clark Law Rev 9:547

Jovanovic M (2017) The Principle of Non-Punishment of victims of trafficking in human beings: a quest for rationale and practical guidance. J Traff Hum Exploit 1:41–76

McClintock F (1998) Prologue: victims and criminal justice. In: Fattah E, Peters T (eds) Support for crime victims in a comparative perspective: a collection of essays dedicated to the Memory of Prof. Frederic McClintock. Leuven University Press, Leuven

Prittwitz C (1999) The resurrection of the victim in penal theory. Buffalo Crim Law Rev 3:109

Silva Sanchéz JM (2008) Nullum Crimen sine Poena? Sobre las Doctrinas Penales de la "Lucha contra la Impunidad" y del "Derecho de la Víctima al Castigo del Autor". Derecho Penal Criminol 29:86–87

Zehr H (2005) Changing lenses – a new focus for crime and justice, 3rd edn. Herald Press, Ontario. (1st ed., de 1990)

positive obligations for states (the establishment of an appropriate legal and administrative framework; the procedural obligation to promote effective investigations where there are signs of trafficking of persons; the imposition of victim protection measures; and the obligation to cooperate with others states).

Cláudia Cruz Santos (claudias@fd.uc.pt) is an Associate Professor at the law faculty of the University of Coimbra (FDUC). She is also a member of the Assembly of the Portuguese Republic since October 2019 and a member of the Board of the Institute of Economic and European Criminal Law (FDUC). Cláudia Santos has been a GRECO (Group of States Against Corruption) expert—Council of Europe. She has several books and articles published on criminal sciences.

Trafficking in Human Beings as an Hourglass Paradigm

Rita Penedo

Abstract This chapter is based on the question "How many of the victims registered by the Member States of the European Union are not actually the same continuously exploited in one or between several countries (continued victimization) and/or exploited more than once but at different times (revictimization)?" Recognizing that it is empirically challenging to gather supportive evidence, it led us to explore the modus operandi of victimization as an (un)interrupted cycle that figuratively portrays THB as an hourglass. This chapter is a retrospective one on a specific country context and it is relevant for this reason, it has been written in 2017. Consequently, the statistical references (e.g., reports) as well as other data should be read having 2017 in mind.

1 Placing the Board and the Pieces

When reading reports on crime statistics and in this case on trafficking in human beings (THB), it is with a strong mind that one does not fall under the temptation of a straightforward usage, especially if to sustain one's own argument.

As a halt to an anthropophagy behavior or to the "obsessive need to measure criminality" (Boutellier 2000), we are adverted at the very beginning that *comparability is to be avoided* (Eurostat 2015) or, *the figures presented should be interpreted with caution* (European Commission 2016).

To make the discussion even more intricate, in most European Union Member States (EU MS) THB does not fall under the category of "volume" crime, and thus to what extent does administrative data and conventional methods of data gathering reveals the seriousness and (full) scale of the crime (del Frate 2010; Maguire 2012)? As pointed out by the United Nations Office on Drugs and Crime (UNODC) (2016a), administrative data is useful to analyze socio-demographics variables and

R. Penedo (✉)
Portuguese Ministry of Home Affairs, Lisbon, Portugal
e-mail: rpenedo@otsh.mai.gov.pt

A. M. Rodrigues, M. J. Guia (eds.), *New Forms of Human Trafficking*,
https://doi.org/10.1007/978-3-031-39732-5_11

elaborate profiles of victims and offenders, but a deeper comprehension of the situation requires a triangulation with other sources and methods.

The debate surrounding statistical cross-national comparability is not new neither its critical evaluation.[1]

Considering all cautions, Von Hofer's considers that cross-national time-series analysis can and should be used if one takes a step back and comprehend beforehand that crime statistics are a construct influenced by three factors (Von Hoffer 2000; Aebi 2008; HEUNI 2014). They are:

1. Statistical factors: the time to which data collection and statistics are referring to (date of reporting vs. date of the event), the counting rules and practices and their changes,
2. Legal factors: the definition and its changes in the Criminal Code, the Code of Criminal Procedure and its implications,
3. Substantive factors: the propensity/opportunity to commit and to report crimes, the risk of detection, the response of criminal justice authorities.

Due to its complexity, each one of the above mentioned elements could be a chapter on their own right. Additionally they are, from our perspective, interdependent (but not necessarily with a causal effect). For instance:

- Within the Statistical factors, the statistical and metadata business process in which one fundamental stage is the assessment of concepts and variables to which data is replying to that lead us to,
- The Legal factors and the (harmonization of) legal definition of THB, of THB victim, of the purposes of exploitation (the results of Protocols', Conventions', and Directives' transpositions') influenced by the,
- Substantive factors or the complexity and nature of THB, constantly adapting, resultant of several causes interconnected with other criminal, social, and economical dynamics (underline idea to the concept of "wicked problems"[2]), that may lead us back to the Legal (e.g., adaptability of the crime—new practices of exploitation—revision of the definition), and to the Statistical factor (e.g., new definition—need for additional information—revision of variables).

Why star with this line of thought? Well, it is our disclaimer as we will sustain our main questioning with reference to some conclusions found in the 2013 and 2015 Eurostat's working paper "Trafficking in Human Beings", the Europol "Situation Report—Trafficking in Human Beings in the EU" (2016), the European

[1] Two international meetings where the collection of statistics on crime at the international level and the problem of comparison was addressed: the *General Statistical Congress for the Purpose of Introducing Unity in the Statistical Documents of all Countries* (Brussels, 1853) and the *International Congress on the Prevention and Repression of Crime, including penal and reformatory treatment* (London, 1872)—at UNODC's "A short history of the collection of UN crime and justice statistics at the international level."

[2] This chapter will not explore this concept but recommends Jernigan S (2016) Human Trafficking as a Wicked Problem: An Analysis of Five Indian NGO Leaders Combating Traffickers.

Commission "Staff Working Document" (2016),[3] and the 2016 UNODC "Global Trafficking in Persons Report".

So, while a common definition of THB is adopted[4] we are aware that the reports reply to different mandates, result from different obligations from the MS to provide data, have different sources, geographical scope, methods and instruments of data and information collection, and use different concepts, or at least terminologies. Additionally, we are also conscious of the fact that the backbone of the reports is the (EU) MS data.

At this level of observation, we are far from harmonization. As an example, let us take the purposes of exploitation, perhaps one out of the three constitutive elements of THB definition that has most changed throughout times (Allain 2014). As a quick reminder, all the instruments in footnote 5 state that the list of the exploitation corresponds to a *minimum* since "National authorities have plenty of scope to broaden the range of exploitative practices to better tailor their legislation to the trafficking situation in their country. In fact, legislators and jurisprudence around the world are continuously reshaping the legal concept of trafficking in persons by including new forms of exploitation in national legal frameworks" (UNODC Annex II 2016c, p. 2).

Maintaining the focus on the statistical dimension, is this relevant? Certainly, as it has a direct impact on national statistics[5] and subsequently, on the overall picture of THB presented in the reports.

With the same impact is the victims' categorization, understood as a division in a system of classification and supported, or not, by the MS.[6] Again, is this relevant? Yes, as again it reflects different legal and also statistical data collection, processing and disseminating metadata systems, with impacts upon (national) statistics.[7]

---

[3] Accompanying the document Report from the Commission to the European Parliament and the Council Report on the progress made in the fight against trafficking in human beings (2016) as required under Article 20 of Directive 2011/36/EU on preventing and combating trafficking in human beings and protecting its victims.

[4] All have as common ground the "Protocol to Prevent, Suppress and Punish Trafficking in Persons Especially Women and Children, supplementing the United Nations Convention against Transnational Organized Crime" (2000). As European agencies, the Eurostat and the Europol and the European Commission reports also make use of the definitions under the "Council of Europe Convention on Action against THB" (2005), and the "Directive 2011/36/EU of the European Parliament and of the Council of 5 April 2011 on preventing and combating trafficking in human beings and protecting its victims, and replacing Council Framework Decision 2002/629/JHA."

[5] In France (Article 225-4-1 of the Penal Code as modified by law n°2013–711 of 5 August 2013), and in The Netherlands (Article 273f of the Dutch Criminal Code) it is considered "*Pimping, sexual assault or abuse*", "*Exploitation of the prostitution*". In Portugal, this is an autonomous crime in the Penal Code (Article 169.°).

[6] The categories used are: *Presumed VoT*—used by Eurostat and European Commission; *Victims/Potential VoT* (comparable to "Presumed")—used by Europol; *Identified VoT by a Relevant authorities*—used by Eurostat and the European Commission; *Identified VoT by State authorities*—used by UNODC.

[7] Europol sources are national competent authorities (law enforcement agencies), whereas the UNODC 2016 report collects core data from state authorities regarding VoT identified by them.

On a brief note, the dimension of victims' categorization would take us to the debate on statistics and state control, Foucault's concept of governmentality (Fried 2014), as well to the debate on the legal and social construction and labeling of victim (Christie 1986; Dignan 2004), or provocatively of "perfect, iconic and deserving victim" (Srikantiah 2007)—statutory language translated in statutory requirements with implications on victim's rights.

The disclaimer is now long, but it acts to recognize that to the questions we all want replies to, such as "What is the profile of THB victims?" "This year there are more victims registered. Is the crime rising?" and "What is the trend as far as the purposes of exploitation?"—examples of the three categories of comparative analyses (HEUNI 2014)—the response must contemplate a metadata prelude.

1.1 All Set

The Europol "Situation Report—Trafficking in Human Beings in the EU" (2016), and the European Commission "Staff Working Document" (2016) present, at the EU MS level, the most recent figures on THB for the time series[8] 2013–2014.

Not going deeper into the EU statistical state of play presented in both reports, the main findings are overall analogous, namely, with reference to:

- the prevalence of EU MS registered Victims of Trafficking (VoT): 65% in the European Commission Document, and 70% in the Europol Report; and,
- the mobility and rotation of registered victims within or between countries.

If also taking into account the 2015 Eurostat' working paper "Trafficking in Human Beings" (time series 2010–2012) used by the European Commission Document as a baseline, as well as its predecessor, the Eurostat's 2013 working paper "Trafficking in Human Beings" (time series 2008–2010), THB is up until 2014 a "European Affair" (Europol 2016). This is described in relation to a clear "(...) consistency in terms of victims' countries of origin, countries of destination,

---

The same is followed by the European Commission, but differs from the previous ones by considering data on presumed + identified VoT (including other sources). Lastly, the Eurostat report in which data sources are the national statistical offices. On a national level, some countries provide data on presumed + identified, while others only on identified. Both have an impact on the size of sample beyond other subsequent issues such the rate of reply per country to each indicator and its variations. Within this last idea we quote UNODC 2016 report "Data on detected victims (total 2012–2015)" was 63,251 and resulted from the reporting of 103 countries. But further disaggregation of victims' data, and also within the time period considered, show that "Reporting from Member States is not uniform. Some countries only provide data for some of the indicators included in the questionnaire." (UNODC 2016b, Annex 1, p. 4). As an example, to the indicator "Citizenship reported" the total was 34,074 and resulted from the reply of 85 countries.

[8]According to OEDC (2007), "A time series is a set of regular time-ordered observations of a quantitative characteristic of an individual or collective phenomenon taken at successive, in most cases equidistant, periods/points of time" (OECD 2007, p. 63).

the forms of exploitation, and the age and gender profile of victims (…)" (European Commission 2016, p. 13).

The same connection between victims' citizenship and regional flows is found in the 2016 UNODC "Global Trafficking in Persons Report" (time series 2012–2014 or most recent), especially seen amongst registered VoT from some Central and Southeastern Europe countries detected in some Western and Southern Europe countries. Although this flow has decreased over the years, "The main origin countries for trafficking victims detected in the EU are other EU countries. In addition, major flows of trafficking also occur within the countries' borders in the form of domestic trafficking" (UNODC 2016a, p. 64).

At a national level (Portugal), similar findings are witnessed by the Observatory on Trafficking in Human Beings from the Portuguese Ministry of Internal Administration (OTSH).[9] As examples to sustain this alignment, let us consider two indicators[10] for the time series 2008–2016:[11]

1. *Percentage of EU MS and of non-EU MS*[12] *registered VoT*.
2. *Number of EU MS and non-EU MS registered citizenship*.

As can be observed in Fig. 1, aside from 2008, between 2009 and 2016 the annual percentage of registers is higher within *EU MS registered VoT* (including national citizens either trafficked domestically or abroad), with an overall average of 69% (*Non-EU MS registered VoT*—31%).

On the other hand, if one observes the *number of reported citizenships*, excluding 2009 and 2010 (but even so, not statistically relevant), a higher number of citizenships is found within *non-EU MS countries* with 70 reported citizenships (*EU MS*—32) (Fig. 2).

In a one-dimensional analysis regarding Finding #1, prevalence of EU MS registered VoT, in Portugal the "European Affair" presents itself in a small set of EU MS citizenships in which the percentage of registered victims is higher if compared to non-EU MS. Additionally, within the set of EU MS citizenships there is a

[9] The OTSH was created in 2008 via the Decree-Law n° 229/2008 of November 27. It is mandated to produce, collect, analyze and disseminate information on THB and other forms of gender violence. Aside other activities, the OTSH is the responsible body for the national monitoring system on THB, but it is not the national official representative for crime and criminal justice statistics—role assumed by the Portuguese Directorate-General for Justice Policy—Ministry of Justice. The OTSH collects disaggregated anonymized data from a network of more than 20 data providers (e.g., Law Enforcement Agencies, Public institutes, NGOs and International organizations).

[10] The sample used in both indicators is the grand total of registered "Presumed VoT" (includes the sum up of "Pending/In Investigation" registers + "Flagged by NGOs/other bodies"), and of registered "Identified VoT" (classified in the monitoring system as "Confirmed VoT by the competent authority"). Not counted, the registers with the classification "Non Confirmed" (by the competent authority), and "Not Considered" (by NGO/other bodies).

[11] Data last updated in August 2017.

[12] In the category "Non-EU MS", EU neighboring countries and third countries are included. We are aware this aggregation is generalist.

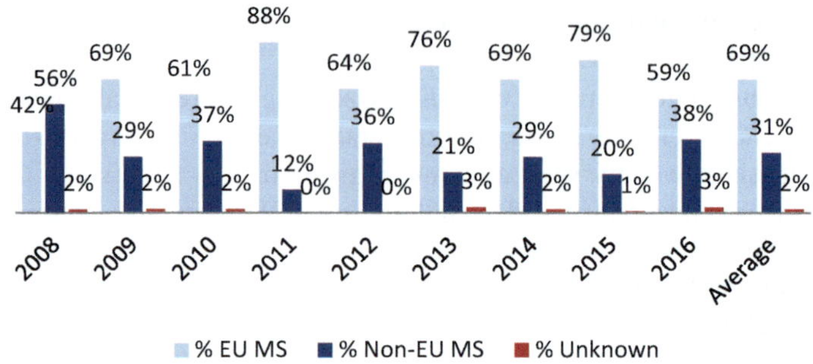

Fig. 1 Percentage of EU MS and non-EU registered VoT (2008–2016). Source of Data: OTSH. Produced by: Rita Penedo

	2008	2009	2010	2011	2012	2013	2014	2015	2016	Total
Nº of EU MS citizenships	2	5	3	2	2	3	5	5	5	32
Nº of Non EU MS citizenships	4	4	3	4	6	10	14	9	16	70
Unknown	1	1	1	2	0	6	3	2	5	21
Total	7	10	7	8	8	19	22	16	26	123

Fig. 2 Number of EU MS and non-EU MS VoT citizenships (2008–2016). Source of Data: OTSH. Produced by: Rita Penedo

recurrence of two EU MS that with a larger number of victims, has an impact on the annual and overall percentage.

But this *fewer countries—more registered VoT* | *more countries—less registered VoT* equation has many complex dimensions to its explanation which from a critical perspective, led us wondering on the state of the "affair".

For the sake of this rational, let us observe 2013, the year with the highest number of Confirmed VoT (n = 150) (Table 1).

If compared with the homologous period, 2013 was an "atypical year" and, as a result, instigated a reorganization of the analysis carried out until that moment. By this we mean that the OTSH looked at the registers beyond the grand total and socio-demographic variables, and self-questioned what was the common denominator to the majority of the registered victims besides sharing the same citizenship? In a straightforward reply, the answer was found in the "Event", seen as a crime of THB.

Going back to Table 1, when we considered the 119 confirmed victims they could not be seen as a sum up, but as units associated to specific events (forgive us for this choice of words as we are talking about persons). In 2013 we found three events: one in which 71 VoT were found, other with 28 VoT, and another one with 15 VoT.

Table 1 2013 EU MS Confirmed VoT description

Year	% of EU MS registered VoT	N° of citizenships
2013	76%	3
Description	From the 76% (Fig. 1), 82% corresponds to 1 citizenship (n = 124)	
	From the 124, 119 are "Confirmed VoT" (majority male—n = 101)	
	The recruitment was a job offer, in some cases by other VoT	
	The victims traveled in group (in some cases couples), by land (van, bus, and taxi/rental car)	
	The exploitation occurred in the same district but in three different contiguous municipalities for the same purpose: THB for labor exploitation in agriculture (olive picking)	
	The main means of control were: withdrawal of personal documentation, control of movements and debt bondage	
	The majority of VoT received assistance (e.g., assisted return to country of origin), but 47 "fled" the site (unknown if whether stayed in Portugal or left the country)	

Source of Data: OTSH
Produced by: Rita Penedo

Consequently, starting from 2014, the OTSH began to analyze the "Person" in connection to the "Event" by typifying this in relation to the number of associated registered victims. Three typologies are used: 1) "Small" (less than 10 VoT), 2) "Medium" (between 10 and 20 VoT), and 3) "Big" (more than 20 VoT).[13]

Going forward, in the 2016 Report (OTSH 2017), the Observatory conducted a simulation exercise, an *alternative scenario*,[14] to see if the "absence" of "Big Events" in a given year(s), would or not maintain the main findings processed and disseminated as a block at a national and European level: the overall *prevalence of Portugal as mainly a destination country, of EU MS victims, from a set group of citizenships, mostly male victims, and trafficked for labor exploitation, in specific territories*.

Aside from the obvious decrease in the annual average rate of change, the simulation exercise also evidenced some variations on the prevalence of certain citizenships, purposes of exploitation and territories, was it not for those "Big Events". But it also led us to two questions and subsequent hypothesis:

1. Do the occurrence of "Big Events" in specific territories corresponds to territories with more events? We need to assess the difference between territories with more victims and territories with more events. They may not be the same and in this sense, we need to inquiry on a long run, what is more disruptive and reflecting a state of social anomie: the number of victims (that "make" annual statistics and headlines), or the number of crimes (maybe with less victims, but more regular over time)?

[13] In the typology of operations/number of victims associated, it is recommended the one presented by UNODC (2014).

[14] For the time series 2011–2016.

2. The categories of the events ("Small", "Medium", and "Big") are fixed in time? The data providers register the victims at the time the crime is reported. But this may or may not coincide with the time of the offense. In most cases it does, but there are others where, for instance, the number of victims associated is registered along 2 or more years as a result of the modus operandi of the network, or because *n* victims fled the site and may be found later on. Consequently, a broader picture is required in the sense that a "Medium" occurrence in a given year can, in a longitudinal analysis, demonstrate to be a "Big Event" (already seen in criminal investigations related to Portugal as a transit country).

From what has been observed, in Portugal "Big Events" are recurrently found in THB for labor exploitation in seasonal agriculture (high-risk sector), where the demand for workforce is higher and thus leading to a higher probability of finding victims often recruited as a group (e.g., 2013 description in Table 1). This "way to do business"—modus operandi—has underneath it, like in any other purpose of THB, push, pull, and facilitating factors (Europol 2016) that need to be simultaneously assess in origin, transit and destination countries and, as such, in the different stages of THB: from recruitment up to the exploitation, and in some cases, even at the ending stage, as according to Europol in what concerns seasonal workers VoT "(…) the exploitative situation is limited in time and victims return to their countries of origin or start a new life at the end of their exploitation (…)" (Europol 2016, p. 26).

Later on we will resume this idea (*exploitation limited in time*), but for now a brief parenthesis.

Typologies applied to countries (origin, transit, and destination) and to stages (the Action in THB definition) are naturally important: they define THB and act as categories to organize and analyze data. However, in practice, they may act in a continuous, fluid manner (Aronowitz 2002) associated to several dimensions, namely, to the structure of the criminal agents and the modus operandi in place. By this we mean that we need to consider the idea of a nonlinear spatiality and temporality of victimization understood as a process/cycle but also as a "(…) material and/or physical and/or psychological (emotional) harm caused by the immediate victimizing event (crime) which can be a single (one-time) (…) [or, and as we will present further on, as a] repeat event (re-victimization, serial or multiple re-victimization)" (Kilchling 2016, p. 14–15). As stated by Makarenko "Although the stages of trafficking appear relatively straightforward, any one chain can take years to complete, and the end of one chain can often act as the first stage of a new chain" (Makarenko 2009, p. 28).

The above recaptures Finding #2: *the mobility and rotation of victims*.

This finding is harder to assess statistically and can be viewed as one of the pieces that explains the difficulties in victims' identification. As presented in the "Research based on case studies of victims of trafficking in human beings in 3 EU Member States, i.e., Belgium, Italy and The Netherlands" (2001): "(…) the high mobility of women periodically moved from one part of Italy to another or between EU countries, [creates] difficulties in measuring this particular target" (Orfano 2001, p. 153), and "The analysis of internal mobility of trafficked women gives remarkable indications on the ever-changing features of the structure of trafficking, of its organisers, and of its victims" (Orfano 2001, p. 172).

To Europol, mobility and rotation is used as a countermeasure to avoid detection (Europol 2016). Subsequently, we question if the concept of Risk applied to THB analysis may fall under the categorization of "Adaptive Risk" as a risk "(…) caused by people that can change their behavior or characteristics in reaction to prevention, protection, response, or recovery measures taken" (US Department of Homeland Security 2010, p. 19)? An example given by Europol (2016) in the analysis of loose networks of THB may reply to the question: "These groups are able to adapt to changing circumstances and quickly respond to new opportunities, shifting their operations to other countries upon detection by law enforcement or if they consider the exploitation to be more profitable elsewhere. The loose structure of the criminal networks thwarts detection, especially of the leaders, even when an operational cell is identified and prosecuted" (Europol 2016, p. 14).

Up to now, the OTSH has primarily analyzed mobility and rotation in the setting of the purpose of exploitation taking as unit the "Person" in relation to the "Event". To illustrate, let us see the 2016 "Big Event" in which out of 22 VoT, 21 where associated to one "Event" in which it was not possible to determine one single district of exploitation (Fig. 3).

As can be seen in Fig. 3,[15] the victims' rotated not only between municipalities of the same district, but also between different districts. The prevalence is especially observed in districts in the south and center of Portugal (Beja, Faro, Santarém and Setúbal), but also between these districts with others in the north of Portugal, namely, between Beja and Santarém with Oporto district.

But we could also evoke the on-an-off trafficking for labor exploitation of Portuguese citizens simultaneously exploited in Portugal and abroad (Spain).

From all the foregoing, *the prevalence of certain EU MS VoT since 2008, the mobility/rotation, the "Person" and the "Event"*, one question emerged in our mind that may reflectively challenge the way we look at the "European (national) Affair". The question is: *"How many victims registered by the Member States of the EU are not actually the same, continuously exploited in one or between several countries (continued victimization), and/or exploited more than once but at different times (revictimization)."*

1.2 First Move: Deadlock

To be honest, this is not a groundbreaking interrogation.

On the first part of the sentence—*How many victims registered by the Member States of the EU are not actually the same…*—that acts as a hypothesis to the second

[15] This event relates to non-EU MS registered VoT, but the modus operandi can be extrapolated to others involving EU MS VoT.

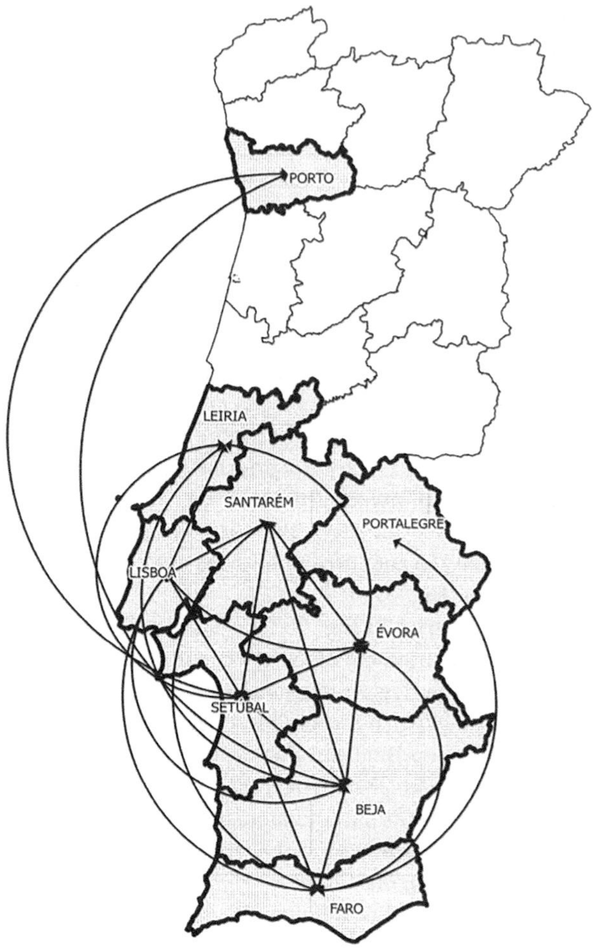

Fig. 3 Mobility of Confirmed VoT in Portugal (2016). Source of Data: OTSH 2017 Report (p. 34). Produced by: Rita Penedo

part, in the final report of the European co-funded project "Tools for the validation and utilization of EU statistics on human trafficking (TrafStat)" (2012–2014) it is stated that within EU, victims "(…) can, and in fact should be, double counted if they are primarily identified in an EU destination country and subsequently referred to or officially received in their EU countries of origin, or any other Member State" (van Dijk et al. 2014, p. 29).

Could this be a part of the explanation for the above overall reported prevalence of victims' citizenships and, consequently, countries' profiles? Probably, as in this scenario, *one plus one does not equal two*.

But to the above, we need to consider (as described) that THB is characterized by a strong mobility and rotation of its victims, and that it thrives from multiples risks that if remain unchanged can result in a higher tendency of former victims to become susceptible to re-trafficking. In both levels lays the question of a likelihood of being double counted, hence the second part of the question: … *continuously exploited in one or between several countries (continued victimization), and/or exploited more than once but at different times (revictimization).*

In an attempt to find some empirical evidence, in 2017 and via the National Rapporteur for Trafficking in Human Beings,[16] the OTSH requested to the Focal Points of the Informal EU Network of National Rapporteurs or Equivalent Mechanisms[17] information on "Presumed" and/or "Identified" VoT registered in their countries—either on their own nationals or foreign citizens, but not Portuguese (other questionnaire annually sent to the Focal Points)—that had mention Portugal as a country of previous exploitation, or as a country of transit.[18]

The result was a deadlock. The data received was insufficient to produce any type of inference, but did it indicate the absence of cases or the non-collection of data? Even so, some countries provided information on cases where Portugal was mention as a previous country of exploitation involving "Presumed" VoT from EU and third countries for the purpose of sexual exploitation, and sexual and labor exploitation, and as a country of recruitment of "Presumed" VoT from a third country.

Concurrently, and with the same aim in mind, the OTSH used two 2016 national occurrences as a case study. They were: (1) Operation *POKHARA*—more than 20 VoT from third countries; (2) A case involving 10 EU MS VoT in the north of Portugal. As sources, the Observatory asked for additional information to the Anti Human Trafficking Unit (UATP) from the Immigration and Border Service, and to the Family Planning Association (APF) Lisbon Multidisciplinary Specialized Team

[16] From the Commission for Citizenship and Gender Equality/Presidency of the Council of Ministries.

[17] Established following Council Conclusions in June 2009. Its role is elaborated in Recital 27 of the Directive 2011/36/EU of the European Parliament and of the Council of 5 April 2011 on preventing and combating trafficking in human beings and protecting its victims, and replacing Council Framework Decision 2002/629/JHA.

[18] The OTSH designed a questionnaire with the following variables: (1) Portugal classification (values: origin, transit, destination); (2) Victims' status (values: presumed or identified); (3) Sex (values: Female, Male, Unknown); (4) Type of exploitation (values: Sexual, Forced Labour, Domestic Servitude, Forced Begging/use for begging, Criminal Activities, Removal of organs, Other, Unknown); (5) Age (open); (6) VoT citizenship (open); (7) Exploiters' citizenship (open).

(for Operation *POKHARA*),[19] and to APF's North Multidisciplinary Specialized Team (for the EU MS VoT case).[20]

Very briefly, the results were:

1. Operation *POKHARA*—several victims indicated that the migratory process initiated in their country of origin (same to the victims' citizenship), having as final destination Portugal. In these situations, some victims reported a third country as transit, while others reported EU MS countries (especially in cases where the means of transportation was airplane). Others reported that the country of destination were other countries (EU MS and others) where they settled for different periods of time (the longest 6 years and the lesser 4 months). In these cases, two VoT self-reported analogous labor situations to the ones experienced in Portugal, in other EU MS countries.
2. Case involving 10 EU MS VoT in the north of Portugal—two VoT reported this to be the first situation of exploitation (lack of wages, threats, body offenses…) although working as seasonal agriculture migrants for several years. The remaining VoT (from three family aggregates) self-reported similar situations in their country of origin. The alleged situations were not reported to law enforcement or other professionals due to lack of sense of empowerment of their rights. While illustrative, once again the results do not allow us to further extrapolations.

Not prepared to declare endgame, it is our ambition to further explore the above question that as an (un)interrupted cycle can figuratively portray THB as an hourglass. The objective is to reflect on what may rest inside the bulbs, and assesses what factors/forces act upon the rotation movement and produces a nonlinear spatiality and temporality of (re)victimization.

[19] Operation *POKHARA*—template with the following variables: (1) Country of Origin; (2) Date of departure; (3) Means of transportation; (4) Country of transit; (5) Means of transportation (4 and 5 to be multiple as much as necessary); (6) Date of entrance in Portugal; (7) Open field to observations. Case in the north of Portugal/EU MS VoT: qualitative information to the following questions: (1) If had work in another country (which?); (2) In which economic activity; (3) Where the working conditions similar to the ones experienced in Portugal; (4) If yes, was that experience shortly after coming to Portugal or did the person return (to where and for how long?); (5) Was the job offer in both situation made by the same person(s); (6) In the previous country and if in similar situation to the one reported in Portugal, was the person contacted or was contacted by any professional (Law Enforcement, NGO, Embassy), and if yes in what way and purpose; (7) If there had been no identification in Portugal was the person to remain in Portugal, working in the same place or intended (was told that) was moving to another region (either in Portugal or abroad).

[20] As the reply to the questions on (a) and (b) depended on self-reported victimization, the OTSH discussed with the Multidisciplinary Teams the best way to insure that this need for data did not result in secondary victimization. As such the information was gathered in several moments along the duration of assistance, in a case per case situation evaluation.

2 THB as an Hourglass

While reflecting on this approach, at first it seemed contradictory to use this image as an hourglass is an instrument for measuring time, a limited amount of time that in its final drop indicates the end. On the other hand, in a more symbolic approach, "(…) the flow of the grains of sand can be compared to the unfolding of all the possibilities included in a cycle of manifestation" (Schuon 2009, p. 4).

In an illustrative manner, the propose paradigm is presented below in Fig. 4.

The subsequent reflection is an exploratory exercise and as such, we will display more triggering questions than replies.

From Fig. 4, and step by step, here are our thoughts:

A – Time and space/socio-ecological setting; B – Stage "Non-Victimization"/ socio-ecological setting; and C – Stage "Victimization"

According to Europol (2016), quoting a UNODC Report (2014) "There are a number of social and economic conditions which influence the actions of both victims and exploiters and facilitate the occurrence of THB. Among these, several push factors are found in the local environment of victims and traffickers, since they often share the same national and cultural background" (Europol 2016, p. 10).

The above sentence displays an introduction to the principles of an ecological approach to crime—contributions of Social Disorganization Theory, from the early body of work from the Chicago School, to Shaw and Mckay, to Bursik and Grasmick, among others (Rhineberger 2003).

We will not revise these contributions, or its critics. Nonetheless, and in a simple manner, the idea is that within the ecological systems (interdependent levels, from individual to societal[21]), some social changes in a given space and time, may or may not act as threats to certain groups of persons and territories, making them (or not) more vulnerable to victimization and in this case to THB (Daniel-Wrabetz, Penedo 2015).

This is the matrix in which the relation between environment and behavior is a fundamental analytical variable, namely, in situations of a breakdown of institutional, group or community ties that act or not as means of social control, impeding or allowing certain criminal or deviant practices to appear. It is in this milieu, and considering the three main agents (the offenders, the victims, and the "clients/beneficiaries") (Vieira et al. 2008) that the change from Stage "Non Victimization" to Stage "Victimization", its sub-process of continued victimization, and the Stage of "Revictimization" is to be analyzed. The Stage of "Non Victimization" is presented as a theoretical dimension, as some experiences of THB have before other situations

[21] Individual ("personal history factors that increase the likelihood of becoming a victim or perpetrator of violence"); Relationship ("relationships that may increase the risk of experiencing violence as a victim or perpetrator"); Community ("settings in which social relationships occur and seeks to identify the characteristics of these settings that are associated with becoming victims or perpetrators of violence"); Societal ("broad societal factors that help create a climate in which violence is encouraged or inhibited") (CDC 2002).

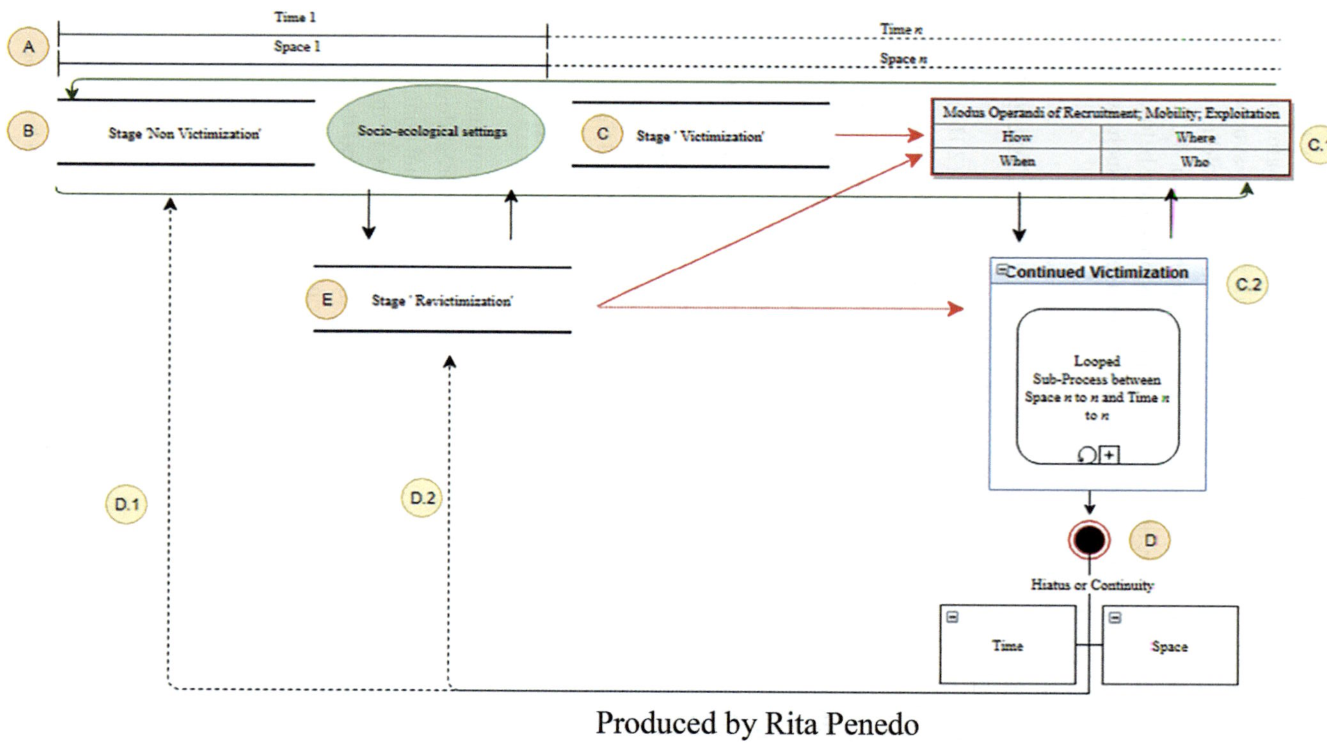

Fig. 4 THB as an hourglass. Produced by: Rita Penedo

of (different) victimization, or at least of vulnerability, that may act upon THB victimization (Couto 2012).

C – Stage "Victimization"/C.1 – Modus Operandi

When observing the Stage "Victimization" we have considered as pertinent the analysis of the modus operandi associated to Recruitment, Mobility and Exploitation as main dimensions. In each, we need to ask: How? Where? When? Who?

The *How* and *Where* can be closely associated to "*Who*". One way to go is to analyze the (previous) relation between victims and offenders/recruiters/exploiters—what is the time and space of social interaction? On one hand, to consider the role of families/isolated individuals in THB offenses, and on the other the role of organized criminal groups, its diversity and the subsequent myriad of models to analyze them—models focusing on the activity, on the structure, or on the social, cultural and historical conditions that facilitate organized crime activity (Le 2012).

To Le (2012), the most comprehensive typology is presented in a UNOCD report (2002) that building upon ten variables (structure; size, violence; ethnic and social identity; activities;[22] trans-border operations; corruption; political influence; cross-over between licit and illicit activities; and cooperation with other organized crime groups), establishes five models: (1) standard hierarchy, (2) regional hierarchy, (3) clustered hierarchy, (4) core group and (5) criminal network.

The description of *How* and *Where* takes us to the type of mobility (also associated to *Who*), in which we propose the following typology: (a) Intra-EU mobility (domestic; intra-regional—short or long distance); and (b) Extra-EU (transregional; transcontinental).[23] The dilation or circumscription in *time* and *space* is connected to the purpose of exploitation, and to the success of the offense or in the eventuality of Stage "Revictimization" to the re-offense in situations that the offenders are (partially or totally) the same.

The *exploitation* may occur in space 1 or the other, but definitely in other time. The *When* (in recruitment) can depend on the type of the "Event" (the size of the "Event" as already described), and to the purpose of exploitation.

C – Stage "Victimization"/C.1 – Modus Operandi/C.2 – Continued Victimization

Continued victimization should be considered as a sub-looped process, linked to the modus operandi of the offense/offenders. It has in its core the mobility/rotation of victims and should be considered as an indicator of the dynamic or patterns of criminal behavior and of social disruption (facilitating factors as described by Europol).

Following the above, we recall the question of the difference between territories with more victims and territories with more events. This evokes the concept of hot

[22] In this variable, we evoke the concept of polycriminality presented in the Europol report (2016).

[23] According to UNODC (2016a), the categories of trafficking flows are considered: "**short-distance** trafficking flows with victims trafficked within national borders or between neighbouring countries; **medium-distance** flows between two countries that do not share a border and with the border of the origin country less than 3500 kilometres away from the closest border of the destination country; and **long-distance** flows in which the border of the origin country is farther than 3500 kilometres away from the closest border of the destination country" (UNODC 2016a, p. 42).

spots, important to crime analysis as a predictive indicator to the *where* and *when* continued victimization and revictimization may (re)occur. While fundamental to the development of intervention strategies, it may also skew interventions and the perception of risk territories and sectors.

In abstract we assume that continued victimization between spaces and times will occur more easily in short distance flows, where the spaces can more easily overlap. At this moment we recall the idea of interpreting the countries typologies (origin, transit, and destination) with more fluidity. (Continued) victimization may be identified for instance in Portugal and abroad. Both are "destination countries" if in this example we are referring to foreigner victims.

One important issue is the need to separate what is continued victimization (mobility and rotation) and what is redistribution more associated to the arrival to space *n* (acting as a hub) and relocation into several sites (Europol 2011, 2016).

D – End/D.1 – End/Stage "Non-Victimization"/socio-ecological setting

By intervention of professionals (law enforcement agencies, NGOs and others), through victims' escape (alone or with help from a third party), by offenders' release (limited exploitation in time—Europol).

Although not explored in this scheme, a call of attention to another type of victimization that may happen at this moment. We are referring to secondary victimization[24] that has an impact on increasing victims' vulnerability and consequently with an (in)direct connection to revictimization.

At this stage, a special attention to the intervention policies in place on the effectiveness of victims' protection, namely, social policies of reintegration and strategies of assisted return, in which a coordinated approach between or within a country is paramount.

There may be a spatiality and temporality hiatus or continuity, and considering once again, the ecological setting in which the "Person" is it may be possible that the same or different offenders "(…) victimize the same target more quickly in the wake of a first victimization if something about the target has changed (a form of temporarily heightened risk heterogeneity)" (Farrell and Sousa 2011, p. 232).

D.2 – End; E – Stage "Revictimization"/socio-ecological setting

As a rule, victimization studies essentially address the victim's personal characteristics (victim-blaming). The present paradigm reflects the personal but also the structural (ecological) factors that if maintained may influence a second victimization situation.

In this scenario it will be essential to analyze: the period that mediated both experiences; the spatial change or permanence that is, if there was a return to the country/region of origin, or spatial permanence (for instance, at the site of exploitation).

In a loop analysis, again the assessment of the modus operandi associated to recruitment, mobility and exploitation, and the *How*, *When*, *Where* and *Who*. These

[24] Understood as the "(…) re-traumatization and the consolidation of primary damages and their consequences which can be reinforced or fortified through relatives and/or social surroundings, through various instances of social control (police, criminal justice system) or through the media" (Kilchling 2016, pp. 14–15).

last two, at a revictimization stage, are quite relevant in the sense of the observation of the relationship between victims and offender(s), especially if they are family members, community members, or elements that usually recruit in a given space.

On an ending, but quite important note, the reflection that "The term 're-trafficking' is a problematic one, and wider debate within research on trafficking is needed to reach a common understanding of the term and to assist accurate comparison between data sets, along with facilitating improved case management. It is difficult to determine at which stage a person can be understood to have experienced re-trafficking" (Jobe 2010, p. 17). Could the same logic be applied to (continued) victimization?

From our perspective, the beginning and end are interconnected if in its basis one considers problematics such social (re)integration, (continued) threats posed by traffickers (being families or groups), and as Jobe describes quoting Davies "(…) the economically driven desire to migrate and a dearth of safe migration options" (Jobe 2010, p. 16).

3 Conclusions

As a sort of conclusion, on a broader scope if data would sustain or decline our questioning, it could also act as a proxy indicator to a critical assessment of:

- Harmonized Monitoring Systems—viewed as methodological settings for the production, collection, treatment and dissemination/sharing of data and information with the objective to better develop and support evidenced based policies and of,
- Prevention policies and national and transnational referral mechanisms—understood as the stages of flagging, identification, (return) assistance and reintegration of victims in the sense that "(...) vulnerability to trafficking may not disappear even after the assistance intervention and its different supports by professionals, especially in situations where they were: structural factors → unemployment, (risk of) poverty or of social exclusion, conflicts (...) [and / or] personal factors → familiar, cognitive, additives, among others".[25]

For now, and open to debate, a first approach to the question *How many victims registered by the Member States of the EU are not actually the same, continuously exploited in one or between several countries (continued victimization), and/or exploited more than once but at different times (revictimization)*?

Acknowledgements This chapter is supported by the Observatory on Trafficking in Human Beings work. The author is gratefully for the helpful comments and suggestions of those who comment it. A special note of appreciation to: Nuno Almeida for the several hours of joint brainstorming,

[25] Non-official translation.

and to Rui Belchior for his support and revision. Finally, a special thanks to the Book Editors for the kind invitation and continuous interest in Human Trafficking research.

References

Aebi M (2008) Measuring the influence of statistical counting rules on cross-national differences in recorded crime. In: Armomma K, Heiskanin M (eds) Justice Systems in Europe and North America 1995–2004. European Institute for Crime Prevention and Control, affiliated with the United Nations (HEUNI) Publication Series 55, Helsinki, pp 200–218. http://www.heuni.fi/material/attachments/heuni/reports/6KkrHLurn/Pages_200-218.pdf

Allain J (2014) No effective trafficking definition exists: domestic implementation of the palermo protocol. Alb Gov Law Rev 14:112–142. http://www.albanygovernmentlawreview.org/articles/vol07_1/7.1.112-allain.pdf

Aronowitz A (2002) The United Nations global programme against trafficking in human beings: research and lessons learned. Int J Comp Appl Crim Just 26(2):258–275. https://www.researchgate.net/publication/232944240_The_United_Nations_global_programme_against_trafficking_in_human_beings_Research_and_lessons_learned

Boutellier JCJ (2000) Editorial. Eur J Crim Policy Res 8(1) https://www.wodc.nl/binaries/ej0001-fulltext_tcm28-75360.pdf

Centers for Disease Control and Prevention (2002) The social-ecological model: a framework for violence prevention. https://www.cdc.gov/violenceprevention/pdf/sem_framewrk-a.pdf

Christie N (1986) Ideal victim. In: Fattah EA (ed) From crime policy to victim policy. Palgrave Macmillan, pp 17–30. https://page-one.live.cf.public.springer.com/pdf/preview/10.1007/978-1-349-08305-3_2

Couto D (2012) Tráfico de Seres Humanos: Perceções sociais, percursos de vitimação e de sobrevivência. Tese de Doutoramento em Psicologia, Área de Conhecimento em Psicologia da Justiça. Orientação Professora Doutora Carla Machado, Professor Doutor Rui Abrunhosa Gonçalves, Professora Doutora Carla Martins. Universidade do Minho. Escola de Psicologia

Daniel-Wrabetz J, Penedo R (2015) Trafficking in human beings in time and space. A socio-ecological perspective. In: Guia M (ed) The illegal business of human trafficking. Springer, Cham, pp 1–19

Del Frate A (2010) Crime and criminal justice statistics challenges. In: Harrendorf S et al (eds) International Statistics on Crime and Justice. European Institute for Crime Prevention and Control, affiliated with the United Nations (HEUNI) Publication Series 64. Helsinki, pp 167–175. https://www.unodc.org/documents/data-and-analysis/Crime-statistics/International_Statistics_on_Crime_and_Justice.pdf

Dignan J (2004) Understanding victims and restorative justice. McGraw-Hill Education, Open University Press. https://books.google.pt/books/about/Understanding_Victims_And_Restorative_Ju.html?id=t9OpffV0Hb8C&redir_esc=y

European Commission (2016) Commission Staff Working Document Accompanying the document Report from the Commission to the European Parliament and the Council Report on the progress made in the fight against trafficking in human beings (2016) as required under Article 20 of Directive 2011/36/EU on preventing and combating trafficking in human beings and protecting its victims, Brussels, 16.5.2016, SWD(2016) 159 final. https://ec.europa.eu/anti-trafficking/sites/antitrafficking/files/commission_staff_working_document.pdf

European Institute for Crime Prevention and Control, affiliated with the United Nations (HEUNI) (2014) European Sourcebook of Crime and Criminal Justice Statistics 2014 Fifth edition. Publication Series No. 80. Helsinki, Finland. http://www.heuni.fi/material/attachments/heuni/reports/qrMWoCVTF/HEUNI_report_80_European_Sourcebook.pdf

Europol (2011) Trafficking in Human Beings in the European Union. Knowledge Product. O8 OC Networks in the South-East European Sphere O2 Analysis and Knowledge. The Hague, 1 September 2011. File NO: 2565-84 https://www.europol.europa.eu/node/468

Europol (2016) Situation Report – Trafficking in Human Beings in the EU. The Hague, February 2016. Document Ref No: 765175. https://www.europol.europa.eu/publications-documents/trafficking-in-human-beings-in-eu

EUROSTAT (2013) Trafficking in human beings. Population and social conditions. Collection: methodologies and working papers. Eurostat. European Union. http://ec.europa.eu/anti-trafficking/sites/antitrafficking/files/trafficking_in_human_beings_-_dghome-eurostat_en_1.pdf

EUROSTAT (2015) Trafficking in human beings. Population and social conditions, statistical working papers. Eurostat. European Union. http://ec.europa.eu/anti-trafficking/sites/antitrafficking/files/eurostat_report_on_trafficking_in_human_beings_-_2015_edition_0.pdf

Farrell G, Sousa W (2011) Repeat victimization and hot spots: the overlap and its implications for crime control and problem-oriented policing. Crime Prev Stud 12:221–240. https://www.researchgate.net/publication/28575337_Repeat_victimization_and_hot_spots_The_overlap_and_its_implication_for_crime_control_and_problem-oriented_policing

Fried S (2014) Quantify this: statistics, the State, and Governmentality. A Thesis submitted to the Faculty of the Graduate School of Arts and Sciences of Georgetown University in partial fulfillment of the requirements for the degree of Master of Arts in Communication, Culture, and Technology, Washington, DC. https://repository.library.georgetown.edu/bitstream/handle/10822/709738/Fried_georgetown_0076M_12673.pdf;sequence=1

Jobe A (2010) The causes and consequences of re-trafficking – evidence from the IOM Human Trafficking Database. International Organization for Migration, Genebra. http://publications.iom.int/system/files/pdf/causes_of_retrafficking.pdf

Kilchling M (2016) Migrants as victims: victimological perspectives of human smuggling and human trafficking. In: Freedom from Fear Magazine Migrant Deadlock - The Abyss of Civilization. Issue n. 12 June 2016. United Nations Interregional Crime and Justice Research Institute and Max Planck Institute, pp 13–19. https://www.mpicc.de/files/pdf3/F3_Magazine_12_Kilchling_migrants_as_victims.pdf

Le V (2012) Organised crime typologies: structure, activities and conditions. Int J Criminol Sociol 2012(1):121–131. http://www.lifescienceglobal.com/pms/index.php/ijcs/article/view/447

Maguire M (2012) Criminal statistics and the construction of crime. In: Maguire M et al (eds) Oxford handbook of criminology, Chapter 8, vol 5th ed. Oxford University Press, pp 206–244. https://www.researchgate.net/publication/265082400_Criminal_Statistics_and_the_Construction_of_Crime

Makarenko T (2009) Organized crime or crimes organized? Isolating and identifying actors in the human trafficking chain. In: Jonsson A (ed) Human trafficking and human security. Routledge, pp 26–47

Observatory on Trafficking in Human Beings (2017) Tráfico de Seres Humanos – Relatório 2016. Observatory on trafficking in human beings. Ministry of Internal Administration. http://www.otsh.mai.gov.pt/Recursos/Pages/default.aspx

Orfano I (2001) Country report – Italy. In: Research based on case studies of victims of trafficking in human beings in 3 EU Member States, i.e. Belgium, Italy and The Netherlands. European Commission, DG Justice and Home Affairs Hippokrates JAI/2001/HIP/023, pp 125–218

Organisation for Economic Co-operation and Development (2007) Data and metadata reporting and presentation handbook. https://www.oecd.org/std/37671574.pdf

Rhineberger GM (2003) Social disorganization, disorder, social cohesion, informal controls, and crime: a reformulation and test of systemic social disorganization theory. A Dissertation Submitted to the Faculty of The Graduate College in partial fulfillment of the requirements for the Degree of Doctor of Philosophy Department of Sociology Western Michigan University Kalamazoo, Michigan. UMI Number: 3123765. http://scholarworks.wmich.edu/cgi/viewcontent.cgi?article=2275&context=dissertations

Schuon F (2009) The Symbolism of the Hourglas. Explanatory notes by editor James S. Cutsinger to World Wisdom's 2009 new edition of the book, pp 1–7. http://www.frithjofschuon.info/uploads/pdfs/articles/117.pdf

Srikantiah J (2007) Perfect Victims and Real Survivors: The iconic victim in domestic human trafficking law. Boston Univ Law Rev 87:157–211. http://www.policeprostitutionandpolitics.com/pdfs_all/Trafficking%20All%20/Law%20Journal%20and%20Academic%20NGO%20UN%20%20Articles%20on%20Trafficking%20All-%20positive%20and%20negative/Law%20Journal%20%20Academic%20NGO%20UN%20Articles%20Neutral/2007%20Boston%20Law%20Review%20trafficking.pdf

United Nations Office on Drugs and Crime (2002) Results of a pilot survey of forty selected organized criminal groups in sixteen countries. Global Programme against Transnational Organized Crime. https://www.unodc.org/pdf/crime/publications/Pilot_survey.pdf

United Nations Office on Drugs and Crime (2014) Global report on trafficking in persons, United Nations publication, Sales No. E.14.V.10, 2014. https://www.unodc.org/documents/data-and-analysis/glotip/GLOTIP_2014_full_report.pdf

United Nations Office on Drugs and Crime (2016a) Global report on trafficking in persons 2016. United Nations publication, Sales No. E.16.IV.6, Vienna. http://www.unodc.org/documents/data-and-analysis/glotip/2016_Global_Report_on_Trafficking_in_Persons.pdf

United Nations Office on Drugs and Crime (2016b) Annex I: Methodology and data coverage. In: Global Report on Trafficking in Persons 2016. United Nations publication, Sales No. E.16.IV.6, Vienna. http://www.unodc.org/documents/data-and-analysis/glotip/GLOTIP16_Annex_I_Methodology.pdf

United Nations Office on Drugs and Crime (2016c) Annex II: The definition of trafficking in persons and the mandate for the Global Report. In: Global Report on Trafficking in Persons 2016. United Nations publication, Sales No. E.16.IV.6, Vienna. http://www.unodc.org/documents/data-and-analysis/glotip/Annex_II_-_Definition_and_mandate.pdf

United States Department of Homeland Security (2010) Risk Steering Committee DHS Risk Lexicon 2010 Edition. https://www.dhs.gov/xlibrary/assets/dhs-risk-lexicon-2010.pdf

van Dijk J et al (2014) Counting what counts: tools for the validation and utilization of Eu statistics on human trafficking. In: Final report of the TrafStat project (HOME/2011/ISEC/AG/THB/4000001960). INTERVICT/Universitat Autònoma de Barcelona. https://www.researchgate.net/publication/279177352_Counting_What_Counts_Tools_for_the_Validation_and_Utilization_of_EU_Statistics_on_Human_Trafficking

Vieira A et al (2008) Roteiro para a Construção de um Sistema de Monitorização sobre o Tráfico de Mulheres para Fins de Exploração Sexual. Projeto Cooperação-Acção-Investigação-Mundivisão. Direção-Geral de Administração Interna, Lisboa

Von Hofer H (2000) Crime statistics as constructs: the case of Swedish Rape Statistics. Eur J Crim Policy Res 8(1):77–89. https://www.wodc.nl/binaries/ej0001-fulltext_tcm28-75360.pdf

Rita Penedo (rpenedo@otsh.mai.gov.pt). Sociologist. In 2006, she joined the Ministry of Internal Affairs in the first national project on trafficking in persons. In 2010, she became a Consultant in the former General-Directorate of Home Affairs where she also assumed the role of National Focal Point in the European Crime Prevention Network. She was also a member of the Board of the Portuguese Association of Sociology. Since August 2013, she is the Director of the Observatory on Trafficking in Human Beings/Portuguese Ministry of Home Affairs, representing Portugal in several European forums, namely, in the European Commission Informal Group of National Rapporteurs and Equivalent Mechanisms on Trafficking in Human Beings jointly with the National Rapporteur on Trafficking in Human Beings.

The Formal Institutions of Control and the Victims of Human Trafficking: From Frequency to Impunity

Maria João Guia

Abstract In this chapter, I will reflect upon a criminological and victimological approach to human trafficking victims. I will question how the formal institutions of control may contribute to the failure of the processes of human trafficking and how that may influence the behaviour of the victim, leading to their loss of trust in the judicial system. The aim of this chapter is to enhance reflections to help the understanding of the failure of convictions in human trafficking cases, mainly because of the refusal of victims to be witnesses in these cases. I will also analyse the pyramid of justice and the selection of information lately appreciated in court. My main conclusion reveals that victims of human trafficking lack confidence in the state system, not only because of already studied factors but also after witnessing system failures. Some also lack knowledge of the formal institutions of control that will influence the whole process.

1 Introduction

Crime and the science that studies it (*criminology*) were objects of speculation until roughly the nineteenth century, at which point a scientific approach emerged (the French anthropologist Paul Topinard[1] has been quoted as the first user of the term 'criminology' in the nineteenth century). For many years, and until the explanations

[1] The term *criminology*, according to Dias and Andrade (2013), was first used in 1879 in the context of the formulation of the causes and consequences of crime (evoking Aristotle and Thomas More, among others, Machado 2008; Wilson 2015).

M. J. Guia (✉)
Ratio Legis - Center of Research and Development of Legal Sciences of the Universidade Autónoma de Lisboa [Project: Corpus Delicti - Studies in Transnational Organized Criminality], Lisboa, Portugal
e-mail: maria.joao.guia@ij.uc.pt

A. M. Rodrigues, M. J. Guia (eds.), *New Forms of Human Trafficking*,
https://doi.org/10.1007/978-3-031-39732-5_12

from the field of behavioural sciences, explanations for why crimes were committed were linked to paranormal phenomena and largely attributed to magic, witchcraft or other elements difficult (if not impossible) to explain. Sciences that study human composition and behaviour (biology, psychology and even psychiatry, just to mention a few) have remitted to individual personality traits many of the motivations for committing crimes, which have allowed the design of treatment programmes for criminals without dissociating themselves from their action in society. Reflection on crime remained for many years centred on crime and aggression, leaving the victims on a lower level of importance.

The rights of victims of crimes have not always been affirmed as a priority of criminology studies. In fact, criminology studies, as the name implies, have sought to focus on the issues of crime, their causes and their explanations. Only at a later stage did the interest in the study of the victim begin to reveal itself, and to some extent by the factors with which it could influence the commission of the crime. From there, a line of research focusing on the victim as an object of study has proliferated and deepened; not only the studies but also the political concerns of states, which, in addition to the repressive and persecutory role of the aggressors, also began to consider the role of the victims of crimes, their rights and the gaps that had previously been relegated to a lower level, leaving the victim forgotten. Of course, the impetus given to specific movements of victims has meant that the pressure on states has been more than rewarded by measures taken in favour of certain victims.

In Europe, however, Directive 2012/29/EU of the European Parliament and of the Council of 25 October 2012, currently under discussion for further updating, the rights of victims of crime have been standardised and the effect has been extended to all victims. It is important to point out that, in the pyramid of justice, the successive stages that find the victim as the first interlocutor, in the preliminary stages of the investigation, imply the selection and/or loss of information until justice is applied in a subsequent phase. In this sense, the formal institutions of control have a fundamental role that can prove to be either very positive or an obstacle to the operationalisation of the various stages of justice.

In this brief chapter, I will address the case of victims of human trafficking, highlighting the specificities of the situation with regard to all other victims, and the search for a hypothesis-making exercise in which certain state staff with purely administrative functions or professionals considered irrelevant in the enforcement of justice may have a positive or negative influence—thus, where they act as key causes of the success/failure of certain crime-processes and where we easily perceive the explanation of the reasons underlying the complete collapse of the application of justice.

2 Criminology, Victimology and the Victims

'The concept of crime: a historical conglomeration of legal, ethical, religious stereotypes and sociological factors—is not a univocal concept' (Dias and Andrade 2013, p. 65). The study of crime,[2] although transversal to several areas of knowledge, has been the object of study of criminology, having gone through different phases of analysis. In fact, criminology seeks to reflect on crime, its causes and its contexts, appreciating not only the endogenous factors influencing the individual who committed the crime but also the social environment that involves such a practice and which contextualises the conduct of the criminal behaviour. The different epochs and approaches of the study of crime can be outlined briefly in the triptych 'aggressor-victim-act'. Thus, not only did criminology address the problem of crime but it also opened a space for a sub-area of criminology to emerge from the interest in understanding the victim's behaviour.

Victimology was, therefore, constructed as the science that deals with the study of the victim of crime in the context of this triple unfolding of the criminal fact. It aims to study the personal characteristics of the victim (biological, psychological, social) and all others that may allow the study of the individual as a victim of the criminal act. This does not mean putting the responsibility for the criminal act on the victim but in understanding what makes one a victim of a crime from social, psychological and legal perspectives in a very simple appreciation.

The study of victimology[3] has been attributed to Benjamin Mendelsohn,[4] as well as other authors such as Hans von Hentig, Marvin Wolfgang and Ernest Roesner. Mendelsohn listed five categories of victims of crime, starting from the ideal victim to the victim as offender. With regard to the weighting and application of penalties, victims were divided into three groups, from the innocent victim to the guilty victim. Von Hentig, for his part, presented a classification of potentially aggressive victims, including the young, the elderly, the mentally ill, the immigrants and those from minorities, as they present a certain characteristic of disadvantage, among other classifications, as referred by the author.

---

[2] Article 1 of the Portuguese Code of Criminal Procedure states that '(a) "Crime" means the set of premises on which the enforcement of a criminal penalty or a security measure depends on the agent'. I will use the Portuguese references to frame some of the arguments.

[3] Historically, a series of legislation could be enumerated at the stage of victimisation that provided for reparation of damages to the victim. This is the case of the Ur-Nammu Code, the Hammurabi Code, the Koran, the Manu Code, the Law of the XII Tables, Mosaic Legislation (elaborated by Moses), Talmudic Law and Roman Law (Spolon and Viana 2016).

[4] Benjamin Mendelsohn (1900–1998) was a Romanian lawyer and a naturalised Israeli professor of criminology at the Hebrew University of Jerusalem who was exiled in the United States of America. He presented the communication 'A New Horizon in Biopsychosocial Science—Victimology' in 1947, advancing the idea that the victim would have to be studied in more detail and with more rigour, rather than being a mere appendage throughout the study of the criminal fact. Therefore, many authors point this fact as a milestone for victimology to becoming an autonomous domain of studies.

The 'modern perspective of the victim' (Santos 2014, p. 53), however, focuses the heart of the debate on the first moment of the victim's/witness testimony and also how the victims deal with the formal institutions of control (and how they are managed), instead of mainly focusing on the intrinsic/objective qualities attributed to the victim, as previously referred. To appreciate the computation of this analysis, it is important to frame the international (and national) conventions that have been published in this area and have contributed to focusing the discourse on the victim. And for that purpose, we will use the human trafficking crime victims as an example.

2.1 The Main Legal Framework on Human Trafficking Crime

The UN Declaration of 1985[5] has been a pioneering document on this subject,[6] and it would be complemented by the Council Framework Decision 2001/220/JHA of 15 March 2001 (no longer in force), the Stockholm Program 2009[7] and Article 82 of the Treaty of Lisbon,[8] as well as Resolution 2011/C 187/01 of 10 June 2011[9] and the Communication from the Commission to Parliament[10] COM (2011) 274 Brussels, 18.5.2011, aimed at strengthening the rights of victims in the European Union (EU). Most recently, Directive 2012/29/EU laid down rules on the rights, support and protection of victims of crime. Victims of human trafficking had specific recommendations published in 2004, with, for instance, the issuing of a residence permit in the country of exploitation.[11]

[5] UN Resolution 40/34 of 29 November 1985, 'Declaration of the Basic Principles of Justice Relating to Victims of Crime and Abuse of Power'.

[6] The Annex of the Declaration of Basic Principles of Justice for Victims of Crime and Abuse of Power (the UN Resolution No. 40/34) defines in para. a) 'Victims' means persons who, individually or collectively, have suffered harm, including physical or mental injury, emotional suffering, economic loss or substantial impairment of their fundamental rights, through acts or omissions that are in violation of criminal laws operative within Member States, including those laws proscribing criminal abuse of power.

[7] Stockholm Program (2009) 'An open and secure Europe serving and protecting citizens'.

[8] Article 82 of the Treaty of Lisbon '2. To the extent necessary to facilitate the mutual recognition of judgments and judicial decisions and police and judicial cooperation in criminal matters with a cross-border dimension, the European Parliament and the Council, by means of directives adopted in accordance with the ordinary legislative procedure, may lay down minimum rules. These minimum rules take into account the differences between Member States' traditions and legal systems. These minimum rules shall cover: (...) (c) The rights of victims of crime'.

[9] Resolution 2011/C 187/01 of 10 June 2011 on a road map for strengthening the rights and protection of victims, in particular in criminal proceedings (known as the 'Budapest Road Map').

[10] Communication from the Commission to the European Parliament, the Council, the European Economic and Social Committee and the Committee of the Regions—Reinforcing victims' rights in the EU Brussels, 18.5.2011 COM (2011) 274 final.

[11] Council Directive 2004/81/EC of 29 April 2004 on the residence permit issued to third-country nationals who are victims of trafficking in human beings or who have been the subject of an action to facilitate illegal immigration, who cooperate with the competent authorities.

Any change in the paradigm regarding how crime came to be seen as a subject not only of the person affected by it but also, and above all, by the state[12] that assumed it with 'growing political-criminal recognition' (Santos 2016, p. 133) implied that the attention given to the victim proliferated. This was also motivated by the fact that a disproportionate focus on the aggressors/traffickers was to the detriment of the victims, who were held to play the 'leading role' in criminal law (since, in most cases, without them the criminal proceedings would not even begin).

It is well known that the more organised victim movements in certain areas have propelled different forces to guarantee more rights to particular types of victims. However, this has been to the detriment of others who, over a period of time, have not seen any improvement in their circumstances.

This is reflected, for example, in more frequent violence against women (especially domestic violence, but not only) and the way in which victims became hierarchised since these victims have access to all the rights while others do not (depending on the crimes that would have harmed them).

The Istanbul Convention is an example of this greater reflection on violence against women, which in Portugal has led to the criminalisation of three new types of crime.[13] Indeed, the problem of violence against women in the EU has been of majour concern. The results of the most comprehensive EU-wide survey were published in 2014 by the EU Agency for Fundamental Rights.[14] They showed a serious problem: 42,000 interviews were conducted with women from 28 Member States, with the main findings showing that 1 in 10 women has been the victim of some form of sexual violence since the age of 15; 1 in 20 has been violated; 1 in 5 has suffered some form of physical and/or sexual violence perpetrated by a current or former partner; and only 14% reported these crimes.

In this work, I intend to deal specifically with victims of human trafficking so I will firstly analyse the crime of human trafficking, seeking to identify the characteristics and difficulties experienced by these victims, and then cross into the premises of the formal institutions of control. This analysis will allow us to understand the extent to which system failure can result from the silent elements of the same system.

---

[12] Regarding publicity in criminal justice, Cláudia Santos (2016, p. 131) mentions that 'crime progressively ceases to be seen as a subject of the victim, his family or group, and becomes understood as a subject of society that comes to be represented by the State'.

[13] As of the Law No. 83° of 5 August 2015, which criminalised forced marriage (Article 154° B), female genital mutilation (Article 144° B) and the crime of stalking (persecution, Article 154° A). Domestic violence has also gained the needed amendments.

[14] FRA, 2014. Violence against women: an EU-wide survey. Main results report (Violence against women: an EU-wide survey. Main results report | European Union Agency for Fundamental Rights (europa.eu).

3 Human Trafficking and Its Victims

Human trafficking is a highly profitable structured organised criminal activity,[15] a priority crime of investigation[16] and considered one of the most profitable crimes[17] alongside trafficking in firearms and drugs.

Most of its victims are still women[18] and young girls because the form of exploitation provided for by law for many years concerned sexual exploitation, even though forced labour has approximately the same estimates, according to the current estimates.[19] However, the crime of human trafficking, due to its relevance, seriousness and often transnational characteristics, has been debated and the prevention of it improved and standardised at an international level.

Thus, in addition to the basic conventions, the Universal Declaration of Human Rights of 1948 (UDHR) and the European Convention on Human Rights of 1950 (ECHR), I highlight a number of international conventions and decisions that have contributed decisively to the fact that in recent years, this phenomenon has been more clearly identified: the United Nations Convention against Transnational Organized Crime of 15 November 2000; the Protocol on the Prevention, Suppression and Punishment of Trafficking in Persons, Especially Women and Children;[20] the Council Framework Decision of 19 July 2002 on combating trafficking in human

---

[15] Article 1, para m of the Portuguese Criminal Code provides that "highly organized crime" means conduct involving crimes of criminal association, trafficking in persons, Trafficking in firearms, trafficking in narcotic drugs or psychotropic substances, corruption, influence peddling, economic participation in business or bleaching.

[16] Article 5 of Law No. 51/2023 of August 28—Portuguese Criminal Policy Law—Biennium 2023–2025—Human Trafficking is again referred in the list of the crimes under priority of investigation.

[17] 'According to data from the United Nations (UN), trafficking in human beings moves around 24 billion euros every year and victimizes more than 2.4 million people a year'. Resolution of the Council of Ministers No. 101/2013, December 31 of the Presidency of the Council of Ministers, 253 SERIES I (pp. 7007–7017).

[18] 'According to the UNODC Report on Trafficking in Persons 2022, the highest number of victims are exploited for forced labour (38,8%), and for sexual exploitation (38,7%). Regarding the other exploitation situations, 10.3% of the victims are related to mixed forms of exploitation, 10,2% with forced criminal activity, 0,9% for forced marriage, 0,7% for exploitative begging, 0,3% for illegal adoption 0,2% removal of organs. From this point of view, from a gender perspective, available data show that women and girls are still the main victims of trafficking in human beings: data from 2020, women (18% of whom were girls) accounted for 60% of victims and men (of which 17% were boys) 40%'.

[19] In Portugal, for example, since the revision of the Criminal Code, with the publication of Decree-Law No. 48/95 of 15 March, the crime of human trafficking (as well as pimping) is now integrated into Sect. I 'Crimes against sexual freedom'. Only with the wording given by Law No. 59/2007, of 4 September, passed the crime of human trafficking (Art. 160) to appear in Chap. IV, 'Crimes against personal freedom', separate from the crime of pimping that was established in Chap. V, 'Crimes against freedom and sexual self-determination'.

[20] Adopted by the General Assembly of the UN of November 15, 2000 (commonly known as the Palermo Protocol).

beings 2002/629/JHA (no longer in force); the Council of Europe Convention on Action against Trafficking in Human Beings, which entered into force on 1 February 2008;[21] the Directive 2011/36/EU of the European Parliament and of the Council of 5 April 2011 on the Prevention of and Fight against Trafficking in Human Beings and the Protection of Victims (currently under revision); and the EU Strategy on Combatting Trafficking in Human Beings (2021–2025). These agreements imply an evolution and convergence of the phenomenon of trafficking in persons that we are dealing with today, and which implies that someone's freedom will soon be manipulated to be exploited sexually, through labour or other forms of exploitation.

The issue of consent is, in this crime, fundamental; it is where the key to exploitation lies because victims' freedom of choice is manipulated in some of the ways specifed in the text of the crime and is therefore considered irrelevant in the assessment of the crime. In any case, such specific characteristics of the contours of this crime imply that its victims also have peculiar behaviours. These include the belief that they have to work, albeit against their will. They feel unable to leave their work environments, showing signs of controlled movements. The prevailing feeling is that they cannot leave where they are for reasons of fear and anxiety of being exposed to any circumstances that imply physical and/or psychological violence. They act as if they were fulfilling orders from third parties. Often, traffickers threaten victims or their family members. Victims may suffer the imposition of debts as a form of manipulation and impediment to resistance. Injuries are not always visible although the offenders can use aggressions or injuries resulting from certain jobs or even resulting from forms of control. These victims become suspicious of the authorities, especially as they are assured of common corruption among the police (which often mirrors the reality of the origin of the victims, making them believe that this is true).

In other cases, and with complete ignorance of the language, the legal situation of the victims in the countries they are exploited in (if they are foreigners) is not regularised, and this is used to blackmail them into thinking they will be denounced and subject to forced return if they refuse to comply with the exploitation. The fact that the victim's documents are often in the possession of another person, or that their documents are forged, counterfeit or false, are recurrent procedures of the networks or perpetrators who traffic people, and it is common for victims to completely ignore the addresses of their home or work.

The fact that these victims are often passive, silent and succumb to their continued exploitation and intimidation implies that they are subjected to manipulative conditions of a physical and a psychological nature. They passively watch demonstrations of impunity of their aggressors, which coincide with low convictions reates, as evidence or elements relevant to produce it in investigations for traffcking in persons often are not visible or may disappear. Victims, therefore, see a reduction in the capacity of the authorities to deal with cases of human trafficking, leaving testimony as an essential evidence for the production of an accusation for this crime.

Despite enumerating many of the constraints that involve victims of human trafficking, and which characterise them in a very peculiar way in relation to victims of

[21] Known as the Warsaw Convention.

other crimes, the selectivity of justice and the way information is lost as it progresses through the formal measures of control impose an additional obstacle on victims of human trafficking in reporting the facts of which they were victims. It implies a further factor of their lack of belief in justice.

Nevertheless, it is possible to list a number of reasons underlying the lack of confidence in the formal control mechanisms which prevents victims from reporting or complaining about the crimes by which they have been or are being victimised. These reasons include the fear and shame [22] they feel of public exposure, social exclusion or even future reprisals (particularly if sexual crimes [23]), especially if the perpetrators are relatives or close friends of the family. Scepticism, lack of trust in police and judicial bodies, and the feeling of a shortage of interest on the part of the formal institutions of control in the occurrences reported by the victims are major reasons for the non-existence of reports or denunciations. We conclude that not only the discredit deposited in the formal institutions of control but also, and mainly, the negative feedback from society in general provide the perpetuation of stigma on the victims, based on the facts they assist but also report to the imaginary of the justice system, and implies that it is not possible to know the criminal reality in fullness.

4 The Formal Institutions of Control and the Bankruptcy of the Processes

It is not my intention at this point to approach the description and explanation of the interactionist perspective, taking 'the way society responds to crime and why it does it' (Dias and Andrade 2013, p. 365). The topic I want to discuss here intends to take the formal institutions of control as object of study. I will take the analysis of the performance of certain elements of these formal control units that integrate the system of functioning of justice through a hypothesis-setting exercise to think about the potential failure of human trafficking cases and how, as such, that may negatively affect its victims, inhibiting them from trusting justice.

I will therefore present five hypotheses[24] going through the various phases of the selection process of justice and in which, at each level, a different invisibility can

[22] According to Peleg-Koriat and Klar-Chalamish (2022), it is interesting to note that if the victims of sexual crimes or domestic violence are male, they become 'invisible and isolated', feel 'discredited and blamed', which prevents them from filing a complaint or denouncing the crime.

[23] According to Fisher et al. (2023) two-thirds of women victims of sexual crimes report them to their relatives, partners and/or friends, but do not report them to the authorities.

[24] These hypotheses will be presented in a very general way because the academic interest is focused solely on the assessment of the effects on the victims and their repercussions on the action of justice.

negatively influence the evolution of the process or even halt its progression in the escalation of justice.

The first hypothesis concerns the specificity of the crime of human trafficking and the lack of knowledge of these characteristics by all the staff that make up the formal institutions of control.

Hypothesis 1
Natalya[25] had just escaped from a sex-trafficking network. Having asked for help from a passerby, she was picked up by a Criminal Police Service (CPS) officer of generic competence who took her as a prostitute. Because she did not speak any Portuguese word, the CPS agent tried, by gestures, to understand her history. As she was a non-national citizen, he immediately contacted the relevant Immigration Service, to check her legal status. As the linguistic difficulty did not allow a full understanding of the facts, the CPS did not give the required credits to her or even to the signs she was showing, not understanding any victim expression, body language, coercion indications of the human trafficking crime in his official report.

As already mentioned in previous sections, human trafficking is a priority crime of investigation. In addition, the competence for its investigation is normally given to Criminal Specialised Police Services. It also has been mentioned, albeit briefly, that the crime of human trafficking has undergone several changes, among which the most striking ones, to use the example of Portugal, are those in 2007[26] and 2013.[27] Although all CPS agents are obliged to follow the legislative amendments to follow-up the cases they have in hands, the truth is that changes to the law are not always easily discernible, nor is there always sufficient training for all CPS officers (and others that may be directly or indirectly involved in the detection of these cases) to accompany, recognise and know how to act to properly recognise signs of a specific crime. The consequence is that this victim, not being recognised as a victim of human trafficking, would have to return to the network of criminals who, being aware she had escaped, would exert physical violence and reprisals against her, causing all other victims who, along with Natalya, were deprived of their liberty and also sexually exploited, to lose faith in the justice system. They would believe there was no way to appeal to the state to benefit from the status of victim and the subsequent rights granted by the Portuguese law.[28] It is, therefore, essential to focus

[25] All names are fictitious and the reports, although based on past facts, do not translate into any specific case, nor was the outcome of the case reported or dealt with here. Only the crucial issue for the argument of this article will be addressed.

[26] Based on Law No. 59/2007 of 4 September, ratified by Law 102/2007 of the 31 October.

[27] As of the Law No. 60/2013 of 23 August, ratified by Law 39/2013 of the 4 October.

[28] Law No. 130/2015 of September 4 transposed Directive 2012/29/EU of the European Parliament and of the Council of 25 October 2012, creating a crime's victim status in Portugal. It has been recently amended, by Law 45/2023 of 17 August.

on the training of the agents of the institutions of control, such as Police, so that they are given all possible knowledge about these cases and thus prevent the credibility of the victims from being affected by cases such as this hypothetical one.

The second hypothesis is the lack of operationalisation of services and the absence of regulations for the granting of documents that allow victims of crimes to receive urgent medical assistance without their identities being revealed or accessed.

Hypothesis 2

Andreas had been beaten up by a network of human trafficking offenders that had exploited him for forced labour. A NGO flagged this case as a victim of human trafficking and accompanied him to one of the CPSs (Criminal Police Service) responsible for the investigation. This CPS issued a simple statement of the reported harassment and indications of human trafficking, which the NGO tried to use in the emergency service of the hospital so this victim could receive urgent and indispensable medical care. Despite the repeated insistence of the NGO not to do it, an invoice was issued by the hospital emergency service for the costs of the urgent medical care and the victim's real name and personal data were compulsorily collected for inclusion in the emergency file.

Portuguese law provides that a victim of domestic violence may complaint to a CPS and be immediately given a document attesting the status of victim,[29] with which free emergency medical care[30] are granted. This victim and children are also entitled to benefit from existing shelters[31] arranged for this purpose. However, this possibility only covered the victims of domestic violence, with other gaps to be filled (under Law No. 130/2015, of September 4), including a document that could allow other victims to be formally immediately reported as victims (such as a human trafficking victim) and receive free and urgent medical support.[32] This has only been recently amended, under Law 45/2023, of 17 August. In addition, hospital services were arranged in such a way as to compulsorily register the real name of the person

[29] Cf. Ordinance N° 138-E/2021, of 1 July, approving the documents proving the attribution of victim status.

[30] Decree-Law No. 128/2012 of June 21.

[31] Law No. 112/2009 of 16 September 2009, in its most recent version introduced by Law No. 57/2021 of 16 August.

[32] Naturally, the practices have shown there are alternatives that allow the problem to be circumvented, which is an unequal treatment because victims of human trafficking are entitled to compensation from the state (by the amendments introduced by Law 121/2015 of 1 September 2015), and only a few benefit from this due to the lack of knowledge of the law and difficulties in accessing the information to submit the request.

being assisted, and they did not allow the use of a fictitious identity (or the name of the entity carrying the victim to protect them).

Thus, any aggressor could, by means of telephone, make a call to the emergency department of a certain hospital, ask for the name of a particular victim and thus easily discover if he or she had entered the emergency service, which would put the victim at risk, by spotting the location. The consequence of allowing the criminal organisation access the hospital emergency records, even if only to locate the victim, if the intention is to carry out threats or revenge, is that victims refrain from reporting their injuries or denouncing the crimes for fear that retaliation for doing so would be much more harmful. Again, if the victim does not feel the support of the state, and hence loses confidence in the formal institutions of control, the process will be seriously compromised. This void was recognised as a serious one, and therefore solved with the amendment of the law later August 2023.

The third hypothesis is that there is no compulsory protocol (which includes sensitive procedures to be carried in person only) that criminal proceedings on human trafficking are required to follow.

Hypothesis 3

Marya was kept in captivity for several weeks and forced to beg by her traffickers. After the situation had been denounced, the victim was identified and the CPS and the Public Prosecutor's Office (PPO) initiated a series of proceedings, and the hearing was promoted for the victim's future memory.[33] According to the judicial map, the statements had to be taken in a city other than the one in which the case was being investigated. Two months after the due diligence, the CPS not having been notified to retrieve the physical paper process[34] and after contact with the bailiff, it was concluded that the physical paper criminal process had been sent by postmail and had gone astray, therefore destroying all the possibilities of continuing the investigation.

This hypothesis, part of the pyramid of justice that has stepped up (having already passed the stages of an identified crime, denounced crime, registered crime and investigated crime), had reached the level where the prosecution would be the next point to be reached. However, and by an almost invisible decision, the physical evidence was lost and, as such, the procedural pieces indispensable for the follow-up process to the next levels disappeared. Speed and effectiveness are, in cases of human trafficking investigation, indispensable for the success of the discovery of

[33] The Portuguese Criminal Procedure Process allows the setting up of a kind of pre-trial where the victim, with all the remaining trial elements (judge, prosecutor and lawyer) record the statements that will be integrally appreciated as proof in the final trial (future memory).

[34] Normally very urgent or serious crimes, criminal processes are only transported in hands by the CPS and never sent by post mail.

the truth of the facts. The effects on the victim can be catastrophic and the lengthening of the time of the investigation by events unrelated to the will of the courts entails increasing difficulties and results in the serious impoverishment in the victim's trust, sometimes achieved with great effort. The process then proceeds to a hearing where the victims decide to change their statements because criminal networks have had time to exert various pressures on them and/or their family members.

The fourth case is related to the way in which formal instances of control fail to follow the procedures of contacting victims, especially when mistakes are made due to the lack of the responsible victim protection.

Hypothesis 4

Raymond was recruited from a poor country to Portugal to work in an agriculture field; he was lodged at the trafficker's home. His schedule was never-ending, he had hardly 5 h daily rest time and a 7-day working week. No registration to the health system was carried out and his legalisation was promised to be solved one day in the future, which never came. Due to a previous health vulnerability, he suddenly felt sick, unconscious, in the public place where he was under exploitation, was brought to hospital and stayed severely ill for many months with a particularly serious prognosis. After his case was initiated in the investigation, and his witness statements were collected at the hospital, it was suggested to the prosecutor that he be brought to the court to confirm his statements, to prevent the loss of witness evidence should he die in the meanwhile. The administrative judicial officer in charge of sending the letter to the victim was not aware or did not pay attention to the complete situation, and sent a notification to the trafficker's house (and not to the hospital were the victim was receiving care or to the police service that was carrying-on the investigation). Therefore, the trafficker, who had not been aware of the investigation, and profiting from the fact that Raymond was vulnerable at the hospital, went to the hospital to try to convince him not to confirm his statements, threatening the victim, thus interfering in the investigation.

This hypothesis is also part of the pyramid of justice that had advanced to a higher level, where the prosecutor was already in charge of producing proof. Nevertheless, it is up to the administrative judicial staff to proceed with the notifications and execute the subsequent actions ordered by the prosecutors (in charge of the investigations). Normally, training and awareness sessions and campaigns target judges, prosecutors and police officers involved in human trafficking investigation and cases, but the administrative judicial staff are not always aware of the infinite number of details to be considered when one is dealing with human trafficking investigations. Of course, this hypothesis would never happen if the administrative staff would have read the whole process or if the prosecutor would point out the address to use to notify the witness (that should have been, in this case, the hospital where he had been staying for several months, the NGO appointed for support or the police service in charge of the investigation and never the trafficker's house). But the way formalities are carried out in the courts, such as entering the current address or contacts of the victims and witnesses in the courts' informatic systems, is not always updated and depends on the way each prosecutor organises his/her work with his/her staff as well as the nature and seriousness of the processes under investigation. The result of such failures is the complete lack of confidence in the system by vulnerable victims, who feel powerless in face of the threats received by traffickers when, as in this situation, they are 'visited' by someone who wants nothing more than to manipulate, harrass or threaten them.

Hypothesis 5

Olena was recruited in her origin country in Eastern Europe to come to Portugal with her younger sister, with the promise of a better life and good conditions. Arriving in Portugal, she was told she had a debt of thousands of euros to pay and, as she did not speak Portuguese language, she was told by the trafficker the only way to pay the debt for her and her sister would be prostitution. She was sent to the woods and forced to prostitute herself and bring money home every day, while she and her sister were victims of physical offenses when she did not bring enough money home. When she was released from this exploitation, after giving her statements to police as a witness, she was asked to confirm her statements in court. Some days before, emotionally coerced, she went to prison to visit the trafficker, who convinced her to lie in court, promising that he would let her go and allow her to bring her sister out of the criminal network, convincing her by saying that the justice system in Portugal was as corrupt as in her origin country. She believed him, and going to court alone, she lied as requested by the trafficker, contradicting her previous statements; he was released a short time later.

The main question in this hypothesis is the special psychological state the victims of human trafficking enter after suffering the violence of being obliged to perform tasks against their will. In this specific case, this victim was possibly suffering from the Stockholm Syndrome, a psychological disturbance that affects mainly victims of human trafficking and domestic violence. Most victims are under this influence or under forms of Post-Traumatic Stress Disorders (PTSD), and the judicial system is only recently understanding the consequences of these psychological disturbances on the production of proof in court. Therefore, not having access to professionals who are specialised in these disturbances, victims of these crimes are often treated as common witnesses and their statements, even if contradictory, are taken following the strict objective parameters of the justice. As human trafficking crimes rely mainly on witness statements for proof, in this case the failure of the justice system was reflected in the lack of witness proof with which to charge the trafficker for his actions; other proof may have been collected but considered insufficient. Psychological support and a physical examination of the victims are the first actions that should be carried out to not only collect objective proof but also, and mainly, to give assistance to victims and empower them with the confidence to rely on the system and not feel abandoned or used by the judicial system.

5 Conclusions

As a final thought, a lot of importance has always been attributed to the study of crime and its aggressor. Only later did the importance of the study of the victim become visible. The victim has been studied in various ways and through various prisms by authors who divided them by groups of diverse victims that, in one way or another, ended up influencing the appreciated judgments. I briefly highlighted some specificities of the crime of human trafficking, presenting some empyrical hypothesis where the evolution of the text of law allowed us to better understand the specific difficulties faced by the victims of human trafficking. Crossing these facts with what we aknowledge from THB crime specificities, it is important to note that the different escalation levels on the pyramid of justice are accompanied by the crucial role that the formal institutions of control exert in the success or failure of THB crime repression.

Therefore, those decisions and actions influence the follow-up of the process in the escalation of the pyramid of justice, functioning as an obstacle or facilitator of the performance of the subsequent levels. Many of these thresholds act quietly and would almost go unnoticed if not for the serious consequences they exert on the victim's trust in the justice system. In the case of human trafficking, this control may reverse the decisions of victims who, fearing retaliation or after excessive delays, become victims of reprisals by criminal networks, functioning as new black figures, but already at the top of the pyramid of justice, in the prosecution, and impeding the exercise of justice to the full.

I therefore leave some thoughts as recommendations:

(a) More awareness and training sessions should be provided to all the staff involved in human trafficking investigations, prosecution and judgement.
(b) A higher focus on the consequences of the mistreatment of such cases should be made, especially by judicial officials, to correct and improve procedures with the aim of putting the "law in books" into trustworthy "law in action", proving or reinforcing the trust of victims in the judicial system.
(c) A clear understanding of the Stockholm Syndrome and PTSD interferences and consequences for the human trafficking victims by judicial staff should be established, and more experts in this field should be requested as a support to courts to produce proof.
(d) An increased network of professionals should act in cases of human trafficking, providing, on the one hand, the necessary support to victims, to protect them

and free them from the criminal networks, and on the other hand, to help the judicial system prosecute the traffickers.

Only in this way, with the involvement of all the intervenients, can victims of human trafficking be confident of receiving from the authorities the much-needed support, and hypotheses such as the ones presented will no longer need to be discussed.

References

Dias JF, Andrade M (2013) O Homem Delinquente e a Sociedade Criminogénea. Coimbra Editora, Coimbra

Fisher BS, Daigle LE, Cullen FT, Turner MG (2023) Reporting sexual victimization to the police and others: results from a national-level study of college women. Crim Justice Behav 30(1):6. https://doi.org/10.1177/0093854802239161

Machado H (2008) Manual de Sociologia do Crime. Biblioteca das Ciências Sociais. Edições Afrontamento, Porto

Peleg-Koriat I, Klar-Chalamish C (2022) Sexual offense victims' responses to the question #WhyIDidntReport? Examining restorative justice as an alternative dispute resolution mechanism. Confl Resolut Q 1–18. https://doi.org/10.1002/crq.21369

Santos C (2014) A Justiça Restaurativa. Um Modelo de Reacção ao Crime Diferente da Justiça Penal. Porquê, Para Quê e Como? Tese de doutoramento em Direito, na especialidade em Ciências Jurídico-Criminais, apresentada à Faculdade de Direito da Universidade de Coimbra, Coimbra Editora

Santos C (2016) Beccaria e a Publicização da Justiça Penal à Luz da Contemporânea Descoberta da Vítima (a alteração ao Código de Processo Penal introduzida pela Lei n.° 130/2015, de 4 de setembro, e o sentido da nova definição de vítima). Revista da Faculdade de Direito da Universidade Lusófona do Porto 7(7)., Publicada online em Julho de 2016:129–147

Spolon PHC, Viana AdP (2016) Aspectos relevantes da vitimologia. In: Âmbito Jurídico, Rio Grande, XIX, n. 146, mar 2016. Disponível em: http://www.ambito-juridico.com.br/site/index.php?n_link=revista_artigos_leitura&artigo_id=16968&revista_caderno=3

UNODC (2022) Global report on trafficking in persons:2022

Wilson JR (2015) The word criminology: a philology and a definition. Criminol Crim Justice Law Soc 16(3):61–82

Maria João Guia (maria.joao.guia@ij.uc.pt) holds a PhD in Law, Justice and Citizenship in the twenty-first century, by the University of Coimbra, Portugal and four Masters Diplomas (Law, Sociology, Translation and Strategic Border Management). She has been an European Commission external expert in the area of 'Security, Liberty and Justice (2014)' after being an alternate member of the Group of Experts on Trafficking in Human Beings. She has been working professionally in criminal investigation, borders, and document control in the area of migration. She is Invited Assistant Professor of Criminology and Researcher of Ratio Legis—Center of Research and Development of Legal Sciences of the Universidade Autónoma de Lisboa [Project: *Corpus Delicti*—Studies in Transnational Organized Criminality], Researcher in the Centre for Legal Research, University of Coimbra and Researcher of *Ius Gentium Conimbrigae*/Centre for Human Rights of the Faculty of Law, University of Coimbra. She lectures on the intersection of sociology, law, and criminology in Post-PhD, PhD, master, postgraduation, degree, and training courses of various areas of knowledge. Maria João Guia is a national expert and researcher in several

European and national projects, namely in the areas of the rights of victims of crimes, human trafficking, and the rights of immigrants. This article has been written within the research activity as Integrated Researcher of Ratio Legis – Center of Research and Development of Legal Sciences of the Universidade Autónoma de Lisboa [Project: Corpus Delicti – Studies in Transnational Organized Criminality]

Human Trafficking in Slovenia: Contemporary Issues

Katja Eman, Gorazd Meško, and Bojan Dobovšek

Abstract Slovenia was (and remains) the main human trafficking path on the Balkan route. In Central and Eastern Europe, it has been increasing since the 1980s. Still, the Balkans and its neighbouring countries only became the region of origin, transit and destination of human trafficking in the 1990s, immediately after the end of humanitarian crises and wars in former Yugoslavia. Trafficking of women for prostitution was the most common type. Due to its geographical position, Slovenia is primarily a transit country for human trafficking, albeit it sometimes acts as a country of origin and destination. The types of human trafficking and its purposes have changed: apart from sexual exploitation, currently include forced begging and petty crimes, labour exploitation or forced labour, trafficking in human organs, tissues and cells, child trafficking. These phenomena have also been on the rise in Slovenia. Its victims generally come from Southern and Eastern Europe. This chapter presents various types of human trafficking of the twenty-first century detected in Slovenia and discusses its dangers and consequences in the future. The authors conclude that Slovenia has a well-developed policy and practice of prevention and assistance to victims of human trafficking, where criminal justice agencies work closely with NGOs.

1 Introduction

The end of the twentieth and the beginning of the twenty-first century are marked by a period of mass migration and the extraordinary rise of Islamist terrorism, mostly known due to the two terrorist organisations, Al Qaeda and the Islamic State

K. Eman (✉)
University of Maribor, Faculty of Justice and Security, Maribor, Slovenia
e-mail: katja.eman@um.si

G. Meško · B. Dobovšek
University of Maribor, Faculty of Criminal Justice and Security, Maribor, Slovenia
e-mail: gorazd.mesko@um.si; bojan.dobovsek@um.si

A. M. Rodrigues, M. J. Guia (eds.), *New Forms of Human Trafficking*,
https://doi.org/10.1007/978-3-031-39732-5_13

(Saltman and Winter 2014). The focus of their activities is in Asia and the Middle East, and these regions are also the origin of mass migration observed in the past decade. Due to the constant threat and lack of conditions for a normal life, refugees leave behind conflict-torn countries, seeking shelter and a better life elsewhere. Kocjančič and Vodlan (2016) emphasise that globalisation facilitates a faster displacement of refugees and migrants, which are exploited by criminal groups. Thus, refugees and migrants quickly become part of a vicious circle of human trafficking and become victims. On the other hand, even in countries closer to Slovenia, poverty and poor living conditions often bring people to make 'bad' decisions which lead them into the claws of human traffickers: young people in search of a better life and greater opportunities; parents selling their children or forcing them to marry in the hope of giving them a normal life; workers accepting low wages and inhumane working conditions because they have to provide for their families, etc. Countries in the Western Balkans region are full of sad stories when it comes to human trafficking, and Slovenia is no exception, since it is the country of origin, transit or destination for trafficked victims.

Human trafficking can be described as the recruitment, sale or transfer of vulnerable individuals or groups between countries with the purpose of exploiting individuals through prostitution, forced labour, slavery or the harvesting of human organs for profit. Victims of human trafficking are constrained through payment, physical force, deception and/or fraud (Čurin 2006; Dobovšek 2012; Milivojevic and Segrave 2012). Moreover, human trafficking is increasingly becoming a highly complex phenomenon, characterised by the involvement of criminal organisations, and usually taking place in multiple countries.

Čurin (2016) points out that human trafficking is a serious crime, often committed by organised crime groups. There are many different definitions of human trafficking in the international arena, which is why the UN Convention against Transnational Organized Crime (UN 2010) represents a major step forward in the identification and definition of trafficking in human beings. The Palermo Protocol (UN 2010) states that human trafficking means any 'recruitment, transportation, relocation, shelter or reception of persons for the purpose of exploitation by threat, use of force or other forms of coercion, abduction, fraud, deception, misuse of powers or vulnerabilities, or giving or receiving payments or benefits in order to achieve the consent of a person who has control over another person. Exploitation involves at least exploiting prostitution or other forms of sexual abuse of persons, their forced labour or services, slavery or similar conditions, servitude or removal of organs'. According to the United Nations Office on Drugs and Crime (UNODC 2016), human trafficking is the second most profitable illegal activity in the world after drug trafficking, which also finances other illegal activities (terrorism, guerrilla forces, etc.).

A decade ago, human trafficking was considered to be only one of the types of crime, however, it is now recognised as a multifaceted phenomenon, which is changing and reaching unknown dimensions due to different social and economic factors. In today's world, everything revolves around the on supply and demand, including the related imagination and deviant tendencies of individuals or society.

Thus, the protection of individuals is of fundamental importance precisely because they are the object of trafficking and, consequently, exploitation (Čurin 2016, p. 2). Therefore, the purpose of this chapter is to present the types of human trafficking of the twenty-first century detected in Slovenia and to discuss the policies aimed at responding to and preventing this type of organised crime. Finally, the authors also discuss the dangers and consequences of human trafficking in the future, with the aim of providing useful solutions.

2 Human Trafficking in Slovenia: Types, Routes, Perpetrators and Victims

Human trafficking involves many different ways of exploiting people. The most common types include forced labour, forced begging, exploitation for sexual services (prostitution, pornography, paedophilia), forced marriage, child trafficking and trafficking in human organs (Dandurand 2012).

The twentieth and twenty-first century are known as the centuries of mass migration. Thus, illegal migration is a concept that is inherent to crime, which is divided into primary crime, i.e. criminal offences committed by illegal migrants, and secondary crime, i.e. criminal offences committed in the scope of activities conducted by organised crime groups. Aas Franko (2007) differentiates between two types of migrants: (1) 'crimmigrants', i.e. migrants who are dangerous, undocumented, potential terrorists and have a criminal background, and (2) 'travellers', i.e. people who can move without restrictions and are therefore privileged. Moreover, illegal migration is often linked to other types of organised crime, such as human trafficking, drug trafficking, firearms trafficking, terrorism and money laundering, and thus represent an even more pertinent security issue (Meško et al. 2018). Therefore, Nikolić-Ristanović (2012, p. 205) notes that human trafficking is a type of crime with a long history, however, changes in the social and economic fields caused by 'globalisation, neoliberal capitalism, transition and the growing number of conflicts resulted in an expansion of human trafficking in all its forms in recent decades'.

2.1 *Types of Human Trafficking*

Other than trafficking in arms, drugs and money laundering, human trafficking is one of the most profitable types of international organised crime, which has serious consequences on the wellbeing and fundamental rights of victims. Apart from gaining profit, the main driving forces and causes of human trafficking include poverty, a growing sex services market in developed countries, the lack of education, poor regulation, demand for cheap labour, demand for victim services and profitability, as human trafficking serves as a good source of income for organised crime groups (Dobovšek 2012; Winterdyk et al. 2012).

The expansion, deepening and, lastly, the origin of human trafficking is caused by numerous factors. Williamson and Prior (2009) highlighted inadequate sanctions and penalties against traffickers, rising poverty and the marginalisation of the poor, very strict migration legislation, and the lack of information on the reality and dangers of trafficking in human beings. Many victims enter into human trafficking voluntarily due to the promises of a good job and higher pay. In some countries, cultural and social differences also undermine young girls and women, thus contributing to their poor decision-making. On the other hand, there are cases of parents selling their children because they believe they are providing them with an opportunity for a better future and saving them from the life of poverty.

As already mentioned, profit is one of the most prominent causes and driving forces of human trafficking. Criminal groups opt for trafficking because of high profits on one hand, and low risks and penalties on the other. Moreover, trafficking does not require a large capital investment (Williamson and Prior 2009, p. 43). The causes of human trafficking and its spread also include the degree of state corruption, the level of state food production, the degree of conflict, the share of population over 14 years of age and the security threat level (e.g. terrorist attacks, military conflicts, religious tensions, etc.), which are inherent to poor and unstable countries.

The types of human trafficking can be divided into the following categories (Winterdyk et al. 2012; Goodey 2012; Smith and Kangaspunta 2012; Kocjančič and Vodlan 2016):

(1) Human trafficking for labour exploitation:
    (a) Forced labour or services (forced begging, forced criminality)
    (b) Slavery, servitude and other types of slavery
(2) Human trafficking for sexual exploitation:
    (a) Bar dancing
    (b) Pornography
    (c) Prostitution
    (d) Forced marriage
(3) Human trafficking for the purpose of recruiting soldiers (child soldiers)
(4) Human trafficking for the purpose of removing human organs
(5) Human trafficking for the purchase of children
(6) Human trafficking as a tool of terrorism (from material support to the direct execution of terrorist attacks)

In Slovenia, the most frequently detected types of human trafficking include trafficking for sexual exploitation (prostitution, bar dance, forced marriage), for labour exploitation (forced begging, forced, slavery and servitude), and for the purchase of children. All these types are presented in detail below.

2.2 Human Trafficking Routes

Due to its geostrategic position, Slovenia acts as a European country of transition in most human trafficking cases (Dobovšek 2012). It used to be a country of destination, origin and transit (Dobovšek 2007) for human trafficking, however, it currently no longer appears to be a country of origin (U.S. Department of State 2010, 2015). Nevertheless, Nikolić-Ristanović (2012) emphasises that most Central and East European countries can be described as countries of origin, even though they also serve as transit routes and points of destination for human trafficking. Surtees (2008a), Europol (2016), the U.S. Department of State Publication (2015) and Goodey (2012) note the recent increase in human trafficking in the Balkan countries, which are generally the countries of origin and transit, and rarely destination points. The Balkans were (Friman and Reich 2007) and still are (Dobovšek 2012) 'attractive' destinations due to the rather chaotic conditions (i.e. previous war, lack of the rule of law, nonworking repressive institutions, the presence of many peacekeeping foreigners, which leads to high demand). Usually, human trafficking destinations include West and South European countries (Nikolić-Ristanović 2012; Kaye and Winterdyk 2012), and countries on other continents, such as Australia and New Zealand, the United States, the United Arab Emirates, South Korea, China, South Africa, Vietnam and Thailand (Europol 2016; U.S. Department of State Publication 2015). According to the media and parliamentary debates, Slovenia is witnessing the issue of legal migration of its young and educated population. Since Slovenia is a member of the EU, many young people seek better opportunities in well-developed EU countries due to unemployment and high housing prices.

Organised crime groups predominantly use three routes for human trafficking in Europe: the Spanish Iberian route, the Italian Apennine route and the Balkan route. The process of mass migration to Europe could be described as a storm on the Iberian route, a hurricane on the Apennine route and a tsunami on the Balkan route. It is commonly believed that Slovenia belongs to the group of countries in the Western Balkans and cannot escape the influence of the Balkan trafficking route(s). According to the UNODC and other reports, trafficking in women, children and men is observed in the Balkans. Women are still most frequently subjected to trafficking for the purpose of sexual exploitation, less frequently for their labour, marriage and other criminal activities, such as trafficking in human organs, etc. Men are most often victims of trafficking for the purpose of forced labour in a variety of sectors, such as construction, forestry, agriculture, and the services sector. Moreover, some men and women, particularly if ill or wounded, are forced to beg. Men are less-frequently trafficked and enslaved for the purpose of sexual exploitation. On the other hand, children are most often trafficked for sexual exploitation, slightly less frequently for the purpose of forced begging, forced labour, adoption, marriage and theft (Dobovšek 2012; Nikolić-Ristanović 2012; U.S. Department of State Publication 2015; Goodey 2012; Smith and Kangaspunta 2012). As a final destination, Slovenia is particularly interesting for the sexual exploitation of women and forced labour and begging for men.

Nikolić-Ristanović (2012, p. 2018) notes that the main human trafficking destination countries include Bosnia and Herzegovina, Croatia, North Macedonia, Montenegro, and Kosovo. People are trafficked in this part of Europe for sexual and labour exploitation, including begging. Most Western Balkan countries are the destinations for the trafficked women and children; however, Montenegro, Croatia and Slovenia also act as destinations for trafficked men. Slovenia was formerly a country of abundant employment opportunities for people from all parts of former Yugoslavia. Today, it has been transformed into a destination for the trafficking in men (who usually possess all required legal documents (Surtees 2008b; Ćopić 2009)) for forced labour. A similar situation may be observed in Croatia, mainly due to the development of tourism and the demand for seasonal work (Nikolić-Ristanović 2012). Furthermore, the growth of sex tourism on the Adriatic coast was also detected (Golubovic-Skec and Radeva-Berket 2010; Goodey 2012). On the other hand, all Balkan countries in general, and Serbia and North Macedonia in particular, have been known as crucial transit countries for all types of illegal trade, including (human) trafficking and smuggling (Nikolic-Ristanovic 2012). Moreover, international agencies (U.S. Department of State Publication 2015; Europol 2016, 2018; Winterdyk et al. 2012; Goodey 2012; Smith and Kangaspunta 2012; Kaye and Winterdyk 2012) find that Balkan countries are increasingly frequently used as the so-called temporary or 'false' destinations for human trafficking towards Western Europe.

2.3 *Perpetrators and Victims of Human Trafficking*

Previous studies on human trafficking in the Balkans (Englund et al. 2008; Jokinen et al. 2011; Europol 2016, 2018; Nikolić-Ristanović 2012; Scheinost 2000; Surtees 2005, 2008a, b) reveal that traffickers are usually citizens of the countries concerned or citizens of neighbouring countries. Moreover, the nationality of recruiters is consistent with the nationality of victims (Lsocik and Wiczorek 2011; U.S. Department of State Publication 2015). In most of Balkan countries (Albania, Bosnia and Herzegovina, Bulgaria, Croatia, Kosovo, North Macedonia, Serbia, Montenegro and Romania) criminal groups, which are composed of both nationals and non-nationals, were detected (Surtees 2008a; Nikolić-Ristanović 2012; Goodey 2012; U.S. Department of State Publication 2015). Although men generally still represent the majority of recruiters, a trend has recently been detected, which points to the increasing number of female recruiters, particularly in women trafficking (Europol 2016), where the previously recruited women are encouraged by traffickers to invite their friends to join them in working abroad (Surtees 2008a). This has been most common in North Macedonia and Serbia. On the other hand, victims in Albania, Montenegro and Kosovo were almost exclusively recruited by men (Nikolić-Ristanović 2012). In numerous human trafficking cases, male-female couples also figure as recruiters/traffickers (e.g. the woman usually recruits the victim, while the man deals with transportation and/or exploitation) (Europol 2018). With respect to Slovenia, which is mostly a country of transition and rarely a destination point, it is important to understand the characteristics and modus operandi of human traffickers from neighbouring countries and beyond, who may only be transiting Slovenia or also work on Slovenia's territory.

In terms of child trafficking, the Balkan countries are replete with numerous sad stories involving children and their parents or other close relatives. In Albania, Kosovo and Serbia, the child traffickers are often the parents of the children or other family members who force them to beg (UNICEF 2004; Ćopić 2009; Kaye and Winterdyk 2012; U.S. Department of State Publication 2015). Also, the recruiters of children trafficked for the purpose of labour exploitation, begging and delinquency, are most often their blood relatives (Surtees 2005; Europol 2016).

Accordingly, Europol's data (2016, 2018) suggest that mafia-style, hierarchical trafficking networks have not been observed on a regular basis in the Balkans. In this part of Europe, criminal groups normally have different organisational structures: 'The relationships among members and management of a criminal enterprise can be vertical, i.e. hierarchical (on a corporative model), but in contemporary societies it is more often horizontal (on a network model)' (Nikolić-Ristanović 2012, p. 209). The so-called local, opportunistic and entrepreneurial criminal enterprise that comprises smaller or larger groups of people and can be of national, regional or international nature or even take the form of a 'family business' (Europol 2016; Luptakova et al. 2004; Nikolić-Ristanović 2012; Kaye and Winterdyk 2012; Herz 2012; U.S. Department of State Publication 2015) have either been taking over the trafficking business in this part of Europe or are a part of a larger trafficking network. Usually, these groups are also involved in other criminal activities, such as drug and firearms trafficking. Nikolić-Ristanović (2012) found that the low-level Balkan traffickers are generally not well-educated, unemployed and without a criminal record. Sometimes, criminal groups use associates known as 'amateur traffickers' (Schloenhardt 1999; Winterdyk et al. 2012; Kaye and Winterdyk 2012), who act as independent individuals performing tasks on an *ad hoc* basis and usually operate in the vicinity of borders, using their own boats, taxis and lorries (Nikolić-Ristanović 2012, p. 210).

Recently, investigators (Europol 2016, 2018; Čurin 2016) have detected greater numbers of trafficking groups in which the persons involved have close family ties or a previous criminal relationship. Moreover, they operate as equals with specifically allocated roles. Sometimes, individual members do not have any previous criminal records (Scheinost 2000; Nikolić-Ristanović 2012; Lsocik and Wiczorek 2011; Herz 2012). Traffickers work in high-, medium- or low-level organised groups (Europol 2018; Spencer et al. 2011), where every phase of trafficking can be carried out by a specialised (medium-level) criminal network, which is, in turn, part of a broader, national or international, criminal network. Similar to the distinctions between criminal groups and networks, the distinctions between individual traffickers themselves also exist. Researchers (Schloenhardt 1999; Scheinost 2000; Nikolić-Ristanović 2012; Winterdyk et al. 2012; Goodey 2012; Smith & Kangaspunta 2012;

Herz 2012) distinguish between individual traffickers according to their key positions in a criminal enterprise:

- Arrangers/investors (investors in human trafficking and supervisors of the overall functioning of the scheme)
- Traffickers at middle-level management (organisers of certain phases/tasks, such as recruitment, transport, accommodation, final exploitation, etc.)
- Low-level traffickers (i.e. amateur traffickers) (deal in various criminal activities and are mainly hired on an ad hoc basis (recruiters of victims; guides and crew members responsible for the transfer of migrants; persons who lease their own flats or houses as temporary accommodation for migrants)

At this point, special attention must be paid to the migration crisis in the 2015–2016 period, which, among other, merely affected the trafficking routes, perpetrators and their modus operandi, and victims. In 2015, thousands of people, who were forced to leave their homes and countries, travelled to Europe through the Balkan migration route (Stanojoska 2016). Over 1,820,000 illegal border crossings were detected through surveillance activities (Frontex 2016) and approximately 900,000 migrants travelled through Greece via the Former Yugoslav Republic of Macedonia, Serbia and Hungary to other parts of Europe, mainly to Austria, Germany, the United Kingdom and Sweden. In October 2015, Hungary closed its borders and, a few days after that, migrants started arriving in Slovenia through its southern border. Unsuccessful attempts to block the migrant flow by sending migrants back to Croatia resulted in the full exposure of Slovenia to the migration crisis (United Nations 2017). The number of daily illegal border crossings was enormous; at the peak of the crisis, more than 11,000 migrants crossed the border, and the end of 2015, police officers dealt with 359,583 foreigners (Policija 2016). Most migrants were citizens of Syria, followed by nationals of Afghanistan, Iraq and Iran. Altogether, over 400,000 migrants, which represents almost a quarter of Slovenia's entire population, crossed the Slovene border during the migration/refugee crisis (Meško et al. 2018, p. 510).

During this massive wave of people, trafficking routes spread to almost every remote path or track. Furthermore, the 'traditional old-fashioned' modus operandi changed because the demand for illegal guidance across state borders increased, which is why some local individuals also participated in the trafficking. These local traffickers were only involved in the illegal transportation of the migrants across the state border and not in any other 'special' type of human trafficking, such as sexual exploitation or trafficking for human organs. On the other hand, organised criminals were extremely quick to exploit such a multitude of people for their illegal businesses of human trafficking. Numerous people, particularly children, were reported missing during this period. Finally, victims in this migration wave originated from Syria, the Middle East and Northern Africa. A large number of illegal migrants represented countless opportunities for offenders of different types of human trafficking, in particular; human trafficking for sexual exploitation, human trafficking for the removal of human organs, and human trafficking for the purchase of children. This unlikely, albeit still possible type of offence relates to human trafficking as a tool of terrorism. The large number of illegal migrants, the extensive migration wave (crossing several countries on the Balkan route) and the phenomenon of new, 'opportunistic' offenders, who only facilitated the transport of illegal migrants once or twice, are particularly complex and make the investigation and prosecution of such crime extremely difficult.

3 Specific Types of Human Trafficking: A Growing Issue of the 21st Century

In 2007, an increase in forced begging (at that time a relatively new type of exploitation) was detected in Slovenia, where minorities or women and children are forced to beg in the street, giving the money received to organised groups (Dobovšek 2012, p. 54). Three years later, in March 2010, the Arab Spring gave rise to the largest migration flow in modern history. Migration has been a daily occurrence until the number of migrants became so high that the so-called 'target countries' were no longer able to accept them. In 2015, during the Syrian crisis, Europe was faced with the largest migration flow since the European colonisation and the Transatlantic Slave Trade (Stanojoska 2016, p. 1857). Europe and other countries soon responded by closing their borders and sometimes by building fences (Meško et al. 2018). Slovenia was one of the countries on the migration route and therefore experienced different types of migration. Most migration flows that crossed Slovenia's borders were economically motivated to and out of the country, as well as illegal migration into the country, characterised by sexual exploitation, forced begging and petty crimes, trafficking in human organs, tissues and cells, trafficking in children and trafficking in human beings for the purpose of labour exploitation or forced labour (Čurin 2016, 2017; Dobovšek and Slak 2016). The aforementioned events led researchers and representatives of the criminal justice system to pay special attention to the 'new' (at least for Slovenia) types of human trafficking: the exploitation of workers, trafficking in children, forced begging and forced criminality.

Human trafficking for the purpose of labour exploitation become a serious problem in Slovenia during the past decade. It is the so-called legacy of the former Yugoslavia when migration of workers among its constituent republics was somewhat usual, therefore, numerous people from the Balkan countries came to work in Slovenia. With the economic crisis, Slovene companies expressed a strong interest for inexpensive foreign labour, particularly in the construction sector. Apart from the deliberate recruitment of people for the purpose of exploitation, 'employers lured workers by false promises regarding remuneration, working conditions and rights they would be able to enjoy once they began work in Slovenia' (Frangež and Bučar Ručman 2017, p. 235). Čurin (2016, 2017) discusses various criminal offences and workers' rights violations in Slovenia, such as: unpaid overtime, failure to pay parts or entire salaries for several months, deregistration from obligatory health and pension insurance schemes, and failure to pay relevant contributions for several years, unpaid sick leave, employment contracts modified by employers without workers' consent, mobbing, bullying and threats of dismissal.

Analyses revealed that migrant workers tolerated all violations and threats because they came from poor backgrounds and because their families' existence back home depended on their work in Slovenia. Most of these workers came from Bosnia and Herzegovina, and rarely from other countries of former Yugoslavia. The Slovene Interdepartmental Working Group for Curbing Human Trafficking (Čurin 2017) found that employers were familiar with workers' personal situations and used them as a mechanism of exploitation. When such cases escalated and were widely reported by the media, Slovenia introduced various changes to its legislation and updated the instructions and rules governing the work of criminal justice agencies with the aim of detecting and putting an end to this new type of modern trafficking. The investigation by the Slovene Police (Čurin 2017) later revealed that Slovene companies employed workers and sent them to other European countries, such as Germany, in which the construction sector had not been affected by the economic crisis.

A literature review (Nikolić-Ristanović 2012; Kocjančič and Vodlan 2016; Meško et al. 2018) and a statistical data analysis (Dobovšek 2012; Čurin 2016, 2017) show that children in Slovenia are rarely exposed to trafficking. Most children who are victims of trafficking, come from abroad and end up in Slovenia. Frangež and Bučar Ručman (2017) believe that a sound system of child protection, which means that children (at risk) live with their families or in foster care instead of on the street, is the main reason why cases of children trafficked from Slovenia remain rare.

Following the crisis in Syria and the mass migration wave, several cases of child trafficking were observed in which smugglers separated children from their parents under the pretence that they would be reunited with their parents or mothers at a later stage. However, children were most often dropped off at major train stations and the Ljubljana train station was one of such spots. Thus, children did not even know where they were, as they were supposed to end up in Italy or in Austria (Čurin 2017; Gov.si 2020).

Trafficked underage migrants in Slovenia were often forced to work in forests and in various waste and raw materials collection, management and sorting centres. Moreover, girls between 14 and 18 years of age, who are the most vulnerable group in terms of sexual exploitation, were recruited by peers, pimps or even their own parents.[1] The same patterns of abuse were identified in other countries (e.g. Romania, Bulgaria, Hungary, Serbia, North Macedonia, and Croatia) in the Balkan Peninsula. Furthermore, certain cases of begging and forced criminality involving children were also detected in Slovenia. Slovenia was a transit country for 15 and 16-year-old boys traveling to work in Italy. When they made a stop and were forced to beg in Slovenia, the reaction was truly negative and many residents called the police,

[1] In Romania, children may also be recruited by their parents for two reasons: (1) they want to give their children an opportunity for a better life, or (2) they are trying to improve their social status by selling one of their children to human traffickers (Frangež and Bučar Ručman 2017, p. 236).

which meant that a rapid response by the police and social services made foreign organised crime groups (e.g. from Romania and Bulgaria) realise that Slovenia was not a suitable place for forced begging (Čurin 2016, 2017).

Other detected cases of child trafficking in Slovenia include forced marriages, typical for the Roma communities, where traditional Roma weddings involve underage Roma girls and are predominantly associated with money, mostly by a debt incurred by the father.[2] The Albanian community is another ethnic group known for arranged marriages. The least often (detected) type of child trafficking in Slovenia is trafficking for the purchase of children—child adoptions. Such cases most often involve future parents, who stay abroad for a few months and return to Slovenia with a new-born alleging that the baby was born abroad (Frangež and Bučar Ručman 2017; Čurin 2017). Furthermore, adoptions from North Macedonia and Russia often raise the suspicion of child trafficking due to payments made for such adoptions.

Human trafficking for the purpose of forced begging and forced criminality involves victims of all ages and genders. Apart from children and minors, forced begging is normally carried out by disabled persons and the elderly. In Slovenia, there were some cases of organised arrivals of beggars, who were forced to 'work' all day, while the leader of the organised crime group took their daily earnings. Victims of this type of trafficking usually come from Romania and Slovakia (Dobovšek 2012; Čurin 2016).

During the past decade, human trafficking as a consequence and a tool of terrorism became a special category of human trafficking. In Slovenia, only three cases of individuals, who were recruited by terrorist groups and went to Syria, were detected, however, the numbers of such individuals in other Balkan countries grew rapidly. This is a new phenomenon in the field of human trafficking; therefore, slightly more attention will be dedicated to it in the subsequent paragraphs.

Terrorists mainly exploit women and girls for the purpose of labour exploitation, housework, (military) warfare and, above all, sexual exploitation and forced marriages. Most recorded cases of human trafficking were carried out for the purpose of recruitment or financing (Escape from hell, 2014). Terrorists often sell captured women (to rich Arabs, who are willing to pay huge sums for women who are still virgins) in order to finance their operations (Keefer 2006). Furthermore, terrorists exploit sexual slavery as a motivational recruitment tool to inspire and attract new members (Merlan 2015). They are promised young brides, which is also one of the most important factors in the psychology of terrorists and in the recruiting process. There are also known cases where terrorists give women as awards in Koran memorisation competitions (ISIS offers female slaves 2015). Hankel (2014) emphasises that most media reports on the link between trafficking and terrorism only refer to sexual exploitation and neglect other types, such as forced child begging, selling organs and labour exploitation (Hankel 2014), since terrorists must often recruit workers, as most residents flee the region where terrorists operate. The next major

[2] Roma girls perceive marriage as a self-evident fact of life and do not identify themselves as victims, since Roma communities define 'Roma weddings' as traditional and customary (Frangež and Bučar Ručman 2017, p. 237).

issue in the terrorist induced human trafficking involves human trafficking for the purpose of war, where people in Iraq and Syria are recruited for military operations carried out by Islamist terrorists (Vodlan 2015). They also recruit and train small children, some as young as 12 years of age, and use them for suicide attacks, patrols and as 'human shields' (U.S. Department of State 2015) or as couriers and even spies (Boghani 2015).

Trafficking in human tissue and organs is also one of the rising types of human trafficking exploited by terrorists. By recruiting foreign doctors, terrorists obtain professional staff who then remove the organs from the fallen members of the Islamic State, prisoners and even from sexual slaves. The obtained tissue and organs are then sent to the black market via Turkey and Saudi Arabia (Blake 2014; Unruh 2015), and funds for the purchase of arms or financing other activities are thus acquired.

The examples described above testify to the fact that Islamist terrorists in particular, use different types of human trafficking, thus contributing to the continued presence and, in some cases, to the increased extent of human trafficking. Therefore, the long-running military focus in the Middle East and Asia is ideal for the development of human trafficking. Dandurand (2012) emphasises that human trafficking is most developed in areas characterised by chaos, where the state is unable to control (illegal) activities on its territory and protect its citizens. In such crisis areas, economic growth is slowing down, which leads to increasing unemployment and vulnerability to exploitation (Benmelech et al. 2010), which is used to the benefit of organised crime networks.

In summary, and returning to Slovenia and human trafficking, the greatest concerns include sexual exploitation, workers' exploitation, child trafficking, forced begging and forced criminality. The labour exploitation represents a particularly interesting issue, since the informal economy is often associated with human trafficking. In Slovenia, the detected cases involve all types of precarious work, temporary work agencies and seasonal workers in agriculture (Dobovšek and Slak 2016). As already mentioned, the most alarming issue in Slovenia is thus associated with the mobility of young people, who were educated and trained in Slovenia, to rich countries with the goal of finding a job and starting a decent life.

4 Policies: Prevention and Suppression of Human Trafficking, and Victim Support

The phenomenon of human trafficking, in all of its dimensions and in terms of organised crime, presents a security threat to Slovenia and particularly to its citizens. As a democratic country, Slovenia is obliged to provide security to its population and also to every victim of human trafficking, regardless of their origin and status. In this context, Slovenia is obliged to design and implement a policy of preventing human trafficking and providing victim protection.

Trends in Europe and across the world point to an increasing need for more effective measures at both systemic and implementation levels. Despite some sort of marginalisation of human trafficking, this type of trafficking is, unfortunately, still on the rise. The reasons for this can be found in exploitative tendencies that are fulfilled by violating the rights of others, the loss of values in a consumer society, the growing demand for cheap labour, and the general poverty experienced by the majority of the population (Farrell 2012). Čurin (2016) stresses that Slovenia has recently witnessed speculations about the very existence of the human trafficking phenomenon, which led to questions as to whether it should be addressed at all and to what extent. The human trafficking phenomenon has repeatedly been reduced to the level of the criminal offence of the abuse of prostitution, either because it would be easier to prove such an offence or simply because of the interlacing of the two offences. This was also the underlying reason for the wider misunderstanding and generalisation of the human trafficking issue.

Human trafficking is intertwined with other areas of social life, such as migration, the (foreign) labour exploitation, the trafficking in children, particularly unaccompanied children, be them applicants for international protection (children refugees) or merely abused minors forced into begging or underage girls in servitude relationships and victims of forced marriages. As a result, human trafficking is a multi-faceted issue that requires a comprehensive and coherent approach (Bruckmüller and Scherman 2012; Dandurand 2012).

Over the last two decades, certain advances were observed in all areas of preventing and combating human trafficking in Slovenia. A fairly effective victim protection and assistance scheme has been put in place, while awareness-raising activities aimed at the general public, as well as individual target groups, and sound education and training of practitioners, have also been conducted. Such a system is somewhat sustainable, but not satisfactory. Despite the fact that the statistical extent of this phenomenon is not alarming in Slovenia, this is not and should not be the reason for the slowdown or even regression of achievements made so far (Čurin 2016). An Interdepartmental Working Group for Curbing Human Trafficking drafts annual reports for the Government of the Republic of Slovenia, outlining both achievements and deficiencies, as well as putting forward proposals for improvements. Čurin (2016) explains that the Group's coordinator tries to act as a rapporteur and, to some extent, the one who draws attention to the necessary systematic upgrades, which is why he or she often expresses constructive criticism of the work done.

The field of human trafficking, its prevention and the fight against it, are defined by a number of international documents, which have been complemented over time, even though they in essence preserve the message regarding the ban of the enslavement of particularly vulnerable categories of persons, i.e. women and children (Čurin 2016). These documents, harmonised with the national legislation (e.g. Criminal Code and other legislative acts), include:

– the United Nations Convention on Transnational Organized Crime, with an associated Protocol to Prevent, Suppress and Punish Trafficking in Persons, Especially

Women and Children, Supplementing the United Nations Convention Against Transnational Organized Crime (Palermo Protocol);
- the Council of Europe Convention on Action against Trafficking in Human Beings (GRETA);
- the European Convention on Human Rights (Article 4);
- Directive 2011/36/EU on Preventing and Combating Trafficking in Human Beings and Protecting Its Victims.

Čurin (2016) analysed the latest GRETA recommendations and the EU Directive 2011/36, and highlighted the following six sets of changes that Slovenia must introduce to meet the requirements set by the international community in the field of preventing and combating human trafficking, and the treatment of victims:

(1) Amending the criminal offence of trafficking (i.e. the introduction of a specific criminal offence of concealing, damaging or destroying of travel or identity documents in relation to human trafficking, and the introduction of a criminal offence of the use of services which are the objects of exploitation as defined in Article 4 of the European Convention on Human Rights, knowing that the person is a victim of human trafficking). In fact, Slovenia met this recommendation by amending Article 113 of the Criminal Code in 2015.
(2) Asset confiscation (i.e. the seizure and confiscation of funds and property obtained by or through the criminal offence of human trafficking, whereas the seized and confiscated assets are used to support victim assistance and protection or for victim compensation and trans-border law enforcement). Slovenia fulfilled this requirement by adopting the Confiscation of Assets of Illicit Origin Act, while asset confiscation is also covered by Articles 74–77 of the Criminal Code. However, it should provide for a more frequent tracking of financial flows accompanied by the seizure and confiscation of criminal proceeds.
(3) Impunity of victims of human trafficking (i.e. the adoption of a provision on the impunity of victims of human trafficking due to their involvement in illegal activities, insofar as they were forced to do so, in order to protect them and avoid further victimisation). In practice, victims of human trafficking, who were forced to commit a crime, are not prosecuted in Slovenia. This is stipulated in Article 23 of the Criminal Code. Pursuant to Article 50 of the Aliens Act, victims of human trafficking, who are legally residing in Slovenia should be authorised to stay for a period of three months by the police. Moreover, victims are free to decide whether to participate as witnesses in criminal proceedings involving a criminal offence of human trafficking.
(4) Protection of victims of human trafficking (i.e. better or fully exploit all available measures to protect victims during and after investigations). Slovene authorities must take additional measures to ensure that victims of trafficking are adequately informed about their rights and existing remedies, and receive assistance during pre-trial and judicial proceedings. It is also necessary to establish appropriate witness protection programmes (e.g. extending special protection procedures to all victims of human trafficking up to the age of 18, taking into account the best interests of the child) and other similar programmes in

order to avoid reprisals, intimidation and the risk of secondary victimisation. In the process of recognising the victim of human trafficking, the Slovene Police must, in a language understood by the victim, inform the victim of the right to help and support, to secure accommodation during the period of recovery and reflection, and the right to participate in criminal proceedings. Agencies, organisations and non-governmental and humanitarian organisations involved in the process of identifying victims of human trafficking are obliged to inform the victims of all available information and their rights. In Slovenia, a project entitled 'Assistance and Protection of Victims of Human Trafficking' has been implemented every year, which attempts to cover all areas of victim assistance.

(5) Compensation to victims of human trafficking (i.e. the adoption of measures to facilitate and provide access to compensation for victims of human trafficking). To this end, a Handbook on the Identification, Assistance and Protection of Victims of Trafficking in Human Beings was adopted in Slovenia, which clearly prescribes all procedures and information that all state bodies and NGOs are obliged to inform the victims of. However, with respect to compensation, the shortcomings of the Crime Victim Compensation Act will have to be addressed.

(6) Training (police and other authorities are still implementing extensive training programmes on human trafficking and have even developed an annual work plan for training programmes):

   (a) Slovene authorities should take further steps to ensure regular training in the field of human trafficking and victims' rights for all relevant professionals (such as judges, prosecutors, lawyers, staff of the administrative units responsible for issuing residence permits, labour inspectors, authorities for the protection of children and social workers). Future training programmes should be designed in a way that will enhance the knowledge and skills of relevant professionals which would enable them to identify victims of trafficking in all types of exploitation and provide them with assistance and protection, guarantee access to compensation for the victims and secure convictions of perpetrators.

   (b) Slovene authorities should intensify training for judges, prosecutors and other relevant experts on human trafficking in order to improve their knowledge and sensitivity on the subject and on the rights of victims of trafficking. Furthermore, the authorities should ensure the practical implementation of existing provisions in the fight against human trafficking beings, in order to allow effective prosecution of perpetrators and punishment, which should be proportionate to the gravity of the offence.

   (c) Slovene authorities should encourage investigative and law enforcement authorities to increase their specialisation in the field of human trafficking with a view to improving the collection of sufficient evidence and the successful prosecution of a large number of perpetrators.

The authors also observe a lack of cooperation between the various ministries responsible in the field of human trafficking, since the bulk of work appears to be shouldered by the Ministry of the Interior and there seems to be too much focus on repression. In addition, good practices should be followed, such as those developed in Italy, where media campaigns are implemented in different countries of origin in order to draw attention to the perilous conditions along traveling routes and at final destinations, as well as the dangers of organised groups. Finally, albeit just as importantly, more work needs to be done to limit the demand for informal types of work.

5 Conclusion

The issue of human trafficking paves the way towards the greater visibility of this serious social phenomenon in the broader lay public, as well as within professional services, including (criminal) justice. The reason for this lies in the intertwining between human trafficking and similar types of phenomena, some of which were mentioned in the beginning of this chapter, as well as in the lack of awareness that such crimes and violations of fundamental human rights are indeed occurring in our environment. Although foreign citizens are currently facing problems arising from the fact that they are a marginalised group at the lower end of the social scale, human trafficking may also affect young people and future generations as they look for new or better life opportunities, adventures and employment. Therefore, a vigorous approach to monitoring European trends in this field and the transposition of international regulations into national legislation, as well as their implementation, is required (Čurin 2016, p. 20).

Human trafficking is rather widely spread in Central and Eastern Europe, which includes the Balkans and Slovenia. Moreover, Western Balkan countries are no longer merely the countries of origin and transit for trafficked persons, but have also increasingly become countries of destination. Slovenia is among them, albeit it is rarely a country of origin, but rather a transit or destination country for the final exploitation of victims. Nevertheless, human trafficking in the Balkans has to be approached from a broader perspective, as programmes aimed at the development and strategies designed to reduce poverty would prevent numerous cases of human trafficking in the region (e.g. victims being sold to traffickers by their relatives due to poverty or examples of low-level traffickers, whose involvement in this criminal activity is stimulated by poverty) (Dobovšek 2012; Nikolić-Ristanović 2012; Kaye and Winterdyk 2012).

Slovenia made a huge step forward in all fields related to perpetrators and victims of human trafficking. Detailed policies and programmes were adopted, and a proper legal basis was established during the past decade which is still being updated in line with international documents and expectations. Nevertheless, there is still a lack of prevention programmes and activities to combat organised crime or human trafficking; thus, activities to prevent human trafficking are left to the individual endeavours of State or non-government and inter-government organisations (Peršolja 2006, p. 51). In addition, there is a lack of cooperation between government agencies and NGOs, which are obliged to take measures in these cases, although a project entitled 'Assistance and Protection of Victims of Human Trafficking' is improving the situation for victims. Furthermore, corruption, weak institutions and the shortcomings in the implementation of the rule of law are crucial barriers to the successful implementation of anti-trafficking measures in the region. To increase their effectiveness, crime control activities must include repressive and preventive measures, whereas all available criminal justice measures should be implemented more vigorously and effectively. Financial institutions should work together with the police according to the 'follow the money' doctrine, which should be prioritised to detect and suppress organised crime on the Balkan route.

The authors agree with Nikolić-Ristanović (2012 p. 214), who stated that future arrangements regarding human trafficking must be based on the security policy adopted by national parliaments, taking into consideration national security aims and ambitions, objective-driven circumstances, threat sources and the level of security culture. The aim of every security policy is to prevent and successfully confront different sources and types of threats, but an inconsiderate policy, waging a repressive war on human trafficking, can eventually do more damage than good. Therefore, countries have to approach human tracking from a broader perspective and tackle several interrelated issues at once (e.g. poverty, lack of social control, non-working anti-human trafficking programmes for victims, etc.).

The analysis of the situation in Slovenia implies that our country has a very well-developed policy of prevention and assistance to victims of human trafficking, where criminal justice agencies work closely with NGOs, to which victims most often turn for help. Furthermore, the Interdepartmental Working Group for Curbing Human Trafficking is very active by annually monitoring the situation in Slovenia and constantly drafting manuals and other methods for preventing and suppressing human trafficking in Slovenia.

It must be admitted that a system of supressing and preventing human trafficking really works only in normal circumstances. During the so-called 'tsunami wave' of migrants in the winter of 2015/2016, Slovenia almost caved into the pressures and challenges related to migration. Thanks to several NGOs, civil defence and firefighters that helped the police and the army in managing the situation on the state border, the security system and the system of support did not collapse. Moreover, Slovene authorities barely handled the migration wave effectively, which is why human traffickers easily crossed the border with hardly any threat of being detected. Nevertheless, the authorities claim to be well prepared for the potential second migration wave, launched by Turkey in the spring of 2020.

On the other hand, there has been an increase in disguised human trafficking, often in the shape of illegal work and, above all, over-work, which is the foundation of an informal economy. The former is particularly problematic, as no taxes are paid to the state budget and workers have no access to health insurance. Therefore, the illegal economy represents a competition to the legal economy, and in some aspects, it even turns into slavery (Dobovšek and Slak 2016). In conclusion, Slovenia's policy of combating human trafficking and the victim protection policy are generally well designed but poorly implemented and are being updated every year. We believe that it would be possible to define the public policy standards and objectives even more precisely, and to provide more resources for its implementation. There is also a need for closer cooperation between public policy actors responsible for the implementation of policies and government agencies which draft, monitor and supervise the implementation of public policies on human trafficking. Closer attention should also be paid to the economic, social and political situation in certain countries, since it can be an indicator for the occurrence of human trafficking when people are forced to search for a better life.

References

Aas Franko K (2007) Globalization and crime. SAGE Publications, Los Angeles

Amnesty International (2014) Escape from hell: Torture and sexual slavery in Islamic State captivity in Iraq. Amnesty International, London. https://www.amnesty.org.uk/files/escape_from_hell_-_torture_and_sexual_slavery_in_islamic_state_captivity_in_iraq_-_english_2.pdf

Benmelech E, Berrebi C, Klor EF (2010) The economic cost of harboring terrorism. J Confl Resolut 54(2):331–353

Blake M (2014) Blood money: How ISIS is selling human organs harvested from living hostages and its own dead soldiers to fund terror across the Middle East. The Daily Mail. http://www.dailymail.co.uk/

Boghani P (2015) Why Afghanistan's children are used as spies and suicide bombers. PBS. http://www.pbs.org/wgbh/pages/front-line/afghanistan-pakistan/isis-in-afghanistan/why-afghanistans-children-are-used-as-spies-and-suicide-bombers/

Bruckmüller K, Scherman S (2012) Crime control versus social work approaches in the context of the "3P" paradigm: prevention, protection, prosecution. In: Winterdyke J, Perrin B, Reichel P (eds) Human trafficking: exploring the national nature, concerns, and complexities. Tylor & Francis Group, Boca Raton, pp 79–102

Ćopić S (2009) The characteristics of male trafficking in Serbia. In: Nikolić-Ristanović V (ed) Male trafficking in Serbia. Victimology Society of Serbia and Prometej, Belgrade, Serbia, pp 81–133

Čurin S (2006) Trgovina z ljudmi – Mednarodne aktivnosti in umeščenost problematike v slovenskem prostoru [Human Trafficking – International action and the situation in Slovenia]. In: Čurin S (ed) Uveljavljanje mednarodnopravnih dokumentov s področja boja proti trgovini z ljudmi [Enforcement of international law documents in the field of fight against human trafficking]. Ljubljana, Ministry of the Interior Slovenia

Čurin S (2016) Kritičen pogled na problematiko trgovine z ljudmi v Sloveniji ob upoštevanju mednarodnih priporočil in evropskega pravnega reda. Pravosodni bilten 37(3):87–101

Čurin S (2017) V Sloveniji na področju trgovine z ljudmi letno beležimo pet do šest obsodilnih sodb. https://radioprvi.rtvslo.si/2017/10/v-sloveniji-na-podrocju-trgovine-z-ljudmi-letno-belezimo-pet-do-sest-obsodilnih-sodb/

Dandurand Y (2012) International cooperation. In: Winterdyke J, Perrin B, Reichel P (eds) Human trafficking: exploring the national nature, concerns, and complexities. Tylor & Francis Group, Boca Raton, pp 207–233

Dobovšek B (2007) Slovenija i reakcija na organizirani kriminalitet [Slovenia and reaction to organised crime]. In: Petrović B, Peršak N (eds) Sigurnost i suradnja kao reakcija na organizirani kriminalitet u srednjoj i jugoistocnoj Evropi [Security and cooperation as a reaction to organised crime in Central and South-eastern Europe]. Pravni fakultet, Sarajevo, pp 117–158

Dobovšek B (2012) The third wave: human trafficking in the Western Balkans. Human Traffick 12(1):51–63

Dobovšek B, Slak B (2016) Economic crisis and "white informal economy" – a slippery slope. Int J Sociol Soc Policy 37(7-8):1–9
Englund C, Viuhko M, Jokinen A, Aromaa K, Resetnikova A, Markina A, Nilsen M (2008) The organisation of human trafficking: a study of criminal involvement in sexual exploitation in Sweden, Finland and Estonia. Swedish National Council for Crime Prevention, Stockholm
Europol (2016) Trafficking of women and children for sexual exploitation in the EU: the involvement of Western Balkans organised crime. www.europol.europa.eu/...Crime.../Western_Balkans_THB_Threat_Assessment.PDF
Europol (2018) Criminal networks involved in the trafficking and exploitation of underage victims in the EU. https://www.europol.europa.eu/publications-documents/criminal-networks-involved-in-trafficking-and-exploitation-of-underage-victims-in-eu
Farrell A (2012) Improving law enforcement identification and response to human trafficking. In: Winterdyke J, Perrin B, Reichel P (eds) Human trafficking: exploring the national nature, concerns, and complexities. Tylor & Francis Group, Boca Raton, pp 181–206
Frangež D, Bučar Ručman A (2017) Specific forms of human trafficking in Slovenia: overview and preventive measures. Police Pract Res 18(3):230–244
Friman HR, Reich S (eds) (2007) Human Trafficking, Human Security, and the Balkans (The Security Continuum). University of Pittsburgh Press, Pittsburgh
Frontex (2016) Risk analysis for 2016 https://frontex.europa.eu/assets/Publications/Risk_Analysis/Annula_Risk_Analysis_2016.pdf. 10.2819/416783.
Golubovic-Skec S, Radeva-Berket M (2010) Trafficking in human beings in Croatia: an assessment focusing on labour exploitation. ICMPD, Vienna
Goodey J (2012) Data on human trafficking: challenges and policy context. In: Winterdyke J, Perrin B, Reichel P (eds) Human trafficking: exploring the national nature, concerns, and complexities. Tylor & Francis Group, Boca Raton, pp 39–56
Gov.si (2020) Boj proti trgovini z ljudmi [Fight against human trafficking]. https://www.gov.si/zbirke/projekti-in-programi/boj-proti-trgovini-z-ljudmi/
Hankel J (2014) ISIS: One of many contributors to trafficking in Syria and Iraq. Human Trafficking Center Blog. http://humantrafficking-center.org/posts-by-htc-associates/isis-one-many-contributors-trafficking-syria-iraq/news/article-2880815/Blood-money-ISIS-selling-human-organs-harvested-living-hostages-dead-soldiers-fund-terror-Middle-East.html
Herz A (2012) Human trafficking and police investigation. In: Winterdyke J, Perrin B, Reichel P (eds) Human trafficking: exploring the national nature, concerns, and complexities. Tylor & Francis Group, Boca Raton, pp 103–128
ISIS offers female slaves as top prizes for Koran competition (2015) MEMRI Jihad and Terrorism Threat Monitor. http://www.memrijttm.org/isis-offers-female-slaves-as-top-prizes-for-koran-competition.html
Jokinen A, Ollus N, Aroma K (eds) (2011) Trafficking for forced labour and labor exploitation in Finland, Poland and Estonia. HEUNI, Helsinki
Kaye J, Winterdyk J (2012) Explaining human trafficking. In: Winterdyk J, Perrin B, Reichel P (eds) Human trafficking: exploring the national nature, concerns, and complexities. Tylor & Francis Group, Boca Raton, pp 57–78
Keefer SL (2006) Human trafficking and the impact on national security for the United States. U.S. Army War College, Carlisle
Kocjančič K, Vodlan A (2016) Trgovina z ljudmi in islamistični terorizem [Human trafficking and Islamist terrorism]. Varstvoslovje 18(1):65–83
Lsocik Z, Wiczorek L (2011) Trafficking for forced labour in Poland. In: Jokinen A, Ollus N, Aroma K (eds) Trafficking for forced labour and labor exploitation in Finland, Poland and Estonia. HEUNI, Helsinki, pp 165–245
Luptakova M, Necada V, Preslickova H, Tvrdlicova K (2004) Trafficking in women: the Czech Republic perspective. Institute of Criminology and Social Prevention, Prague
Merlan A (13.8.2015) How ISIS uses rape and sexual slavery as a recruiting tool and a business. Jezebel. http://jezebel.com/how-isis-uses-rape-and-sexual-slavery-as-a-recruiting-t-1723848987

Meško G, Hacin R, Pirnat U, Eman K (2018) Migration issues in Slovenia: beyond the rhetoric of university-level criminology and crime prevention education for sustainable development. In: Kury H, Redo S (eds) Refugees and migrants in law and policy: challenges and opportunities for global civic education. Springer, Cham, pp 495–527

Milivojevic S, Segrave M (2012) Evaluating responses to human trafficking: a review of international, regional, and national counter-trafficking mechanisms. In: Winterdyk J, Perrin B, Reichel P (eds) Human trafficking: exploring the national nature, concerns, and complexities. Tylor & Francis Group, Boca Raton, pp 233–264

Nikolić-Ristanović V (2012) Human trafficking between profit and survival. In: Šelih A, Završnik A (eds) Crime and transition in Central and Eastern Europe. Springer, New York, pp 205–227

Peršolja T (2006) Boj proti trgovini z ljudmi [The fight against human trafficking]. In: Čurin S (ed) Uveljavljanje mednarodnopravnih dokumentov s področja boja proti trgovini z ljudmi [Enforcement of international law documents in the field of fight against human trafficking]. Ljubljana, Ministry of the Interior Slovenia

Policija [Police] (2016) Letno poročilo o delu policije za 2015 [Annual report on the work of the Police 2015]. http://www.policija.si/images/stories/Statistika/LetnaPorocila/PDF/LetnoPorocilo2015_popravljeno.pdf

Policija [Police] (2017) Letno poročilo o delu policije za 2016 [Annual report on the work of the Police 2016]. http://www.policija.si/images/stories/Statistika/LetnaPorocila/PDF/LetnoPorocilo2016_popravljeno.pdf

Policija [Police] (2018) Letno poročilo o delu policije za 2017 [Annual report on the work of the Police 2017]. http://www.policija.si/images/stories/Statistika/LetnaPorocila/PDF/LetnoPorocilo2017_popravljeno.pdf

Policija [Police] (2019) Letno poročilo o delu policije za 2018 [Annual report on the work of the Police 2018]. http://www.policija.si/images/stories/Statistika/LetnaPorocila/PDF/LetnoPorocilo2018_popravljeno.pdf

Policija [Police] (2020) Letno poročilo o delu policije za 2019 [Annual report on the work of the Police 2019]. http://www.policija.si/images/stories/Statistika/LetnaPorocila/PDF/LetnoPorocilo2019_popravljeno.pdf

Saltman EM, Winter C (2014) Islamic State: the changing face of modern Jihadism. Quillam Foundation, London

Scheinost M (2000) Transnational organised crime and cross-border trafficking in human beings in the Czech Republic. In: Van Duyne PC, Ruggiero V, Scheinost M, Valkenburg W (eds) Cross-border crime in a changing Europe. Tilburg University, IKSP, Praha, pp 37–55

Schloenhardt A (1999) Organised crime and the business of migrant trafficking: an economic analysis. Crime Law Soc Change 32:203–233

Smith CJ, Kangaspunta K (2012) Defining human trafficking and its nuances in a cultural context. In: Winterdyk J, Perrin B, Reichel P (eds) Human trafficking: exploring the national nature, concerns, and complexities. Tylor & Francis Group, Boca Raton, pp 19–38

Spencer J, Broad R, Aroma K, Junninen M, Markina A, Saar J et al (2011) Organised crime, corruption and movement of people across borders in the new enlarged EU: a case study of Estonia. Finland and UK. HEUNI, Helsinki

Stanojoska A (2016) Migrant and Refugee crisis in Europe: was Pandora's box open? J Liberty Int Aff 1(1):10–15

Surtees R (2005) Second annual report on victims of trafficking in South-Eastern Europe. International Organization for Migration, Geneva

Surtees R (2008a) Traffickers and trafficking in Southern and Eastern Europe: considering the other side of human trafficking. Eur J Criminol 5:39–68

Surtees R (2008b) IOM global database thematic research series: trafficking of men - A trend less considered. The case of Belarus and Ukraine. International Organization for Migration, Geneva

U.S. Department of State Publication (2015) Trafficking in Persons Report: July 2015. U.S. Department of State Publication, Washington DC

UNICEF (2004) Trafficking in children in Kosovo: a study on protection and assistance provided to children victims of trafficking. UNICEF, Priština

United Nations (UN) (2010) UN Convention against Transnational Organized Crime. https://www.unodc.org/unodc/en/organized-crime/intro/UNTOC.html

United Nations (2017) Report of the United Nations High Commissioner for Refugees. United Nations, New York. https://digitallibrary.un.org/record/1303980?ln=zh_CN

United States Department of State (2010) Trafficking in persons report. United States Department of State, Washington

UNODC (2016) Transnational organized crime: The globalized illegal economy. http://www.unodc.org/toc/en/crimes/organized-crime.html

Unruh B (2015) More reports of ISIS human-organ trafficking. WND. http://www.wnd.com/2015/08/more-reports-of-isis-human-organ-trafficking/

Vodlan A (2015). Trgovina z ljudmi kot varnostna grožnja sodobni državi (primer Slovenije) (Magistrsko delo) [Trafficking in human beings as a security threat to the modern state (Slovenia's example) (Master's thesis).]. Ljubljana: Fakulteta za družbene vede

Williamson C, Prior M (2009) Domestic Minor sex trafficking: a network of underground players in the Midwest. J Child Adolescent Trauma 2:46–61

Winterdyk J, Perrin B, Reichel P (eds) (2012) Human trafficking: exploring the national nature, concerns, and complexities. Tylor & Francis Group, Boca Raton

Katja Eman is an Associate Professor of Criminology at the Faculty of Criminal Justice and Security, University of Maribor, Slovenia. She is the author of Environmental Crime and Criminology: Crime Phenomena and Development of a Green Criminology in Slovenia (Scholar's Press 2014) and co-editor of the Water, Governance, and Crime Issues (Springer 2020). She participated in research on water crimes in Europe (2016-2017) and is currently a lead researcher in the EU research project SHINE on sexual harassment in nightlife city areas (2020-2023) (katja.eman@um.si).

Gorazd Meško is a Professor of Criminology at the Faculty of Criminal Justice and Security, University of Maribor, Slovenia. He was a lead editor of books entitled Trust and Legitimacy in Criminal Justice: European Perspectives (Meško & Tankebe; Springer, 2015), Handbook on Policing in Central and Eastern Europe (Meško, Fields, Lobnikar & Sotlar; Springer, 2013) and Managing and Understanding Threats to the Environment (Meško, Dimitrijević & Fields; Springer 2011), and Water, Governance, and Crime Issues (Eman, Meško, Segato & Migliorini; Springer 2020). He participated in a research project on water crimes in Europe (2016-2017) and is currently a lead researcher in a national research project on safety and security in local communities (2019–2024) (gorazd.mesko@um.si).

Bojan Dobovšek is a Professor of Criminology at the Faculty of Criminal Justice and Security, University of Maribor, Slovenia. He was an editor of the book entitled Corruption, Fraud, Organized crime, and the Shadow Economy (Edelbacher, Kratcoski & Dobovšek 2016), Advances in Police Theory and Practice series, and author of article 'Economic Crisis and "White Informal Economy" – A Slippery Slope'. International Journal of Sociology and Social Policy. He is a researcher on organised crime, corruption, and financial crime (bojan.dobovsek@um.si).

How Organized is Labour Trafficking? On the Involvement of Organized Criminal Groups in Labour Exploitation

Masja van Meeteren and Joanne van der Leun

Abstract Human traffickers are usually depicted in public discourse as evil villains: the crème de la crème of organized crime. Although this image has also been dominant among scholars for a long time, it has become increasingly controversial. On the one hand, this debate is fuelled by discussions amongst criminologists on criminal networks, on the other hand by the expansion of the legal definition of the crime since 2005. Apart from sexual exploitation, various other forms of human trafficking are distinguished now, including labor exploitation. This chapter explores the question of which organizational forms play a role in labor exploitation. Through a review of the empirical research literature on labor exploitation, the authors show that in the field of labor exploitation, there is probably less involvement in criminal syndicates or criminal networks that maintain contacts with other criminal networks. In many cases, labor exploitation is committed by individuals or family businesses, or smaller loosely organized networks that are not necessarily embedded in other criminal networks. For researchers and policymakers alike, it is therefore advisable not to approach labor exploitation exclusively from the perspective of transnational organized crime.

1 Introduction

Although human trafficking features high on policy agendas (Goodey 2008), it is certainly not a new or a recent problem. For many years, millions of people are estimated to be victims of trafficking in human beings (Datta and Bales 2013). According to different estimates, human trafficking allegedly is the third largest

M. van Meeteren (✉)
Radboud University, Faculty of Law, Nijmegen, The Netherlands
e-mail: masja.vanmeeteren@ru.nl

J. van der Leun
Leiden University, Leiden Law School, Leiden, The Netherlands
e-mail: j.p.vanderleun@law.leidenuniv.nl

A. M. Rodrigues, M. J. Guia (eds.), *New Forms of Human Trafficking*,
https://doi.org/10.1007/978-3-031-39732-5_14

criminal enterprise worldwide, after the trade in arms and drugs (Weizer 2014). Various sources also suggest that it is a growing and extremely lucrative phenomenon due to the high revenues to be made and limited chances of getting caught (Shelley 2010). This chapter discusses human trafficking that takes place outside of the realm of sex work and focuses on labor trafficking.

Legislation on human trafficking has long been restricted to sex trafficking and has been the domain of nation states. Since 2000, the punishment of human trafficking—including labor trafficking—has been regulated internationally and laid down in the Palermo Protocol of the United Nations. Since then, many countries have implemented the most important principles in their national legislation. The Palermo Protocol was part of the International Convention Against Organized Transnational Crime. As a result, in policy circles, human trafficking has from the outset been framed as a form of organized crime. International attention to the establishment of the protocol also arose as a result of a number of specific cases of organized crime. Today, human trafficking is still commonly framed as a problem of organized crime Viuhko (2018).

According to Europol, human traffickers are "professionals and organized criminals," and groups and networks involved in human trafficking meet the criteria for organized crime (Europol 2011). Stories about how women are transported to the West to work in prostitution are widely known. Also in the media these stories feature prominently, often discussing in detail the role of organized crime and portraying the perpetrators as the ultimate villain. Reports of NGOs and government agencies also suggest that it is a form of crime involving mainly organized crime groups (Tripp and McMahon-Howard 2015). Viuhko (2018, p. 182) likewise observes that traffickers are often portrayed as "ideal-kinds-of-offenders," that is as "hardened criminals who are members of organised crime groups." Researchers likewise suggest that organized groups play a large role in human trafficking and argue that traffickers seem to represent the ultimate criminals. Shelley (2010) for example writes that "many are among the most vicious of criminals." While this thought has been commonplace among scholars for a long time, nowadays, the idea that this image is not supported by empirical evidence seems to be gaining support. Keo et al. (2014, p. 204) for example state:

> The literature is replete with unsubstantiated, extraordinary estimates of the extent and profitability of the phenomenon, as well as unsupported claims about its control by organized crime syndicates.

Furthermore, the involvement of organized groups in human trafficking may have also changed over the years because the crime itself has changed as well. Whereas trafficking in human beings used to mainly refer to trafficking in women, today, the broad definition of human trafficking includes much more forms than sexual exploitation only. Perhaps these other forms of exploitation, such as labor exploitation, involve other types of traffickers with other organizational structures than those involved in sex trafficking. Based on a review of the empirical research literature, this chapter investigates which perpetrators and what forms of organization play a role in labor trafficking. The answer to this question has important consequences for combatting labor exploitation and for scholars studying this phenomenon.

2 Labor Trafficking

In most countries, the definition of trafficking is derived from the UN Convention against Transnational Organized Crime and the associated Palermo Protocol. The protocol provides a guiding definition of trafficking as follows: "the recruitment, transportation, transfer, harbouring or receipt of persons, by means of the threat or use of force or other forms of coercion, of abduction, of fraud, of deception, of the abuse of power or of a position of vulnerability or of the giving or receiving of payments or benefits to achieve the consent of a person having control over another person, for the purpose of exploitation." The concept of human trafficking thus incorporates a multitude of situations that were not previously seen as trafficking in human beings, including labor exploitation or labor trafficking. In this chapter, we will use both terms interchangeably.

Labor trafficking refers to exploitation that takes place in the domain of work and income but that does not concern sexual exploitation. It concerns cases of labor exploitation that are serious enough to qualify as human trafficking and therefor surpass mere bad employment practices. As the definition of human trafficking above has already shown, it concerns labor that takes place under the threat of or with the use of violence or other forms of coercion, of extortion, fraud, deception, abuse of power or abuse of a vulnerable position, for the purpose of exploitation.

In a recent example of labor trafficking from the Netherlands, the perpetrator exploited various immigrants who were illegally residing in the Netherlands by having them work in a laundry business under very poor conditions. While temperatures were very high, the employees were not allowed to open any window so there was insufficient ventilation. Employees were not given protective clothing while working with chemicals and some of the machines were unsafe. In addition, the victims had to work six or seven days a week, much more than had been agreed, usually until the work was completed (often for more than 12 hours at a time). To work as efficiently as possible, some of the employees slept in the workplace under appalling conditions for a fee. Payment of wages hardly took place. The perpetrators promised that wages would be paid later or used to arrange residence documents, which subsequently did not happen. So there was deception. The illegal status of the workers put them in a vulnerable position. There were no contracts or payslips and the employees involved could not turn to authorities or the courts. By working with this cheap workforce, the perpetrators were able to generate high turnover for a long period of time at very low costs. The court found that the deception and abuse violated the victims' personal freedom and human dignity, and sentenced the perpetrator to 12 months of imprisonment.

Although labor exploitation can be assumed to occur much more frequently than sex trafficking (Weizer et al. 2014a), empirical research is still scarce (Cockbain et al. 2018). The fact that both law enforcement and victim support are still more focused on exploitation that takes place in the sex industry contributes to this bias (Farell et al. 2020). To the extent that exploitation outside the sex industry is studied, the research is primarily legal (Weizer et al. 2014b). To date, the most important data available to researchers are data from law enforcement and victim support, which are inherently problematic to generalize from. Estimates of the size of the phenomenon or statements about its character are often intended to encourage parties to take action or emphasize the importance of a tough-on-crime approach, which does not always benefit the validity of the statements made (Tyldum 2010). Nevertheless, the scarce social science research on labor exploitation that does exist shows that there are some questions about the degree of criminal organization that is usually involved in labor exploitation (De Vries 2019; Viuhko 2018).

3 Conceptualizing Organized Crime

To analyze what forms of organization play a role in labor exploitation, it is important to understand the various conceptualizations of organized crime that are used in the literature. Therefore, we first discuss the most important insights from criminological research on how organized crime can be conceptualized.

There have been a lot of studies by criminologists into criminal activities that are assumed to require a certain degree of cooperation or organization (Bruinsma and Bernasco 2004). According to Finckenauer (2001), it is important to distinguish between the criminal activities which may require a certain degree of organization, and the partnerships in which these activities are being undertaken. Criminologists generally assume that human trafficking is a form of crime that requires organization. For example, there are activities concerning recruitment, transportation, and actual exploitation itself. However, the organization of these processes can in principle be done by one individual and do not require partnerships. In addition, not all the activities actually need to take place.

An important example of human trafficking in the Netherlands in which not all activities took place is known as the "Chinese Hospitality Case" from 2009. It concerned Chinese employees without a residence permit who worked 11 hours a day, six days a week and were housed in the restaurant where they worked. They did not speak Dutch, were unfamiliar with Dutch society and lived in isolation. However, they were not recruited in China but came to the Netherlands themselves with the aim of making money. They simply approached the restaurant themselves to ask for work. There was no question of a debt relationship or other obligation to the restaurant. In theory, the victims were free to leave at any time. Because they were afraid of being deported, the victims did not dare to go to the police, although they were hardly paid at all for their work. The employer took advantage of their vulnerable position, which in this case was "only" about exploitation and not about recruitment. It clearly shows that not all phases in labor trafficking have to be organized.

Criminal relations exist in many types and sizes, and therefore there are various concepts in use, that are not always as clearly defined. The "bureaucracy model" has long dominated the debate on organized crime. Organized crime has been conceptualized as "a bureaucratic organization with a pyramid structure, a strict hierarchy, a clear division of tasks, a code of conduct and an internal sanctioning system" (Weerman and Kleemans 2005). Such organizations are also described as criminal syndicates or mafia-like criminal organizations. Today, partnerships are increasingly studied from the perspective of social networks (Bruinsma and Bernasco 2004). Partly due to this, the term "criminal network" has become popular "as an indication of the structure of groups involved in organized crime." This is not just a change of perspective but also a real change due to developments in communication technology and transport possibilities.

Unfortunately, in the scientific literature on human trafficking and organized crime, it is not always clear what definitions authors use. In case authors do provide a definition, it is often derived from the policy definition of the United Nations. In their most recent Organized Crime Threat Assessment Europol notes:

> Since the year 2000, the United Nations Convention against Transnational Organized Crime has provided an internationally shared definition of an organised criminal group as a group of three or more persons existing over a period of time acting in concert with the aim of committing crimes for financial or material benefit.

Europol notes that this definition is less and less consistent with the reality of flexible and fluid networks. Moreover, it is clear that by using this definition, provided that the goal is materially benefit, a group of people engaged in crime can be defined as an organized criminal group quite easily.

For the above reasons, this chapter links up with this common conceptualization of organized crime, but also looks beyond this definition. It is investigated to what extent (1) criminal syndicates, (2) criminal networks of three or more persons, and (3) individuals or couples are involved in labor exploitation. The third category is added because in recent years stories have increasingly been published about human trafficking that takes place by individuals (Keo et al. 2014). As such, all cases of labor exploitation that do not meet the threshold of the Europol definition of three or more persons can be listed in that category.

4 Literature Research

For this chapter, we have conducted a literature research. We have searched for English and Dutch research literature using various search terms such as human trafficking and organized crime. In addition, in various bibliographies we found leads to new articles and books. Our literature research is limited to the last 17 years, because the Palermo Protocol was drawn up in 2000 and a literature review was published in 2002, which outlined the results of previous years (Bruckert and Parent 2002).

What is striking in more recent international literature on labor exploitation is that it is almost never explicitly analyzed what the role of organized crime is in this form of trafficking. The vast majority of research is conducted among victims (Serie et al. 2018). In interviews they explain, for example, about the violence, deception, and poor working conditions, but not about the way in which the perpetrators organized the exploitation. They probably usually have no insight into this. Nevertheless, various statements are made, for example based on estimates from experts in the field. According to Farrell et al. (2008), a survey of law enforcement officials in the United States shows that nine out of ten think that human trafficking is linked to criminal networks. In a book chapter on human trafficking in Europe, Shelley (2010, p. 226) warns not to underestimate the role of organized groups:

> Human trafficking is not as small-scale and disorganized as some would suggest." And "many traders in humans are sophisticated criminals who only lack the infrastructure and organization of drug traffickers operating within Europe.

Although at the beginning of her book, Shelley indicates that her findings are based on various empirical sources, it remains unclear on what Shelley bases these specific warnings and to what extent such statements also apply to traffickers in labor exploitation.

Furthermore, many studies do not analyze the entire perpetrator spectrum, but explicitly focus on the involvement of groups. For example, Shelley writes that she explicitly limits herself to reporting on human trafficking committed by groups and not by individuals. Although some authors acknowledge that cases not involving groups exist, they are often not examined. Leman and Janssens (2015, p. 10) point out that cases involving individuals or very small groups do not have the priority of the Public Prosecutor. They note that in their analysis of 63 investigations (of which 27 cases of labor exploitation) they have unwillingly paid less attention to individual or small-scale human trafficking networks, because these were less well represented in the files. They assert that "they do exist, more so even than is generally accepted, but they do not appear in the files." Because the authors do not discuss this further and the focus of the book is on completely different questions than the central questions posed here, this book was not included in our literature study. However, their observation is relevant.

Overall, there seems to be a bias towards groups both in investigation and research. Most criminologists seem less interested in analyzing the entire perpetrator spectrum and focus on the larger cases. In addition, those interested in studying individual, less organized forms of human trafficking face practical problems regarding the availability of data. Studies with an explicit focus on organized groups have not been included in the literature research due to this bias, nor have studies with a focus on children. Furthermore, this literature review only included studies that discussed exploitation in relation to criminal law and not labor law. Because the definition of labor exploitation we use here is related to human trafficking, studies that discuss "minor" forms of abuses in the labor market or precarious work have not been included in this review. It should be remembered that human trafficking and labor exploitation have been criminalized in various countries around the world.

We only included studies based on empirical research. Most of these studies discuss various forms of trafficking and do not always separately report on labor exploitation. Such studies have been included and where possible we tried to distinguish labor exploitation. If we had included only studies that specifically address the question of the role of organized crime, we would have very few studies to discuss. We therefore tried to distil the necessary information as much as possible from the details provided. In some publications this worked out better than in others. Studies that exclusively focus on sexual exploitation are not included in our review. As a result, many studies on human trafficking have not been included. The studies included varied from articles in international scientific journals to national policy documents.

5 The Involvement of Organized Crime Syndicates in Labor Trafficking

In a study by Keo et al. (2014), p. 21 interviews were held with prisoners convicted for human trafficking in Cambodia. Only one human trafficker was part of a criminal syndicate. This respondent said that trafficking in human beings was not part of the regular activities of the syndicate but that he had developed the human trafficking activities independently from the syndicate on his own initiative. Although this study reports both labor exploitation and sexual exploitation, this specific case concerned sexual exploitation and not labor exploitation.

Tripp and McMahon-Howard (2015) examined 24 judicial human trafficking cases in Atlanta. Only one of the 24 cases showed the involvement of a syndicate, and this was also a case of sexual exploitation rather than labor exploitation. Postma and Van Wijk (2012) analyzed 27 criminal investigations into labor exploitation. Their analysis shows that in some cases there are "groups of more than five people who organized the process of recruitment, employment and housing through a defined division of tasks."

According to Europol (2016), there are criminal syndicates involved in trafficking in human beings. Europol states that it is likely that human trafficking is one of the central activities of criminal syndicates involved in human trafficking due to the organization and planning it requires, especially when it comes to large groups of victims. In addition, syndicates are involved in various other offenses that support exploitation such as human smuggling, document fraud and money laundering, and in some cases also in criminal activities that are not related to the exploitation, such as drug trafficking, extortion, theft, and social security fraud. Europol (2016), however, mentions various forms of exploitation but does not clarify whether such syndicates are involved in sexual exploitation only or also in the field of labor exploitation.

In all other studies investigated here, there is no mention of the involvement of organized crime syndicates. Overall, only the study done by Postma and van Wijk

(2012) brings forward evidence for the involvement of organized crime syndicates in labor exploitation.

6 Criminal Networks of Three or More Persons

In the period 2013–2104, Europol received nearly 6000 reports about organized crime groups that would be involved in trafficking in human beings. Of these, 90% were involved in prostitution and 5.6% in labor exploitation. This resulted in 142 reports in 2013 and 190 reports in 2014. According to Europol (2016), trafficking in human beings is likely to be mainly committed by small groups operating independently as well as in collaborative relationships with other crime groups. According to Europol, the typical criminal group involved in labor exploitation consists of a structure of loosely organized networks linked by shared origin or ethnicity. Such groups are flexible and can quickly adapt to changing circumstances.

Levenkron (2007) studied the court records of 325 people traffickers in Israel. It remains unclear how many of these cases involve labor exploitation. Nevertheless, none of these records showed that large-scale organized networks are involved in trafficking in human beings. In most cases, individuals or small, loosely organized networks were involved. Other studies also show evidence of the involvement of loosely organized networks of three or more people in labor exploitation. The vast majority of the cases of labor exploitation (23 out of 27) analyzed by Postma and van Wijk (2012) involved some form of collaboration. At the same time, they also note that the collaboration was not large-scale. The suspects generally did not really work with other people, but ran a company with three or more people. In two cases, two suspects ran the company and hired a third (also Chinese) person to intimidate or assault the victims.

In the context of the Dutch National Threat Assessment 2017, completed criminal investigations on labor exploitation over the period 2011–2015 were analyzed. This concerned 58 investigations conducted by the labor inspectorate or the police on labor exploitation and criminal exploitation. Article 140Sr (criminal organization) was charged in only five of these investigations. In the context of this Dutch National Threat Assessment, organized crime was defined as a partnership consisting of at least two people. Based on this definition, 40 of the 58 cases meet this requirement. It is not clear in how many cases it concerns labor exploitation. It is striking that the bar on the number of people involved with two people is lower than the definition we use here (three people or more). Therefore, a number of cases will actually have to fall under the third category, but it is not possible to determine for how many of these cases this should be so.

Moreover, the authors of these studies question the criminal nature of the networks in which they are embedded. Of the 21 human traffickers interviewed by Keo et al. (2014), five were linked to three independent, small-scale networks. The three networks to which the five human traffickers belonged consisted of three to six individuals. Keo et al. (2014) mention that these traffickers have entered into a partnership without clearly defined roles and responsibilities. These were primarily temporary partnerships to make money quickly, and not long-term partnerships. According to Keo et al. (2014, pp. 214–215), the characteristics of these networks therefore did not correspond to common definitions of criminal organizations. They continue:

> Their accounts did not suggest that they belonged to a criminal organization, but rather that they merely happened to be acquainted. (…) Each of the three networks we uncovered consisted of three to six individuals who had formed an informal alliance without clearly defined roles and responsibilities or a hierarchy. These networks were family or friend-based, weak, amateurish, and had no clearly formulated plan. They were based on the temporary partnership of a few individuals looking for ways to make quick money

Unfortunately, it remains unclear whether one of the five cases involved labor exploitation, or whether they were all cases of exploitation in prostitution. Tripp and McMahon-Howard (2015) also concluded that in the labor exploitation cases, there were no cases where suspects were part of an organized network or that suspects had received help from a criminal network.

Cockbain and Brayley-Morris (2017) analyzed three cases of labor trafficking in the casual construction industry involving Irish traveler offending groups. So clearly, such groups are organized crime groups. It is discussed here because the authors also note that their involvement in labor exploitation seemed to be rather opportunistic. Each case involved multiple offenders—groups of three, five, and seven respectively, linked by close familial ties of kinship and marriage. Ten out of the 15 offenders in these cases had been previously convicted of in total 110 offenses. Their criminal records pointed towards an opportunistic and generalist approach to offending, of which labor exploitation just incidentally formed part. Only one of the 110 prior convictions could be lined to labor trafficking.

Overall, a modest number of studies points at the presence of organized crime groups in labor trafficking, and when they do, labor trafficking does not seem to represent their core business. Their engagement in labor trafficking seems rather opportunistic and perhaps even incidental. Moreover, the networks seem small scale, and in some cases, amateurish.

7 Individuals or Partnerships

Europol (2016) barely mentions cases in which an individual or only two people organize human trafficking. They only notice that it sometimes occurs in case of local exploitation or when only little victims are involved, but do not actually discuss this any further. Presumably this also relates to Europol's mission, which is more focused on transnational organized crime. In other studies, attention is paid to cases in which human traffickers operated individually or with a single partner.

Of the 21 human traffickers in prisons in Cambodia interviewed by Keo et al. (2014), p. 15 operated individually. This study includes cases of exploitation in the sex industry (19) and cases of labor exploitation (2). Only one of the two labor exploitation cases is actually described. In this case, there seems to be an independently operating perpetrator named Karot. He was convicted of exploiting two children he transported to Thailand to work in a plantation. He had previously transported groups of Cambodian illegal workers to Thailand. He then arranged a subcontracting contract with the plantation specifying what work the workers would carry out. For this, he negotiated one lump sum payment with the owner. He paid the workers part of the lump sum payment with a distribution key that he invented himself. He then also worked on the plantation to generate sufficient income for himself. Karot was not part of a criminal network but had set up this arrangement himself and on his own. It is not clear how the traffickers operated in the other case of labor exploitation.

The Tripp and McMahon-Howard (2015) study, which examined 24 human trafficking files in Atlanta, found that in 67% of these files, the suspects were not part of an organized network and had not been assisted by a criminal network. Moreover, it turned out that in all cases of labor exploitation there was an individually operating perpetrator who arranged the victim's arrival and subsequently exploited him or her in his own household. Exploitation in households often involves individuals or couples. For example, Owens et al. (2014) also found that the human traffickers involved in the employment of persons in domestic work acted as both recruiters and employers, and that only a few were involved in a criminal network. Wilson and Dalton (2008) analyzed 15 cases of human trafficking in Toledo and Columbus from the news. Five of these cases domestic work, with the traffickers operating alone or as a couple. It was also noted that the suspects were prominent doctors or business people who recruited their victims transnationally.

Van Meeteren and Wiering (2019) analyzed eight investigative police files on labor trafficking in Chinese restaurants in the Netherlands. In total 13 perpetrators were connected to these files: the restaurant owners. Most restaurants in the files are owned by a man and a woman (husband and wife), and in most cases both were seen as suspects. In some cases only the men were singled out. Although some restaurant owners relied on legitimate recruitment agencies for a supply of workers, the exploitation itself was organized by the restaurant owners themselves and there were no signs that the recruitment agencies took part in that.

Viuhko (2018) analyzed 11 court cases of human trafficking in Finland, including both cases of sexual exploitation as well as labor exploitation. She found that in the cases of labor trafficking it concerned people in the restaurant or service sector who had been exploited by only one person or a couple and where the perpetrators were relatives of the victim. She notes that "there are few signs of organised crime involvement related to labor exploitation in Finland" (Viuhko 2018, p. 187). And that "the role of organised crime is somewhat clearer in the cases related to trafficking for sexual exploitation."

A similar observation was made in a Canadian study by Beatson et al. (2017) in which 36 cases of labor exploitation were studied. The role of criminal networks was not explored explicitly, but the authors noted laterally:

> It is noteworthy that, from our sample, it appears that labour trafficking is less tied to organized crime than sex trafficking. Apart from a very few cases in our sample, most employers seem to have been private individuals or entrepreneurs engaged in legitimate small or medium-sized businesses whose practices over time evolved from deception to other forms of labour exploitation.

Moreover, these employers were not all private households but they were self-employed or employed in farms, factories, restaurants, and several small businesses. Therefore, it does not seem to be the case that labor exploitation involving perpetrators operating individually or in tandem only concern domestic work.

The analysis of Postma and van Wijk in the Netherlands shows that in only four cases the suspects acted entirely individually. In the great majority of cases, therefore, there was some form of cooperation, although it could consist of only two people. The collaboration often took place "in a smaller context within a regular company or family." For example, in the hospitality industry, "partners or family members often ran a restaurant in pairs and were jointly responsible for the exploitation of their staff. They generally did not cooperate with other people."

The same picture emerges in literature that was not included in the review because the inclusion conditions were not met, such as in the study by Hiah and Staring (2016). Based on qualitative research in the Chinese catering industry in the Netherlands, the labor relations between Chinese employers and their illegally staying employees are described. Although no explicit attention is given to the degree of organization or links to criminal networks, a clear picture emerges of couples or families who are responsible for the employment of their staff without the intervention of others. Cases are described of Chinese employees who have come to the Netherlands on their own and who work at a restaurant owned by a Chinese couple. The authors then show that both employers and employees do not seem to be aware that under Dutch law the conditions under which work is done can be seen as labor exploitation. A study by Bloch and McKay (2014) also shows that employers do not always operate with criminal motives, but sometimes have the idea that they are helping employees, for example by providing irregular migrants with a job they desperately need. In such cases, employers do not see themselves as exploiters or human traffickers. In addition, little organization needs to be involved in labor exploitation and employers act relatively independently.

From the studies described above the picture emerges that the perpetrators involved in labor exploitation are more heterogeneous than commonly suggested in literature on trafficking. In addition, the perpetrators involved in labor exploitation have a link with legitimate business structures, and much less with criminal organizations. Levenkron (2007, p. 97) notes:

> In contrast to traffickers of women for prostitution, whom it is easy and convenient to abhor, traffickers in construction and slavery are respectable companies, decent folks, usually without criminal records, without a blot on their names. They are viewed as normative citizens, and it would seem that, because of this image, the police find it difficult to investigate and prosecute them.

This quote illustrates that in cases of labor exploitation, it is likely that there is a completely different group of perpetrators than in cases of exploitation in prostitution. Although there may be a degree of organization, there seems to be a clear link with legitimate organizations and not so much with criminal organizations. In her analysis of court files on labor exploitation, De Vries (2019) shows how this crime can occur within legitimate market structures. Her study highlighted how regular market-based and personal relations in the marketplace linked more than 200 firms to labor trafficking and exploitation. This does not mean that legitimate and illegitimate organizations have nothing to do with each other. Illegitimate organizations are increasingly trying to operate in the legitimate atmosphere. But there is obviously a difference with the sex industry.

8 Conclusions

Myths are plentiful when it comes to human trafficking. The idea of labor trafficking as large-scale organized crime is one of them. Not because it does not exist, but because this is certainly not the only picture. With this analysis of national and international research literature we attempted to gain more insight into the role of organized crime in labor exploitation. Our analysis shows that there appears to be little empirical evidence for the involvement of criminal syndicates in labor exploitation. There are some studies that mention the involvement of criminal networks. The main reason to speak of criminal networks is in such cases that the networks consist of three or more persons and that they themselves engage in crime, namely labor exploitation. In only a few cases was there also involvement in other forms of crime, or the reverse, involvement in labor exploitation seemed an incidental opportunistic act apart from more regular involvement in other forms of crime. However, most cases that emerge in the empirical research literature are cases where individuals, households or small businesses are responsible for exploitation. In some cases, exploitation only takes place locally, and in other cases individual employers are responsible for the entire process from recruitment to the actual abusive work situation. Labor exploitation therefore does not necessarily appear to require so much organization that, by definition, several people should be involved.

For various reasons, however, based on the data that were available we cannot say anything conclusive about the extent to which organized crime is active in the field of labor exploitation. First, because there is still little research available on traffickers, and that what is usually available is about sex trafficking, not about labor exploitation. Labor exploitation is still an under-researched area, vastly overshadowed by research on sexual exploitation. To the extent that the involvement of organized crime is empirically demonstrated, it mainly concerns exploitation in the sex industry and not labor exploitation. But the evidence base is too meagre to say anything conclusive.

Second, research findings come from such diverse countries in the world that one may wonder whether these data can be compared across countries, and to what extent they can be translated from one context to the other. For example, Bruckert and Parent (2002) argue that there are relatively many amateurs in Asia and that the relationship between human trafficking and organized crime depends on local contexts. Based on large-scale empirical research in Finland, Poland and Estonia, Jokinen and Ollus (2011) conclude that involvement of organized crime groups differs between the three countries. In Poland, there are cases of involvement of organized crime groups, but in the Finnish and Estonian data there were no direct indications of organized crime involvement. It would be interesting to further analyze the regional differences we observe. Unfortunately, given the limited number of studies and cases in the context of this chapter, this is not possible. In any case, it is clear that the results from other countries should be translated to other contexts only with the utmost caution.

Third, research has to deal with a systematic bias in the data that is available for research. Researchers usually rely on data from criminal investigations, while the investigation of organized groups usually has more priority than the investigation of individual perpetrators. Postma and van Wijk (2012) encounter few individuals in the files of the Inspectorate SZW. This is not surprising given the working methods of this investigation service. The Inspectorate uses a risk model whereby data files of various authorities about companies are linked to calculate risk scores (Bogaerts et al. 2010). Exploitation within households is much less encountered in this way. In addition, part of labor exploitation is unlikely to be recognized as such because it is more likely to be perceived as illegal work (Van der Leun and Van Schijndel 2016).

Fourth, the question of involvement of criminal groups is dependent on the measurements used. Unfortunately, researchers use different definitions or do not make explicit how they define organized crime, which makes research not always easy to compare. It is clear that the international policy-based definition of organized crime has a very low threshold (groups of three or more people without clear structure), while the public image of organized crime groups is quite different (large well-oiled criminal networks with hierarchical control) (Finckenauer 2005).

Although there is much to be said about the generalizability of our findings, they clearly show that the image of organized crime is by no means the only image and probably not the dominant one. Moreover, we have argued that not all parts of the entire perpetrator spectrum of labor exploitation are well in sight, both in criminal investigations and in criminology.

Not only the degree of organization of the networks involved in labor exploitation deviates from the dominant image. The nature of the networks and individuals involved in labor exploitation also appears to be different. For example, many perpetrators turned out to be private households or family members who run a small business together. In such cases, the question of whether these perpetrators have links with criminal environments is an interesting one. By extension, it can be relevant in labor exploitation to make a distinction between labor exploitation that arises from business economic opportunistic motives and labor exploitation that arises in criminal environments. In any case, follow-up research would do well to investigate the entire perpetrator spectrum of labor exploitation.

In view of the foregoing, it is also advisable to not only approach the perpetrator spectrum from perspective of transnational organized crime, but also to look at the phenomenon from the perspective of, for example, organizational criminology and business administration. In the combat of labor trafficking, the priority clearly does not lie with the more small-scale and less organized labor exploitation, but these forms should also be considered in the design of an effective approach. For example, in some cases, a strategy of prevention or an administrative policy focusing on fines can be more effective than a criminal law approach. The rather one-sided image of the "violent organized gang" that is being reproduced over and over can also disguise a type of problem that may be more common in numbers and that requires a different approach.

References

Beatson J, Hanley J, Ricard-Guay A (2017) The intersection of exploitation and coercion in cases of Canadian labour trafficking. J Law Soc Policy 26:137–158

Bloch A, McKay S (2014) Employment, social networks and undocumented migrants. The employer perspective. Sociology 1:38–55. https://doi.org/10.1177/0038038514532039

Bogaerts A, Plooij P, Zoetekouw R (2010) De bestrijding van arbeidsuitbuiting. Werkwijzen en bevindingen van de SIOD, *Justitiële Verkenningen* 7:68–79

Bruckert C, Parent C (2002) Trafficking in human beings and organized crime. A literature review. Royal Canadian Mounted Police

Bruinsma G, Bernasco W (2004) Criminal groups and transnational illegal markets. A more detailed examination on the basis of the Social Network Theory. Crime Law Soc Change 1:79–94

Cockbain E, Brayley-Morris H (2017) Human trafficking and labour exploitation in the casual construction industry: an analysis of three major investigations in the UK involving Irish Traveller offending groups. Policing 12(2):129–149

Cockbain E, Bowers K, Dimitrova G (2018) Human trafficking for labor exploitation: the results of a two-phase systematic review mapping the European evidence base and synthesizing key scientific research evidence. J Exp Criminol. https://doi.org/10.1007/s11292-017-9321-3

Datta MN, Bales K (2013) Slavery in Europe. Part 1, estimating the dark figure. Human Rights Q *4*:817–829

De Vries I (2019) Connected to crime: an exploration of the nesting of labour trafficking and exploitation in legitimate markets. Br J Criminol 59(1):209–230. https://doi.org/10.1093/bjc/azy019

Dutch National Threat Assessment (2017) Mensenhandel – Arbeidsuitbuiting, criminele uitbuiting en gedwongen dienstverlening. Inspectie SZW, The Hague

Europol (2011) Trafficking in human beings in the European Union. Europol, The Hague

Europol (2016) Situation report. Trafficking in human beings in the European Union. Europol, The Hague

Farell A, Bright K, de Vries I, Pfeffer R, Dank M (2020) Policing labor trafficking in the United States. Trends Org Crime 23:36–56

Farrell A McDevitt J, Fahy S (2008) Understanding and improving law enforcement responses to human trafficking. Northeastern University, The Institute on Race and Justice, 2008, https://www.ncjrs.gov/pdffiles1/nij/grants/222752.pdf

Finckenauer JO (2001) Russian transnational organized crime and human trafficking. In: Kyle D, Koslowski R (eds) Global human smuggling. Comparative perspectives. John Hopkins University Press, Baltimore, pp 305–324

Finckenauer JO (2005) Problems of definition. What is organized crime? Trends Organ Crime 3:63–83. https://doi.org/10.1007/s12117-005-1038-4

Goodey J (2008) Human trafficking: sketchy data and policy responses. Criminol Crim Just 8(4):421–442

Hiah J, Staring R (2016) But the Dutch would call it exploitation'. Crimmigration and the moral economy of the Chinese catering industry in the Netherlands. Crime Law Soc Change 66(1):83–100

Jokinen A, Ollus N (2011) Trafficking for forced labour: project summary and conclusions. In: Jokinen A, Ollus N, Aromaa K (eds) Trafficking for forced labour and labour exploitation in Finland, Poland and Estonia. HEUNI, Helsinki, pp 312–323

Keo C, Bouhours S, Broadhurst R, Bouhours B (2014) Human trafficking and moral panic in Cambodia. ANNALS Am Acad Polit Soc Sci 1:204

Leman J, Janssens S (2015) Human trafficking and migrant smuggling in Southeast Europe and Russia. Criminal entrepreneurship and traditional culture. Palgrave MacMillan, Houndmills, p 10

Levenkron N (2007) Another delivery from Tashkent. Profile of the Israeli Trafficker. Hotline for Immigrant Workers, Tel Aviv

Owens C, Dank M, Breaux J, Banuelos I, Farrell A, Pfeffer R (2014) Understanding the organization, operation and victimization process of labor trafficking in the United States, Urban Institute Crime and Justice research report

Postma D, Van Wijk J (2012) Op het land in plaats van achter het raam. Aard en omvang van arbeidsuitbuiting in Nederland. PROCES 91(5):327–339

Serie CMB, Krumeich A, van Dijke A, de Ruiter E, Terpstra L (2018) Seks trafficking views: a qualitative study into their perceptions of the victim-offender relationship. J Human Traffick 4(2):169–184

Shelley L (2010) Human trafficking. A global perspective. Cambridge University Press, Cambridge

Tripp TM, McMahon-Howard J (2015) Perception vs. reality. The relationship between organized crime and human trafficking in metropolitan Atlanta. Am J Crim Just 4:732–764. https://doi.org/10.1007/s12103-015-9315-5

Tyldum G (2010) Limitations in research on human trafficking. Int Migr 5:1–13. https://doi.org/10.1111/j.1468-2435.2009.00597.x

Van der Leun JP, Van Schijndel A (2016) Emerging from the shadows or pushed into the dark? The relation between the combat against Trafficking in Human Beings and Migration Control. Int J Law Crime Just:26–42

Van Meeteren MJ, Wiering E (2019) Labour trafficking in Chinese restaurants in the Netherlands and the role of Dutch immigration policies. A qualitative analysis of investigative case files. Crime Law Soc Change 72(1):107–124

Viuhko M (2018) Hardened professional criminals, or just friends and relatives? The diversity of offenders in human trafficking. Int J Comp Appl Crim Just 42(2–3):177–193

Weerman FM, Kleemans E (2005) Criminele groepen en samenwerkingsverbanden. Een overzicht. Tijdschrift voor Criminologie 2:114–127

Weizer R (2014) New directions in research on human trafficking. ANNALS Am Acad Polit Soc Sci 1:6–24

Weizer R, Kay J, Winterdyk J, Quarterman L (2014a) Beyond criminal justice. A case study of responding to human trafficking in Canada. Canadian J Criminol Crim Just 1:23–48

Weizer R, Joarder MAM, Miller PW (2014b) The experiences of migrants trafficked from Bangladesh. ANNALS Am Acad Polit Soc Sci 1:141–161

Wilson JM, Dalton E (2008) Human trafficking in the Heartland. Variation in law enforcement awareness and response. J Contemp Crim Just 3:296–313

Masja van Meeteren is a Professor of Criminology at Radboud University (Nijmegen, the Netherlands). Masja researches approaches to crime control and their (unintended) consequences at the intersection of crime and migration. On the one hand, she focuses on legislation, policy and discretionary actions and decisions by and about actors involved in criminal justice and administrative enforcement; on the other, she focuses on manifestations of crime that are closely related to migration, such as human trafficking or human smuggling (m.vanmeeteren@jur.ru.nl).

Joanne van der Leun is a Professor of Criminology at and Dean of the Leiden Law School, Leiden University the Netherlands. Her research interests are irregular migration, migration control, human trafficking and policies in the field of crime and migration. She is one of the initial members of the CINETS steering group (www.crimmigrationcontrol.com) and member of the Working Group "Immigration, Crime and Citizenship" of the European Society of Criminology. She is a member of the Dutch Advisory Committee on Migration Affairs (ACVZ), an independent body which advises the Dutch Government and Parliament on migration issues (j.p.vanderleun@law.leidenuniv.nl).

Human Trafficking in Brazilian Law: The New Legal Definition

Artur de Brito Gueiros Souza

Abstract This chapter aims to analyze the crime of human trafficking, considering both the phenomenon on a global scale as well as the situation in Brazil. Therefore, the chapter discusses the legal evolution of this crime in the history of Brazil, from the Brazil Empire to the insertion of the country into the globalized world. Specifically, this chapter analyzes the controversy involving the new legal definition of the crime of human trafficking, which was brought by Law No. 13.344/2016, whose meaning is different from that previously existing. The text also aims to verify whether, with the enactment of the new Article 149-A, there was *abolitio criminis* of facts that were considered criminal based on the prior legislation.

1 Introduction

Despite its recognized seriousness, human trafficking has received deficient legal treatment in Brazil. The different types of human trafficking, whether internally (considering the vast extension of our territory and our equally enormous social inequality) or abroad, were defined in different ways, such as the crime of reducing a person to a condition analogous with slavery, recruitment of workers for emigration purposes, crimes of sexual exploitation, or removal of organs, or even the illegal adoption of minors. The law addressed conducts defined in the Brazilian Penal Code (BPC) and in specific legislation, although without any rational systemization.

Despite the existence of crimes covered in several different laws, the official data indicated that, between the years 2005 and 2011, thousands of Brazilians and foreigners (most of whom are women and children) were victims of these criminal practices (BRASIL. Relatório Nacional sobre Tráfico de Pessoas: Consolidação dos dados de 2005 a 2011). One of the factors that contributed to the alarming human

Artur de Brito Gueiros Souza (✉)
State University of Rio de Janeiro (UERJ), Faculty of Law, Rio de Janeiro, Brazil
e-mail: arturgueiros@uerj.br

A. M. Rodrigues, M. J. Guia (eds.), *New Forms of Human Trafficking*,
https://doi.org/10.1007/978-3-031-39732-5_15

trafficking numbers very likely was precisely the absence of any standardization in our Criminal Law as related to international standards, with the consequent lack of legal clarity and the impunity of members of criminal organizations specialized in the highly lucrative "business" involving the illegal exit of Brazilians into foreign lands and the illegal entry of foreigners into Brazil.

Based on this, and through the country's signing of the "Additional Protocol to the United Nations Convention Against Transnational Organized Crime Associated with the Prevention, Suppression and Punishment of Trafficking in Persons,"[1] Law No. 13.344/2016 established a new national policy for addressing human trafficking. Besides providing uniform treatment for preventing and repressing this crime, Law No. 13.344/2016, which amended BPC, joined the types of human trafficking under a single definition (Article 149-A). Under these terms, pursuant to Law No. 13.344/2016, the criminal categories from Articles 231 and 231-A, of BPC, which addressed international human trafficking for sexual exploitation and human trafficking for the purpose of sexual exploitation, respectively, were fully and expressly revoked. The other offenses mentioned above were partially and implicitly revoked.

If, on one hand, the lawmaker acted well by establishing updated and unified legislation, on the other, it caused controversy related to a possible abolition of the crime (*abolitio criminis*). This is because the prior legal provisions used the typical structure of prohibiting the promotion or facilitation of trafficking for the purposes of prostitution or sexual exploitation. The new Article 149-A of the BPC describes the more extensive typical structure using eight verbs (serving as agent, luring, transporting, etc.), but tied the existence of the crime to the agent's use of a serious threat, violence, duress, fraud, or abuse. It should be noted that, in the prior legislation, this condition did not exist, since the crime was considered committed only when there was the trafficking of persons for prostitution.[2]

The objective, therefore, is to discuss this issue, aiming to offer a possible solution for the contentious occurrence of *abolitio criminis*. Accordingly, it offers a brief analysis of the historical evolution of the classification of crime in Brazil. After that, the text covers the controversy, seeking an adequate solution to effectively combat the reprehensible practice of human trafficking.

---

[1] Enacted in Brazil through Decree No. 5.017/2004.

[2] Cf. instructed by Edmilson da Costa Barreiros Jr.: "By any means, this does not ignore the many controversial aspects of the new text, which innovated in describing the means of execution ('... through serious threat, violence, duress, fraud, or abuse...'). This, for some, would imply the reduction of *jus puniendi* through retraction by the lawmaker. Of the five types chosen, three already existed in previous texts and two (duress and abuse) were added to the text" (Barreiros JR., Edmilson da Costa).

2 Regulatory Development of the Crime of Human Trafficking in Brazilian Law

It is not possible to discuss the regulatory development of the repression of human trafficking without first covering the trafficking of Africans brought, sold, and subjugated to the atrocious system of slavery that has existed since our discovery (in the year 1500) until the middle of the period of the Brazilian Empire. It was only through Law No. 581/1850, enacted after pressure from the British Empire, that the "trafficking of Africans" became prohibited.[3] According to Nina Rodrigues, originating from different "nations" and "distinct cultures," the survivors of the awful Atlantic voyages had been captured from among tribes and cultures then located in Cape Verde, Mozambique, Portuguese Guinea, Congo, Sudan, Angola, and Mina Coast, among other regions of Africa.[4] Despite the fact that the trafficking of slaves had been prohibited in 1850, as paradoxical as it might seem, slavery in of itself was only abolished quite late in Brazil, in 1888, through Law No. 3.353, which became known as the "Aurea Law."[5]

Based on this historic record, the international trafficking of people who, in thesis, are not subjected to slavery or servitude, is a long-standing criminological phenomenon in Brazil.[6] It is interesting to observe that the commitment by the countries in the sense of preventing and repressing trafficking was part of the first efforts

[3] See Article 1 of Law No. 581/1850: "Brazilian vessels found in any part, and foreign vessels found at the ports, inlets, anchored out, or in territorial waters of Brazil, that have slaves on-board, whose importing is prohibited (…) or which has unloaded said individuals, shall be apprehended by the authorities, or by Brazilian warships, and considered importers of slaves. Those that did not have access to slaves on-board, or which have not unloaded them nearby, but which are found to show signs of employing the trafficking of slaves, shall be equally apprehended, and considered guilty of an attempt to import slaves" (in http://www.planalto.gov.br/ccivil_03/leis/lim/LIM581.htm).

[4] Cf. Rodrigues (1982), p. 19. Further, according to the author: "It is needless to discuss the precise date on which black slaves were first introduced in Brazil. Nearly half a century before its discovery, the African slave trade existed in Europe, and Portugal served as its headquarters. Black slavery in Brazil is, therefore, a contemporary phenomenon of its colonization" (Idem, p. 15).

[5] Cf. "Article 1 Slavery in Brazil has been declared extinct since the date of this law" (in http://www.planalto. gov.br/ccivil_03/leis/lim/LIM3353.htm.

[6] Between the turn of the nineteenth century and twentieth century, thousands of women and children who survived hunger, poverty, and the European *pogroms* were "trafficked" to Rio de Janeiro and São Paulo through a connection departing from the ports of Marseilles (France) and Odessa (currently the Ukraine) with passage through Buenos Aires (Argentina). They came to "supply" the male demand for paid sex, as if they were mere "merchandise," as part of a criminal activity dominated by the so-called international pimps (Souza 2006, p. 184). According to Beatriz Kushnir, Argentina, and especially the city of Buenos Aires, "was known from 1880 to 1930 as the largest global center for the prostitution trade" (Kushnir 1996, p. 69). In a book he wrote nearly 100 years ago, author Evaristo de Moraes stated that one of the conclusions from the 5th Paris Penitentiary Conference (1895) was that the "disgraced victims" of trafficking to the more populated cities of South America nearly all originally came from Austria-Hungary, Russian Poland, Italy, Romania, and France (Moraes 1921, p. 323).

toward collaboration on criminal matters. In this sense, there was the celebration of the "International Convention on the Repression of Trafficking of White Women" in Paris (1902), which required countries, among them Brazil, to reform their criminal law based on what had been established. In compliance with this international commitment, there was the enactment of Law No. 2.992/1915, which, changing the Penal Code from 1890, defined "pimping and trafficking of women."[7]

Under Article 278 of that law, it was considered a crime to "maintain or exploit brothels, induce women, whether abusing of their weakness or poverty, whether humiliating them through intimidation or threats, and presenting them for prostitution, providing, either on one's own behalf or someone else, under your own or someone else's responsibility, any assistance or support for the commerce of prostitution. Sentence: one- to three- year prison term, plus a fine. § 1. Luring, attracting, or misleading, to satisfy the lewd lusts of others, any minor, whether a virgin or otherwise, even with the misuse of their consent; luring, attracting, or misleading, to satisfy the lewd lusts of others, any adult woman, virgin or otherwise, employing for this purpose threat, violence, fraud, trickery, abuse of power, or any other means of duress; retaining by any of the aforementioned means, even if due to debts incurred, any woman, either an adult or minor, virgin or not, in a house of prostitution, forcing her to participate in prostitution. Sentence: the same as in the provisions above. § 2. The crimes covered in Article 278 and § 1 of the aforementioned article will be punishable in Brazil even if one or more of the acts constituting the violations covered in the same have been practiced in a foreign country."

Some decades later, with the enactment of the Brazilian Penal Code (BPC) of 1940, a more succinct wording was offered for the crime in question. With the section "trafficking of women," Article 231 of the BPC states: "Promoting or facilitating the entry into national territory of a woman that enters to exercise the practice of prostitution, or the exit of a woman who will exercise this practice abroad. Sentence: three- to eight-year prison term."

The legal provision of Article 231 of the BPC was in effect for approximately 65 years until it was amended, already in the 21st century, for Law No. 11.106/2005. At the same time, as anticipated, other offenses were created to prevent and repress other human trafficking conducts, even though not focused on the purpose of prostitution. This is how the BPC itself was changed to better regulate the crime of reduction to a condition analogous with slavery, with this crime classified as "reducing someone to a condition analogous with slavery, whether by subjecting this

[7] At the start of the twentieth century, Evaristo de Moraes reported that "despite the legislator's sincerity and morally remediating intentions of the top authorities, it would not be legitimate to rely, for this and other topics, on the impartiality of the subordinate executors of laws," responsible for repressing pimping and prostitution, primarily of foreigners of a Semitic origin. Based on his own words: "With respect to those who exploit prostitution, for example, we have only witnessed as of the date this essay was written, the trend to persecute those of the Israeli ethnicity and religion, the most well-known to pimps, with complete indifference for the others, even national citizens, which are as or more dangerous. In this case, similarly to other social relations—concluded Evaristo de Moraes – equality before the law gives way to conveniences of all kinds" (Idem, pp. 338–339) (highlights from original).

individual to forced labor or exhaustive work hours, or by subjecting said individual to degrading work conditions, either by restricting his or her movement by any means, based on some debt incurred with the employer or representative. Sentence: two- to eight-year prison term, plus a fine, in addition to a sentence corresponding to the violence."[8]

Law No. 8.069/1990 (Brazil's Child and Adolescent Statute), in Article 239, regulated the crime of illegal adoption: "Promoting or assisting with the execution of the act designed to send the child or adolescent abroad, failing to observe the legal formalities or with aims of earning profit: Sentence: four- to six- year prison term, plus a fine."

Law No. 9.434/1997, in its Article 14, classified the crime of the illegal removal of organs: "Removing tissue, organs, or body parts from a person or cadaver, failing to comply with the provisions of this law. Sentence: two- to six-year prison term, and a daily fine ranging from 100 to 360 days."[9]

As anticipated, Law No. 11.106/2005 gave new wording to "trafficking of women," changing the wording to call it "international human trafficking." "Promoting, intermediating, or facilitating the entry on national territory of people who come to exercise prostitution or the exit of people to exercise this practice abroad. Sentence: three- to eight-year prison term, plus a fine. (…) § 2 If there is the use of violence, serious threat, or fraud, the sentence is a five- to 12-year prison term, and a fine, in addition to the sentence corresponding to the violence."

Law No. 11.106/2005 also introduced the crime of "domestic human trafficking" in Brazil in Article 231-A of the BPC: "Promote, intermediate, or facilitate on national territory the recruitment, transport, transfer, lodging, or sheltering of people who come to exercise prostitution. Sentence: three- to eight-year prison sentence, plus a fine."

A few years later, Law No. 12.015/2009, once again changed the BPC, offering a new wording, both for international and domestic trafficking, removing the verb "intermediate" from the text. The text reads as follows: "Article 231. Promoting or facilitating the entry, into national territory, of someone who comes there to exercise the practice of prostitution or another form of sexual exploitation, or the exit of someone who comes to exercise it abroad. Sentence: three- to eight-year prison term. § 1 Incurs the same sentence as the person who serves as agent, lures, or purchases the trafficked individual, as well as, aware of this condition, the person who transports, transfers, or lodges said individual. § 2 The penalty is doubled if: (…) IV – there is use of violence, serious threat, or fraud."[10]

As stated, Law No. 13.344/2016 once again amended the BPC, and gave new wording for the crimes of human trafficking, joining the two in Article 149-A, with multiple verbs: "Negotiating, luring, recruiting, transporting, transferring,

[8] Text based on Law No. 10.803/2003.

[9] The §§ of the cited Article 14 of Law No. 9.434/1997 cover the qualified types related to economic motivation, bodily injury of a serious nature, or even the death of the victim.

[10] Domestic human trafficking had wording similar to the one used for international trafficking, naturally containing the elements of displacement *within* the national territory.

purchasing, lodging, or sheltering a person, through serious threat, violence, coercion, fraud or abuse, with the purpose of: I - removing their organs, tissues or body parts; II - subjecting them to conditions analogous to slavery; III - subjecting them to any type of servitude; IV - illegal adoption; or V - sexual exploitation. Sentence: four- to eight-year prison term, plus a fine."[11]

It is also important to observe the political-criminal trend of transferring categories of crime, which in the Penal Code, protect the sexual dignity from "crimes against customs" to "crimes against the person." This is what can be exemplified with the occurrence of violent kidnapping or that which uses fraud, from the former Article 219 of the BPC, which was later transported to Article 148, subsection V of the BPC (a type of illegal kidnapping), pursuant to Law No. 11.106/2005. It can be imagined that, in the future, all sexual crimes come to be cataloged right at the start of the BPC, within the sphere of crimes against people, considering the close relationship with the greater principle of human dignity.[12]

3 The Controversy Associated with the Abolishment of the Crime

An in-depth reading of Law No. 13.344/2016 reveals the lawmaker's scope in the sense of its progress to confront human trafficking in its many different forms based on an interdisciplinary approach (human dignity, non-discrimination, transversal nature of the dimensions of gender, sexual orientation, attention to victims, and particularly, children and adolescents).

Generally, there was a criminal and procedural upsurge in the cited phenomenon, notably through cooperation between the international justice system and public safety agencies.[13] Furthermore, the law established the adoption of guaranteeing measures to block financial transactions, as well as the subsidiary application of Law No. 12.850/2013 (Criminal Organization Law), reinforcing the role of the

---

[11] Under § 1 of Article 149-A, BPC, the penalty is increased from one-third to one-half if: I—the crime is committed by a civil servant during the exercise of his or her duties or the pretext of exercising them; II—the crime is committed against a child, adolescent, elderly person, or person with a disability; III—the agent makes use of the special relationship of kinship, among others; IV—the victim of human trafficking is removed from the national territory.

[12] In an exactly opposite sense to the political-criminal trend, Law No. 13.445/2017 – Migration Law – still on the topic of *vacatio legis*, introduced the crime of *promotion of illegal migration* into the title associated with the protection of sexual dignity: "Article 232-A, BPC. Promote, by whatever means and with the intent of obtaining some economic advantage, the illegal entry of foreigners into national territory or the entry of Brazilian citizens into a foreign country. Sentence: two- to five- year prison term, plus a fine."

[13] In this sense, human trafficking no longer includes the requirement of the victim's entry into or exit from the national territory. Furthermore, the international character of a crime of this nature leads to an increase in the sentence (cf. Article 149-A, § 1, sub-section IV of the BPC).

police and Public Prosecutor's Office, and increased rigor when granting parole, among other measures.

In this sense, upon analyzing the new Article 149-A of the BPC, Luiz Regis Prado observes that the legal asset protected would resemble the crime of reduction to a condition analogous with slavery, that is, "human freedom, and particularly, personal dignity, considering that the victim, even if consenting to the trafficking, does so because of violence, a serious threat, duress, fraud, or abuse, and is treated here as *mera res*, as a thing or object, that is taken from one place to another with utter disregard for his or her moral integrity."[14]

Nevertheless, a controversial legislative technique was used to elaborate the type covered by the new Article 149-A of the BPC, as seen in the comparison of structures in the current wording of the crime compared to previous wordings, which are described above. If previously there was nothing in the text about the victim's agreement or lack of it, and the promotion of trafficking with the person's knowledge that he or she would leave the country to work as a prostitute,[15] the new wording alludes that serving as agent, luring, transport, etc., takes place based on serious threat, violence, fraud, duress, or abuse; or in other words, against the victim's express or tacit will.

One hypothetical example—based on the professional experience of the signatory as Federal Prosecutor responsible for investigating and criminally prosecuting those people involved with said illegal practice—can illustrate the understanding of the problem:

> Before the effective date of Law No. 13.344/2016 (that is until the new law), individual "A," without being involved with some criminal organization, lures women "B" and "C" for the purpose of exercising the practice of prostitution in a brothel located along the side of the road in a certain European country. Women "B" and "C" are aware of the sexual nature of the activity to which they will be subjected on European soil, with it certain that "A" did not use violence, serious threat, or fraud, providing only the passport, purchase of clothing, winter clothes, meals, and airline tickets (Brazil-Europe) for the flight taken by "B" and "C."

Accordingly, in the case taken as an example, it can be verified that "A," besides not belonging to any criminal organization, did not use violence, serious threat, or fraud to promote *lato sensu* the exit of "B" and "C" to exercise prostitution on foreign soil. Before Law No. 13.344/2016 went into effect, this would certainly be a crime (old Article 231-A, of the BPC, described above), with "use of violence, serious threat, or fraud," serving only to associate a more serious conviction with the crime. Accordingly, through a fast reading of (the new) Article 149-A, BPC,

[14] Prado (2017), p. 210.

[15] Cf. "It does not matter whether she/he knew whether he/she would be prostituted, if she/he married a foreigner based on spontaneous will, whether she/he agreed to be transported to work in another state/country, and upon arriving to the destination site, became a victim of some type of exploitation. Consent is irrelevant, since the individual is ill-informed, and therefore, such consent would not be valid. (…) The lack of alternatives means that these victims, even when aware of the risks during transport and in certain cases, suspicious of the promises of a better life in other cities /countries, surrender to the trafficking network" (*Relatório Nacional sobre Tráfico de Pessoas* ("National Report on Human Trafficking") cit., p. 8).

apparently there was indeed the phenomenon of abolition of the crime (*abolitio criminis*), making the exemplified conduct of "A" atypical (non-criminal) based on the new law.

Nevertheless, special attention should be given to the elements of "abuse" and "duress" introduced by Law No. 13.344 in the crime of human trafficking.[16] In the case above, it can be concluded that "B" and "C" incurred a debt with "A" (costs to issue the respective passports and international airline tickets, along with other expenses). Removing the theoretical possibility of "philanthropy" or the "unpretentious" donation of money, it is interesting to consider whether "A" did not take advantage (*abuse*) of the vulnerable financial situation[17] of women "B" and "C," expecting at least the reimbursement of the amounts spent, to be provided with the money earned from prostitution.[18]

As expressed by Edmilson Barreiros Jr.:

> It is not possible to understand this element [of abuse] as typical without understanding that the different types of vulnerability, protected by International Treaties and Conventions, are included therein. The experience of International Law and the fight against human trafficking presumes a more in-depth understanding of this concept. The law should not fight against the reality when there is a compatible interpretation for reasonable regulation. Discarding *vulnerability*, which maximizes the risks of victimization through human trafficking, would imply the undue reduction in the Brazilian government's role in the global effort against this *global crime*.[19]

It cannot be ruled out that, besides taking advantage of the situation of economic vulnerability, there is also, in the case at hand, "duress," also established in the text of Article 149-A, BPC, by Law No. 13.344/2016. In the case analyzed, there was resistible or irresistible (moral) duress (the type does not matter) for "B" and "C" to return, with the money earned from prostitution, the money for the inducement expenses incurred by "A."

---

[16] According to Edmilson Barreiros Jr., "the case under examination is not that simple, considering that the elements 'duress' and 'abuse' were not *inserted*, but rather *explained*, since they were punishable and quite frequent in the cases covered under the previous laws." (Barreiros JR., Edmilson da Costa. *Op. cit.*, p. 4).

[17] On the issue of vulnerability within the sphere of Mercosur, Ela Wiecko de Castilho indicates that "the region of Mercosur constitutes primarily an origin and destination region, and on a smaller scaler, one marked by transit. It was observed that there was a diversity of vulnerability factors that constitute favorable scenarios for the expansion of trafficking networks, including: (a) factors associated with socio-cultural dimensions, primarily gender inequality, gender violence, discrimination of specific social groups (indigenous peoples, individuals of African descent, transsexuals); (b) factors associated with social-economic dimensions such as social exclusion and poverty, social impact, and the development models that exist in the impacted region, and the migration from the rural areas to urban zones; c) factors associated with migratory barriers in the destination countries" (Castilho 2014, p. 152).

[18] In this regard, Luiz Regis Prado explains that the "abuse" mentioned in the crime should be understood based on the case that the agent makes use of the "condition of vulnerability of the victim, as in the case of extreme poverty or hardship, family or personal strife, mourning, etc." (Prado 2017, p. 211).

[19] Barreiros JR., Edmilson da Costa. *Op. cit.*, p. 20.

In my opinion, through these two elements (abuse and duress), the supposed abolition of the crime would be discarded. On this point, it is important to recall the words used for the first incrimination (Law No. 2.992/1915), mentioned in the previous item, to interpret "abuse" in the current law as something similar to the abuse of "weakness or poverty," as well as "duress" as being similar to practices of duress "due to debts incurred."

By any means, if it is understood that the succession of criminal laws resulted in the solution of normative-criminal continuity, without *abolitio criminis*, there is an observed *novatio legis in mellius* associated with the elements of violence, serious threat and fraud from (revoked) Article 231 of the BPC. There was also *novatio legis in pejus* associated with the same elements of (revoked) Article 231-A. In other words, the three- to eight-year prison terms, which were doubled, from Article 231 of the BPC, were greater than the four- to eight-year prison terms from Article 149-A of the BPC, although greater than the two- to six-year prison terms, doubled, which exist in Article 231-A of the BPC.

However, in 2019, the Superior Court of Justice of Brazil (STJ), when judging an appeal brought by convicted of the crime of human trafficking, found that in certain situations the abolition of crime actually occurred. According to the Court, the new Article 149-A did not "embrace" the conduct previously provided for in the old Article 231 (*caput*), since it brought as a definition of the crime the practice of trafficking through serious threat, violence, coercion, fraud, or abuse. On the other hand, the abolition did not occur in the hypothesis of the previous §§ 2 Article 231, which was thus "achieved" by the current Article 149-A, BPC.[20]

4 Conclusion

Based on the National Report on Human Trafficking, many people have fallen victim to the network of trafficking worldwide. Improved living conditions, a better job, a foreign husband, the dream of living in a developed country, and having access to certain consumer goods have been indicated in literature as the main reasons that people who are in situations of vulnerability take the risk and leave their territories for other cities and countries in search of opportunities.[21]

Paradoxically, in today's globalized world, instead of decreasing in intensity, human trafficking has grown exponentially, notably due to transnational criminal organizations that unscrupulously exploit the hardships resulting from environmental disasters, poverty, famine, and war, as well as other nature or man-made disasters. There has been the contemporary establishment of that which was deplorably described as "modern-day slavery or servitude," which especially affects children, adolescents, and women.

[20] AREsp N. 1.267.282. STJ. 5ª T. Pub. DJe 13/05/2019.

[21] Relatório Nacional sobre Tráfico de Pessoas ("National Report on Human Trafficking"), cit., p. 5.

In this sense, Brazilian lawmakers have realized the need to enact more appropriate legislation for preventing and repressing human trafficking in all its different forms. However, the possible abolition of crime is a controversial issue in Brazilian law. Despite those who, like the signatory, believe that abolition has not occurred, Brazilian jurisprudence seems to be moving towards abolition, at least in the basic form of the definition of human trafficking.

References

Barreiros JR, Edmilson da Costa. Abuse and vulnerability in human trafficking, under the terms of Federal Law No. 13.344/2016, in published form

Brasil. Relatório Nacional sobre Tráfico de Pessoas: Consolidação dos dados de 2005 a 2011 (National Report on Human Trafficking: Consolidation of Data from 2005 to 2011). https://www.unodc.org/documents/lpo-brazil/noticias/2013/04/2013-04-08_Publicacao_diagnostico_ETP.pdf

Castilho EWde (2014) Exploração sexual no tráfico de pessoas: (Sexual exploitation in human trafficking): (in)definition. In: Conceito e tipologias de exploração. Cadernos temáticos sobre o tráfico de pessoas (Concept and Types of Exploitation. Theme-Based Booklets on Human Trafficking) Vol. 1. Michelle Gueraldi (Org.). Brazilian Ministry of Justice, Brasília

Kushnir B (1996) Baile de Máscaras. Mulheres judias e prostituição (Masquerade Ball. Jewish Women and Prostitution). Imago, Rio de Janeiro

Moraes E (1921) Ensaios de Patologia Social. Vagabundagem, alcoolismo, prostituição e lenocínio (Social Pathology Essays. Vagrancy, Alcoholism, Prostitution, and Pimping). Leite Ribeiro, Rio de Janeiro

Prado LR (2017) Curso de Direito Penal Brasileiro (Course in Brazilian Criminal Law) vol. 2, 15th edn. Revista dos Tribunais, São Paulo

Rodrigues N (1982) Os Africanos no Brasil (Africans in Brazil). 6th edn. University of Brasília, Brasília

Souza AdeBG (2006) Presos estrangeiros no Brasil. Aspectos jurídico e criminológicos (Foreign prisoners in Brazil. Legal and criminological aspects). Lumen Juris, Rio de Janeiro

Artur de Brito Gueiros Souza is an Associate Professor of Criminal Law at the State University of Rio de Janeiro (UERJ), Post-doctorate in Economic Criminal Law at the University of Coimbra (UC), and Federal Circuit Prosecutor at Rio de Janeiro. He is also the Scientific Coordinator of the Corporate Crime and Compliance Research Center at the State University of Rio de Janeiro (www.cpjm.uerj.br), and author of scientific books and articles in the area of Criminal Law and Economic & Corporate Criminology (arturgueiros@uerj.br).

Trafficking in Persons Vis-à-Vis the Recent Jurisprudence of the Inter-American Court of Human Rights: Lessons for Brazil

Ana Cláudia Ruy Cardia Atchabahian and Felipe Chiarello de Souza Pinto

Abstract The present work aims to, starting from qualitative research based on primary and secondary sources' document analysis, as well as the legal literature of international law and international human rights law, study the theme of human trafficking under the protective view of the Regional Human Rights Protection Systems, notably through a critical analysis of the recent decision produced by the Inter-American Court of Human Rights in the case of *Fazenda Brasil Verde vs. Brazil* to try to obtain grounds for comprehension of the subject in the international landscape and invoke the applicability of its conclusions to the national doctrine and jurisprudence.

1 Introduction

With the development of our society into a postmodern condition, the crime of trafficking in persons—well known to both Brazilian and international communities—has been subject to deep changes in its outlines and means.

The development of globalization in its various aspects has allowed a crime which had previously been characterized solely based on the use of physical force as a means to guarantee further exploitation to be transformed so as to also consider the occurrence of vitiated consent, under which the deepest aspirations of individuals to secure better living conditions, both economically and socially, are taken into account with the ultimate purpose of facilitating the victims' oppression—an oppression which is also adapted to the new social reality, which increasingly considers the human being as a mere commodity.

Aware of such changes in the kind of activity developed by those responsible for such modern slavery practices, international law has considered these new paradigms upon the consolidation of sources capable of ensuring the effective protection

Ana Cláudia Ruy Cardia Atchabahian (✉) · F. C. de Souza Pinto
Mackenzie Presbyterian University, Faculty of Law, São Paulo, Brazil
e-mail: ana.cardia@mackenzie.br; felipe.chiarello@mackenzie.br

A. M. Rodrigues, M. J. Guia (eds.), *New Forms of Human Trafficking*,
https://doi.org/10.1007/978-3-031-39732-5_16

of individuals subjected to human trafficking. For this purpose, efforts in several different spheres of international law have been made in the last two decades, such as the development of the Palermo Protocol, which focuses on the international aspect of trafficking in persons, and the active involvement of the International Labor Organization in combating slavery and related crimes within labor relations, both of which are interdependent and interrelated actions, as well as the expansion of the jurisdictional activity of international courts and of regional Human Rights Courts, which, by means of their jurisprudence, create the possibility of a positive interference in the reality of countries which currently violate such rights.

The present work intends to analyze the main outlines of this new form of modern slavery, chiefly represented by the trafficking of human beings for their subsequent labor exploitation. Thus, the present work shall analyze the evolution of the concept of said crime both at local and international levels, as well as the contribution of international human rights law to the fight against said crime, and especially make a critical evaluation of the recent jurisprudence of the Inter-American Court of Human Rights in the paradigmatic decision of the *Fazenda Brasil Verde vs. Brazil* case to further develop the discussions on this matter at the international and especially at the local level.

For the development of the present research, primary sources (official documents from international organizations and domestic bodies), secondary sources (academic works) as well as jurisprudence related to the subject will be used. The method used to reach the main conclusions will be the inductive method.

2 Concept and Global and National Reality of Human Trafficking

The crime of trafficking in persons has common characteristics in the various jurisdictions of the international community. Thus, the present topic shall start by presenting the main outlines of said crime to ultimately be able to compare the local reality related to this crime inside the individual countries—emphasizing the Brazilian reality—to the transnational context in cases where more than one jurisdiction is involved in the consummation of said crime.

2.1 *Trafficking in Persons: Main Outlines*

Trafficking in persons is a phenomenon recognized by the international community since the most ancient times. Although it was initially related to a context of slavery of chiefly black people in the West, with the development of today's globalized society, said crime has been subject to several changes to encompass broader contexts, aimed at all people, and especially at those who are subject to extreme conditions of socioeconomic and cultural vulnerability. [1]

This globalizing context currently contributes to the propagation of human subjection to commodification. Thus, the reduction of an individual to the status of an object by other individuals or by companies managed thereby turns out to be a tragic natural consequence of a society which tends to value consumer goods more than human qualities. [2] On the trivialization of human exploitation, in this new social model, individuals are the first ones to be subjected to the most inhuman and degrading forms of oppression, since the use of their workforce does not even require capital investments to be made for the effective pursuit of the company's economic activities (Laky 2014, p. 71). Due to its high profitability, trafficking in persons currently alternates statistically between second and third positions among the world's most profitable illegal activities, along with trafficking in arms and drugs, with an annual volume of transactions valued at approximately 150 billion Dollars. It is estimated that 21 million people are currently victims of forced labor, which means that trafficking constitutes a necessary part of this form of modern slavery (ILO).

Trafficking in persons may either occur locally within states or transcend their territorial boundaries. The main features of this crime are related to the use of force or to the misleading of workers who will be recruited and eventually subjected to situations of labor exploitation for various purposes. Therefore, the exploitative activities which currently constitute what is known as contemporary slavery, or modern slavery, are understood to be interdependent and, in this context, trafficking constitutes the logical precedent of all the other crimes. Thus, there is no exploitation where the crime of trafficking in persons does not constitute its direct precedent (Nogueira et al. 2014).

There are several other crimes, such as sexual exploitation, trafficking in organs, trafficking in arms, trafficking in drugs, weapons, pedophilia, homicides, document forgery, extortion, corruption, and money laundering, which are co-related to the crime of trafficking in persons (Ministério Público Federal 2014, p. 11). Also, there certainly are aggravating factors for such crime, especially female vulnerability—it is currently estimated that the majority of trafficked persons are women (Vieira and Charf 2016, p. 19). However, statistics have been giving special attention to the rapid changes which are taking place in this kind of exploitation, including the increase in the number of men involved (UNODC 2016, p. 6). It is clear, therefore, that the crime of trafficking in persons follows the demand of exploiters for different forms of oppression.

[1] Said vulnerability is often directly related to slavery, as in the Brazilian case.

[2] "Deviating from a project under which the community would act as a defender of the universal right to a decent and dignified life and going towards one under which the promotion of the market would confer sufficient guarantee to the achievement of universal opportunity to self-enrichment further deepens the suffering of the new poor, adding insult to all of its injuries, interpreting poverty with humiliation and with the denial of the consumers' freedom, now identified with humanity" (freely translated from Portuguese) (Bauman 1998, p. 34).

Therefore, trafficking in persons in its broad and current meaning is intrinsically related to the existence of false promises of better living conditions, generally associated with a situation of trust between trafficker and trafficked person (UNODC 2016, p. 7), which ends up directly resulting in the vitiation of the consent given by individuals submitted to this kind of exploitation; the retention of documents, or retention due to indebtedness, which prevents individuals from easily detaching themselves from their situations of oppression; and in several other forms of exploitation, correlated to other crimes, whose definition under domestic and international legal systems is also necessary.

2.2 *Its Transnational Dimension: A Crime That Knows No Boundaries*

The transposition of the outlines established in the previous item to a cross-border context, where two or more jurisdictions are involved in the consummation of modern slavery crimes, constitutes what is known as international trafficking in persons. In this kind of criminal activity, the invisibility of individuals and their commodification surpasses the territorial borders of states, which makes it even more worrying since it involves migrants in a serious state of economic and social vulnerability. [3]

With the expansion of migrations, it is well known that migrants often do not have the means to afford to leave their country of origin in search of better living conditions and are therefore easily seduced by recruiters, which are sometimes linked to international criminal organizations. [4] As a result, migrants manage to enter other jurisdictions (by illegal means, and even with illicit documentation provided by recruiters), but enter into financial debt with their imagined "benefactors" due to the transportation and food initially provided by the latter, and develop great fear of them in case of termination or flight from this relationship. Migrants under such circumstances often receive death threats from their recruiters. Also, even in cases where the migration is considered legal under the laws of the country of destination, in some situations, migrants have their documents confiscated and retained by traffickers or even by the employers who receive them, a situation which ties them through invisible chains to a reality of fear and exploitation. Migrants who

[3] "In a broad sense, given that this is a non-ethical phenomenon, it also does not discriminate the objects to be transacted. The conditions to which 'Bolivians' in Sao Paulo, 'workers from the East' in Western Europe, families from the Maghreb who invade Spain and Italy, and Brazilian women who prostitute themselves in Portugal and Spain are subjected are not very different" (Laky 2014, p. 71).

[4] In this case, it is also noteworthy that, at present, international criminal organizations in many cases have greater economic, financial, and structural power than states: "(…) organized crime has also grown exponentially and governments are greatly concerned that organized crime is now better financed, equipped and organized than governments" (Global Rights 2007 p. 39). In this regard, see Durães et al. (2014).

manage to flee the chains imposed by their exploiters are offered little or no help at all: they often find themselves adrift in a community which is unaware of their status as victims and which effectively denies them any protection and are ultimately regarded as the true dregs of society (Bauman 2017; Laky 2014, pp. 72-73).

Despite the history of existence of this crime, the concrete indication of this reality with regard to its outlines and the routes used by the traffickers is only contemporary. Until very recently it was still very difficult to recognize trafficking networks without confusing them with traditional migratory networks or even with migratory networks formed by private family and friendship circles. This also constitutes further proof of the new subterfuges created by traffickers to ensure the invisibility of the crime of trafficking in persons, often leading state agents to error (Ministério da Justiça 2011). In 2016, a report published by the United Nations Office on Drugs and Crime (UNODC) estimated the existence of approximately 500 different trafficking routes in the last four years, which consolidates the understanding that no state is immune to the crime of trafficking in persons (UNODC 2016, p. 5).

Another factor which helps perpetuating the silence about the existence of this kind of exploitation is the fear that people subjected to such degrading conditions have of denouncing those who have exploited them, which may derive from issues related to their own safety or, in the case of illegal migrants, from the fear of being deported and returned to their country of origin, which they initially decided to leave. There is therefore a need for intense international cooperation among countries as an attempt to effectively combat international trafficking in persons and ensure due protection for the victims.

Also, due to the marginalization of migrants, which is another consequence of this crime in its transnational (Bauman 1999) form, it is necessary to strengthen domestic laws aimed at expanding the rights and guarantees of migrants, in the broadest sense of the term. It is becoming increasingly difficult to prevent and combat international trafficking in persons without laws capable of granting migrants benefits identical or similar to those of nationals.

2.3 *Trafficking in Persons and the Brazilian State*

On Brazil's situation in the treatment of trafficking in persons, Brazil is considered a country of origin, destination and circulation of trafficked persons, and has more than 200 national and international trafficking routes within its borders. [5] Statistics point out alarming numbers of people trafficked in Brazil in the latest years, the majority of whom are women. [6] Also, between 2005 and 2011, 337 national victims

[5] For further definition of the human trafficking routes found in Brazil, see Leal and Leal (2002, pp. 71–106). For a more summarized approach, at both domestic and international levels, see Barbosa (2010), pp. 45–49.

[6] Specifically, on the trafficking of women in Brazil, it is worth mentioning the study conducted by Associação Mulheres pela Paz on the specificities of said crime in the five regions of Brazil (Vieira

of trafficking for sexual exploitation were identified in other jurisdictions, as well as 135 Brazilians who were trafficked for slave labor in 18 different countries (Brazil 2011, p. 32).

Such data should, however, always be questioned and reassessed, given the regional peculiarities related to trafficking and the fear of victims to denounce this kind of crime, as well as their difficulty in recognizing the extent of the Brazilian territory.

In recent years, with the escalation of the current migratory situation (which, combined with voluntary migration, also presents a rapidly expanding contingent of refugees (Bauman 2017), Brazil became the recipient of a large number of migrants, who, in search of greater dignity of treatment and better wages, submit to working under inhuman and degrading conditions, performing various kinds of jobs. Only in recent years 14 hundred people have been rescued in São Paulo while living under slavery-like conditions, especially working in textile companies. [7] Although regional specificities generate different forms of exploitation in different markets, the circumstances which attract people in vulnerable conditions in other jurisdictions to Brazil, as analyzed in the previous items, remains, since it is related to the eternal intrinsic condition of human mobility.

On modern slavery in Brazil, the country has turned its attention to this problem soon after the international combination of efforts to combat trafficking was consolidated through the Palermo Protocol of 2000, which will be further detailed in the following items. Based on international concerns, Brazil has, in a joint effort between government, international organizations and civil society organizations, analyzed the main issues related to local and international trafficking in Brazil and found alarming results, published in the Survey on Trafficking in Women, Children and Adolescents for the Purposes of Commercial Sexual Exploitation—PESTRAF. [8]

In 2004, Brazil also ratified the Palermo Convention, published by Decree No. 5,015, of March 12, 2004, [9] and has, since 2008, been implementing a number of National Policies to combat trafficking in persons (Brazil 2006), developed in partnership with federal agencies and the civil society and aimed at establishing guidelines and actions related to victim protection and reintegration into society, prevention and repression of trafficking in persons in a wide range of public and

---

and Charf 2014, pp. 35–171).

[7] In this regard, see BBC Brasil. 'A vida no Brasil não é normal, é só 'trabalho', conta boliviana que foi escravizada em SP. http://www.bbc.com/english/noticias/2015/01/150127_boliviana_escravizada_ms. Also, the NGO Repórter Brasil has conducted a survey on the main slave labor inspections carried out jointly by the Ministry of Labor (Ministério do Trabalho), the Labor Public 'Prossecurtor's Office (Ministério Público do Trabalho), the Federal Police and the Federal Highway Police between 1995 and 2015, of great value to the present work. In the Municipality of São Paulo, it has been verified that more than 80% of the companies inspected were related to the textile sector. Repórter Brasil. Dados sobre trabalho escravo no Brasil. http://reporterbrasil.org.br/dados/trabalhoescravo/.

[8] Leal and Leal (2002 pp. 71–106). For a more summarized approach, at both domestic and international levels, see Barbosa (2010).

[9] BRASIL. *Decree No. 5,015, of March 12, 2004.*

private national agencies. These measures have been consolidated in the First National Plan to Combat Trafficking in Persons, of 2008 (Brazil 2008), as well as in its revised version (which has also been subject to intense debates at local level [10]), namely, the II National Plan to Combat Trafficking in Persons, of 2013 (Brazil 2013a, b). In 2018, the III National Plan to Combat Trafficking in Persons was implemented (Brazil 2018).

From an institutional point of view, the fight against trafficking in persons relies on the work of the Ministry of Justice (*Ministério da Justiça*), the Federal Public Prosecutor's Office (*Ministério Público*), the Federal Police, the Federal Union's Public Defender's Office (*Defensoria Pública da União*), the Federal Union's Attorney General's Office (*Advocacia-Geral da União*), the Special Secretariat for Policies for Women (*Secretaria Especial de Políticas para as Mulheres*), and the Judiciary, among other public organizations, which have been increasingly adding value and bringing updated data to this debate. Brazilian civil society organizations also play an important role in disseminating the main features related to this crime. The Brazilian government also has an important role in participating in national and international campaigns to prevent and combat this criminal activity, [11] among which the campaign carried out jointly with the United Nations Office on Drugs and Crime (UNODC) and the European Union to combat trafficking in persons and the migrants smuggling, [12] called Global Action to Prevent Trafficking in Persons and Migrant Smuggling (Glo.Act, UNODC), is worthy of note and demonstrates Brazil's concern with the promotion of international cooperation to combat such crimes.

From a legal perspective, the crime of trafficking in persons is provided for in the Brazilian Criminal Code. Initially described in Articles 149 and 207 of said normative document, the crime later came to be regulated by Articles 231 and 231-A as well, due to the enactment of Law No. 12,015, of August 7, 2009. These changes were criticized at the time by scholars and applicators of the norm, since the rules only mentioned the crime of trafficking in persons for purposes of sexual exploitation (Brazil 2011). Thus, in 2016, with the enactment of Law No. 13,344, [13] of October 6, 2016, [14] Articles 231 and 231-A of the Criminal Code were repealed, and

---

[10] For more information on the processes which resulted in the two national plans.

[11] For an overview of all national campaigns aimed at combating trafficking in persons, see Brasil. Ministério da Justiça e Segurança Pública. Campanhas. http://www.justica.gov.br/sua-protecao/trafico-de-pessoas/campanhas.

[12] The present work makes a brief note to emphasize that the terms trafficking in people and smuggling of migrants are not synonymous. Smuggling of migrants means a crime which involves the obtainment of a financial or material benefit from the unlawful entry of a person into a state in which that person is not a natural or resident. This crime requires the actual consent of the migrant but does not require their further exploitation to qualify as such and is always a transnational crime. United Nations Office on Drugs and Crime. Tráfico de pessoas e contrabando de migrantes. https://www.unodc.org/lpo-brazil/pt/trafico-de-pessoas/.

[13] BRASIL. *Law No. 13,344 of October 6, 2016.*

[14] Interestingly sanctioned weeks before the final decision on the *Fazenda Brasil Verde vs. Brazil* case was handed down by the Inter-American Court of Human Rights.

a more comprehensive rule for that crime, provided for in the new Article 149-A, was thenceforth to be observed by new interpreters of Brazilian law. In addition to the Criminal Code, there are also specific provisions on children's rights in the Child and Adolescent Statute.

On the protection of migrants who have been victims of this kind of crime, Law No. 13,344 also provides for the international trafficking in persons. However, the statutes are still analyzed and interpreted in the light of Law No. 6,815/80 ("Alien Statute"), [15] a norm which was implemented during the Brazilian dictatorial period. Its moment of implementation is reflected in the very wording of its provisions, which ultimately considers migrants as actual threats to the country. Therefore, on this topic, the entry into force of the new Migration Act, [16] approved in May 2017 with a *vacatio legis* of 180 days, is urgent, since its aim is precisely to ensure humanized treatment to migrants in Brazil, who, as mentioned, often suffer doubly the miseries of their displacement.

Notwithstanding all the norms and public policies, whose existence is of paramount importance to the present moment, the occurrence of this kind of exploitative activity is still largely neglected by public and private agents, who, while ignoring the internal legal system, contribute to ensure the invisibility of this crime. The past which Brazil currently strives to forget still haunts our contemporaneity—and an example of that is, as will be seen below, its recent international condemnation for inaction of its agents on the commission of these crimes.

Now that the main features of human trafficking in its internal and international forms have been addressed, the next subject to be analyzed shall be its regulation under international law.

3 The Disclosure of an Invisible Crime: Human Trafficking Under International Law

Trafficking in persons in its modern configuration has only been addressed by international law as of the year of 2000, [17] with the publication of the Additional Protocol [18] to the United Nations Convention against Transnational Organized Crime, also known as the Palermo Protocol. [19] Until that moment, this criminal activity had,

---

[15] BRASIL. *Law No. 6,815, of August 19, 1980.*

[16] BRASIL. *Law No. 13,445, of May 24, 2016.*

[17] For more details on the preparatory works of the UN Convention against International Organized Crime, as well as on the Palermo Protocol, see Brazil 2013.

[18] BRASIL. *Decree No. 5,017, of March 12, 2004.*

[19] By that date, other international initiatives had been enacted, such as the Treaty of Paris, signed in 1814 by England and France, as well as the Geneva Convention of 1956. However, none of the rules prior to the Palermo Protocol addressed trafficking in persons taking into account the typical modern outlines of that form of labor exploitation. For more details on the history of international rules regarding this subject.

notwithstanding its existence, either voluntarily or involuntarily passed unnoticed to legislators, public policy enactors and interpreters of domestic and international law, which further corroborates the argument herein defended on the invisibility and commodification of trafficked and subsequently exploited individuals.

On the definition of trafficking in persons established by the Protocol, its Article 3, line "a", reads as follows:

> For the purposes of this Protocol:
> (a) 'Trafficking in persons' shall mean the recruitment, transportation, transfer, harbouring or receipt of persons, by means of the threat or use of force or other forms of coercion, of abduction, of fraud, of deception, of the abuse of power or of a position of vulnerability or of the giving or receiving of payments or benefits to achieve the consent of a person having control over another person, for the purpose of exploitation. Exploitation shall include, at a minimum, the exploitation of the prostitution of others or other forms of sexual exploitation, forced labour or services, slavery or practices similar to slavery, servitude or the removal of organs.

The crime of trafficking in persons, as understood in its broadest sense—to encompass as many violations as possible and even include the situation of migrants under vulnerable conditions, as seen above – has thus three essential aspects, namely: the actions carried out by the recruiting agents, the means used for such recruitment and the purpose of the victims' exploitation (UNODC 2014). For the possible actions of recruiters, the wording of the article highlights the recruitment, transportation, transfer, harboring, or receipt of persons. The means employed may, in turn, correspond to the use of threats, force, or other forms of coercion, abduction, fraud, abuse of power, position of vulnerability, or giving or receiving payments or benefits to obtain the consent of a person having control over another person, for the purpose of exploitation. Lastly, the purpose of the exploitation may be the prostitution of others or other forms of sexual exploitation, as well as forced labor or services, slavery (or similar labor practices), servitude, or the removal of organs.

International law has thus encompassed human trafficking in several aspects, irrespective of socioeconomic or gender issues. Any action whatsoever carried out for the purpose of exploitation may be considered as trafficking. Moreover, this provision has also eliminated the stigma related to the consent of the victim, [20] since, as mentioned, said consent is ultimately vitiated through various means, due to the truly disproportionate relation existing between perpetrator and victim (Siqueira and Quinteiro 2013). This has been an extremely important step towards the decriminalization of victims, who were often considered as criminals due to an erroneous understanding regarding the assumption of their acquiescence. Nonetheless, nearly two decades after the publication of the Protocol, victims are often still unaware of

[20] In this same sense, the provision of Article 3, item "b", which establishes: "b) The consent of a victim of trafficking in persons to the intended exploitation set forth in subparagraph a) of this article shall be irrelevant where any of the means set forth in subparagraph a) have been used."

their own condition, [21] which reinforces their vulnerability and, even more shockingly, cause them to be judged by society as the ones responsible for their own submission to crime (Vieira and Charf 2016, p. 23).

The Palermo Protocol also contains provisions on the criminalization of recruiting agents; assistance and protection to victims, including guidelines for their repatriation in the case of immigrants; means for preventing the crime; exchange of information between governments and training of their agents; measures to be taken at the borders of jurisdictions; and provisions on the documentation presented by trafficked persons. Notwithstanding the broad scope of the international norm, each state may, at its own discretion, define the scope of application of the references established in the Palermo Protocol upon the enactment or amendment of domestic legislation on this subject, provided that the necessary protection to victims of human trafficking is observed.

In addition to the Protocol, in 2002, the United Nations High Commissioner for Human Rights established a number of principles and guidelines [22] to be observed by states and non-state actors and subjects for the effective prevention and combat against the crime of trafficking in persons, which reinforces its connection with the expansion of internal and international migration. Despite the *soft law nature* [23] of the document, the recommendations made therein are of great value for the establishment of a domestic normative framework and for the institution of public policies and international cooperation mechanisms providing protection for the victims and punishment for the perpetrators of that kind of crime.

With regard to the International Labor Organization (ILO), Convention No. 29, [24] of 1930, has laid the foundations for the definition of forced or compulsory labor. However, this convention did not give any specific determinations regarding the precedent of such practices, which, for this work, would correspond to trafficking.

Still on sources produced by the ILO, the recently enacted Protocol to the Convention (2014) is also worthy of note and provides, under Article 2, item "d", for the need to protect individuals, particularly migrant workers, from any abusive and fraudulent practices during their recruitment and harboring process, and refers, albeit indirectly, to the need of identifying the outlines of the criminal activity which will lead to the exploitation of individuals by means of forced or compulsory labor. All the sources above must necessarily be read in conjunction with other international law and international human rights law instruments and which, although not

[21] Ministério da Justiça. Jornadas transatlânticas: uma pesquisa exploratória sobre tráfico de seres humanos do Brasil para Itália e Portugal. Brasília: 2011. http://www.justica.gov.br/yua-protecao/trafico-de-pessoas/publicacoes/anexos-pesquisas/jornadastransatlanticas.pdf/view.

[22] Officer of the High Commissioner for Human Rights. Recommended Principles and Guidelines of Human Rights and Human Trafficking. http://www.ohchr.org/Documents/Publications/Traffickingen.pdf.

[23] For this work, the definition of *hard law* and *soft law* is merely didactic. Both types of legal instruments are herein understood as having the same normative force, for the sake of the greater effectiveness of international law and the protection to the human rights derived therefrom.

[24] The Convention has been internalized by Brazil by means of Decree No. 41,721 of June 25, 1957.

mentioned in the present research, provide guidelines and protective parameters to potential victims of trafficking, such as children, migrant workers, women, etc. (Piovesan and Kamimura 2013). It is based on a systemic interpretation of such rules that a true protective system for the victims of human trafficking shall be consolidated.

Other instruments of great value for international law may be found among the works and research produced by international non-governmental organizations [25]—which, despite not being the object of the present work, are the basis for much of the information mentioned herein – in addition to the work of International Courts, which have been ensuring an evolutionary interpretation of the treaties referred to herein by means of their jurisprudence. This last aspect shall be further investigated below, specifically in relation to the Courts of Human Rights.

4 Transnational Crime, Global Solutions: The Contribution of the Regional Human Rights Courts in Its Protective and Transformative Dimensions

Trafficking in persons, as seen in the previous items, may either take place within a given state's internal borders or transcend the borders of various jurisdictions. Thus, the transnationality defended herein refers not only to the second aspect, but also to the fact that this kind of crime is consummated at internal/domestic level in various countries in a very similar fashion, which ensures the transnational nature of its *modus operandi*.

Therefore, regardless of whether the crime is committed at the internal/domestic or international level, the attempts which have so far been made in the global legal system to have it regulated have been responsible for ensuring its main outlines as they are known today.

International human rights law is widely known to be the branch of international law focused on establishing minimum protective standards and ethical references (Piovesan 2015, p. 45) to be followed by states upon the development of domestic rules and public policies. Moreover, it is also widely understood that human rights instruments should particularly apply upon the failure or inaction of states, demonstrating their counter-majoritarian character in relation to the actors of the international community, thus representing the last protective hope for individuals who have been neglected in their own jurisdictions (Ramos 2016, pp. 182–183). Thus, although there is no specific convention to combat trafficking in persons [26] under

[25] On the importance and influence of NGOs in international law, see Menezes (2005, p. 71).

[26] Much is being said about the nature of the Palermo Protocol, especially as to whether or not it is a human rights treaty. Although the subject matter of said rule is intrinsically related to the protection of individuals, its nature is internationally recognized as that of a treaty of international law, since it was created by the United Nations Commission on Crime Prevention and Criminal Justice.

international human rights law, there is a great variety of sources of law in this field and that the role of the Regional Human Rights Systems is of particular importance, since their specific courts have been able to construct, by means of their jurisprudence, evolving interpretations of the human rights conventions from which they have derived, in such way to ensure that contemporary situations are not covered under the rug of impunity in the signatory states. Thus, the present work demonstrates the richness of the plurality of sources in postmodern international law, as well as the importance of their effective dialogue for the protection of human rights.

Among the broad range of sources and bodies of international law, the bodies dedicated to the exclusive analysis and application of international human rights law are also worthy of note. In addition to the subjects which constitute the so-called global system for the protection of human rights, there are the regional systems, especially represented by the European, inter-American and African systems.

On the functioning of these systems, one item is common to all of them: the existence of Regional Courts, which are capable of handing down decisions to states which recognize their jurisdiction, while taking into account the particularities of the socioeconomic and cultural contexts of each state. These decisions, as further explained below, must be properly implemented by the Member States (Piovesan 2015, pp. 100–101).

Especially on this last aspect, the importance of the role of Regional Human Rights Courts in relation to the possibility of transforming cultures which are currently understood to violate human rights and provide greater protection to the rights of individuals living in the jurisdictions to which their decisions are addressed. This is because, as mentioned, given that Regional Human Rights Courts act essentially upon the failures or inactions of the states which recognize their authority, this protective and transforming dimension corresponds to a natural consequence of the exercise of their jurisdiction at the international level.

With these brief considerations in mind, the present work will now focus on the point specifically related to the importance of the decisions of the Inter-American Court of Human Rights in transforming the protective standards mainly related to combating all forms of human trafficking and exploitation which correspond to modern slavery. This is what shall be analyzed below by means of the analysis of the decision handed down in the *Fazenda Brasil Verde vs. Brazil* case.

This explains the statement made in the present work on the lack of specific normative instruments inherent to international human rights law referring to this subject.

5 The Contribution of the Inter-American Court of Human Rights to the Fight Against Trafficking in Persons in the *Fazenda Brasil Verde vs. Brazil* Case

As mentioned, once the importance of international rules and decisions for the discussion on the fight against trafficking in persons has been demonstrated, the present work will now proceed to the analysis of the recent decision of the Inter-American Court of Human Rights in the *Fazenda Brasil Verde vs. Brazil* case and ultimately point out the main lessons to be observed by the Brazilian state regarding its conduct in relation to this subject.

5.1 Trafficking in Persons in the Inter-American System of Human Rights

The American Convention on Human Rights, in its Article 6, establishes the prohibition of slavery and servitude, as well as the possible violations of human rights resulting from such acts. The prohibition on trafficking in persons is included among the paragraphs of the article, namely, in Art. 6.1, which establishes the following definition: *"6.1. No one shall be subject to slavery or to involuntary servitude, which are prohibited in all their forms, as are the slave trade and traffic in women."*

Thus, the rule only explicitly mentions the crime of trafficking in women and slaves, and does not mention trafficking in persons in its most general meaning.

The analysis of the jurisprudence of the Inter-American Court of Human Rights on cases involving potential violations of Article 6 leads to the conclusion that the Court had not until very recently analyzed a case in which a thorough analysis and interpretation of the article was required. [27] The decision handed down in the *Fazenda Brasil Verde vs. Brazil* case, which will be further analyzed below, was a leading-edge and paradigmatic one in this sense, for which reason it deserves due attention in the present work.

5.2 The Fazenda Brasil Verde vs. Brazil *Case: A New Paradigm*

The *Fazenda Brasil Verde vs. Brazil* case was analyzed by the Inter-American Court of Human Rights between the years 2015 and 2016. Specifically related to the occurrence of human rights violations in Fazenda Brasil Verde, a farm located in the

[27] This fact is actually mentioned in the decision, in its para 244. Inter-American Court of Human Rights. *Fazenda Brasil Verde vs. Brazil* case. Series C, No. 318. Decision of October 20, 2016.

municipality of Sapucaia, south of Pará state, the decision of the case was handed down on October 20, 2016 and has consolidated the understanding of said international Court in the sense that trafficking in persons and other forms of slavery-like exploitation constitute forms of what is currently known as "modern slavery".

These violations, occurred and documented between the late 1980s and the early 2000s, had been analyzed internally by the Brazilian state, but were not given due attention by administrative and judicial authorities upon their examination, which is in fact what motivated the admission of the case by the Court.

In one word, the dispute was related to the practice of internal trafficking in persons and slavery of workers hired to work in the cutting of *juquira* weed [28] in Fazenda Brasil Verde, owned by João Luiz Quagliato Neto at the time. Recruiters enticed workers by *promising* [29] good wages and decent living conditions, including housing and food, and often left their families hoping that they would also ensure better living conditions in their homelands. As soon as they arrived at their workplace, however—which was located far from the main urban centers, in the thick of the Amazon rainforest—they faced inhuman and degrading conditions of housing and work, including workdays of more than twelve hours, retention of their work and identity documents and death threats in case of exit or flight from the farm, as well as the disappearance of workers who questioned their condition. Also, the workers were in debt from the very beginning: initially with the recruiters, who asked them to pay for the trip to their workplace, in addition to any food and lodging expenses, and subsequently with their employers, who deducted from their compensations the value of the utensils used for the accomplishment of their work and even of the lodging and the food provided to them, leaving them without any remuneration at the end of the working period. [30] Thus, in addition to the practice of trafficking, the exploitation of the workforce under slavery-like conditions and the practice of debt bondage were also present.

In spite of the complaints made by workers who managed to escape from that context, as well as the inspections carried out in different periods by representatives of the Federal Police and the Labor Prosecutor's Office, which resulted in judicial claims and administrative procedures, [31] there was no effective internal punishment for the perpetrators of such violations, which is why civil society entities submitted a petition to the Inter-American Commission on Human Rights, which subsequently led to its analysis by the Court belonging to the same system.

---

[28] A native plant of the region.

[29] In Portuguese, "gatos" – name commonly used to refer to employees hired to recruit workers under this type of exploitation.

[30] Details on the degrading conditions to which the workers of Fazenda Brasil Verde were subjected can be found in paras 163 to 173 of the ruling.

[31] For a detailed chronology of the judicial and administrative measures that were carried out domestically, see paras 128 to 188 of the decision.

The decision, rightly concluded in relation to the crime of subjection of workers to slavery-like working conditions, [32] has established important considerations regarding the crime of trafficking in persons, especially in relation to the interpretation given by the Court to Article 6.1 of the American Convention on Human Rights. [33]

The decision gives an extensive and evolutionary interpretation [34] to said instrument, as well as to other international sources of similar nature [35] to extend the provision on the prohibition of trafficking—which, under the American Convention, only expressly encompasses the crimes of trafficking in women and slaves—to any category of persons who are subsequently subjected to a condition of vulnerability, which confirms the theory defended herein with regard to the crime of trafficking in persons being the main precedent for the occurrence of other forms of exploitation of individuals.

This evolutionary interpretation of said instrument has not only considered the dialogue between international sources of law and international bodies, [36] such as the Vienna Convention on the Law of Treaties, the Palermo Protocol, the Council of Europe Convention on Action against Trafficking in Human Beings, the understandings of the Working Group on Contemporary Forms of Slavery, but also the dialogue between International Courts, especially represented by the analysis of the precedent established by the European Court of Human Rights in the *Rantsev v. Cyprus and Russia* case, [37] which contains considerations about trafficking in persons and the appropriation of workers by employers, which also corroborates our argument on the "commodification" of individuals and the possibility of their appropriation by other persons, as mentioned and defended in the previous items of the present work. The prohibition of this criminal activity is also compared to a *jus*

[32] In this regard, see the article published by the non-governmental organization Repórter Brasil: Repórter Brasil. Eu fui escravo. http://reporterbrasil.org.br/brasilverde/reportagem.html.

[33] For this work, the decision of the Inter-American Court in the *Fazenda Brasil Verde vs. Brazil* case will be analyzed only on the issue of trafficking in persons. Nonetheless, the decision outstandingly stands out in its analysis of the crime of subjecting individuals to conditions similar to slavery and debt bondage, for which reason the reading of the complete document is highly recommended so that the reader may make their own conclusions on the subject of modern slavery as a whole.

[34] Paragraphs 281 to 290 of the decision.

[35] On the possibility of the American Convention being interpreted in accordance with other international instruments, see paras 78 and 79 of the decision.

[36] In this regard, Paulo Borba Casella provides the following definition: "No international legal system is built by the mere superposition, which is more than the mere sum of domestic legal systems, placed side by side. It is necessary to have a set of principles, norms and institutions also at the international level." The harmonious analysis of international rules for the construction of the interpretation made by the Inter-American Court of Human Rights in the present case demonstrates this search for the required harmony and dialogue also at the international level. Casella (2008), p. 712.

[37] Paragraphs 284 to 289 of the decision.

cogens rule, [38] i.e., a rule which cannot be derogated by states, due to the fact that it is not subject to any statutes of limitation in accordance with international law. [39] To transcend the literal meaning given by Article 6.1 of the American Convention for the crime of trafficking in persons and provide a broader interpretation for that provision was an equitable decision of the Inter-American Court of Human Rights which shows that the Court too has been following the international community's evolution with regard to its actions against the crimes which constitute contemporary slavery.

Also, one of the criterion considered by the Court to support the arguments presented in its decision was related to the condition of socioeconomic vulnerability of the individuals submitted to this kind of exploitation, which made this the very first time that a case was decided based on a country's historical structural discrimination. [40] The misery to which the workers were previously subjected was also a condition for their consent based on the false promises made by the recruiters. Once again, the Court has highlighted a reality which does not only permeate Brazilian society—with its social inequalities, often derived from its own past as a former slave society—but also other jurisdictions submitted to that Body and which currently present similar practices.

Therefore, while presenting a new interpretation of Article 6.1 of the American Convention, in compliance with the latest sources of international law, this decision has created an important precedent for the fight against human trafficking, which is why its effects must be analyzed with regard to Brazil.

5.3 *The Necessary Dialogue Between Legal Systems: Lessons for Brazil*

In addition to Brazil's mandatory compliance with the resolutions made by the Inter-American Court of Human Rights in the decision—since it has recognized the resolutions made by said court and is therefore bound by its decisions—due to the paradigmatic nature of the decision, which directly involves the Brazilian government, it is clear that Brazil is required to comply with said resolutions in accordance with international human rights law.

Therefore, said decision must be considered not only in situations of internal trafficking in persons, but also where said crime takes place at an international level, given the increasing number of immigrants in a situation of vulnerability who have settled in the Brazilian territory in search of better living conditions (Pinto et al. 2017).

As stated in the decision, it is not enough to simply abstain from practices aimed at the trafficking and exploitation of individuals. Positive measures are required,

[38] On *jus cogens* rules, see Trindade (2010).

[39] Paragraphs 249 to 258 of the decision.

[40] Paragraphs 81 to 100 of the decision.

such as the existence of a proper legal framework for the protection of such individuals, as well as prevention policies and practices allowing agents to act effectively in relation to complaints regarding this subject. [41] Situations which generate the demand for labor exploitation in Brazil must also be eliminated, [42] despite their ambitions for development.

It is thus necessary to improve the existing public policies aimed at combating modern slavery in Brazil—which, as seen above, are already considered to be progressive when compared to those of other jurisdictions—as well as to provide effective training for public and private agents dealing with potential victims. Such measures, if effectively put into practice, shall enable the Brazilian government to avert international condemnations for the inaction of its agents, as seen in the *Fazenda Brasil Verde vs. Brazil* case, as well as to obtain greater success in the protection of human rights in Brazil.

This improvement must also encompass the judicial decisions given by Brazilian courts on crimes of human trafficking and slave labor after the international decision. The same applies to the interpretation of the new Brazilian legislation aimed at combating internal and international trafficking in persons, namely, Law No. 13,344/2016, along with the rules amended thereby, as well as of the national policies established for that same purpose; and, with regard to the international trafficking in persons, to the urgent entry into force of the Migration Act. Domestic and international legal systems must therefore be properly reconciled in this regard, and Brazilian courts must also perform a true and effective review of the Brazilian legislation with regard to its compliance with the inter-American rule and its new interpretation, and that by means of a systemic interpretation between domestic and international legal systems, [43] thus avoiding erroneous interpretations exclusively based on the domestic legislation currently in force. Also, the understandings of the Inter-American Court of Human Rights on the interpretation and application of international legal cooperation treaties aimed at repressing the crime of trafficking in persons must also be observed.

It is true that there is a number of obstacles to the effective realization of these rights and to the fight against forced labor in Brazil, some of which have been listed by the Inter-American Court of Human Rights in the decision, such as: the great extent of the Brazilian territory, which brings difficulties to the inspection of the public policies currently in force; the resistance of national judicial and executive bodies to the publication of the list of employers found to be engaged in slavery-like

[41] Paragraph 320 of the decision.

[42] In this respect, the Inter-American Court of Human Rights mentions the UN Guiding Principles on Business and Human Rights, which, although not incorporated by Brazilian, must be strictly observed by all jurisdictions in today's postmodern globalized community. On this subject, see Cardia (2015).

[43] Still on the conventionality control, as well as to the necessary dialogue between legal systems, see Bogdandy et al. (2013).

practices with their employees ("slave labor dirty list" [44]), deemed as one of the main forms of constraint and popular pressure against the perpetrators of such violations; and the absence of adequate training and structure on the part of the various national agencies engaged in preventing and combating this kind of crime. [45] However, although Brazil's current situation does not allow the effective protection of human rights on aspects mentioned below, such obstacles must never hinder the due incorporation of international rules into the domestic legal system, for which reason the present work defends the observance of the rulings set forth in the international instrument as an excellent source of lessons for the Brazilian government [46] on the fight against trafficking in persons and other forms of exploitation derived therefrom, thus avoiding impunity with regard to the protection of the rights of its workers [47] and ensuring the transnational nature (Menezes 2005, pp. 199–205) of international law in relation to the domestic law.

6 Conclusion

Trafficking in persons has historical roots in all of the jurisdictions of the international community. Although it has been accepted as common practice for a long time, and constitutes the driving force of many other kinds of violations such as slavery and servitude, human trafficking has been abolished internationally, but has not completely disappeared in the today's postmodern society which is still taking shape and gaining strength.

Being currently one of the crimes comprised under what is known as modern slavery and considered, for the present work, as the ultimate precedent of the other forms of exploitative crimes against human beings, the trafficking in persons no longer necessarily uses physical force to oblige workers to submit to inhuman and degrading conditions. On the contrary, it increasingly resorts to the strength of the dreams of those who, immersed in a context of socioeconomic misery, seek better living conditions, being deceived into engaging in exploitative kinds of labor which, as seen above, ratifies the interdependence between the crimes of human trafficking and slavery.

[44] Ministério do Trabalho. Cadastro de empregadores que tenham submetido trabalhadores a condição análoga à de escravo. http://trabalho.gov.br/component/content/article?id=4428.

[45] Paragraph 468 of the decision.

[46] It is also well known that the decision of the Inter-American Court, in itself, will not be able to change Brazil's normative and public policy framework. However, its importance in constraining the Brazilian government (*"name and shame"*) to move towards greater effectiveness in protecting national and migrant workers subject to exploitation is an important and driving factor.

[47] This is in fact the keynote of postmodern international law, as defined by Paulo Borba Casella: "The law and the state are only justified by their ultimate goal: the human being. They must serve as instruments for the life of man, and not the opposite. This is what the focus and the conceptual keynote of postmodern international law emphasizes" (Casella 2008, p. 669).

As part of an advanced process of globalization, where voracious consumption of goods overlaps the consolidation of human relations, individuals subjected to human trafficking are relegated to the category of mere commodities, and are thus easy prey for those who own the means of production and seek to maximize profits in the performance of their activities. Although it is a historical relationship, its new outlines seem to have turned it into the rule in the current social scenario.

Brazil, which has historically tolerated exploitative practices of human beings for labor purposes, still today prostrates itself before the international community as a perpetrator of contemporary forms of slavery. We broke the physical chains that bound black slaves in 1888, but we are still tied to the exploitative forms of labor related to the vitiated consent of people who, in search of relief from their historic situation of misery, submit to inhuman and degrading working conditions. The paradigmatic decision of the Inter-American Court of Human Rights in the *Fazenda Brasil Verde vs. Brazil* case did nothing more than portray this historical picture of Brazil represented by all of the 128 victims rescued from that farm between the years of 1997 and 2000, demonstrating the need not only for Brazil to improve its existing normative instruments and update its rules aimed at providing greater protection to migrants, but also to change the national community's mentality in relation to the labor exploitation of those who need help the most.

Thus, Brazil's effective compliance with the resolutions set forth in said decision is essential for the country to take the lead in preventing and protecting the victims of trafficking in persons, at both domestic and international levels. As seen throughout the present work, the subject of international trafficking in persons has become increasingly important given the large number of immigrants in a situation of vulnerability who have been arriving and settling here. For this purpose, a transnormative perspective must be adopted in such way as to consider both domestic and international rules, with an effective conciliation between legal systems and a correct incorporation of international rules and resolutions into the domestic legal system. Hopefully, with such measures, Brazil will no longer be in the dock before international courts and will finally implement its policies for combating the crime of trafficking in persons.

References

Barbosa CYS (2010) Tráfico internacional de pessoas. Núria Fabris Ed, Porto Alegre

Bauman Z (1998) *O mal-estar da pós-modernidade.* Translation by Mauro Gama, Cláudia Martinelli Gama. Zahar, Rio de Janeiro

Bauman Z (1999) *Globalização*: as consequências humanas. Translation by Marcus Penchel. Zahar, Rio de Janeiro

Bauman Z (2017) *Estranhos à nossa porta.* Trans. Carlos Alberto Medeiros. 1ª ed. Zahar, Rio de Janeiro

BBC Brasil. 'A vida no Brasil não é normal, é só trabalho', conta boliviana que foi escravizada em SP. http://www.bbc.com/english/noticias/2015/01/150127_boliviana_escravizada_ms

Bogdandy AV, Piovesan F, Antoniazzi MM (2013) Direitos Humanos, democracia e integração jurídica: emergência de um novo direito público. Elsevier, Rio de Janeiro
Brasil (2011) Relatório nacional sobre tráfico de pessoas: Consolidação dos dados de 2005 a 2011. Brasília
Brasil. Ministério da Justiça e Segurança Pública. Campanhas. http://www.justica.gov.br/sua-protecao/trafico-de-pessoas/campanhas
Brasil. Decree No. 5,015, of March 12, 2004
Brasil. Decree No. 5,017, of March 12, 2004
Brasil. Law No. 13,344, of October 6, 2016
Brasil. Law No. 13,445, of May 24, 2016
Brasil. Law No. 6,815, of August 19, 1980
Brasil. Secretaria Nacional de Justiça (2006) Política Nacional de enfrentamento ao tráfico de pessoas. SNJ, Brasília
Brasil. Secretaria Nacional de Justiça (2008) Plano Nacional de enfrentamento ao tráfico de pessoas. SNJ, Brasília
Brasil. Secretaria Nacional de Justiça (2013a) II Plano Nacional de enfrentamento ao tráfico de pessoas. SNJ, Brasília
Brasil. Secretaria Nacional de Justiça (2013b) Tráfico de Pessoas: Uma abordagem para os Direitos Humanos. Ministério da Justiça, Brasília
Brasil. Secretaria Nacional de Justiça (2018) III Plano Nacional de enfrentamento ao tráfico de pessoas. SNJ, Brasília
Cardia ACR (2015) Empresas, direitos humanos e gênero: desafios e perspectivas na proteção e no empoderamento da mulher pelas empresas transnacionais. Buqui, Porto Alegre
Casella PB (2008) Fundamentos do Direito Internacional Pós-Moderno. Quartier Latin, São Paulo
Durães TF, Corrêa N, Damasceno ECC, Tavares JP (2014) Tráfico internacional de pessoas e outros trânsitos. Editora Espaço Acadêmico/Editora Puc Goiás, Goiânia
Global Rights (2007) Combating Human Trafficking in the Americas: a guide to international advocacy. Washington
Inter-American Court of Human Rights. *Fazenda Brasil Verde vs. Brazil Case.* Series C, No. 318. Decision of October 20, 2016
Laky T (2014) Tráfico Internacional de Mulheres: Nova Face de uma Velha Escravidão. 2ª edn. Editora Prismas, Curitiba
Leal ML, Leal MFP (2002) Pesquisa sobre Tráfico de Mulheres, Crianças e Adolescentes para fins de Exploração Sexual Comercial – PESTRAF. CECRIA, Brasília
Menezes W (2005) Ordem global e transnormatividade. Unijuí, Ijuí
Ministério da Justiça. Jornadas transatlânticas: uma pesquisa exploratória sobre tráfico de seres humanos do Brasil para Itália e Portugal. Brasília: 2011. http://www.justica.gov.br/yua-protecao/trafico-de-pessoas/publicacoes/anexos-pesquisas/jornadastransatlanticas.pdf/view
Ministério do Trabalho. Cadastro de empregadores que tenham submetido trabalhadores a condição análoga à de escravo. http://trabalho.gov.br/component/content/article?id=4428
Ministério Público Federal. Procuradoria Federal dos Direitos do Cidadão (2014) Diálogos da Cidadania: Tráfico de pessoas: conhecer para se proteger. Brasília
Nogueira C, Novaes M, Bignami R (2014) Tráfico de Pessoas: Reflexões para a compreensão do trabalho escravo contemporâneo. Paulinas, São Paulo
Officer of the High Commissioner for Human Rights. Recommended Principles and Guidelines of Human Rights and Human Trafficking. http://www.ohchr.org/Documents/Publications/Traffickingen.pdf
Organization of American States. *American Convention on Human Rights.*
Pinto EVC, Perazzolo JR, Barroso LR, Silva MAM, Cicco MC (2017) Refugiados, Imigrantes e Igualdade dos Povos. Quartier Latin, São Paulo
Piovesan F (2015) Direitos Humanos e Justiça Internacional: um estudo comparativo dos sistemas regionais europeu, interamericano e africano. 6ª ed. Saraiva, São Paulo

Piovesan F, Kamimura A (2013) Tráfico de pessoas sob a perspectiva de direitos humanos: prevenção, combate, proteção às vítimas e cooperação internacional. In: BRASIL. Secretaria Nacional de Justiça. Tráfico de Pessoas: uma abordagem para os direitos humanos. Ministério da Justiça, Brasília, pp 105–131

Ramos AC (2016) Teoria geral dos direitos humanos na ordem internacional. 6ª ed. Saraiva, São Paulo

Repórter Brasil. Dados sobre trabalho escravo no Brasil. http://reporterbrasil.org.br/dados/trabalhoescravo/

Repórter Brasil. Eu fui escravo. http://reporterbrasil.org.br/brasilverde/reportagem.html

Siqueira P, Quinteiro M (2013) Tráfico de pessoas: quanto vale o ser humano na balança comercial do lucro? A escravidão no século XXI. Ideias & Letras, São Paulo

Trindade AAC (2010) *International law for humankind: towards a new jus gentium*. The Hague Academy of International Law. Martinus Nijhoff Publishers, The Netherlands

United Nations. Office of the High Commissioner (2014). *Human Rights and Human Trafficking. Factsheet No. 36*. New York and Geneva

United Nations Office on Drugs and Crime (2016) 2016 Global Report on Trafficking in Persons. United Nations, New York

United Nations Office on Drugs and Crime. Global Action against Trafficking in Persons and the Smuggling of Migrants. https://www.unodc.org/unodc/en/human-trafficking/glo-act/index.html

United Nations Office on Drugs and Crime. Tráfico de pessoas e contrabando de migrantes. https://www.unodc.org/lpo-brazil/pt/trafico-de-pessoas/.

Vieira V, Charf C (2014) Mulheres e homens trabalhando pela paz contra o tráfico de mulheres e a violência sexual, 1ª edn. Associação Mulheres pela Paz, São Paulo

Vieira V, Charf C (2016) Percepção da sociedade sobre o tráfico de mulheres. Associação Mulheres pela Paz, São Paulo

50 For Freedom. http://50forfreedom.org/

Ana Cláudia Ruy Cardia Atchabahian holds a PhD and Master in International Law from the Pontifical Catholic University of São Paulo. She is a Professor of Private International Law at the Mackenzie Presbyterian University; member of the International Law Association—Brazilian Branch (ILA-Brazil) and Advisor to the Latin American Section of the Global Business and Human Rights Scholars Association. She is a coordinator of "Mack DH&E: Business and Human Rights" Study Group and of the Research Group "Invisible People: Prevention and Combat of Internal and International Human Trafficking", both from the Mackenzie Presbyterian University. She is also a member of the Human Rights Commission at the Brazilian BAR Association, São Paulo Section (OAB/SP); a lawyer and ESG consultant in São Paulo, Brazil (ana.cardia@mackenzie.br).

Felipe Chiarello de Souza Pinto is a Provost and Professor of the Political and Economic Law Master and PhD Program at the Mackenzie Presbyterian University. He is currently the Deputy Coordinator of Academic Programs of the Law Area of CAPES-MEC, member of the Law Committee in the SciELO Program/FAPESP; Paulista Academy of Legal Letters, and Mackenzie Academy of Letters. Felipe has a PhD degree in Law from the Pontifical Catholic University of São Paulo. He was a member of the Scientific Technical Council, the Superior Council, and of the Law Committee of CAPES-MEC. He is the leader of the research group State and Economics in Brazil attached to the Post-Graduate Program on Political and Economic Law at the Mackenzie Presbyterian University, where he coordinates some researches in human rights such as "Invisible People" and "Technology and Democracy" (felipe.chiarello@mackenzie.br).

GPSR Compliance

The European Union's (EU) General Product Safety Regulation (GPSR) is a set of rules that requires consumer products to be safe and our obligations to ensure this.

If you have any concerns about our products, you can contact us on ProductSafety@springernature.com

In case Publisher is established outside the EU, the EU authorized representative is:

Springer Nature Customer Service Center GmbH
Europaplatz 3
69115 Heidelberg, Germany

Batch number: 10732044

Printed by Printforce, the Netherlands